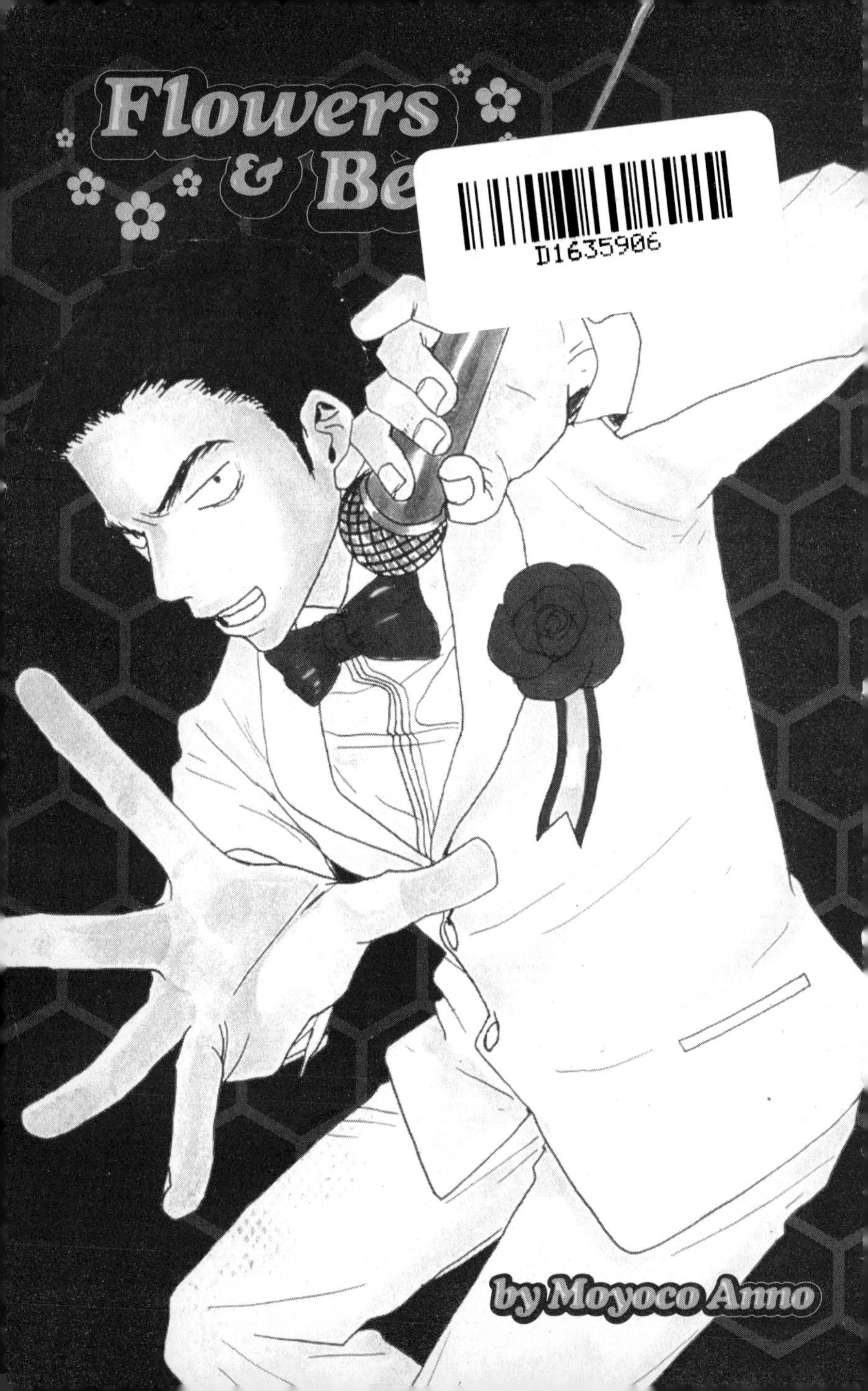
Flowers
& Be
by Moyoco Anno

Flowers and Bees Vol. 2

Editor's Choice Edition

Story and Art by

Moyoco Anno

English Adaptation/Carl Gustav Horn
Translation/Yuji Oniki
Lettering & Touch-Up/William Schuch
Cover and Graphic Designer/Izumi Evers
Editor/Carl Gustav Horn

Managing Editor/Annette Roman
Editor-in-Chief/William Flanagan
Sr. Director of Licensing & Acquisitions/Rika Inouye
Production Manager/Noboru Watanabe
Vice President of Marketing/Liza Coppola
Sr. Vice President of Editorial/Hyoe Narita
Publisher/Seiji Horibuchi

Printed in Canada

Published by VIZ, LLC.
P.O. Box 77010
San Francisco, CA 94107

Editor's Choice Edition
10 9 8 7 6 5 4 3 2 1
First printing, January 2004

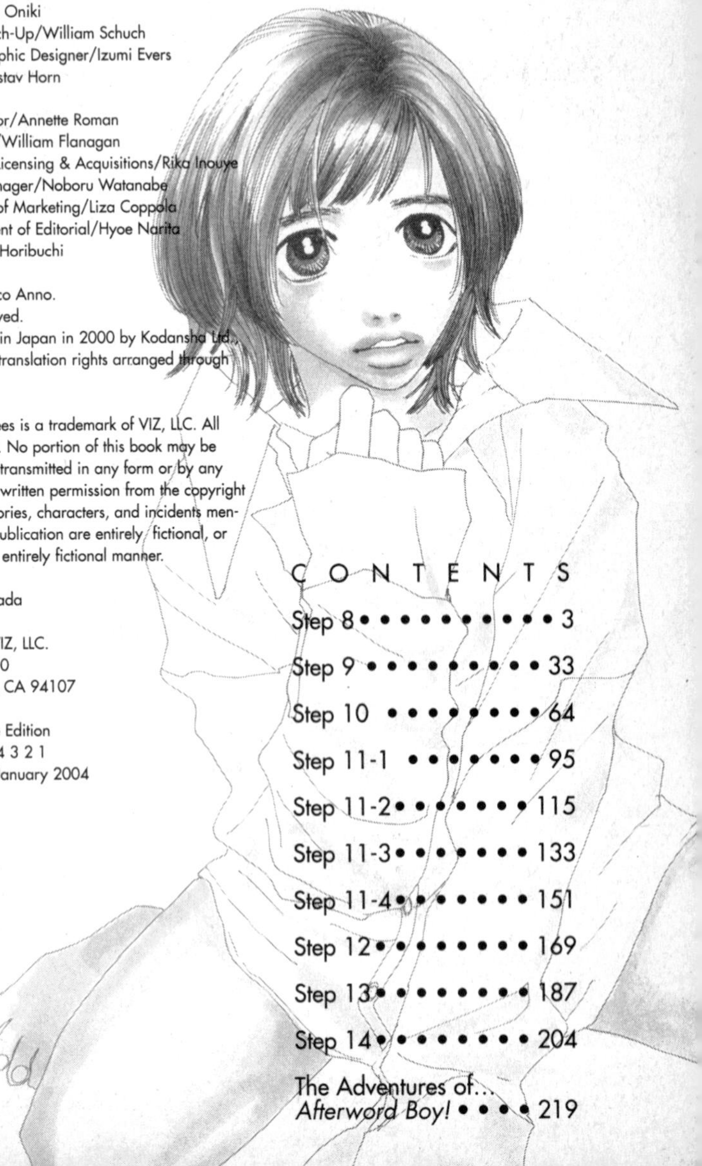

CONTENTS

Step 08

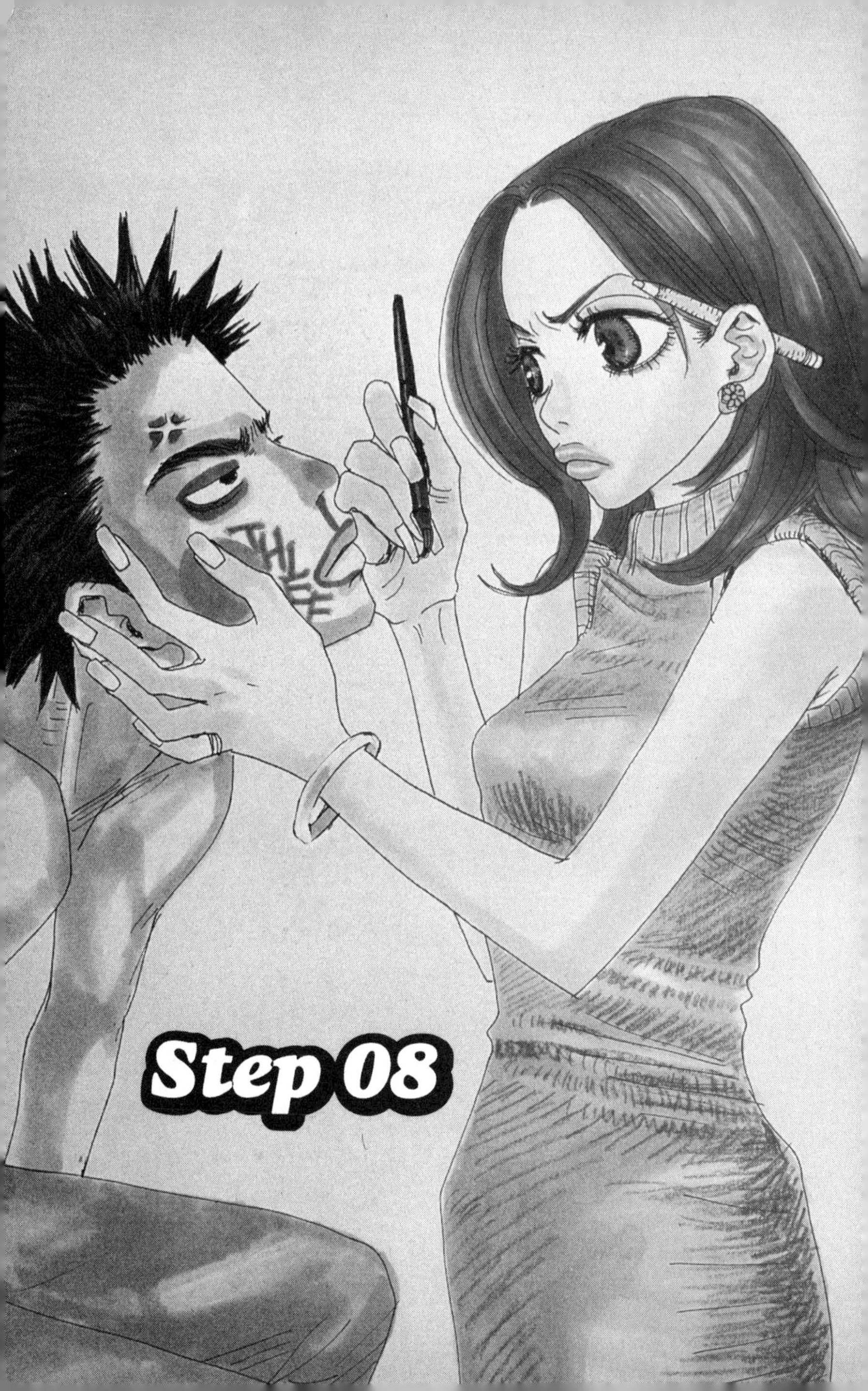

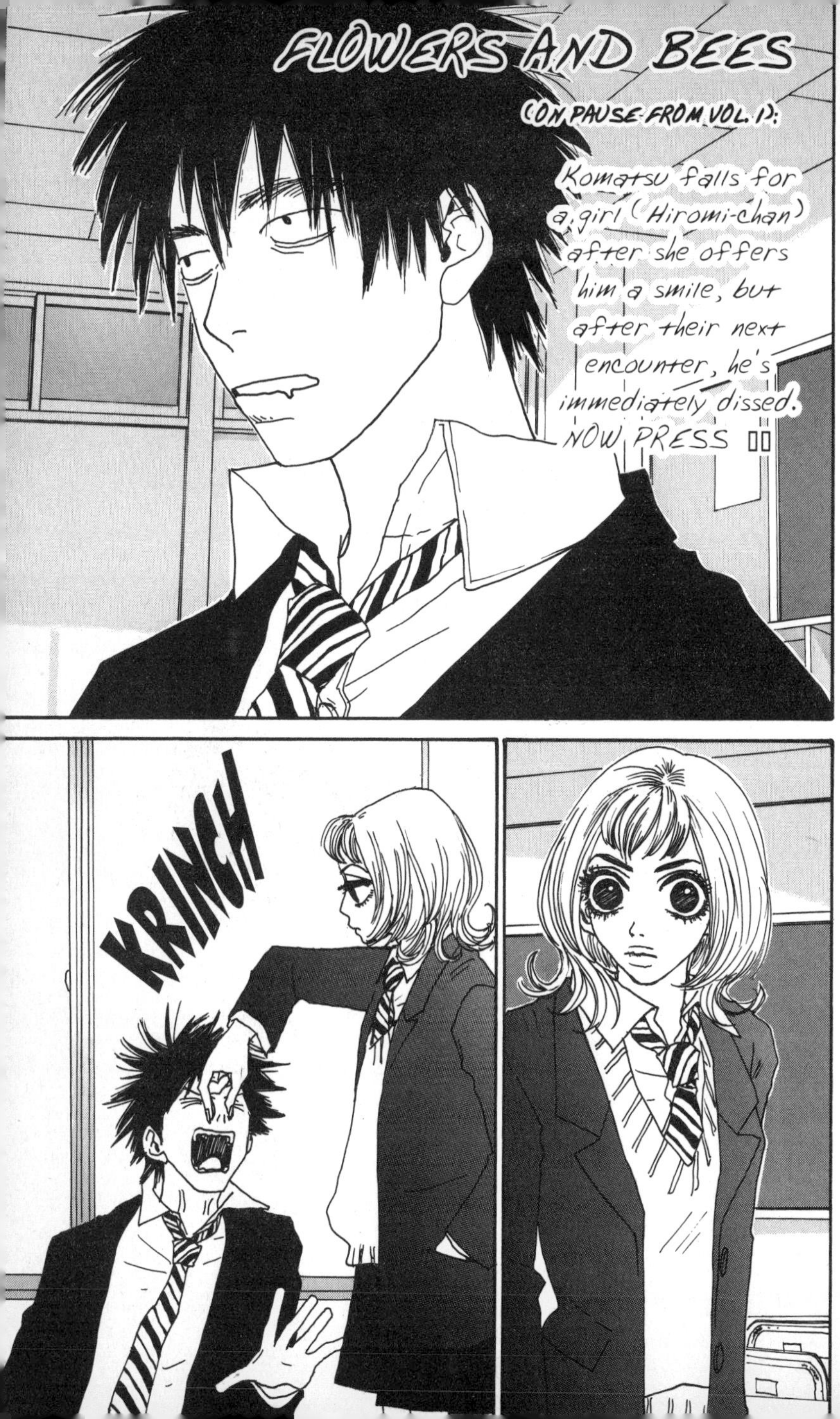
FLOWERS AND BEES
(ON PAUSE FROM VOL. 1):
Komatsu falls for a girl (Hiromi-chan) after she offers him a smile, but after their next encounter, he's immediately dissed. NOW PRESS ▯▯
KRINCH

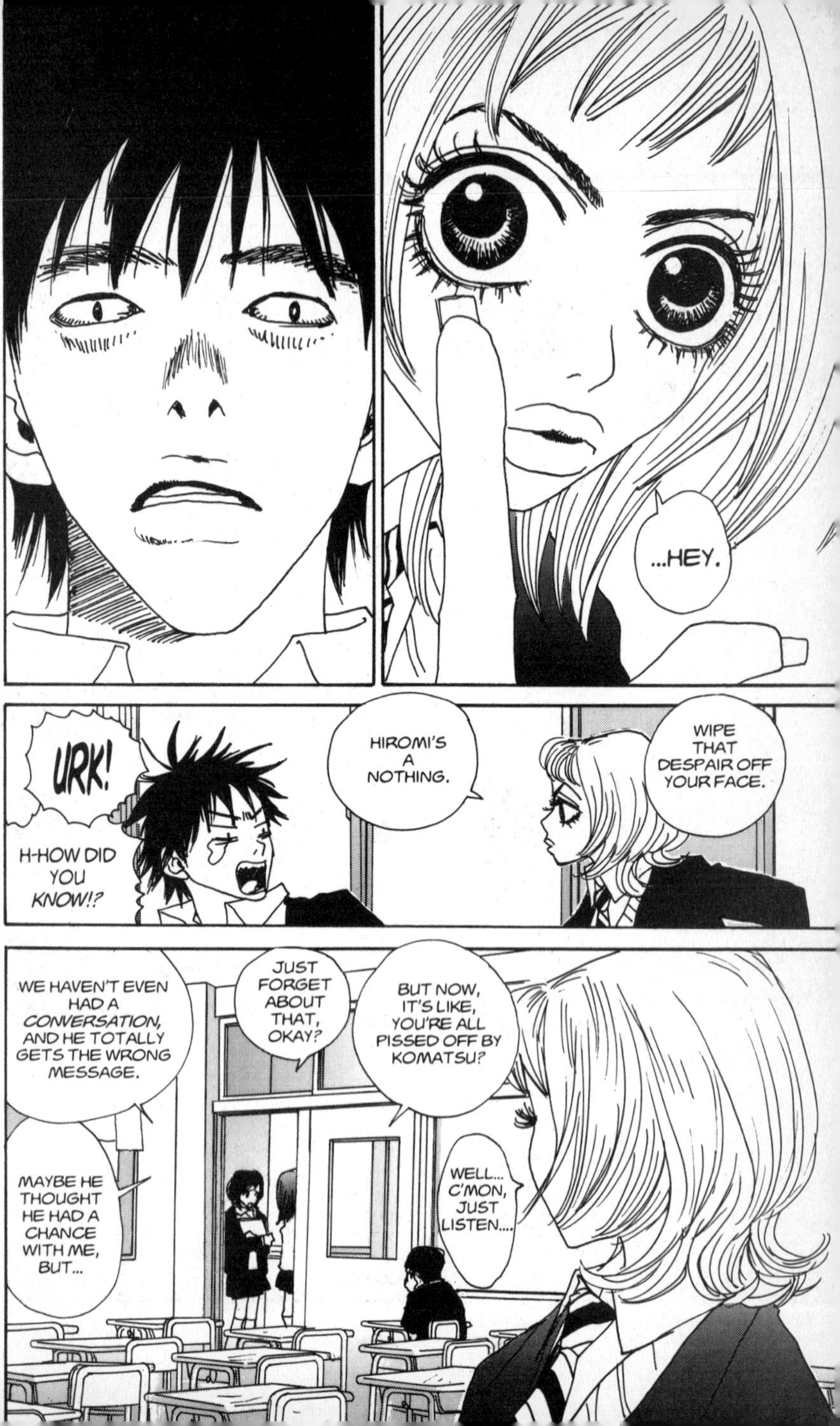
...HEY.
WIPE THAT DESPAIR OFF YOUR FACE.
HIROMI'S A NOTHING.
URK!
H-HOW DID YOU *KNOW*!?
BUT NOW, IT'S LIKE, YOU'RE ALL PISSED OFF BY KOMATSU?
JUST FORGET ABOUT THAT, OKAY?
WE HAVEN'T EVEN HAD A *CONVERSATION*, AND HE TOTALLY GETS THE WRONG MESSAGE.
WELL... C'MON, JUST LISTEN....
MAYBE HE THOUGHT HE HAD A CHANCE WITH ME, BUT...

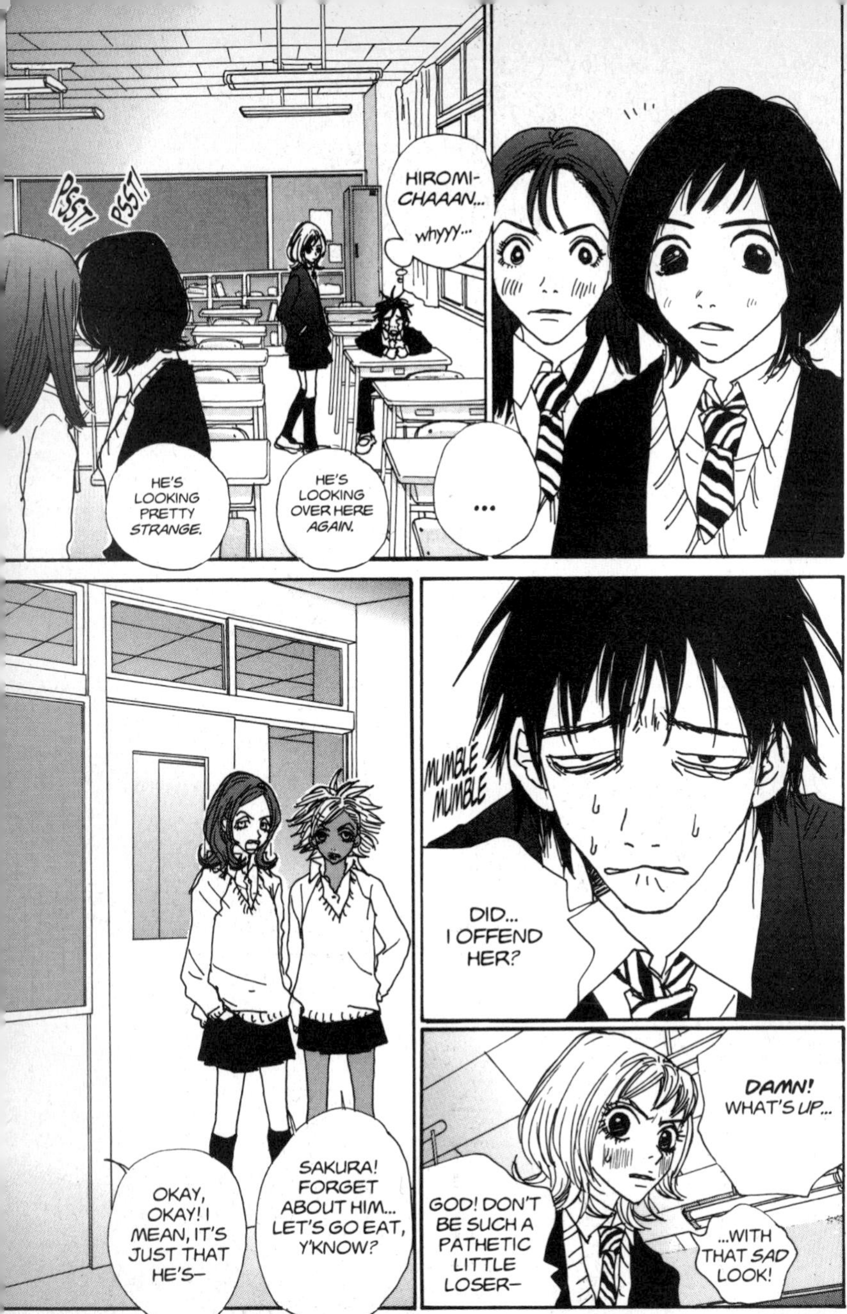
HIROMI-CHAAAN... whyyy...
...
PSST! PSST!
HE'S LOOKING OVER HERE AGAIN.
HE'S LOOKING PRETTY STRANGE.
MUMBLE MUMBLE
DID... I OFFEND HER?
DAMN! WHAT'S UP...
...WITH THAT SAD LOOK!
GOD! DON'T BE SUCH A PATHETIC LITTLE LOSER—
SAKURA! FORGET ABOUT HIM... LET'S GO EAT, Y'KNOW?
OKAY, OKAY! I MEAN, IT'S JUST THAT HE'S—

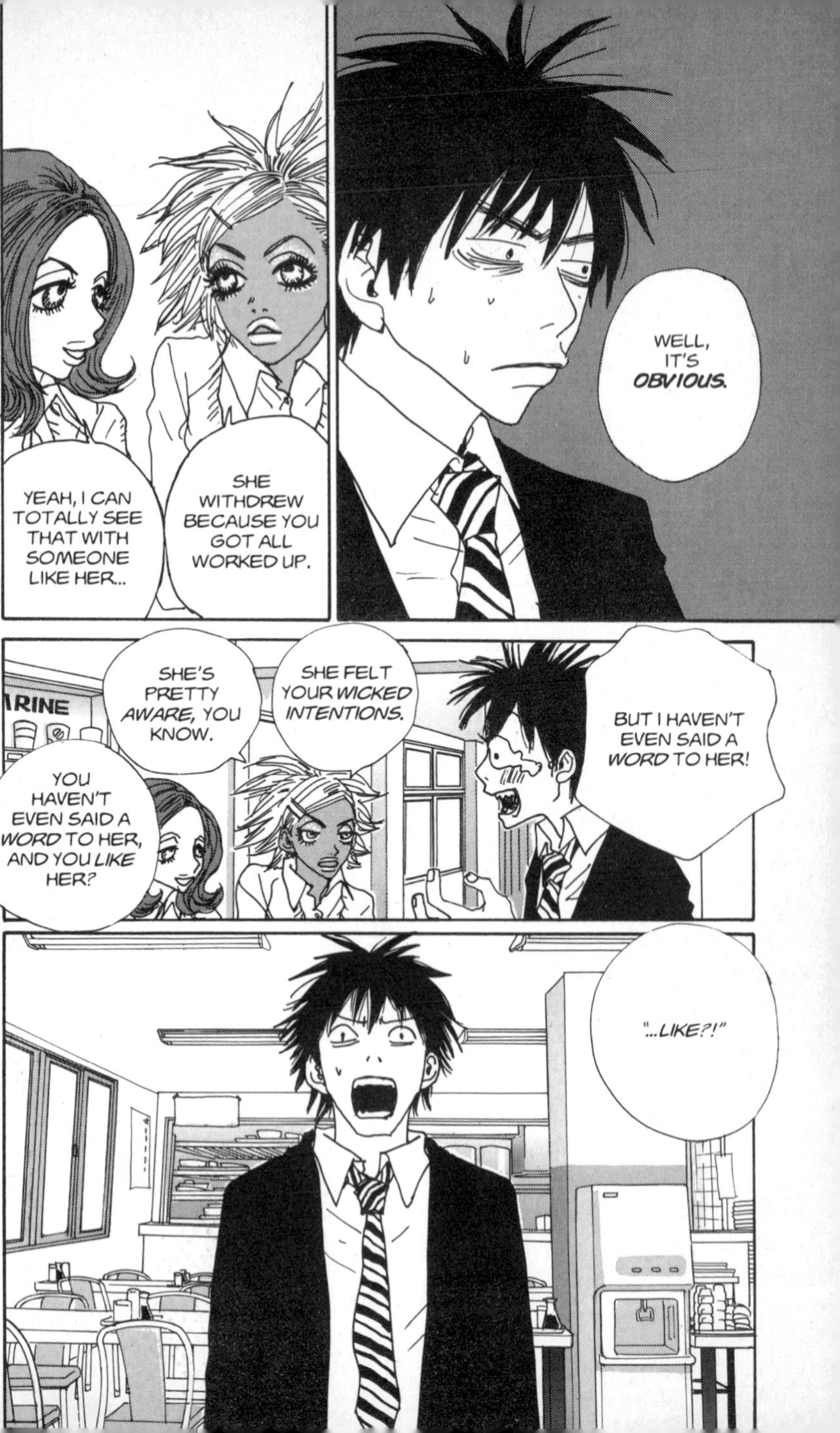
WELL, IT'S *OBVIOUS.*
SHE WITHDREW BECAUSE YOU GOT ALL WORKED UP.
YEAH, I CAN TOTALLY SEE THAT WITH SOMEONE LIKE HER...
BUT I HAVEN'T EVEN SAID A *WORD* TO HER!
SHE FELT YOUR *WICKED INTENTIONS.*
SHE'S PRETTY *AWARE,* YOU KNOW.
YOU HAVEN'T EVEN SAID A *WORD* TO HER, AND YOU *LIKE* HER?
"...LIKE?!"

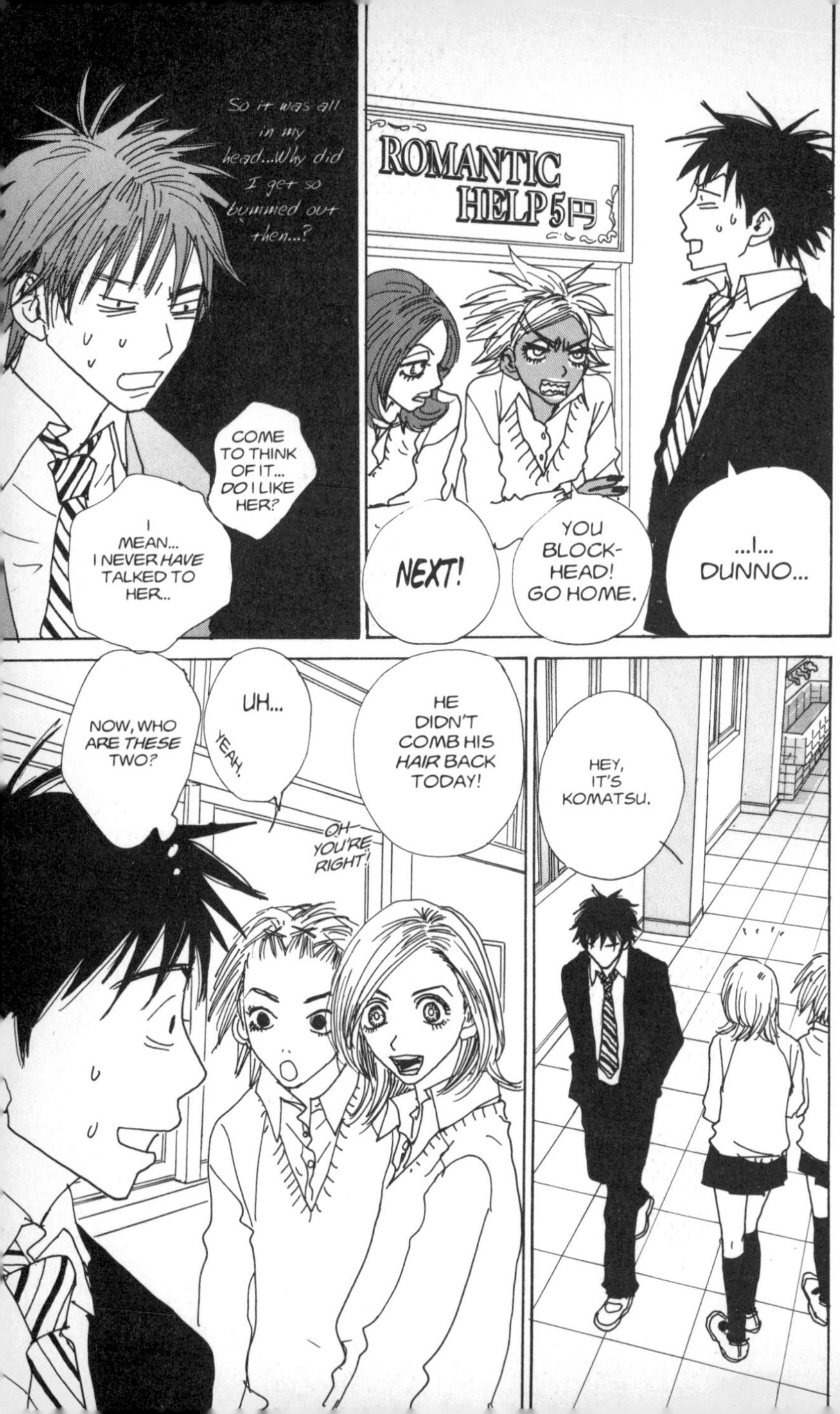
ROMANTIC HELP 5円
...I... DUNNO...
YOU BLOCK-HEAD! GO HOME.
NEXT!
So it was all in my head...Why did I get so bummed out then...?
COME TO THINK OF IT... DO I LIKE HER?
I MEAN... I NEVER *HAVE* TALKED TO HER...
HEY, IT'S KOMATSU.
HE DIDN'T COMB HIS *HAIR* BACK TODAY!
OH YOU'RE RIGHT!
UH... YEAH.
NOW, WHO ARE *THESE* TWO?

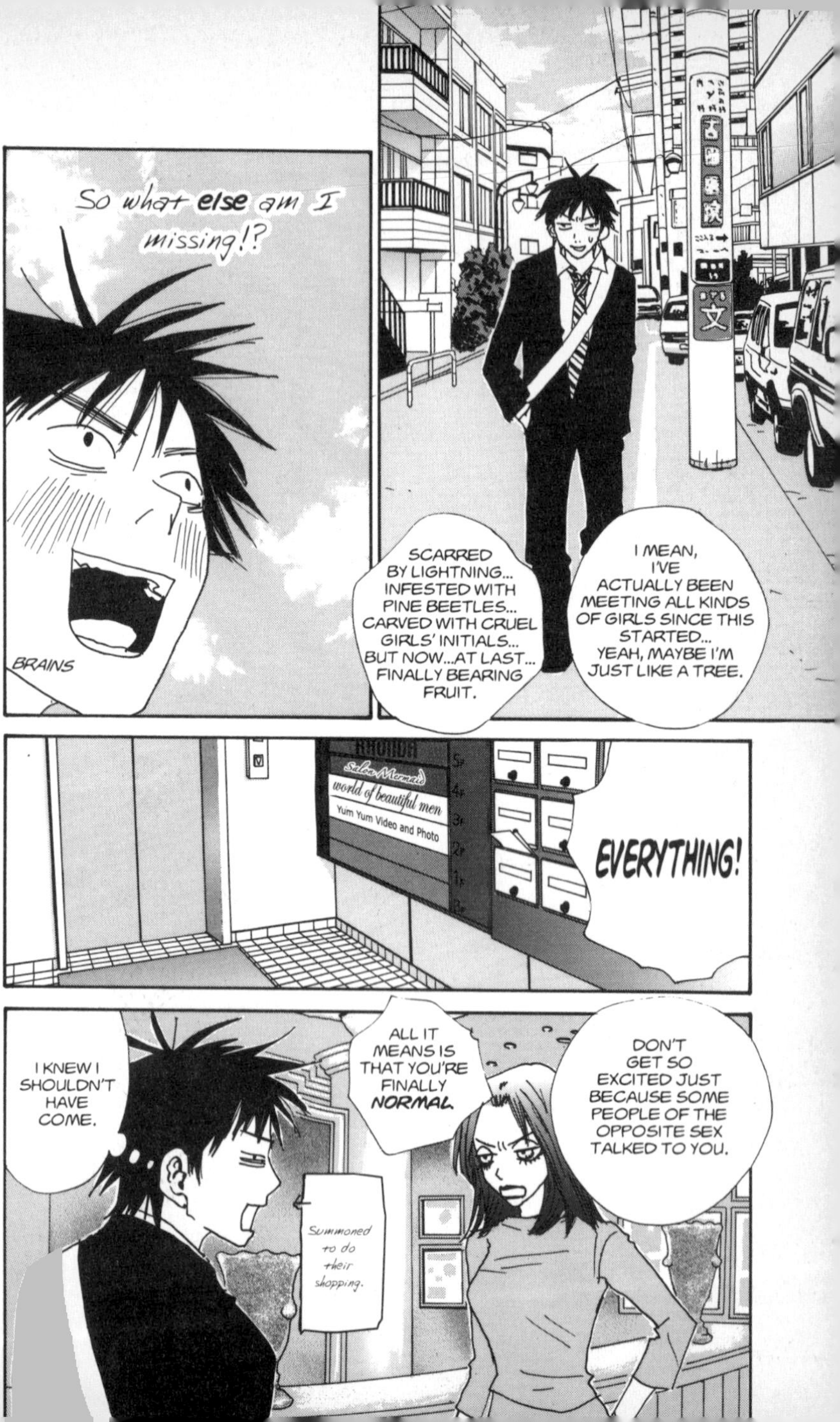

I MEAN, I'VE ACTUALLY BEEN MEETING ALL KINDS OF GIRLS SINCE THIS STARTED... YEAH, MAYBE I'M JUST LIKE A TREE.
SCARRED BY LIGHTNING... INFESTED WITH PINE BEETLES... CARVED WITH CRUEL GIRLS' INITIALS... BUT NOW...AT LAST... FINALLY BEARING FRUIT.
So what else am I missing!?
BRAINS
Salon Mermaid
world of beautiful men
Yum Yum Video and Photo
EVERYTHING!
DON'T GET SO EXCITED JUST BECAUSE SOME PEOPLE OF THE OPPOSITE SEX TALKED TO YOU.
ALL IT MEANS IS THAT YOU'RE FINALLY NORMAL.
I KNEW I SHOULDN'T HAVE COME.
Summoned to do their shopping.

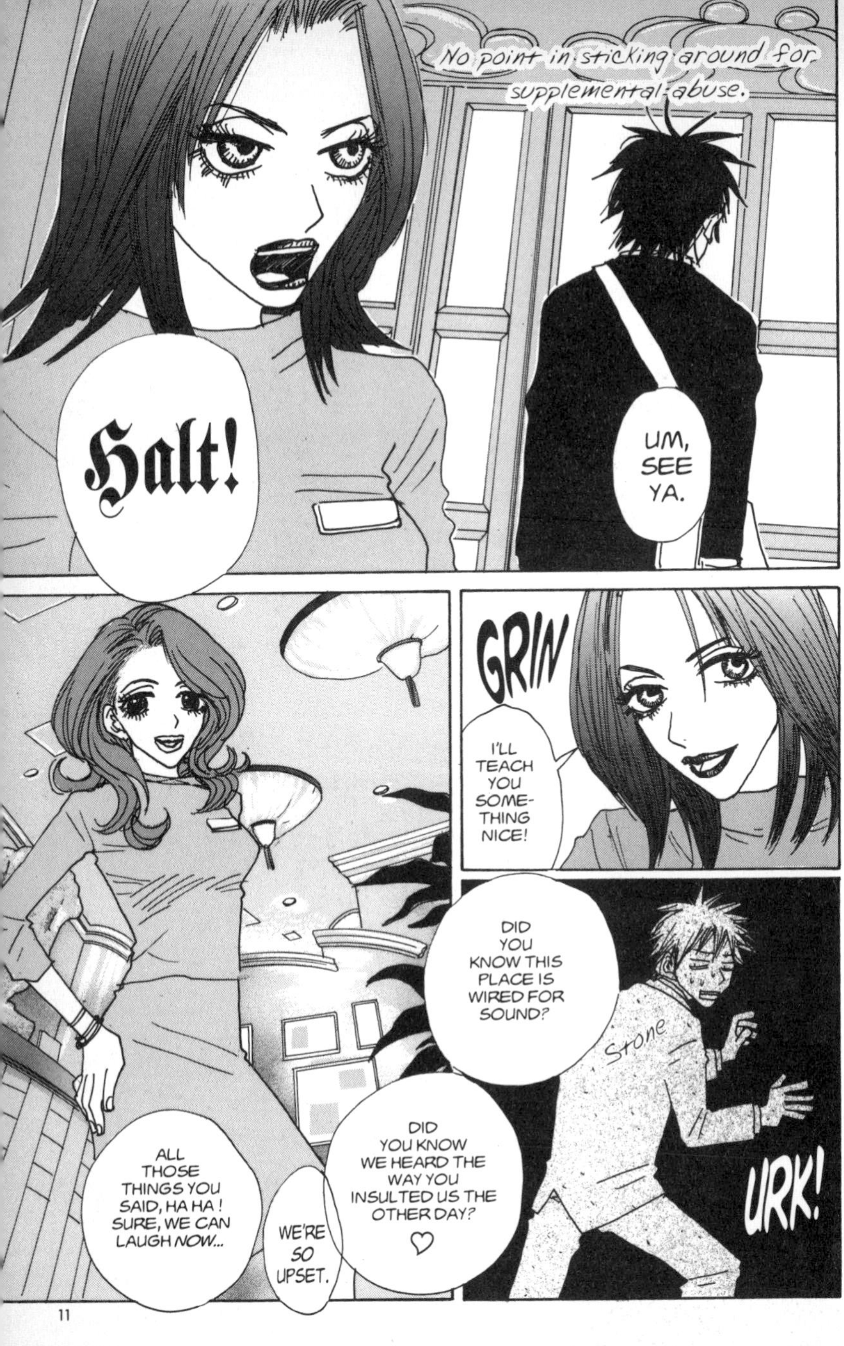
No point in sticking around for supplemental abuse.
UM, SEE YA.
Halt!
GRIN
I'LL TEACH YOU SOME-THING NICE!
DID YOU KNOW THIS PLACE IS WIRED FOR SOUND?
Stone
URK!
DID YOU KNOW WE HEARD THE WAY YOU INSULTED US THE OTHER DAY? ♡
WE'RE SO UPSET.
ALL THOSE THINGS YOU SAID, HA HA! SURE, WE CAN LAUGH NOW...

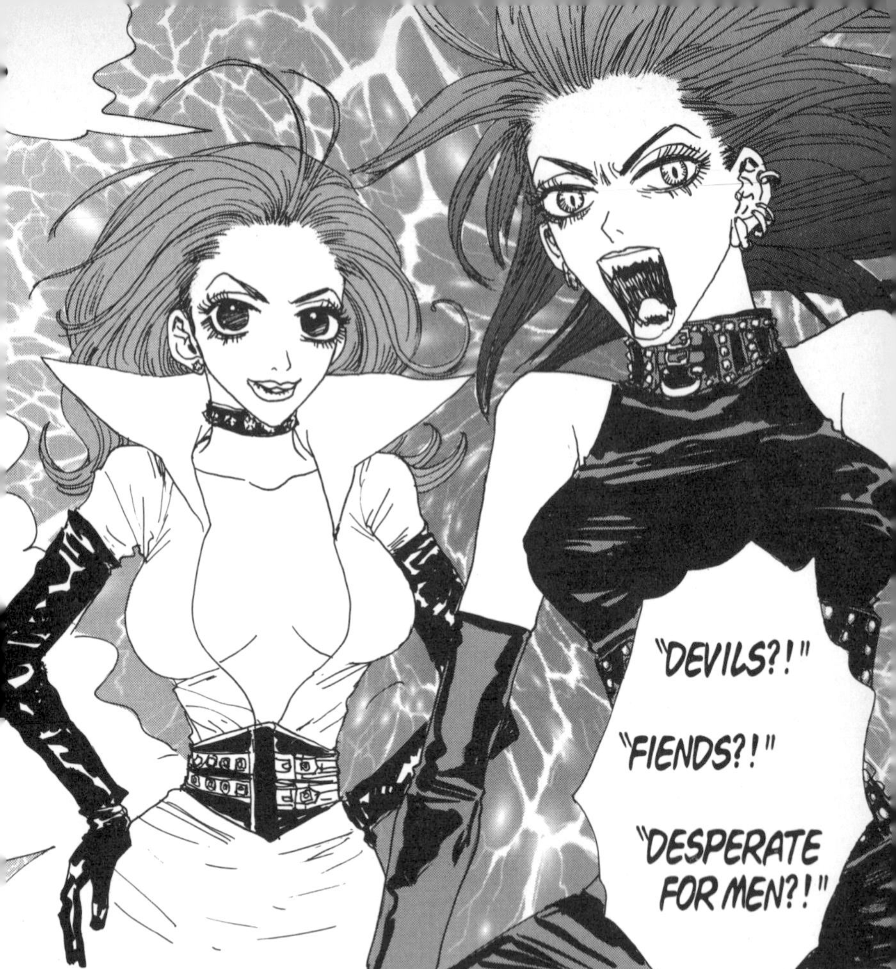
"DEVILS?!"
"FIENDS?!"
"DESPERATE FOR MEN?!"
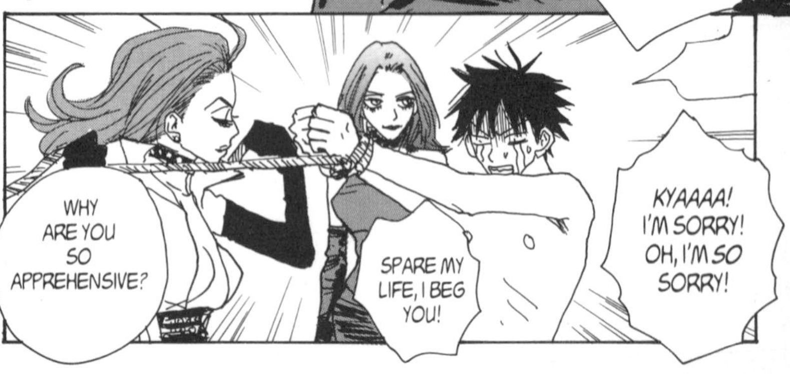
KYAAAA! I'M SORRY! OH, I'M SO SORRY!
SPARE MY LIFE, I BEG YOU!
WHY ARE YOU SO APPREHENSIVE?

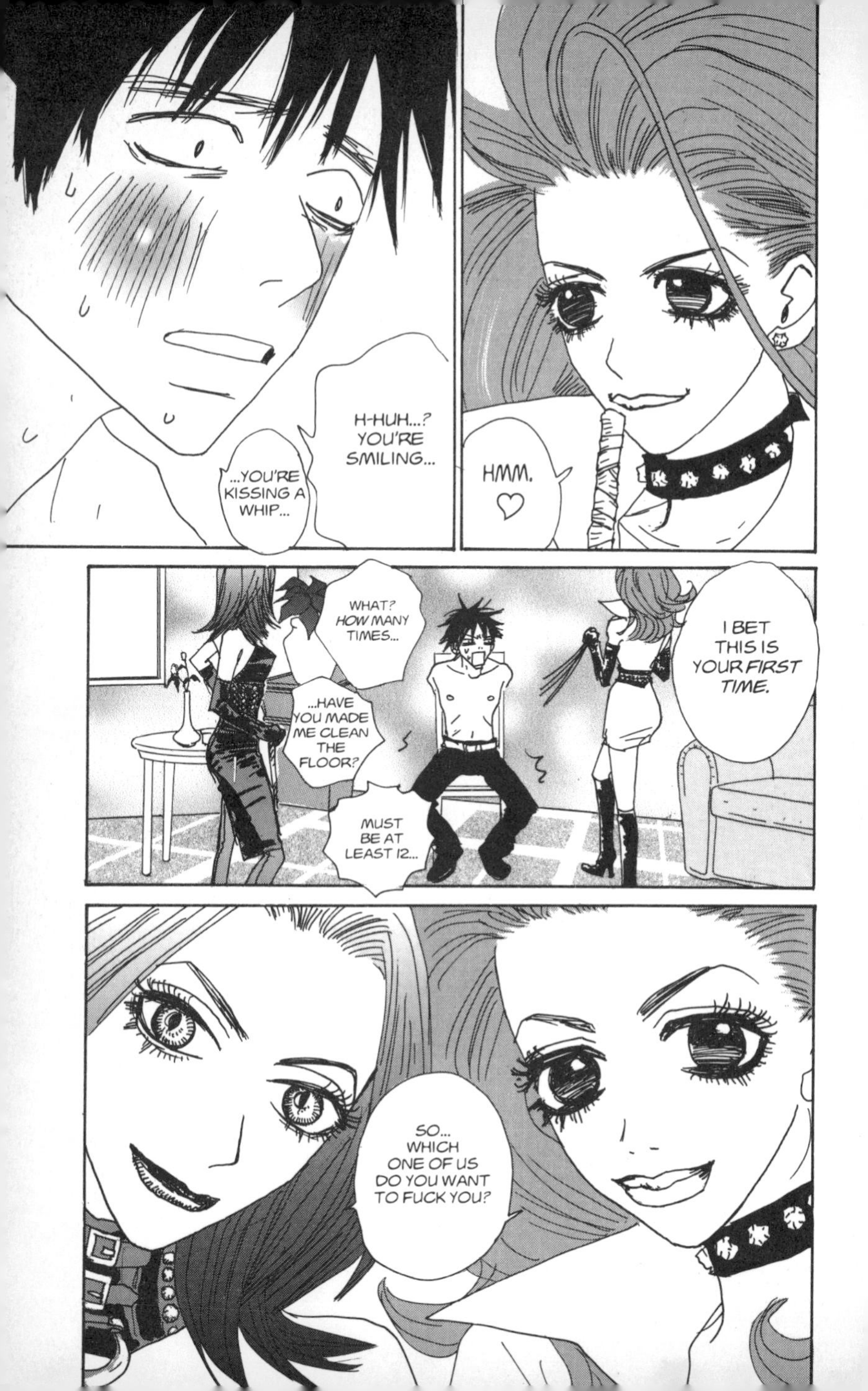
HMM. ♡
H-HUH...? YOU'RE SMILING...
...YOU'RE KISSING A WHIP...
I BET THIS IS YOUR *FIRST* TIME.
WHAT? *HOW MANY* TIMES...
...HAVE YOU MADE ME CLEAN THE FLOOR?
MUST BE AT LEAST 12...
SO... WHICH ONE OF US DO YOU WANT TO FUCK YOU?

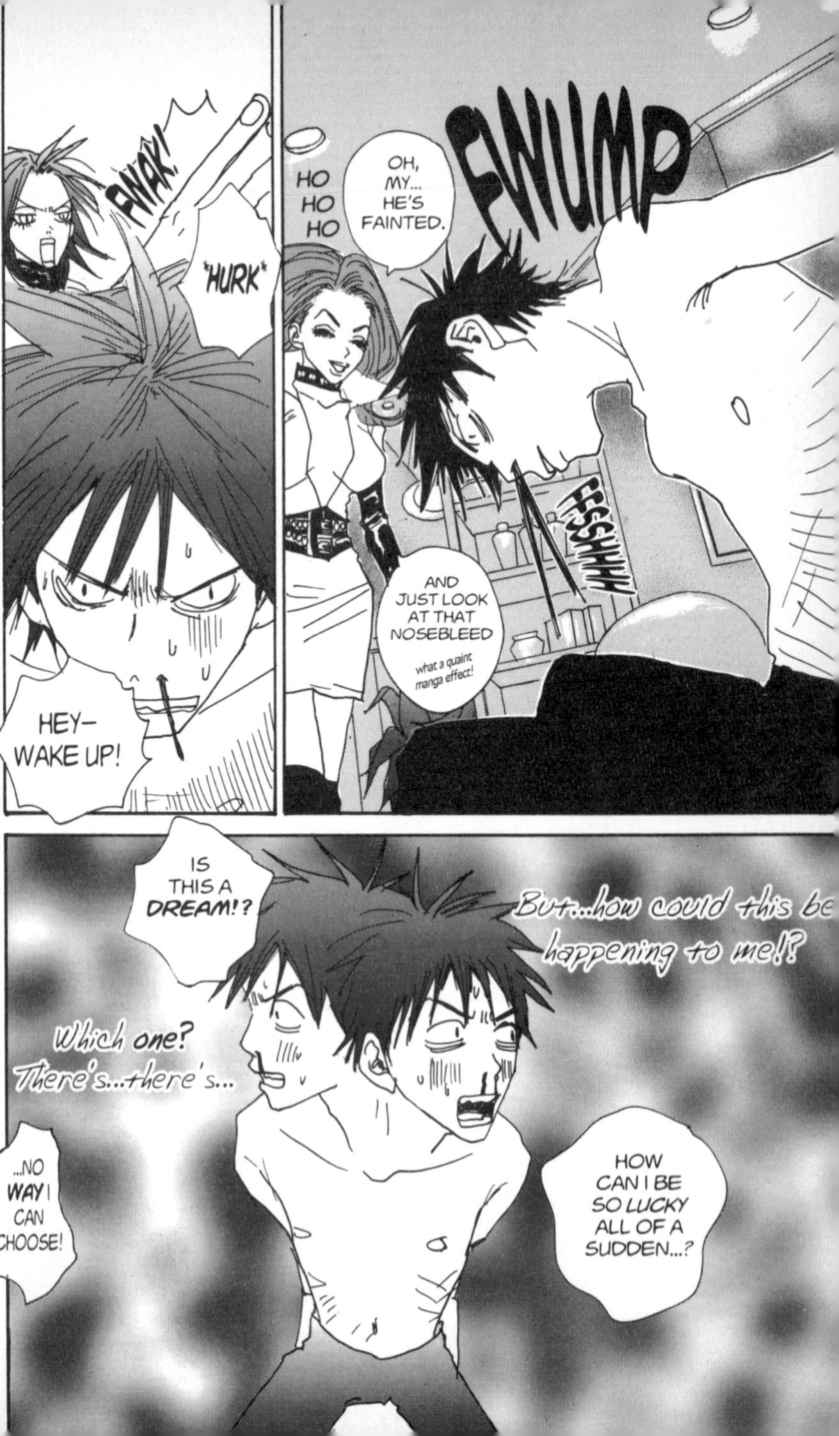
FWUMP
HO HO HO
OH, MY... HE'S FAINTED.
FSSHHH
AND JUST LOOK AT THAT NOSEBLEED
what a quaint manga effect!
FWAK!
HURK
HEY— WAKE UP!
But...how could this be happening to me!?
IS THIS A DREAM!?
Which one? There's...there's...
HOW CAN I BE SO LUCKY ALL OF A SUDDEN...?
...NO WAY I CAN CHOOSE!

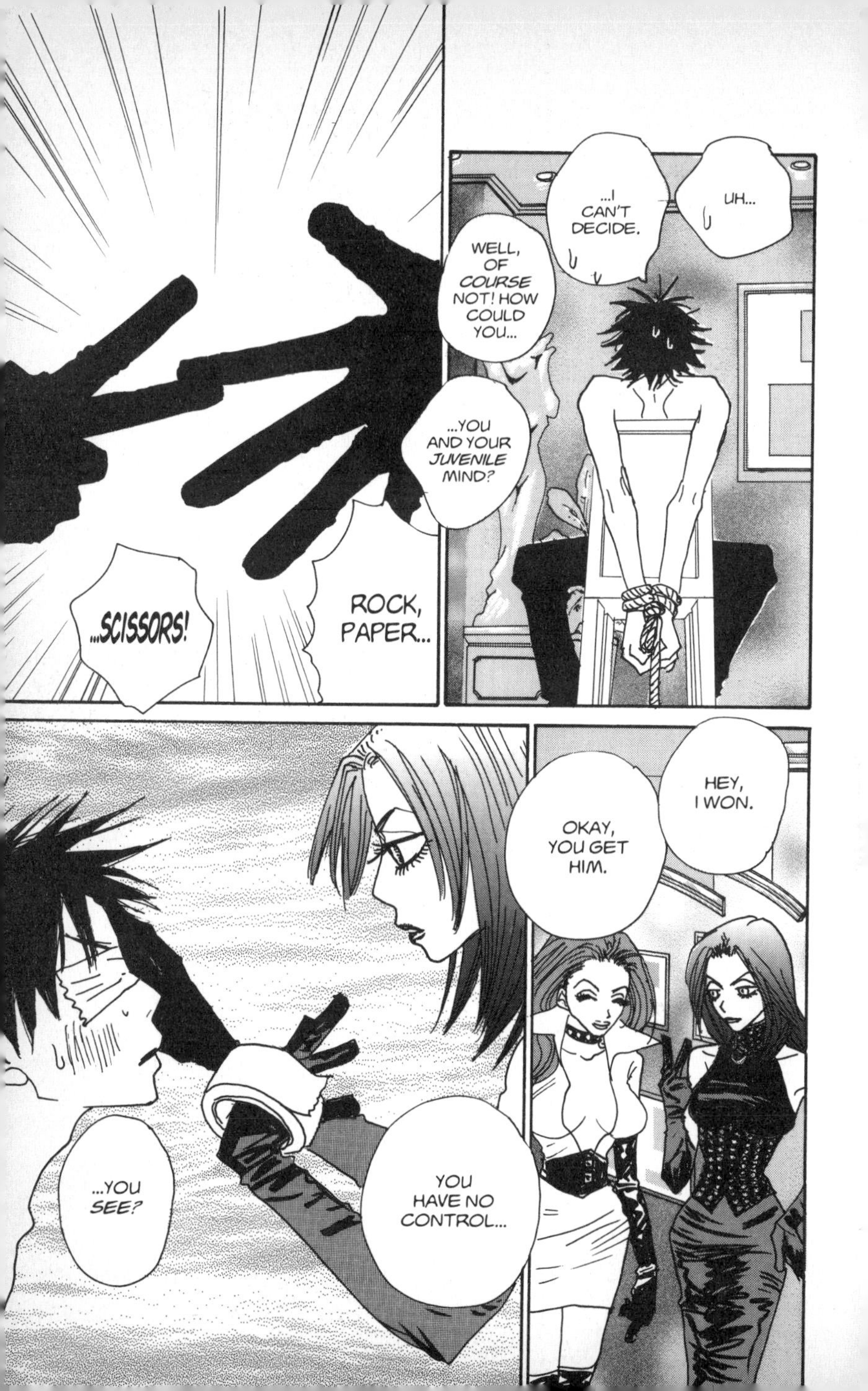
UH...
...I CAN'T DECIDE.
WELL, OF COURSE NOT! HOW COULD YOU...
...YOU AND YOUR JUVENILE MIND?
ROCK, PAPER...
...SCISSORS!
HEY, I WON.
OKAY, YOU GET HIM.
YOU HAVE NO CONTROL...
...YOU SEE?

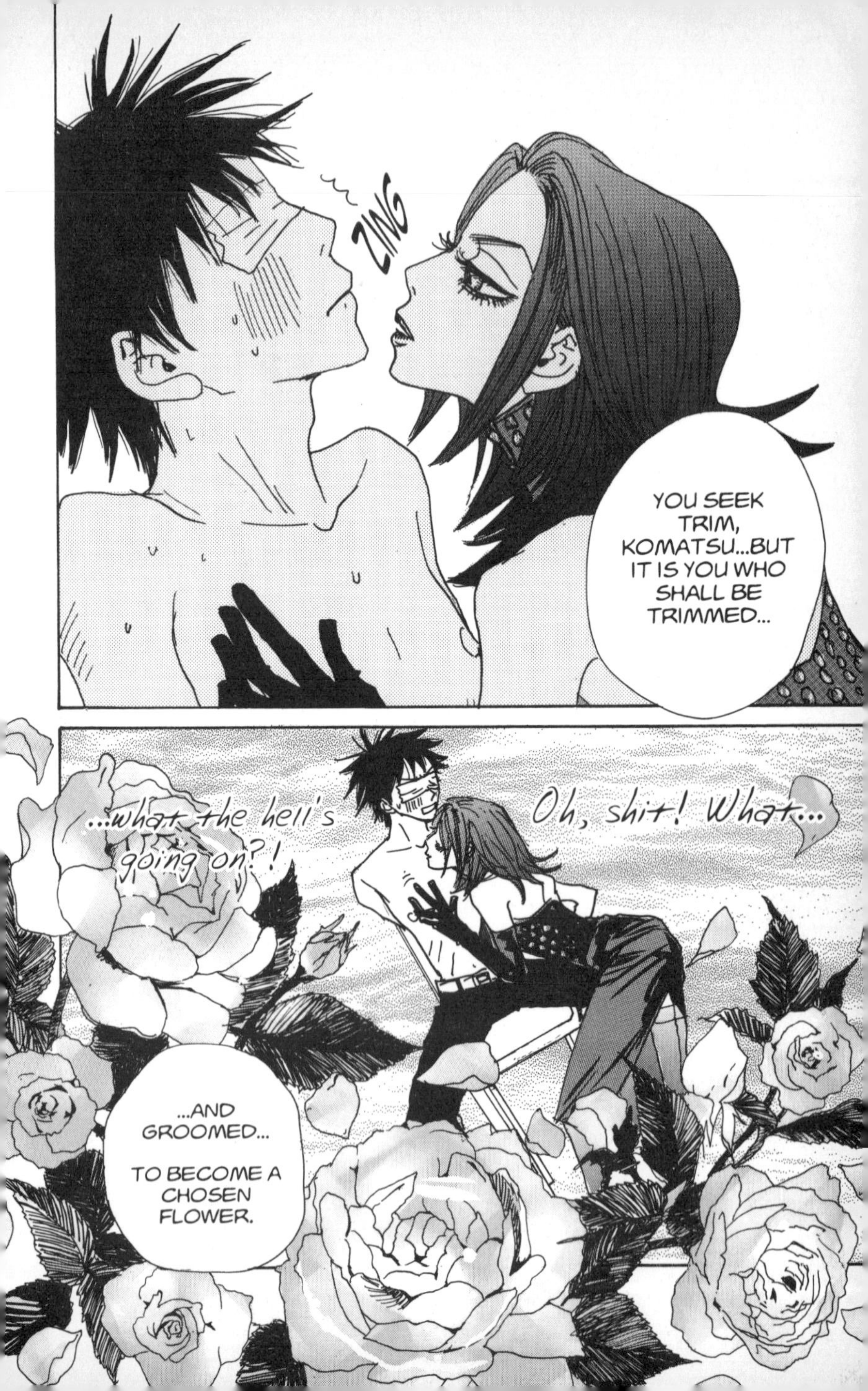
ZING
YOU SEEK TRIM, KOMATSU...BUT IT IS YOU WHO SHALL BE TRIMMED...
Oh, shit! What...
...what the hell's going on?!
...AND GROOMED...
TO BECOME A CHOSEN FLOWER.

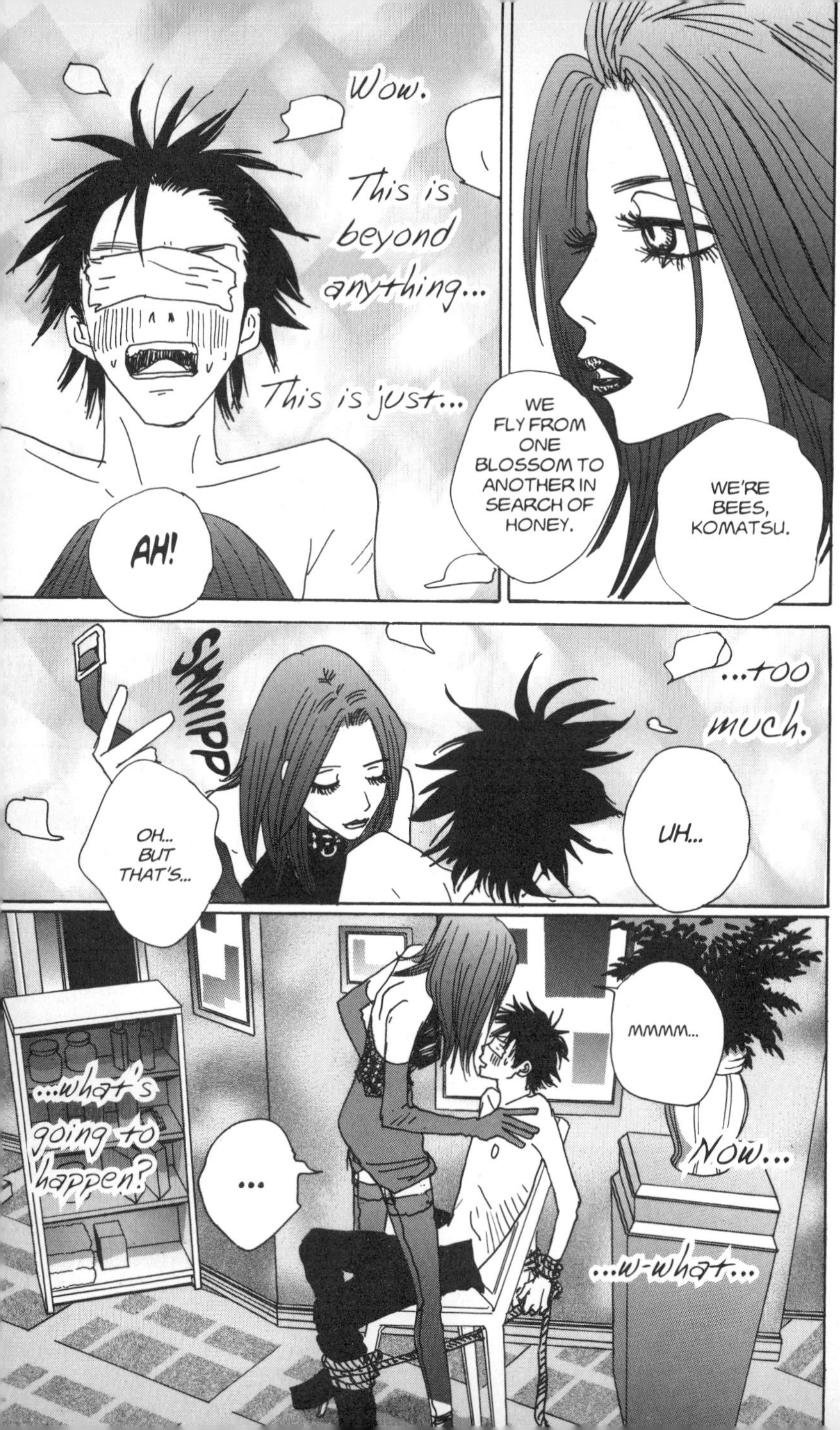
WE'RE BEES, KOMATSU.
WE FLY FROM ONE BLOSSOM TO ANOTHER IN SEARCH OF HONEY.
Wow.
This is beyond anything...
This is just...
AH!
...too much.
UH...
SHWIPP
OH... BUT THAT'S...
MMMM...
Now...
...w-what...
...
...what's going to happen?

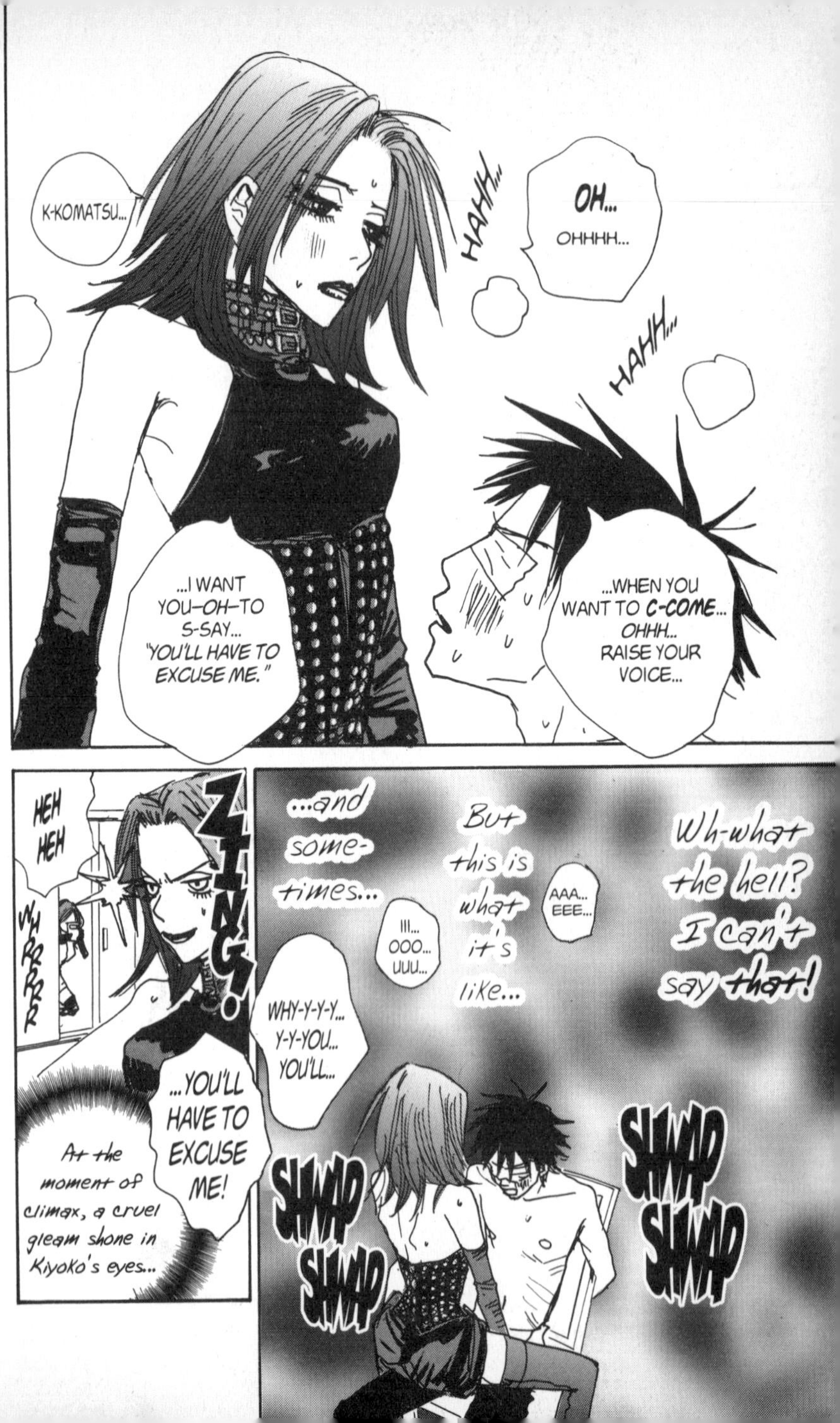
OH... OHHHH...
HAHH...
HAHH...
K-KOMATSU...
...WHEN YOU WANT TO C-COME... OHHH... RAISE YOUR VOICE...
...I WANT YOU—OH—TO S-SAY... "YOU'LL HAVE TO EXCUSE ME."
Wh-what the hell? I can't say that!
AAA... EEE...
But this is what it's like...
III... OOO... UUU...
...and some-times...
WHY-Y-Y-Y... Y-Y-YOU... YOU'LL...
SHWAP SHWAP
SHWAP SHWAP
ZING!
HEH HEH
WHRRRRR
...YOU'LL HAVE TO EXCUSE ME!
At the moment of climax, a cruel gleam shone in Kiyoko's eyes...

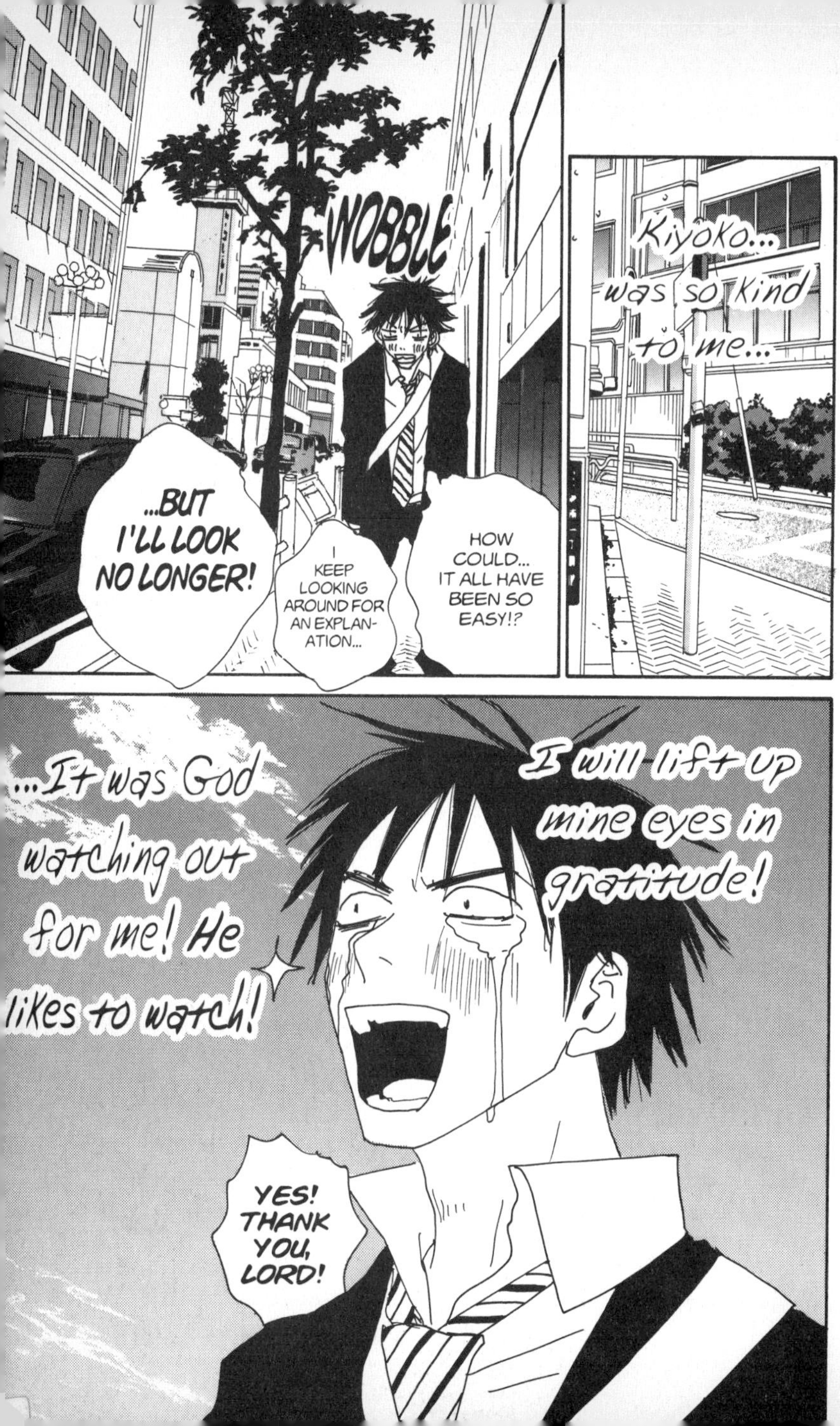

Kiyoko... was so kind to me...
WOBBLE
HOW COULD... IT ALL HAVE BEEN SO EASY!?
I KEEP LOOKING AROUND FOR AN EXPLANATION...
...BUT I'LL LOOK NO LONGER!
I will lift up mine eyes in gratitude!
...It was God watching out for me! He likes to watch!
YES! THANK YOU, LORD!

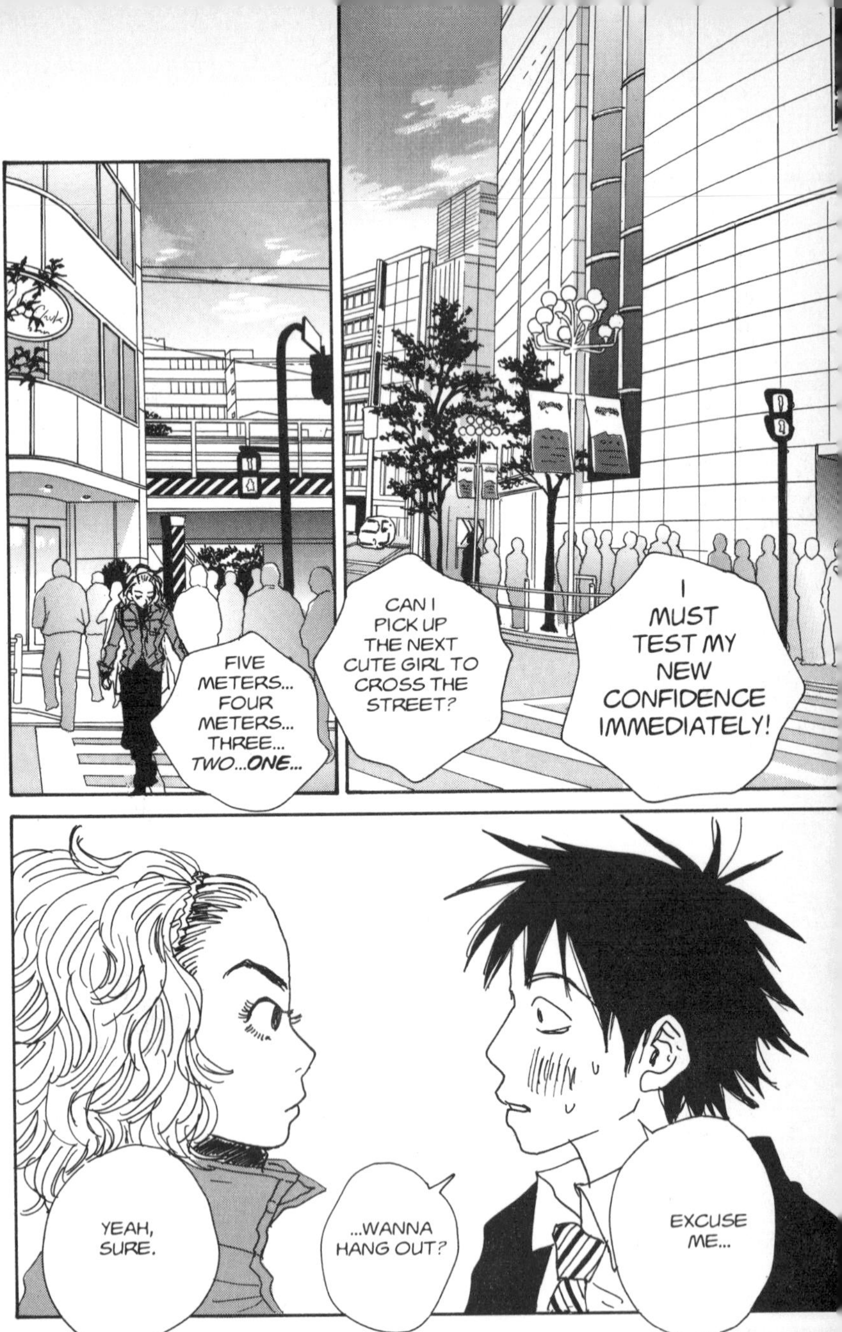
I MUST TEST MY NEW CONFIDENCE IMMEDIATELY!
CAN I PICK UP THE NEXT CUTE GIRL TO CROSS THE STREET?
FIVE METERS... FOUR METERS... THREE... TWO...*ONE*...
EXCUSE ME...
...WANNA HANG OUT?
YEAH, SURE.

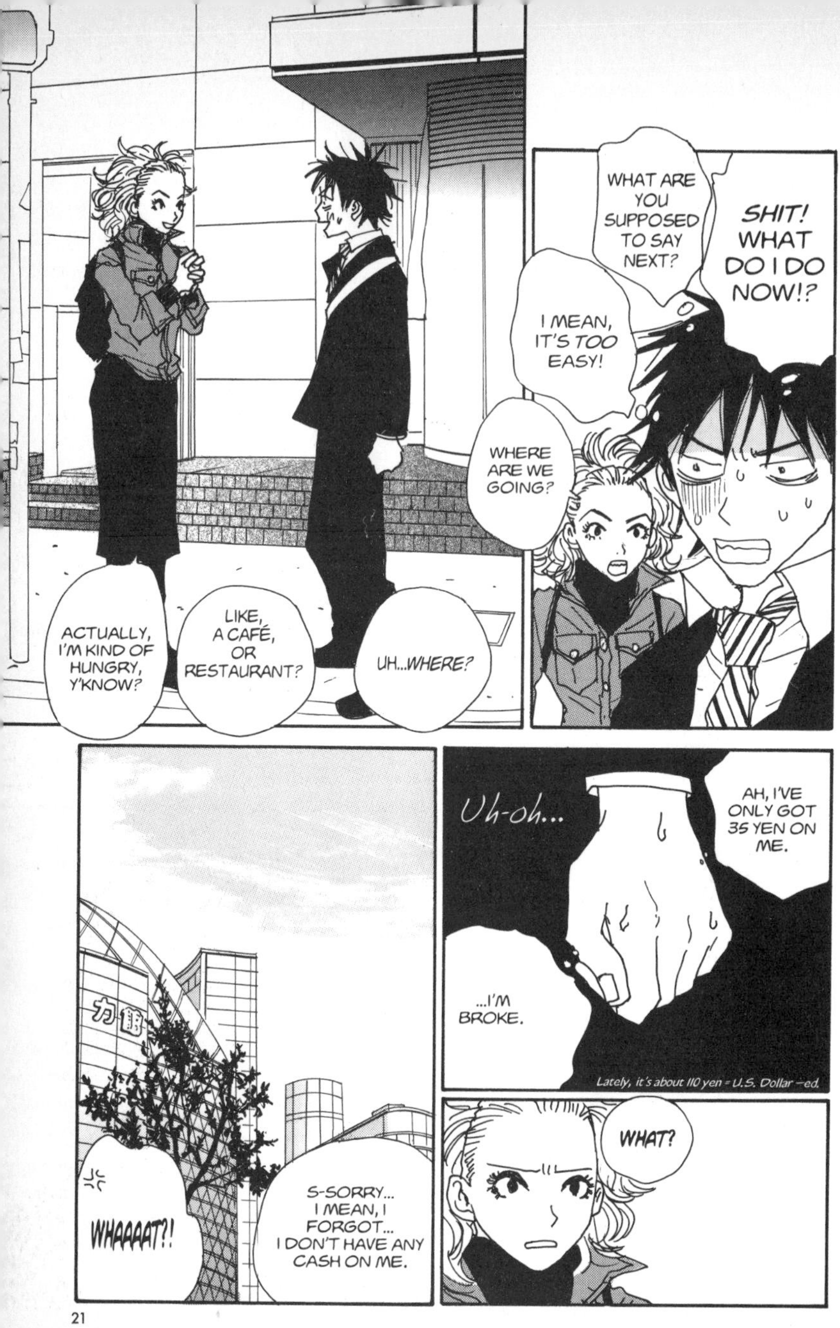
SHIT! WHAT DO I DO NOW!?
WHAT ARE YOU SUPPOSED TO SAY NEXT?
I MEAN, IT'S *TOO* EASY!
WHERE ARE WE GOING?
UH...*WHERE?*
LIKE, A CAFÉ, OR RESTAURANT?
ACTUALLY, I'M KIND OF HUNGRY, Y'KNOW?
AH, I'VE ONLY GOT 35 YEN ON ME.
Uh-oh...
...I'M BROKE.
Lately, it's about 110 yen = U.S. Dollar —ed.
WHAT?
S-SORRY... I MEAN, I FORGOT... I DON'T HAVE ANY CASH ON ME.
WHAAAAT?!

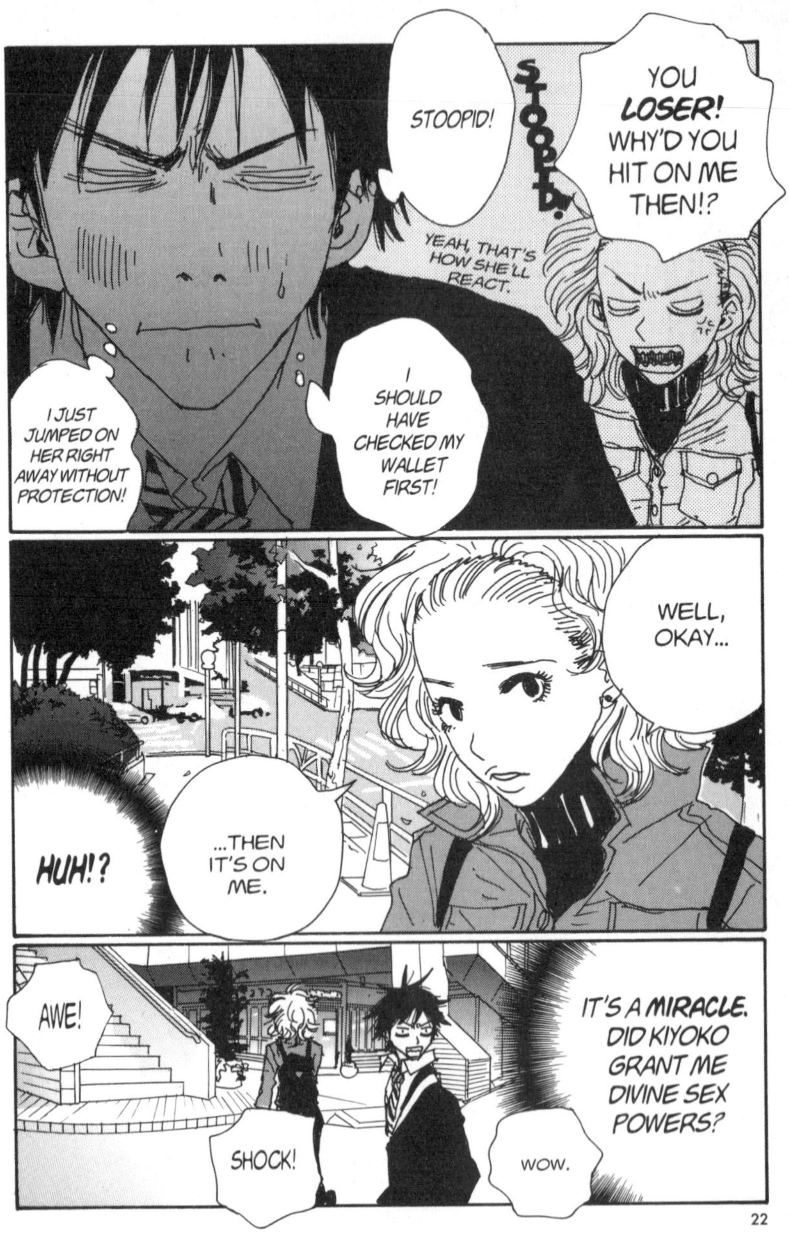
YOU LOSER! WHY'D YOU HIT ON ME THEN!?
STOOPID!
STOOPID!
YEAH, THAT'S HOW SHE'LL REACT.
I SHOULD HAVE CHECKED MY WALLET FIRST!
I JUST JUMPED ON HER RIGHT AWAY WITHOUT PROTECTION!
WELL, OKAY...
...THEN IT'S ON ME.
HUH!?
IT'S A MIRACLE. DID KIYOKO GRANT ME DIVINE SEX POWERS?
WOW.
SHOCK!
AWE!

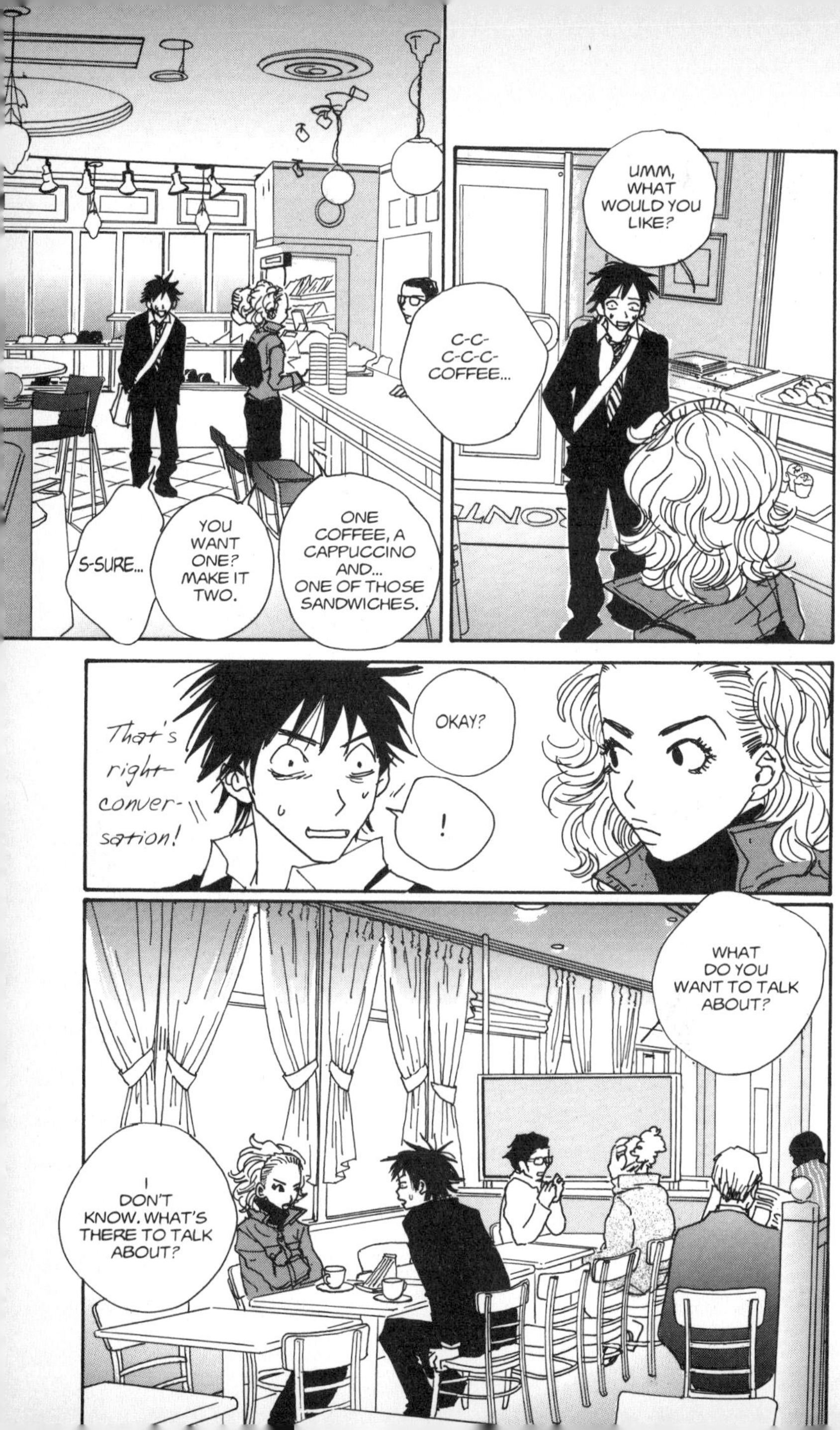
UMM, WHAT WOULD YOU LIKE?
C-C- C-C-C- COFFEE...
ONE COFFEE, A CAPPUCCINO AND... ONE OF THOSE SANDWICHES.
YOU WANT ONE? MAKE IT TWO.
S-SURE...
OKAY?
!
That's right- conversation!
WHAT DO YOU WANT TO TALK ABOUT?
I DON'T KNOW. WHAT'S THERE TO TALK ABOUT?

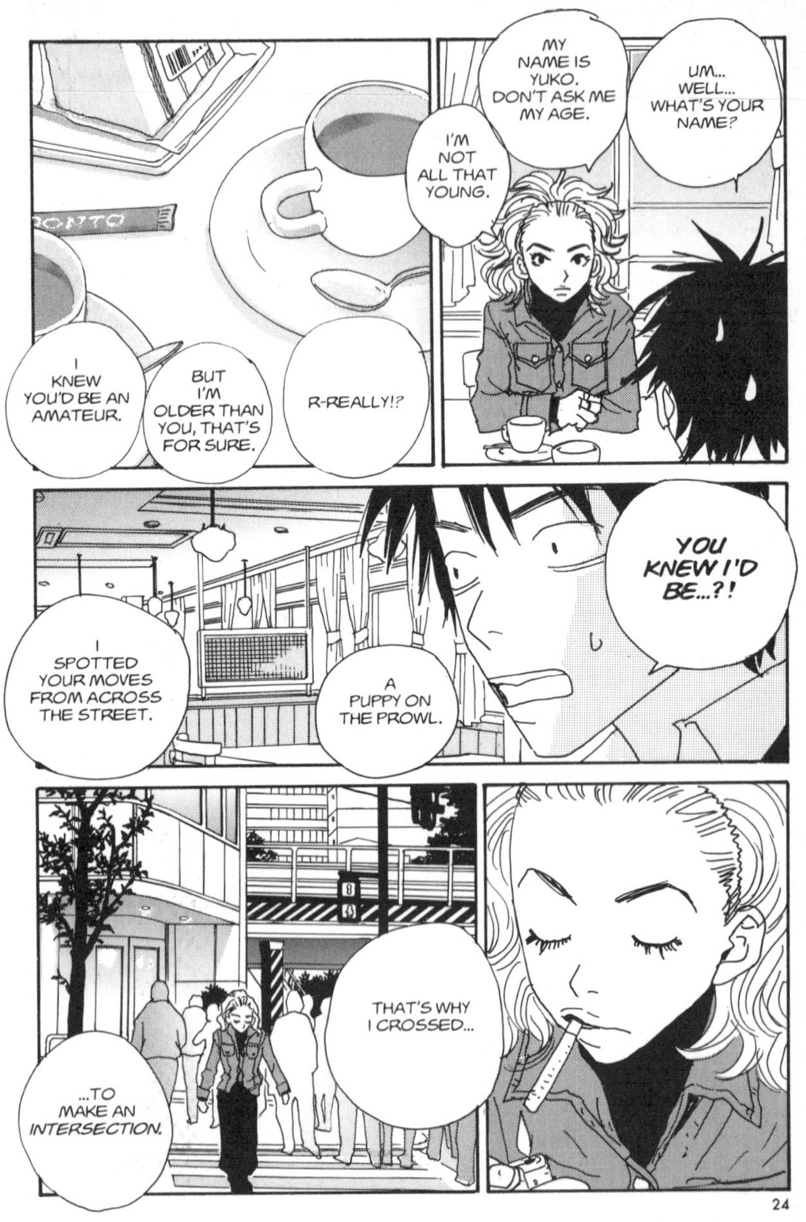
UM... WELL... WHAT'S YOUR NAME?
MY NAME IS YUKO. DON'T ASK ME MY AGE.
I'M NOT ALL THAT YOUNG.
R-REALLY!?
BUT I'M OLDER THAN YOU, THAT'S FOR SURE.
I KNEW YOU'D BE AN AMATEUR.
YOU KNEW I'D BE...?!
A PUPPY ON THE PROWL.
I SPOTTED YOUR MOVES FROM ACROSS THE STREET.
THAT'S WHY I CROSSED...
...TO MAKE AN INTERSECTION.

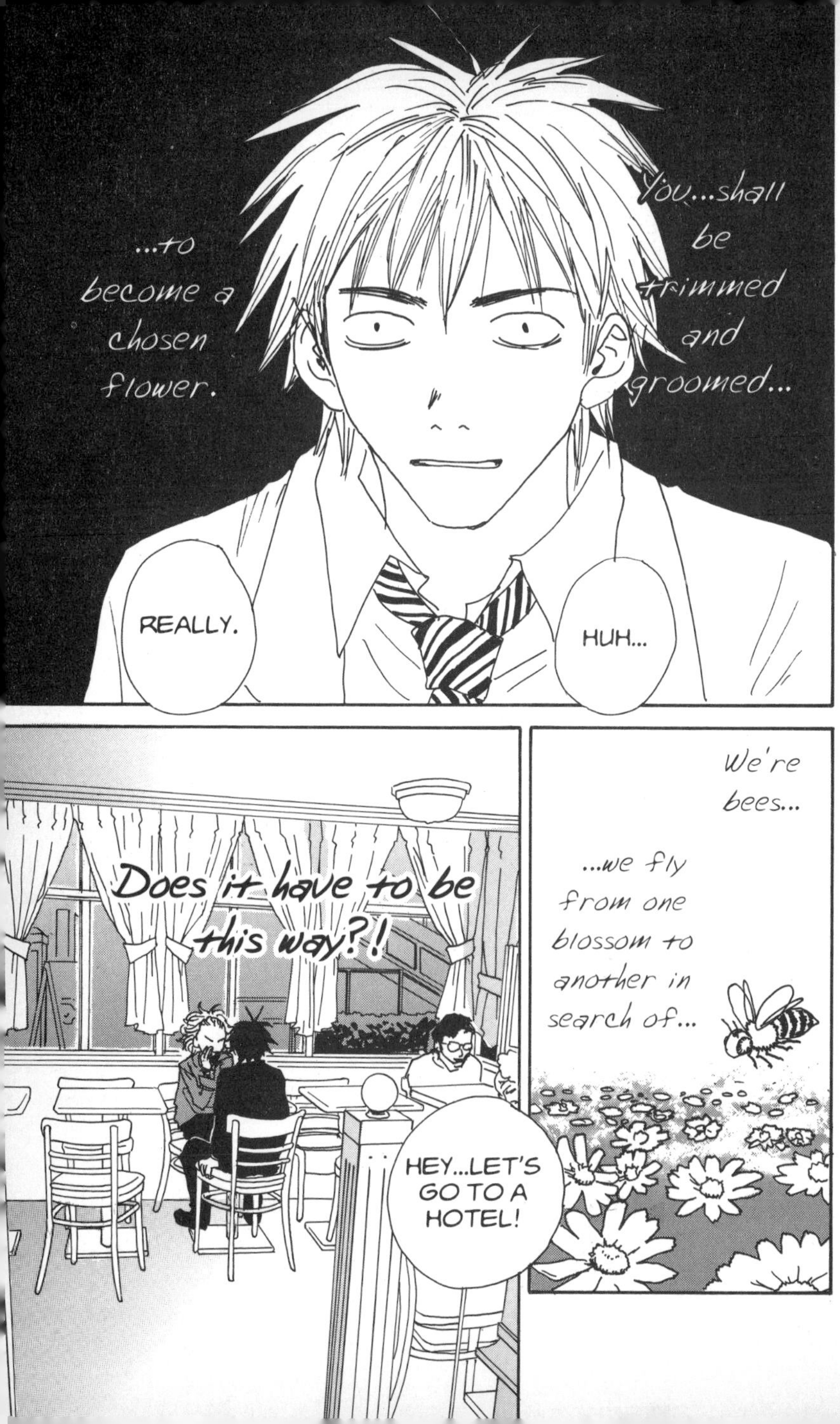
You...shall be trimmed and groomed...
...to become a chosen flower.
HUH...
REALLY.
We're bees...
...we fly from one blossom to another in search of...
Does it have to be this way?!
HEY...LET'S GO TO A HOTEL!

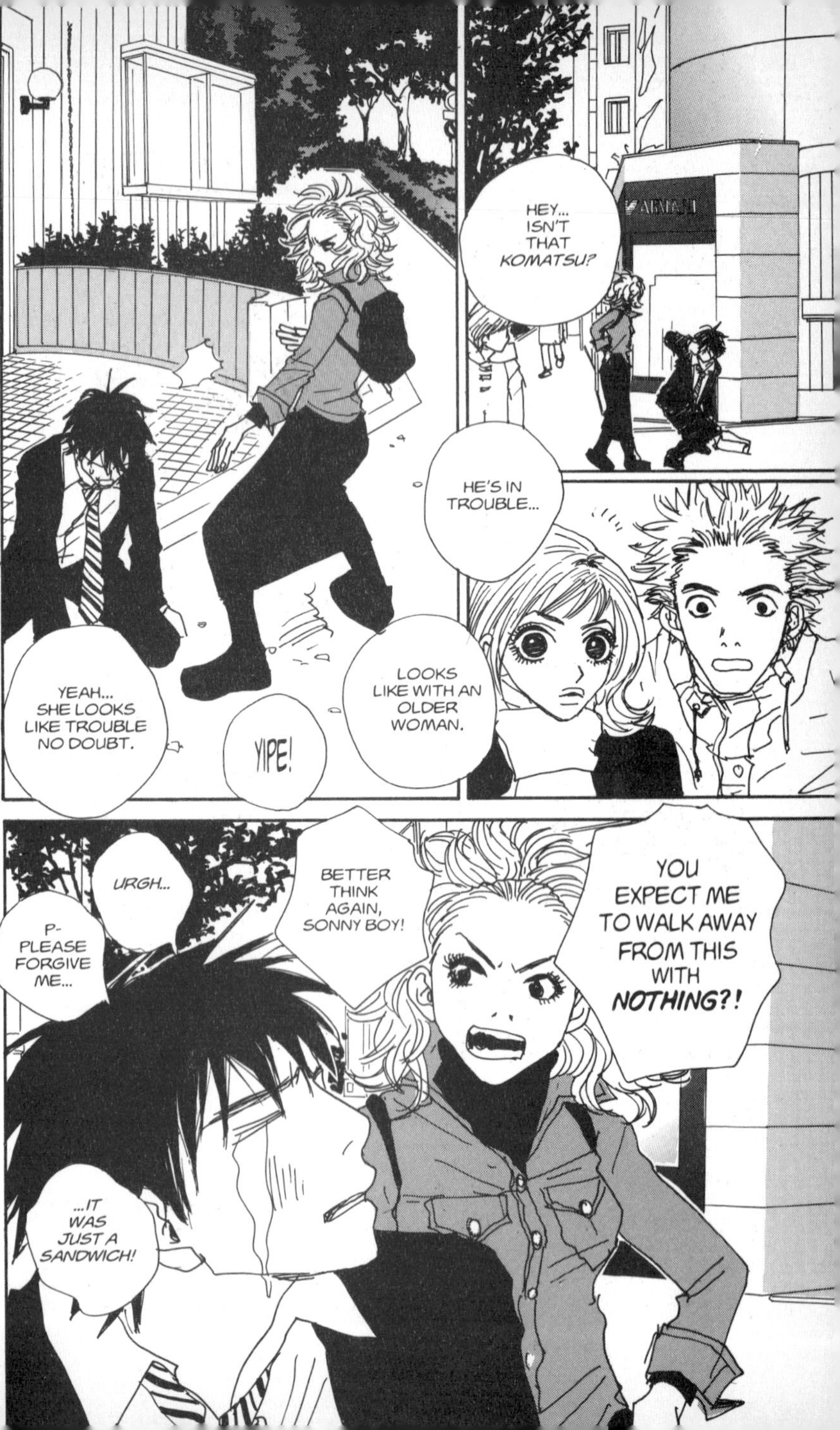

HEY... ISN'T THAT KOMATSU?
HE'S IN TROUBLE...
LOOKS LIKE WITH AN OLDER WOMAN.
YIPE!
YEAH... SHE LOOKS LIKE TROUBLE NO DOUBT.
YOU EXPECT ME TO WALK AWAY FROM THIS WITH NOTHING?!
BETTER THINK AGAIN, SONNY BOY!
URGH...
P- PLEASE FORGIVE ME...
...IT WAS JUST A SANDWICH!

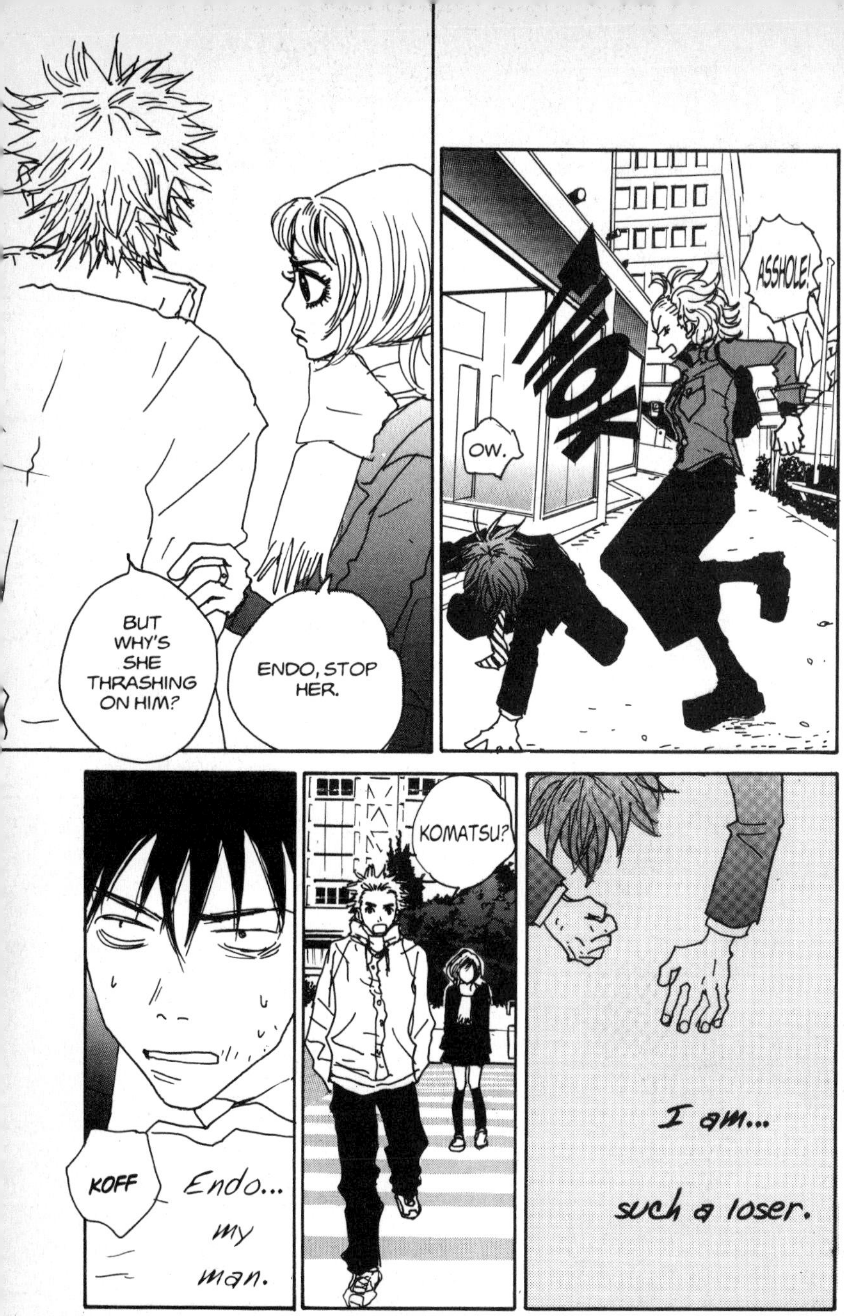
ASSHOLE!
THOK
OW.
ENDO, STOP HER.
BUT WHY'S SHE THRASHING ON HIM?
I am... such a loser.
KOMATSU?
Endo... my man.
KOFF

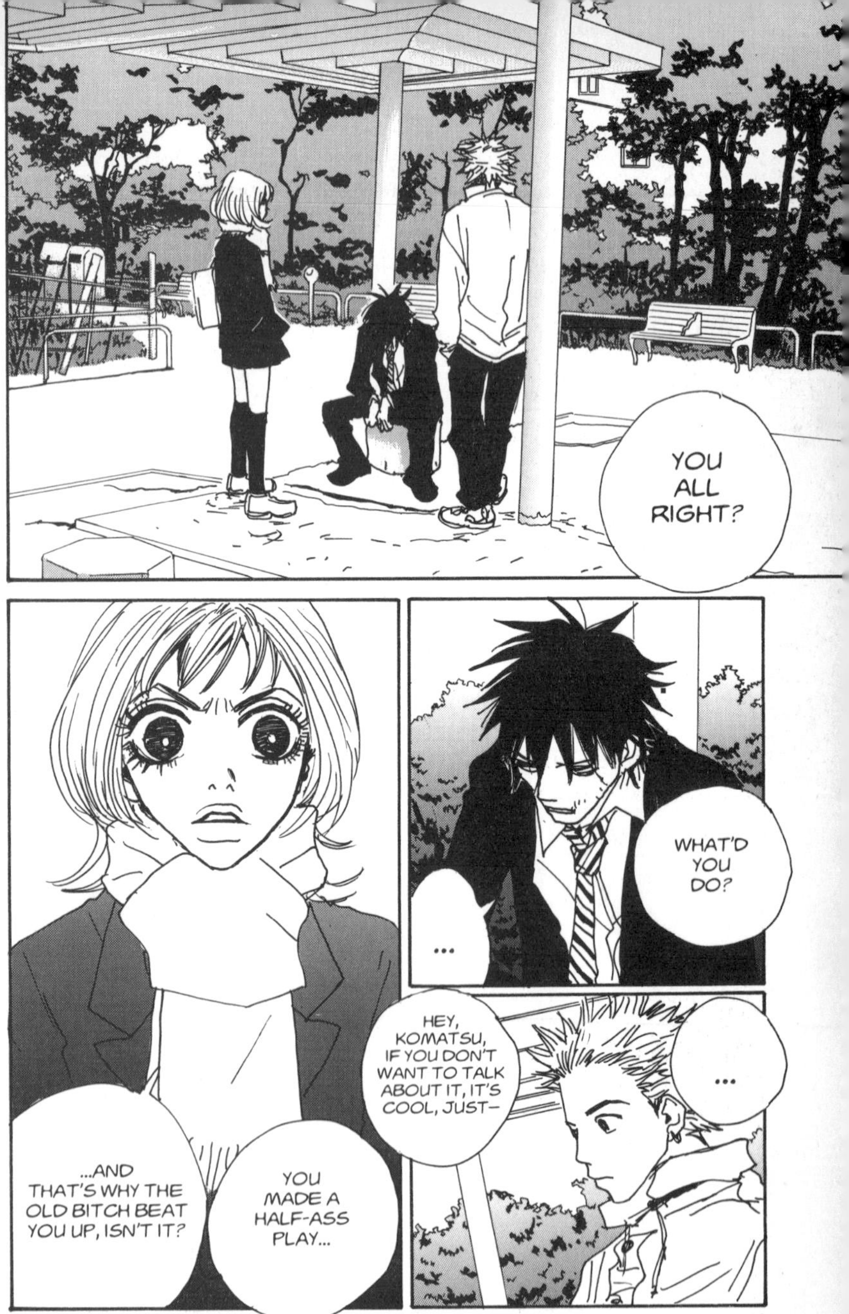

YOU ALL RIGHT?
WHAT'D YOU DO?
...
...
HEY, KOMATSU, IF YOU DON'T WANT TO TALK ABOUT IT, IT'S COOL, JUST—
YOU MADE A HALF-ASS PLAY...
...AND THAT'S WHY THE OLD BITCH BEAT YOU UP, ISN'T IT?

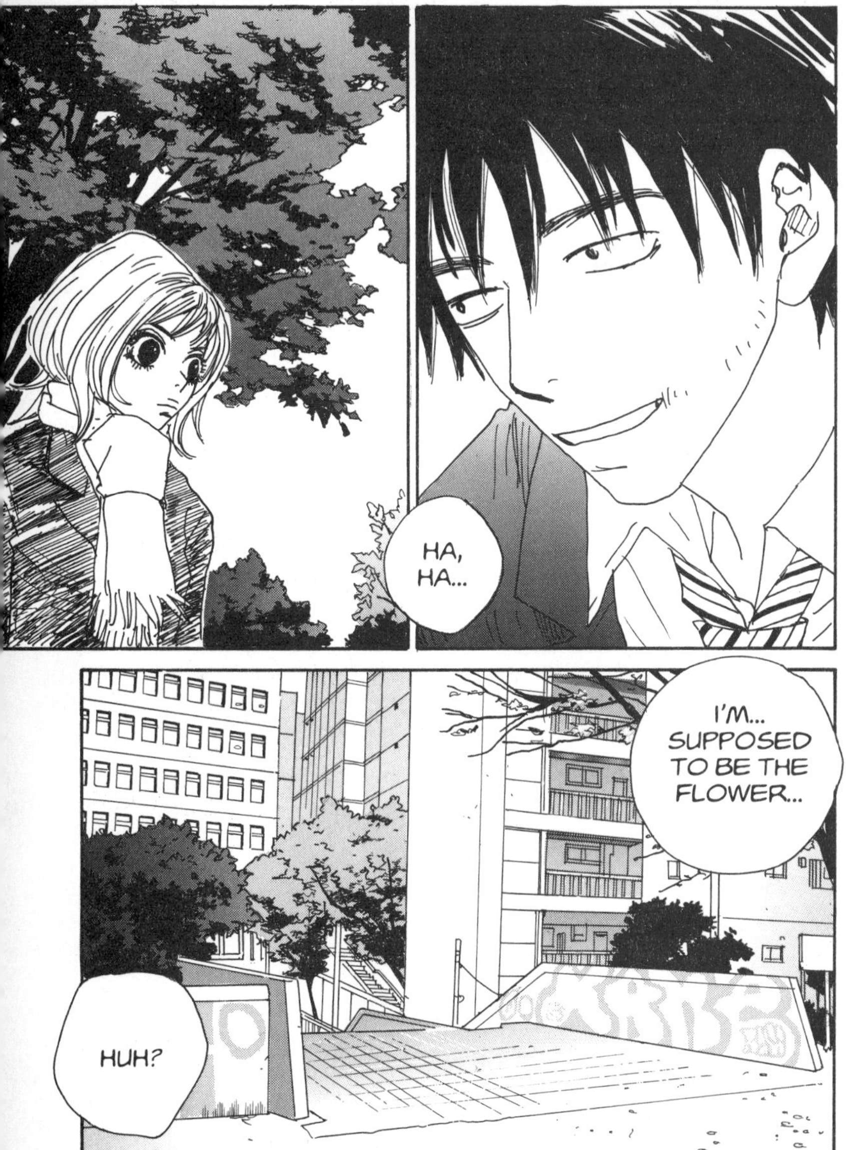
HA, HA...
I'M... SUPPOSED TO BE THE FLOWER...
HUH?

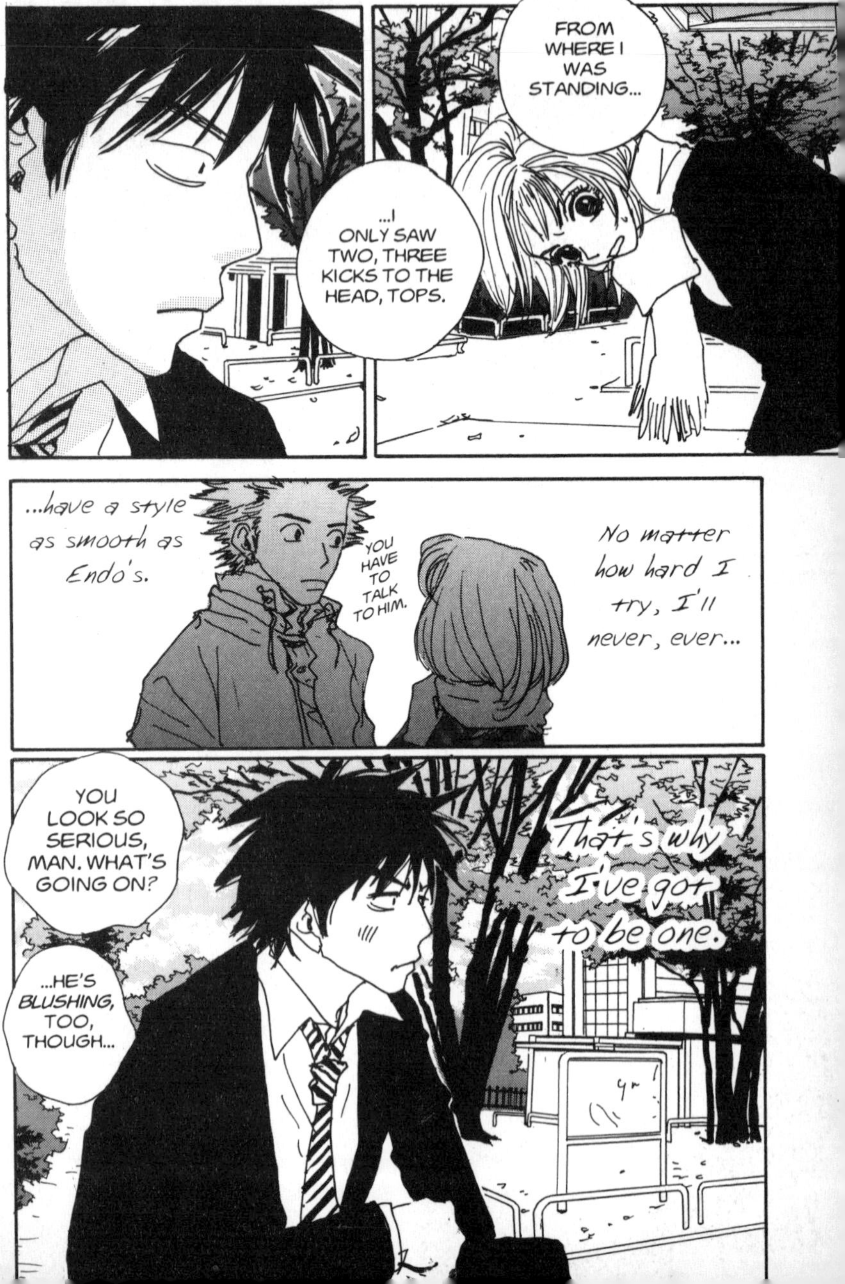
FROM WHERE I WAS STANDING...
...I ONLY SAW TWO, THREE KICKS TO THE HEAD, TOPS.
No matter how hard I try, I'll never, ever...
YOU HAVE TO TALK TO HIM.
...have a style as smooth as Endo's.
That's why I've got to be one.
YOU LOOK SO SERIOUS, MAN. WHAT'S GOING ON?
...HE'S BLUSHING, TOO, THOUGH...

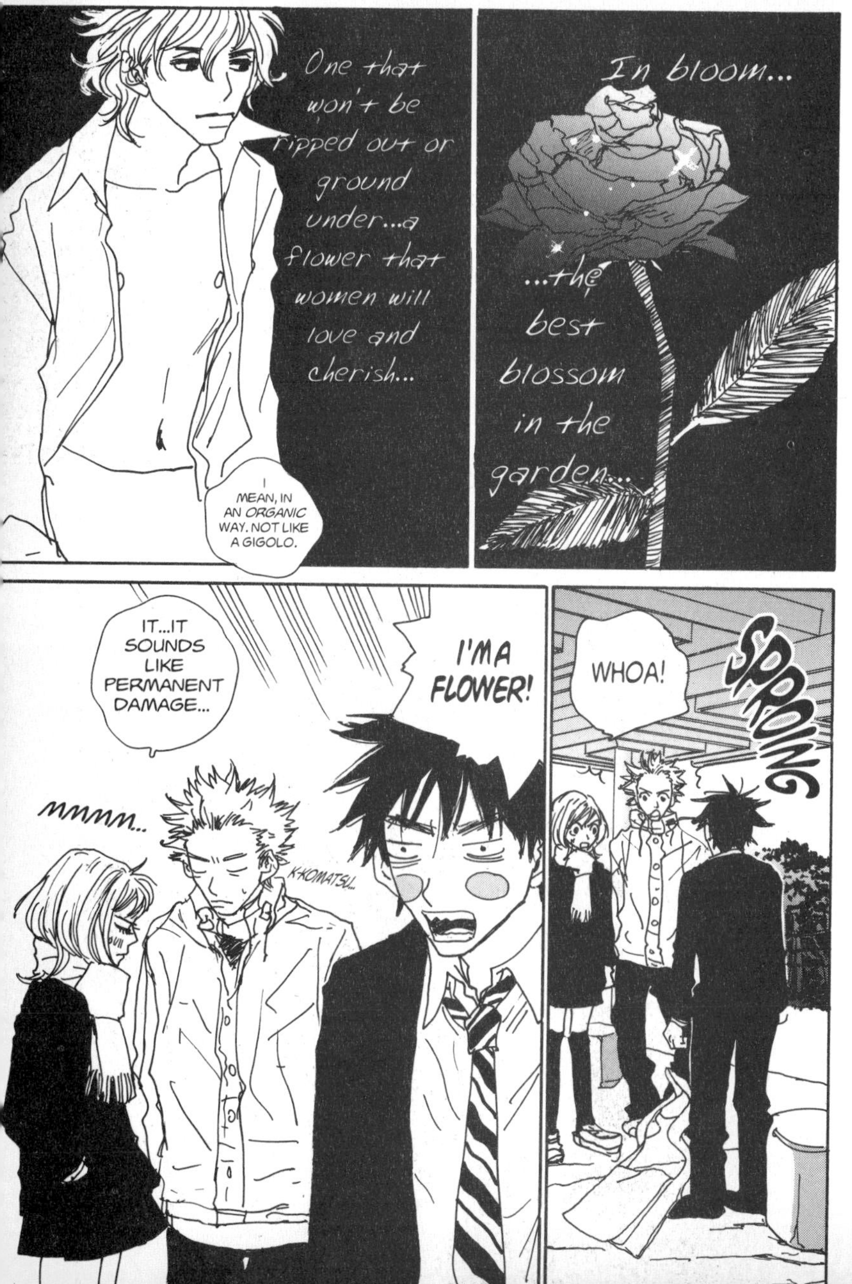

In bloom...
...the best blossom in the garden...
One that won't be ripped out or ground under...a flower that women will love and cherish...
I MEAN, IN AN *ORGANIC* WAY. NOT LIKE A GIGOLO.
SPROING
WHOA!
I'M A FLOWER!
IT...IT SOUNDS LIKE PERMANENT DAMAGE...
K-KOMATSU...
mmmm...

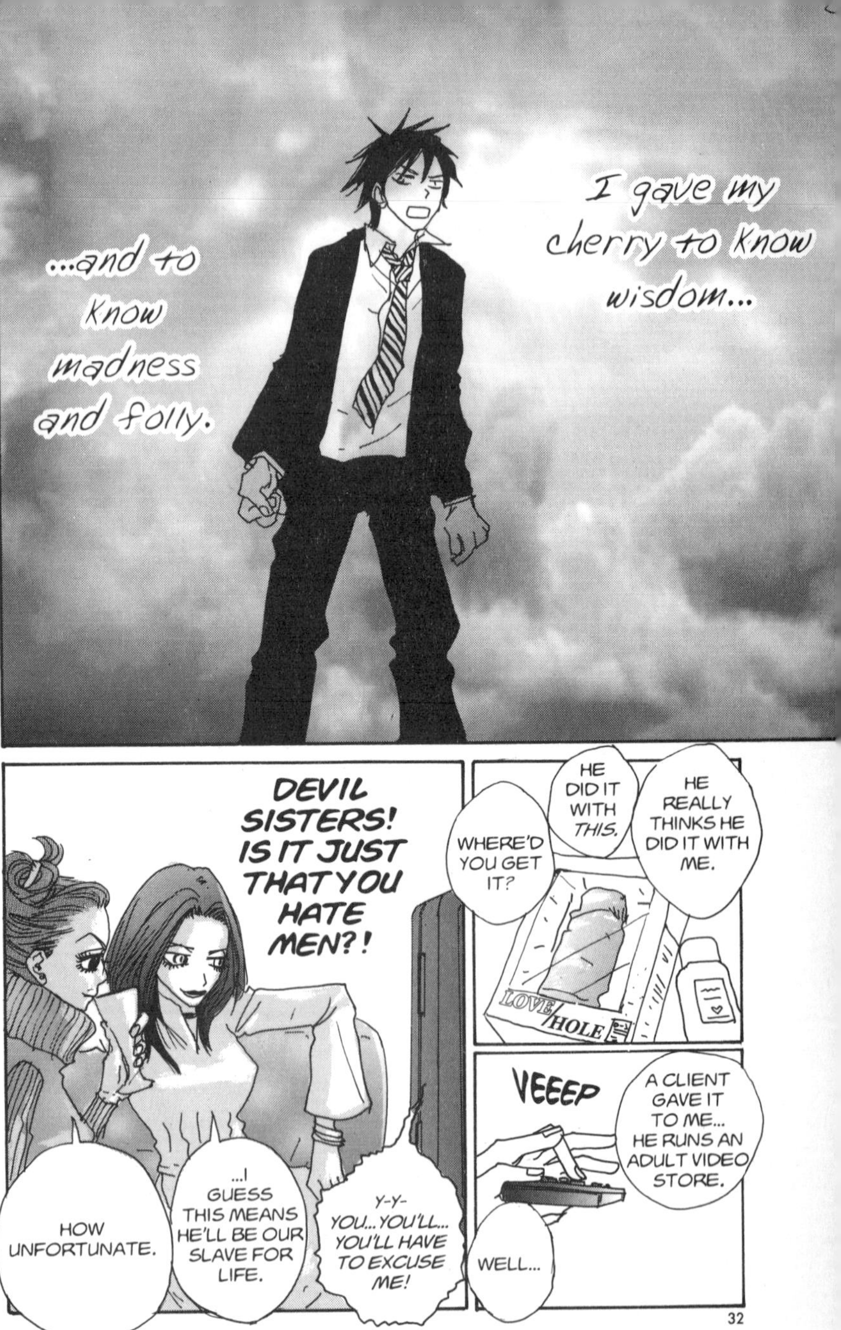
I gave my cherry to know wisdom...
...and to know madness and folly.
HE REALLY THINKS HE DID IT WITH ME.
HE DID IT WITH THIS.
WHERE'D YOU GET IT?
LOVE HOLE
A CLIENT GAVE IT TO ME... HE RUNS AN ADULT VIDEO STORE.
VEEEP
WELL...
DEVIL SISTERS! IS IT JUST THAT YOU HATE MEN?!
Y-Y- YOU... YOU'LL... YOU'LL HAVE TO EXCUSE ME!
...I GUESS THIS MEANS HE'LL BE OUR SLAVE FOR LIFE.
HOW UNFORTUNATE.

Step 09

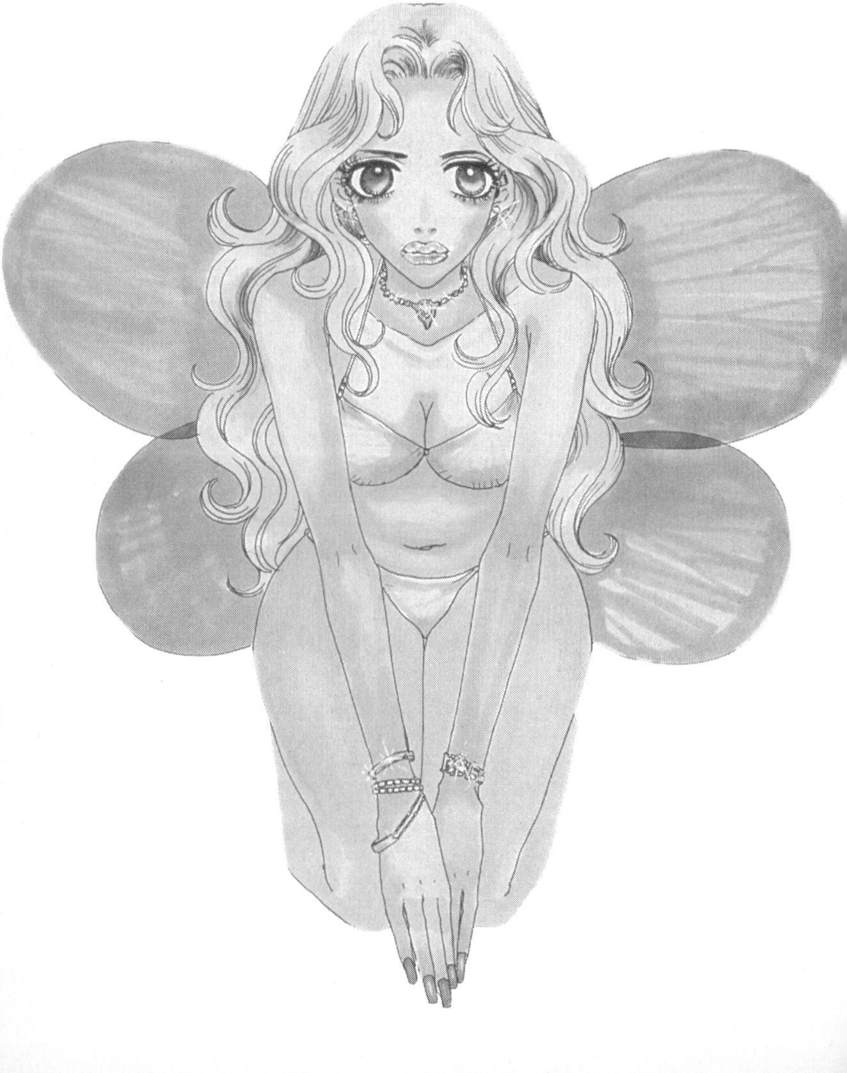

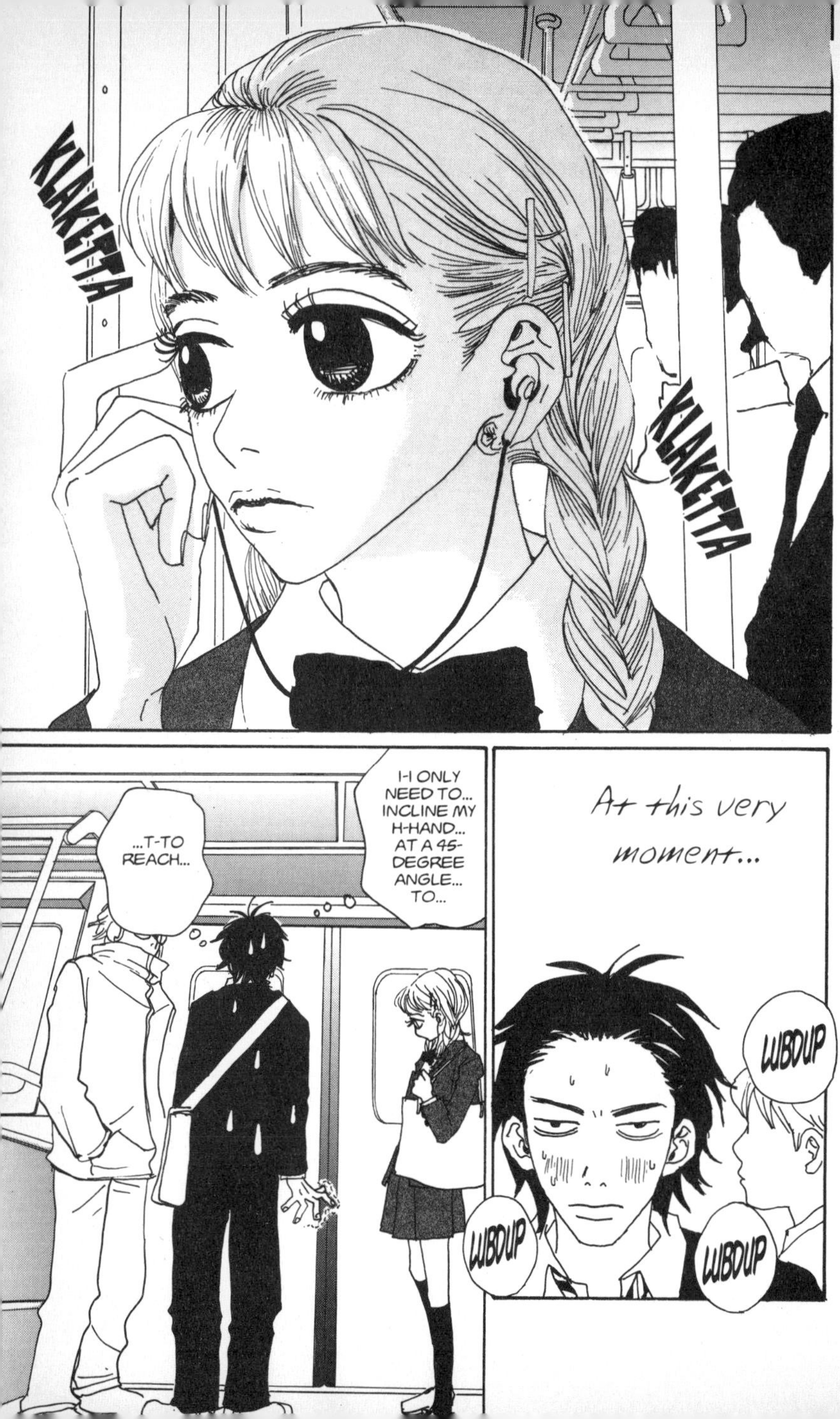
KLAKETTA
KLAKETTA
At this very moment...
LUBDUP
LUBDUP
LUBDUP
I-I ONLY NEED TO... INCLINE MY H-HAND... AT A 45-DEGREE ANGLE... TO...
...T-TO REACH...

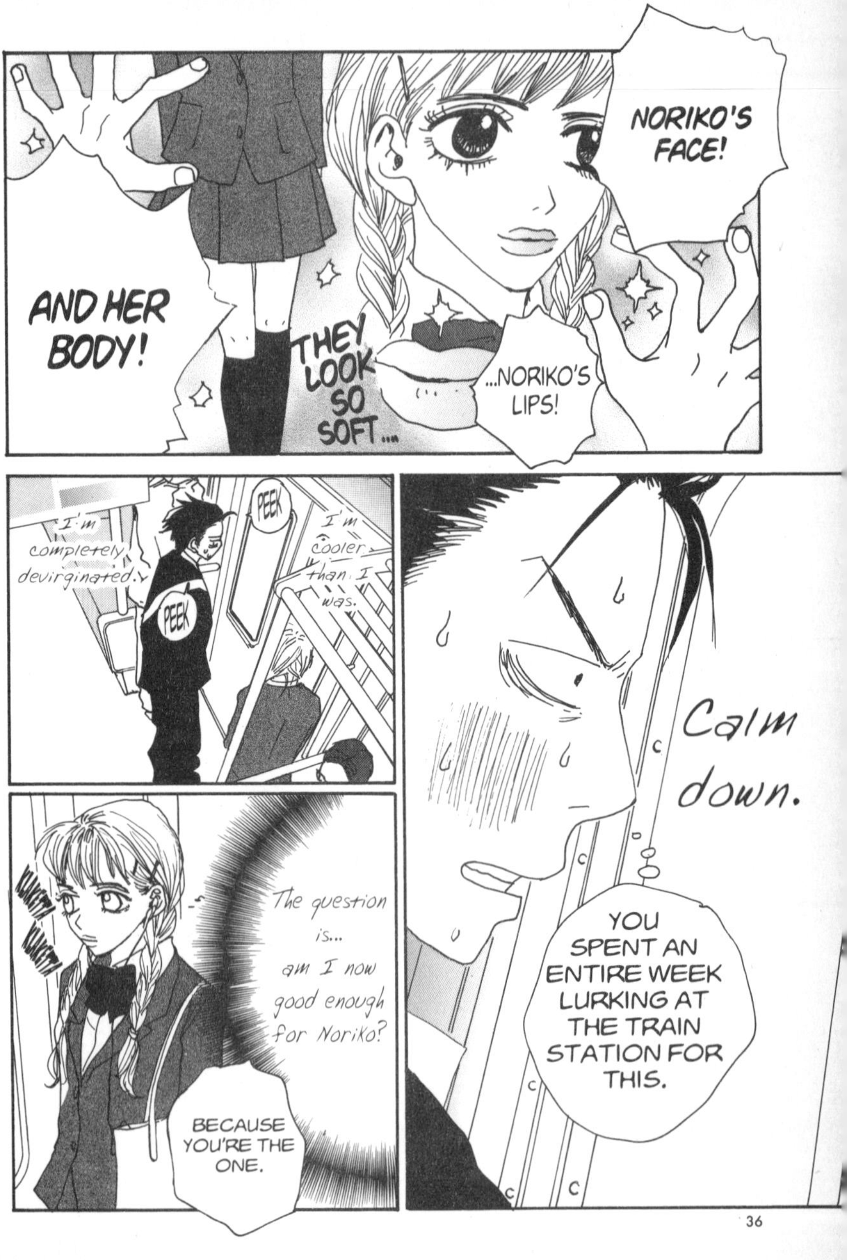
NORIKO'S FACE!
...NORIKO'S LIPS!
THEY LOOK SO SOFT...
AND HER BODY!
Calm down.
YOU SPENT AN ENTIRE WEEK LURKING AT THE TRAIN STATION FOR THIS.
I'm cooler than I was.
PEEK
I'm completely devirginated.
PEEK
The question is... am I now good enough for Noriko?
BECAUSE YOU'RE THE ONE.

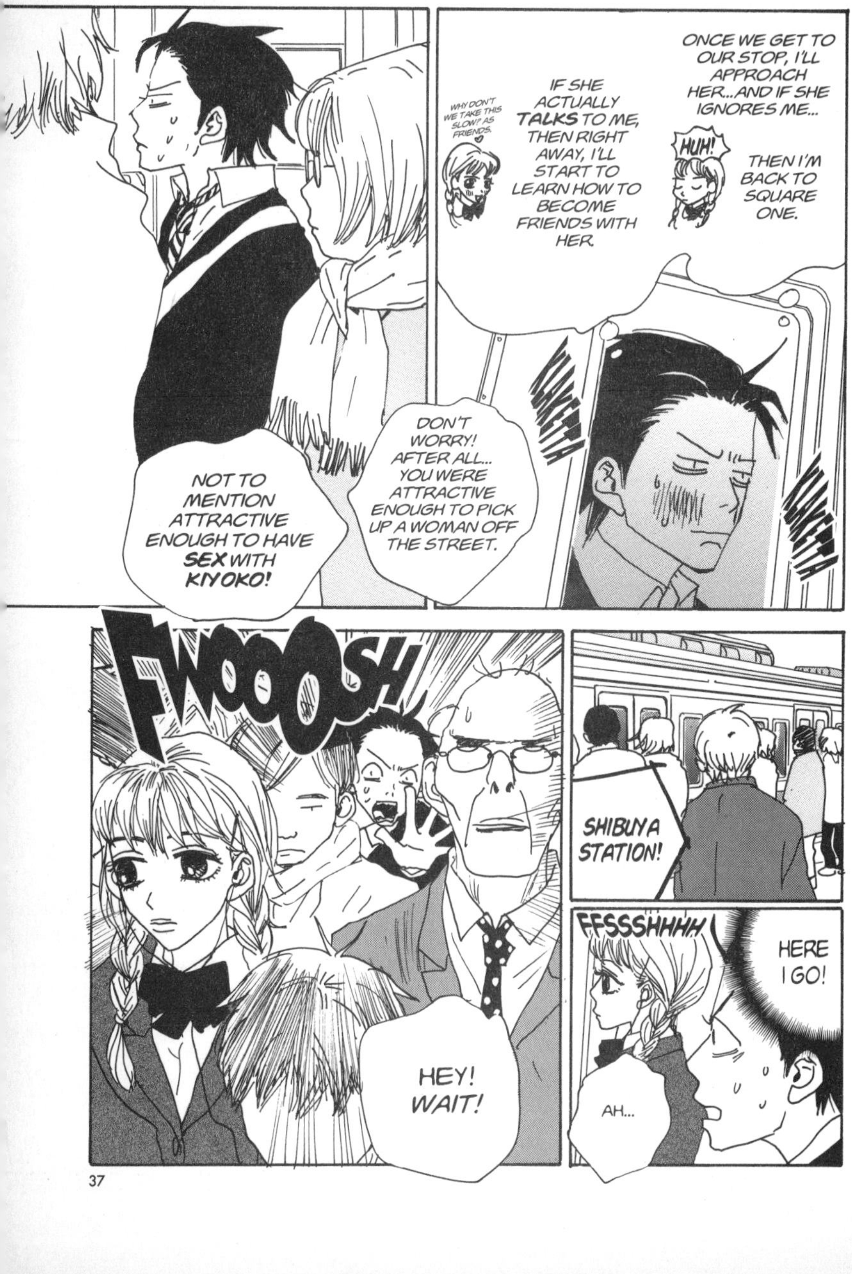
ONCE WE GET TO OUR STOP, I'LL APPROACH HER...AND IF SHE IGNORES ME...
HUH!
THEN I'M BACK TO SQUARE ONE.
IF SHE ACTUALLY TALKS TO ME, THEN RIGHT AWAY, I'LL START TO LEARN HOW TO BECOME FRIENDS WITH HER.
WHY DON'T WE TAKE THIS SLOW? AS FRIENDS. ♡
DON'T WORRY! AFTER ALL... YOU WERE ATTRACTIVE ENOUGH TO PICK UP A WOMAN OFF THE STREET.
NOT TO MENTION ATTRACTIVE ENOUGH TO HAVE SEX WITH KIYOKO!
SHIBUYA STATION!
FFSSSHHHH
HERE I GO!
AH...
FWOOOSH
HEY! WAIT!

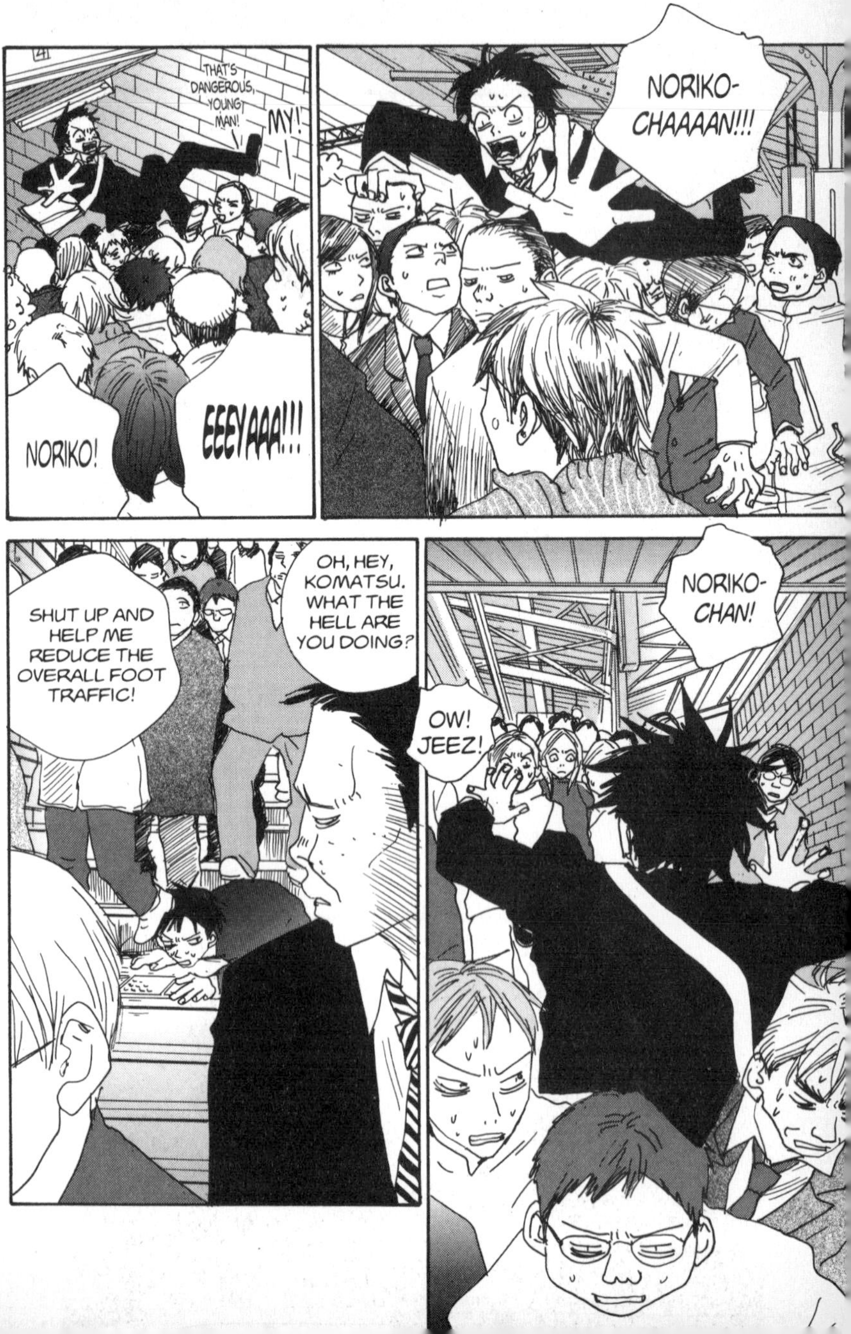
NORIKO-CHAAAAN!!!
MY!
THAT'S DANGEROUS, YOUNG MAN!
EEEYAAA!!!
NORIKO!
NORIKO-CHAN!
OW! JEEZ!
OH, HEY, KOMATSU. WHAT THE HELL ARE YOU DOING?
SHUT UP AND HELP ME REDUCE THE OVERALL FOOT TRAFFIC!

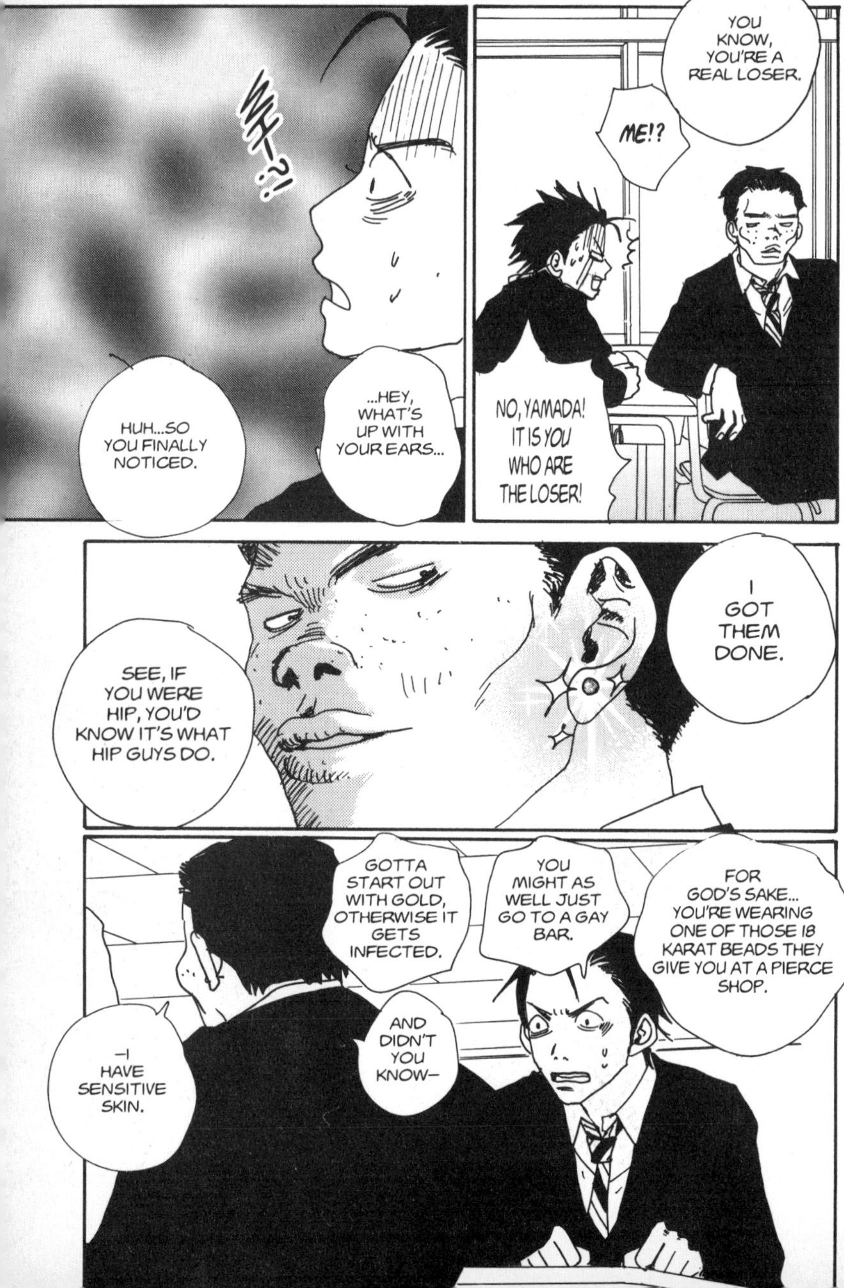
YOU KNOW, YOU'RE A REAL LOSER.
ME!?
NO, YAMADA! IT IS YOU WHO ARE THE LOSER!
...HEY, WHAT'S UP WITH YOUR EARS...
HUH...SO YOU FINALLY NOTICED.
I GOT THEM DONE.
SEE, IF YOU WERE HIP, YOU'D KNOW IT'S WHAT HIP GUYS DO.
FOR GOD'S SAKE... YOU'RE WEARING ONE OF THOSE 18 KARAT BEADS THEY GIVE YOU AT A PIERCE SHOP.
YOU MIGHT AS WELL JUST GO TO A GAY BAR.
GOTTA START OUT WITH GOLD, OTHERWISE IT GETS INFECTED.
AND DIDN'T YOU KNOW—
—I HAVE SENSITIVE SKIN.

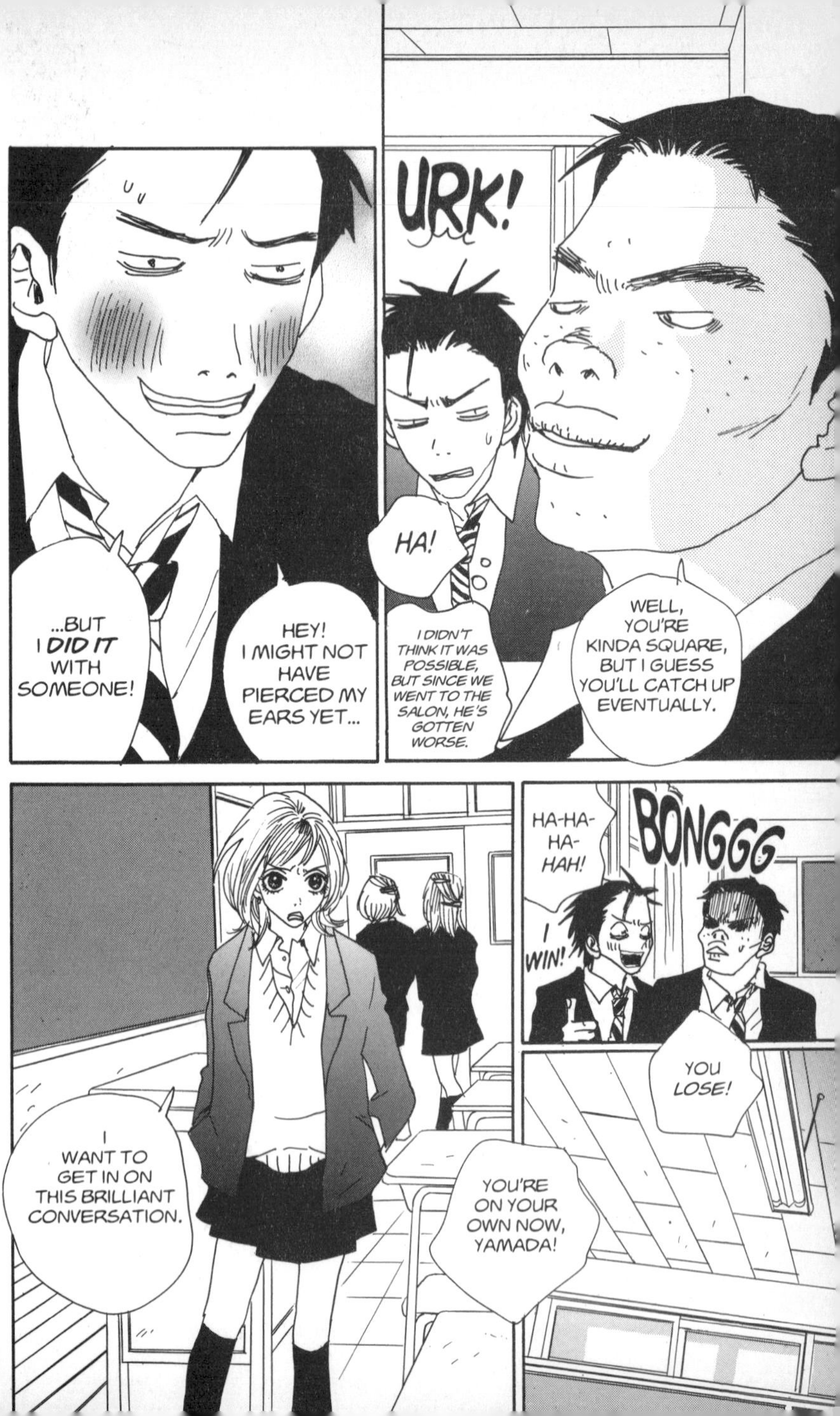
WELL, YOU'RE KINDA SQUARE, BUT I GUESS YOU'LL CATCH UP EVENTUALLY.
URK!
HA!
I DIDN'T THINK IT WAS POSSIBLE, BUT SINCE WE WENT TO THE SALON, HE'S GOTTEN WORSE.
HEY! I MIGHT NOT HAVE PIERCED MY EARS YET...
...BUT I **DID IT** WITH SOMEONE!
BONGGG
HA-HA-HA-HAH!
I WIN!
YOU LOSE!
YOU'RE ON YOUR OWN NOW, YAMADA!
I WANT TO GET IN ON THIS BRILLIANT CONVERSATION.

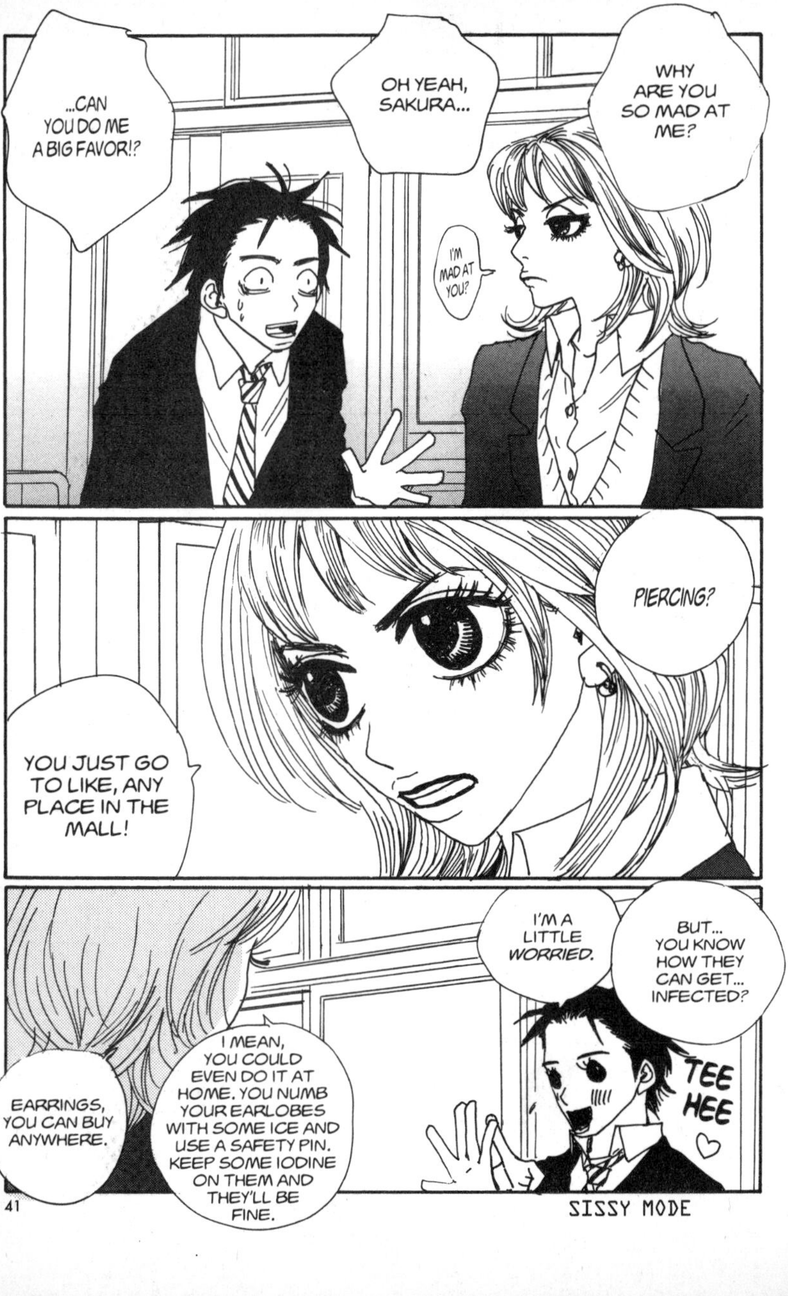
WHY ARE YOU SO MAD AT ME?
I'M MAD AT YOU?
OH YEAH, SAKURA...
...CAN YOU DO ME A BIG FAVOR!?
PIERCING?
YOU JUST GO TO LIKE, ANY PLACE IN THE MALL!
BUT... YOU KNOW HOW THEY CAN GET... INFECTED?
I'M A LITTLE *WORRIED.*
TEE HEE
I MEAN, YOU COULD EVEN DO IT AT HOME. YOU NUMB YOUR EARLOBES WITH SOME ICE AND USE A SAFETY PIN. KEEP SOME IODINE ON THEM AND THEY'LL BE FINE.
EARRINGS, YOU CAN BUY ANYWHERE.
SISSY MODE

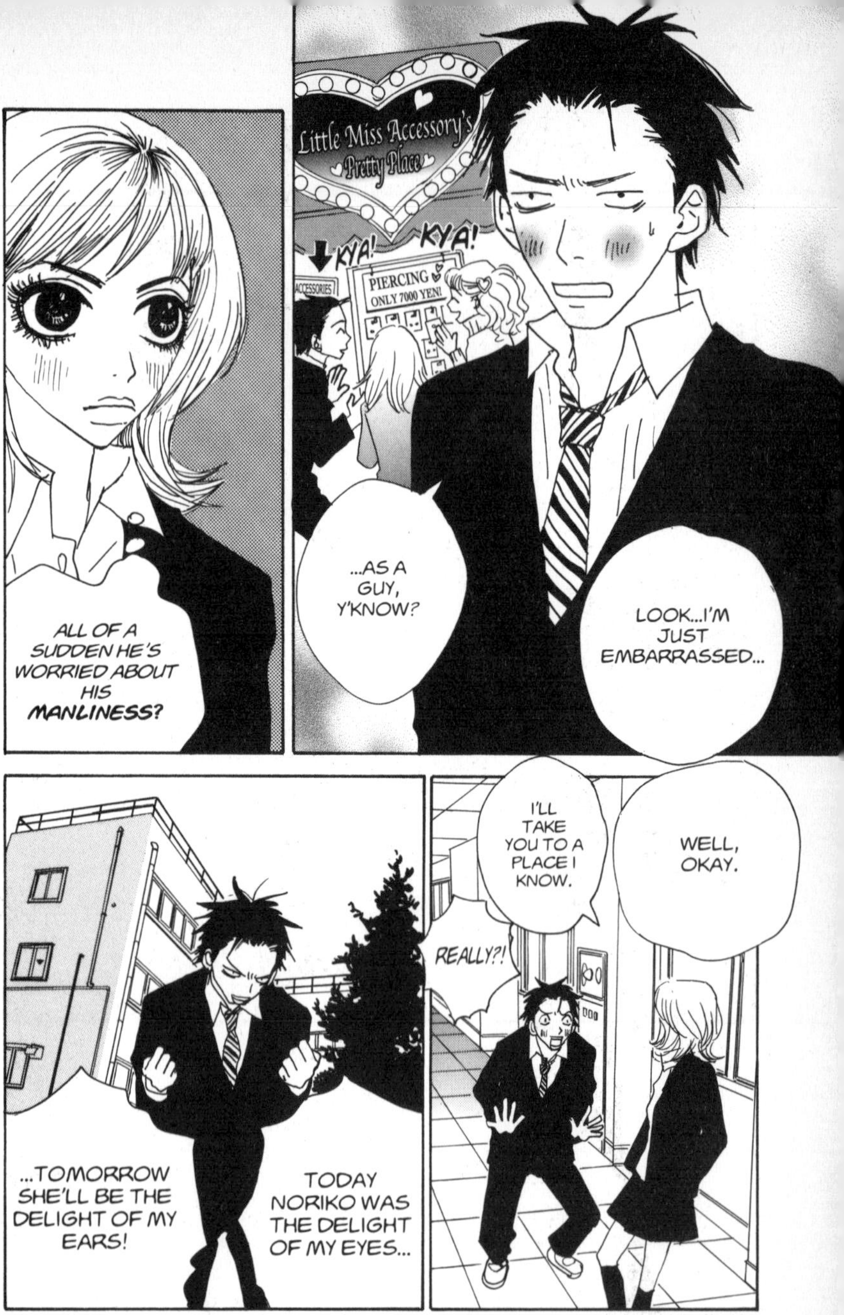
Little Miss Accessory's
Pretty Place
KYA!
KYA!
ACCESSORIES
PIERCING ONLY 7000 YEN!
LOOK...I'M JUST EMBARRASSED...
...AS A GUY, Y'KNOW?
ALL OF A SUDDEN HE'S WORRIED ABOUT HIS **MANLINESS?**
WELL, OKAY.
I'LL TAKE YOU TO A PLACE I KNOW.
REALLY?!
TODAY NORIKO WAS THE DELIGHT OF MY EYES...
...TOMORROW SHE'LL BE THE DELIGHT OF MY EARS!

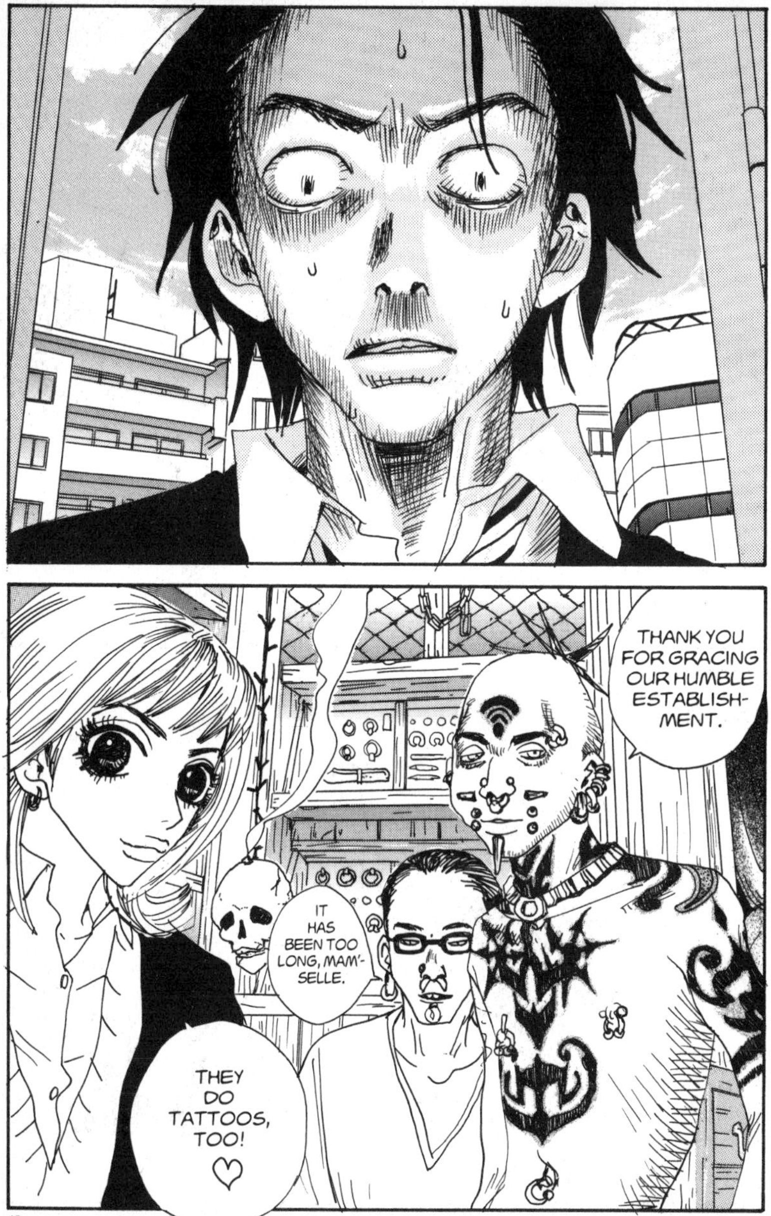
THANK YOU FOR GRACING OUR HUMBLE ESTABLISH-MENT.
IT HAS BEEN TOO LONG, MAM'-SELLE.
THEY DO TATTOOS, TOO! ♡

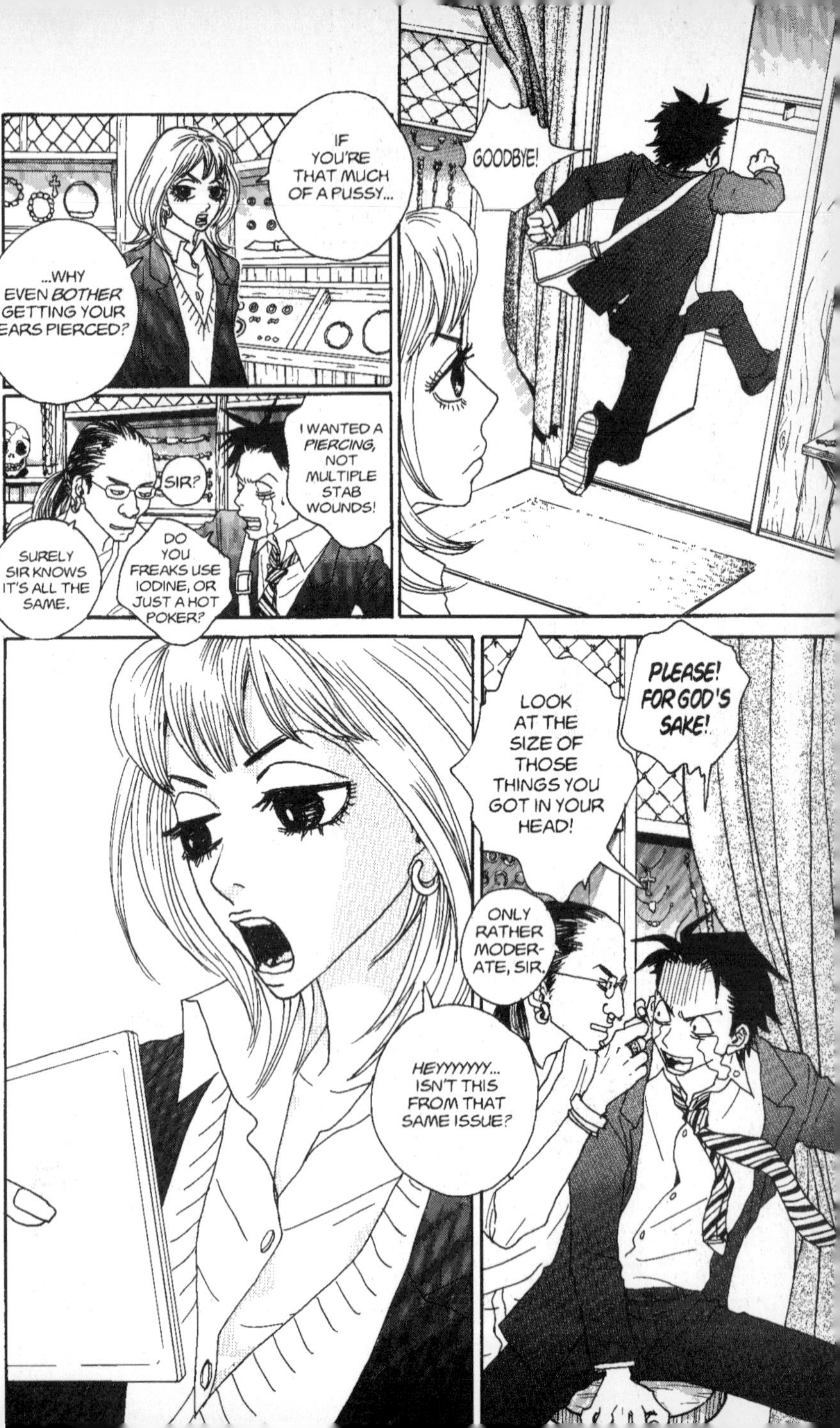
GOODBYE!
IF YOU'RE THAT MUCH OF A PUSSY...
...WHY EVEN BOTHER GETTING YOUR EARS PIERCED?
I WANTED A PIERCING, NOT MULTIPLE STAB WOUNDS!
SIR?
DO YOU FREAKS USE IODINE, OR JUST A HOT POKER?
SURELY SIR KNOWS IT'S ALL THE SAME.
PLEASE! FOR GOD'S SAKE!
LOOK AT THE SIZE OF THOSE THINGS YOU GOT IN YOUR HEAD!
ONLY RATHER MODER-ATE, SIR.
HEYYYYYYY... ISN'T THIS FROM THAT SAME ISSUE?

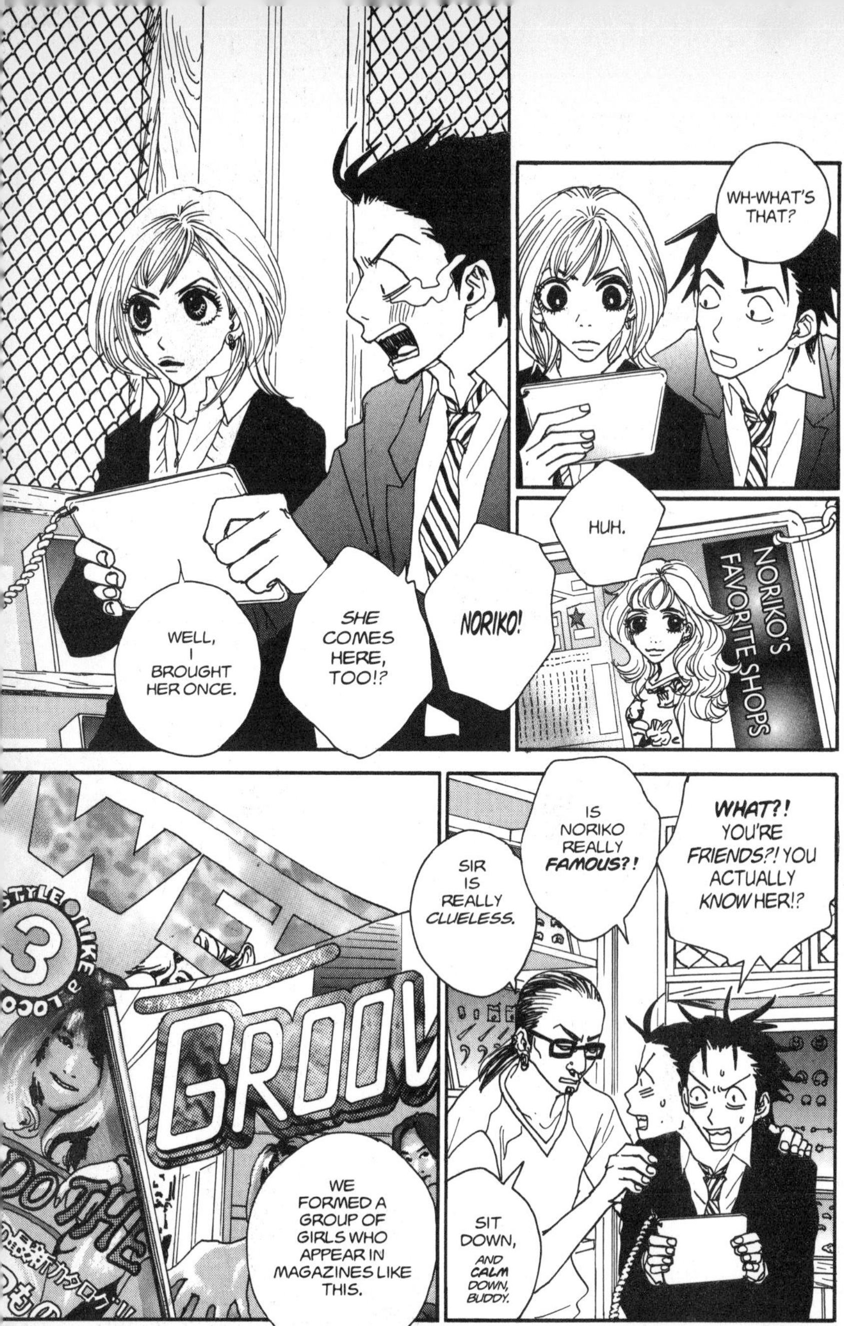
WH-WHAT'S THAT?
HUH.
NORIKO'S FAVORITE SHOPS
NORIKO!
SHE COMES HERE, TOO!?
WELL, I BROUGHT HER ONCE.
WHAT?! YOU'RE FRIENDS?! YOU ACTUALLY KNOW HER!?
IS NORIKO REALLY FAMOUS?!
SIR IS REALLY CLUELESS.
SIT DOWN, AND CALM DOWN, BUDDY.
WE FORMED A GROUP OF GIRLS WHO APPEAR IN MAGAZINES LIKE THIS.
GROOV

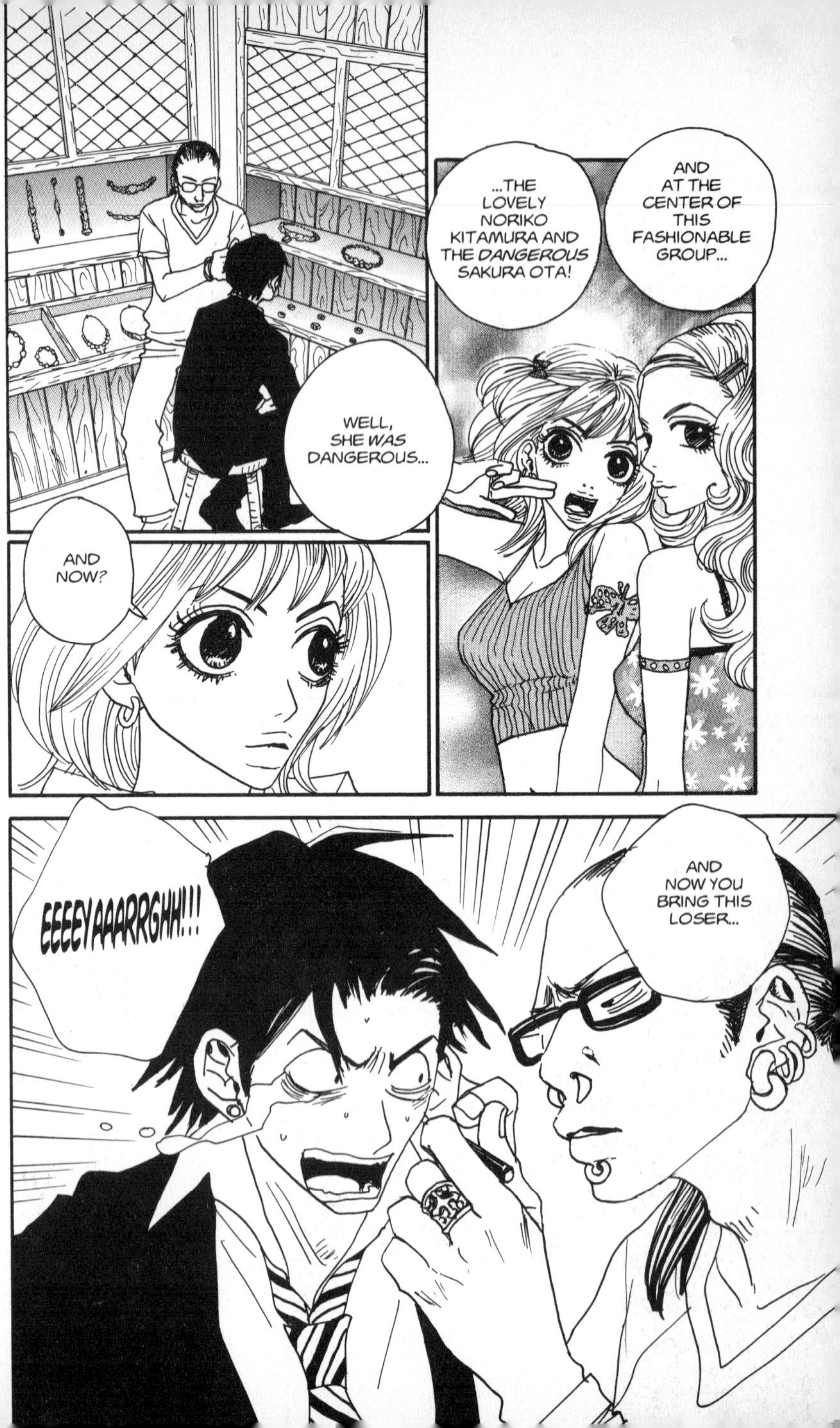
AND AT THE CENTER OF THIS FASHIONABLE GROUP...
...THE LOVELY NORIKO KITAMURA AND THE *DANGEROUS* SAKURA OTA!
WELL, SHE *WAS* DANGEROUS...
AND NOW?
AND NOW YOU BRING THIS LOSER...
EEEEYAAARRGHH!!!

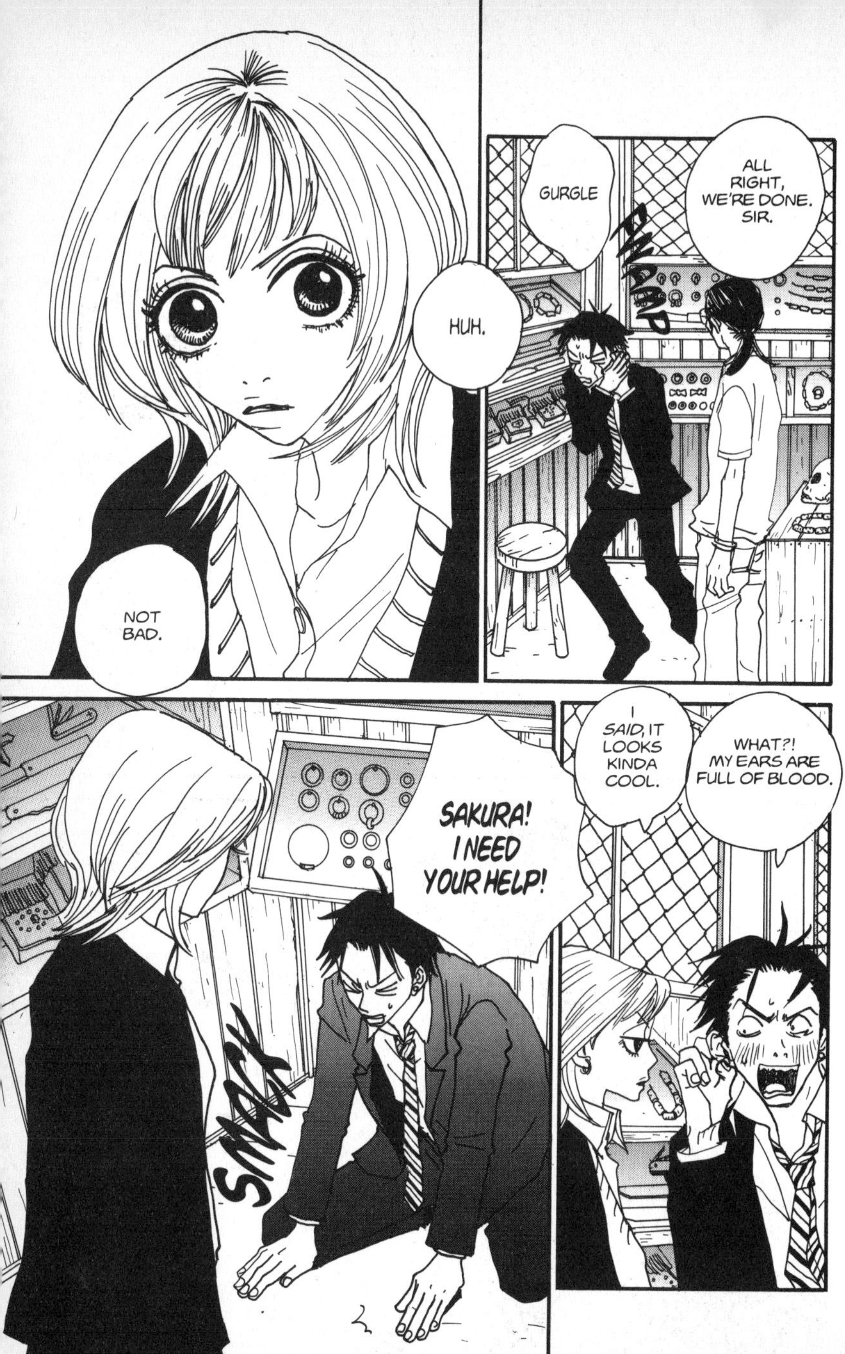
ALL RIGHT, WE'RE DONE. SIR.
GURGLE
PWAMP
HUH.
NOT BAD.
WHAT?! MY EARS ARE FULL OF BLOOD.
I SAID, IT LOOKS KINDA COOL.
SAKURA! I NEED YOUR HELP!
SMACK

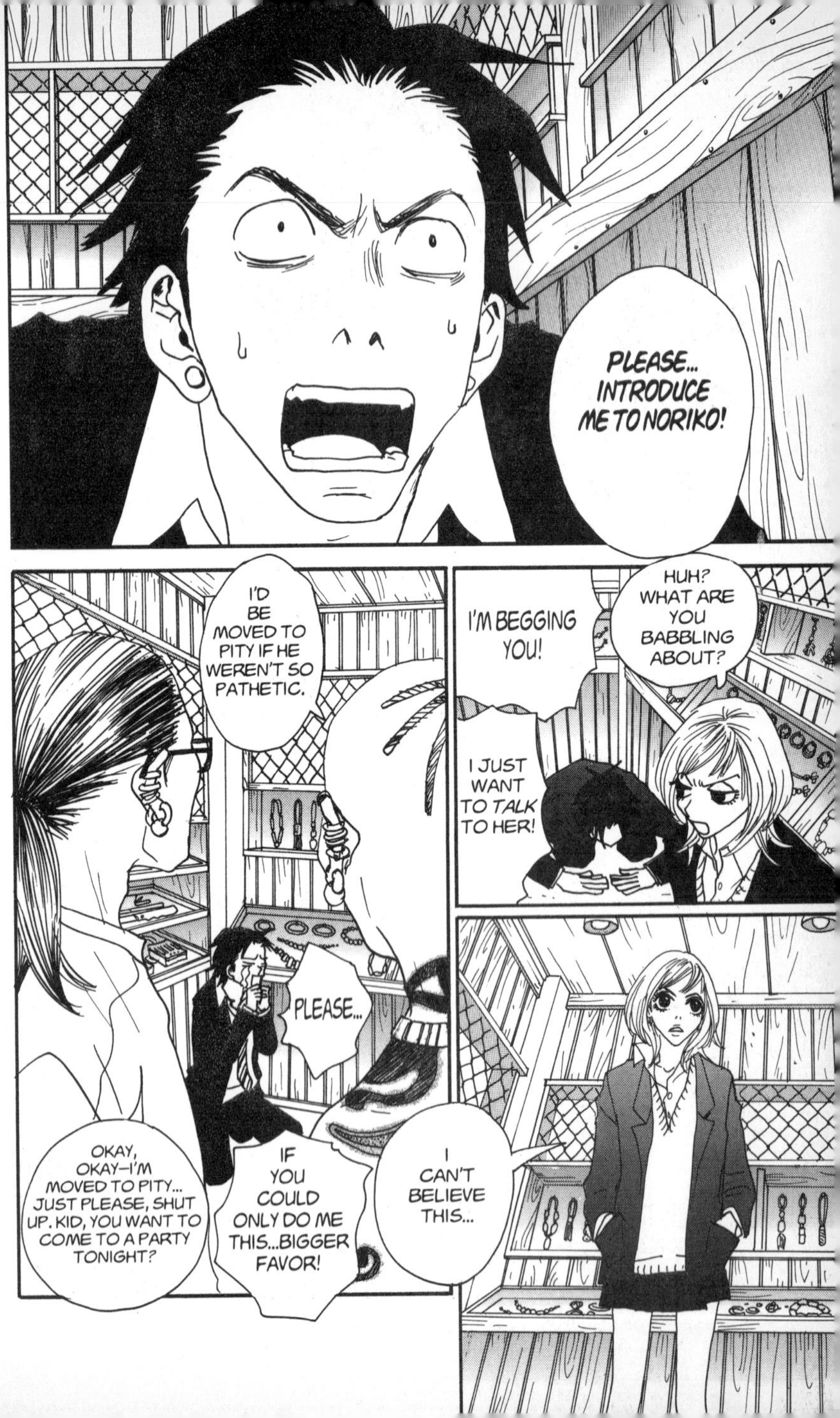
PLEASE... INTRODUCE ME TO NORIKO!
HUH? WHAT ARE YOU BABBLING ABOUT?
I'M BEGGING YOU!
I JUST WANT TO TALK TO HER!
I CAN'T BELIEVE THIS...
I'D BE MOVED TO PITY IF HE WEREN'T SO PATHETIC.
PLEASE...
IF YOU COULD ONLY DO ME THIS...BIGGER FAVOR!
OKAY, OKAY—I'M MOVED TO PITY... JUST PLEASE, SHUT UP. KID, YOU WANT TO COME TO A PARTY TONIGHT?

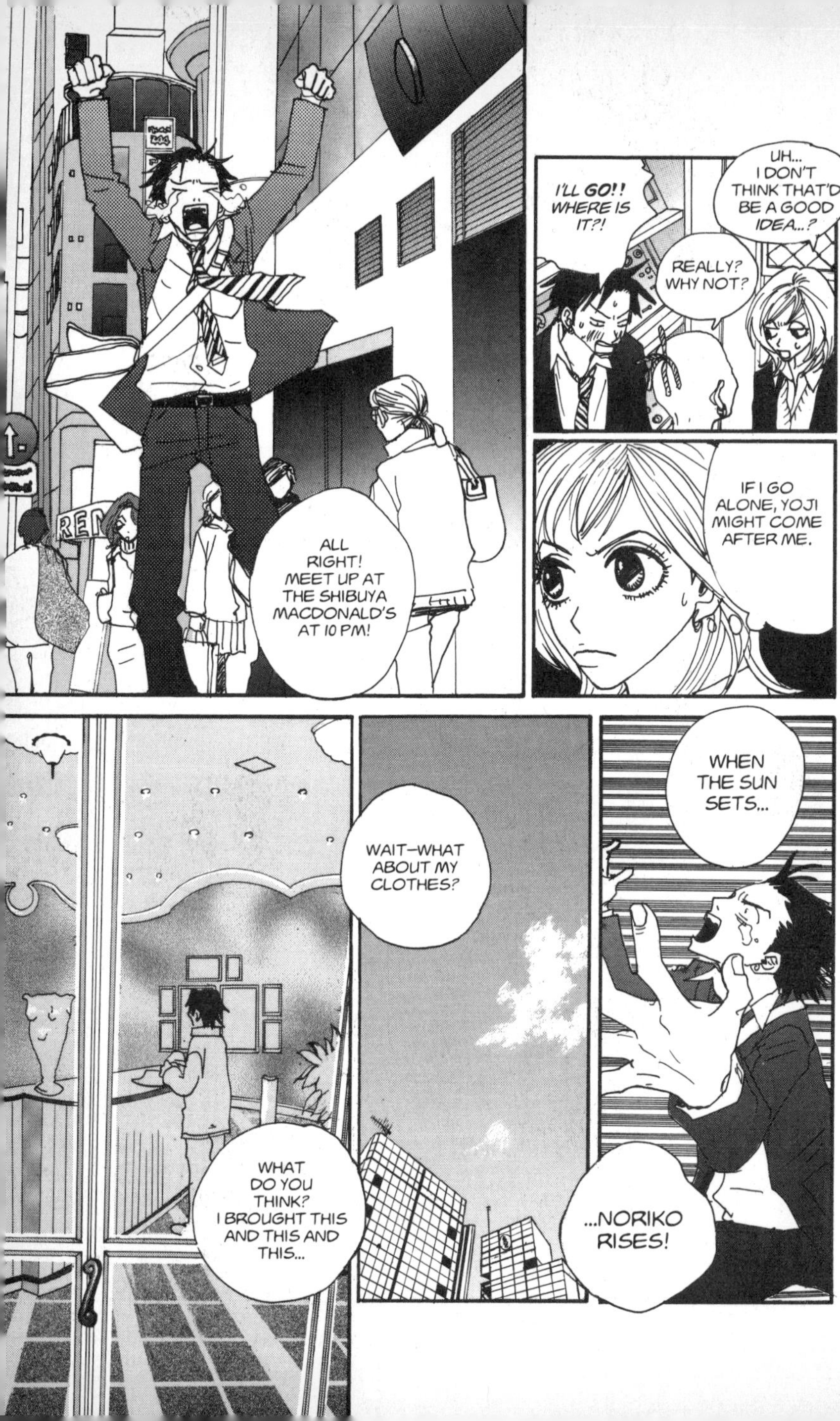
I'LL GO!! WHERE IS IT?!
UH... I DON'T THINK THAT'D BE A GOOD IDEA...?
REALLY? WHY NOT?
IF I GO ALONE, YOJI MIGHT COME AFTER ME.
ALL RIGHT! MEET UP AT THE SHIBUYA MACDONALD'S AT 10 PM!
WHEN THE SUN SETS...
...NORIKO RISES!
WAIT—WHAT ABOUT MY CLOTHES?
WHAT DO YOU THINK? I BROUGHT THIS AND THIS AND THIS...

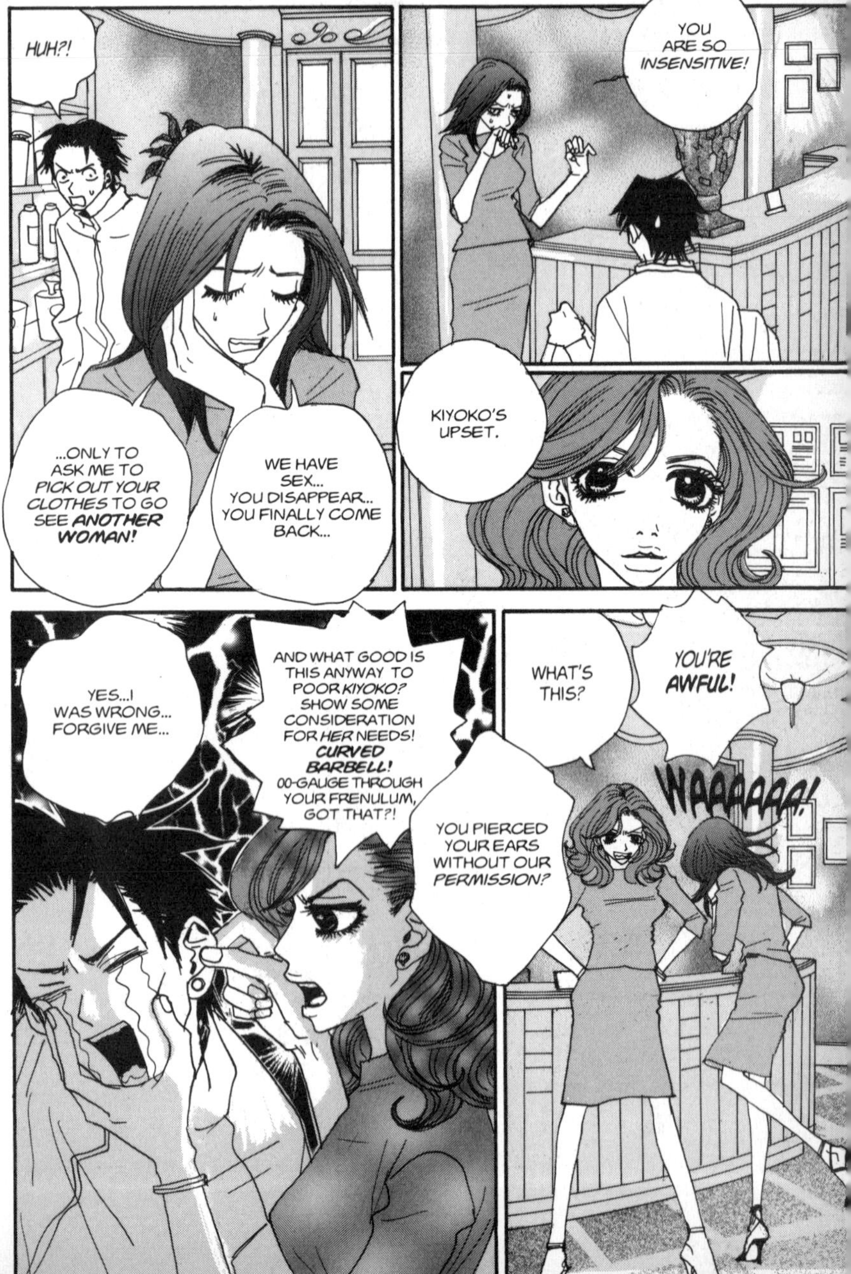

YOU ARE SO INSENSITIVE!
KIYOKO'S UPSET.
HUH?!
WE HAVE SEX... YOU DISAPPEAR.. YOU FINALLY COME BACK...
...ONLY TO ASK ME TO PICK OUT YOUR CLOTHES TO GO SEE ANOTHER WOMAN!
YOU'RE AWFUL!
WHAT'S THIS?
WAAAAAA!
YOU PIERCED YOUR EARS WITHOUT OUR PERMISSION?
AND WHAT GOOD IS THIS ANYWAY TO POOR KIYOKO? SHOW SOME CONSIDERATION FOR HER NEEDS! CURVED BARBELL! 00-GAUGE THROUGH YOUR FRENULUM, GOT THAT?!
YES...I WAS WRONG... FORGIVE ME...

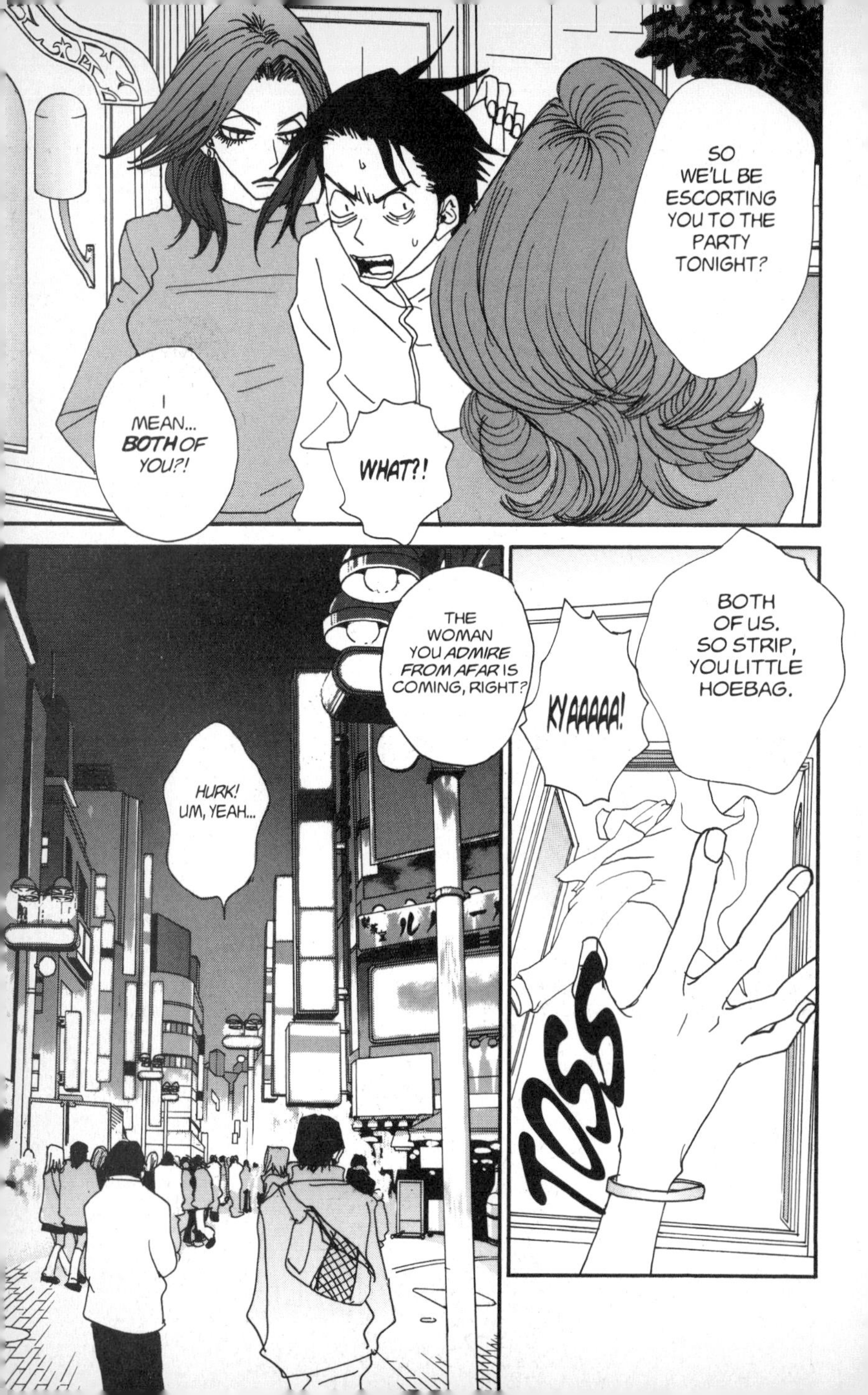
SO WE'LL BE ESCORTING YOU TO THE PARTY TONIGHT?
WHAT?!
I MEAN... BOTH OF YOU?!
BOTH OF US. SO STRIP, YOU LITTLE HOEBAG.
KYAAAAA!
TOSS
THE WOMAN YOU ADMIRE FROM AFAR IS COMING, RIGHT?
HURK! UM, YEAH...

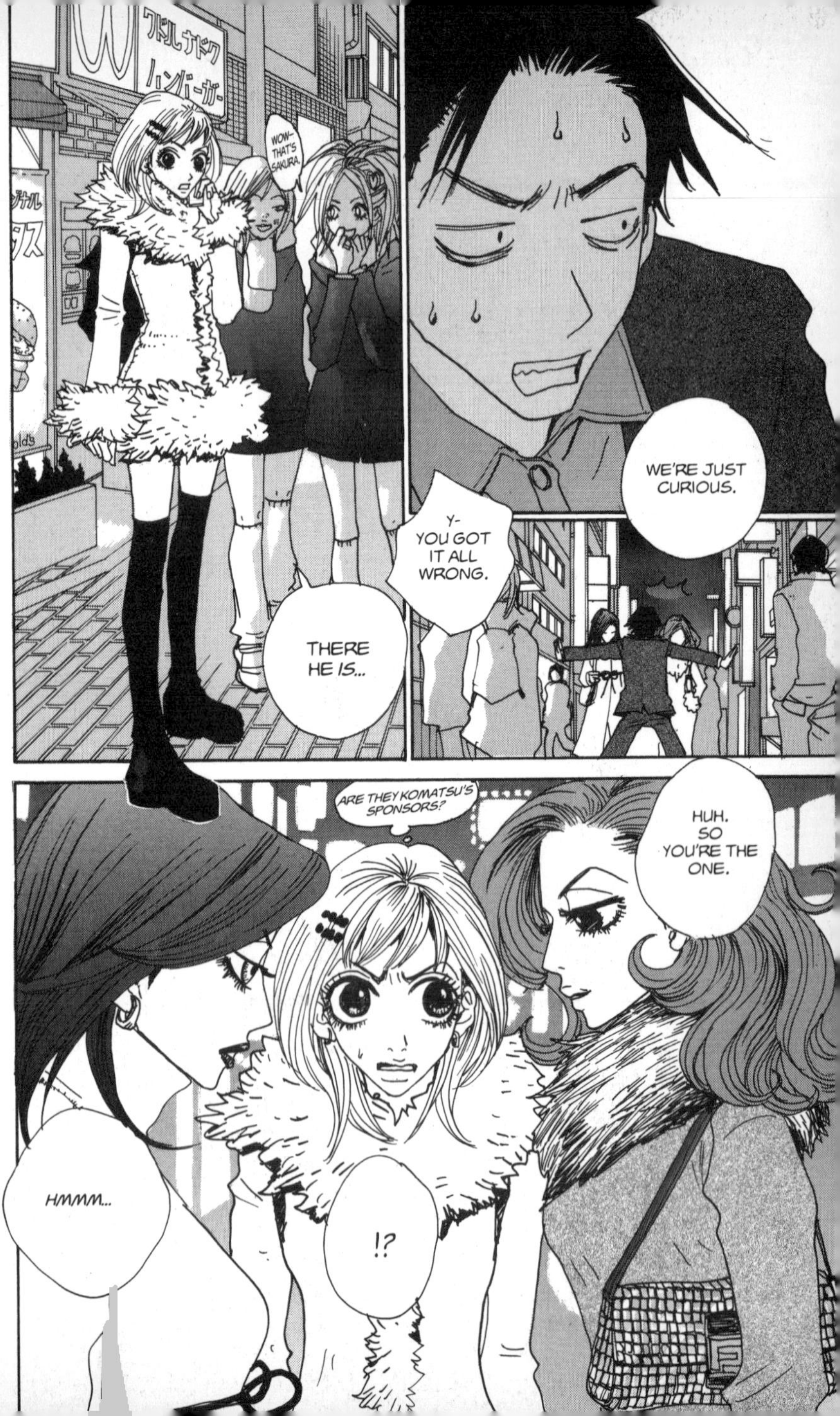
WE'RE JUST CURIOUS.
Y- YOU GOT IT ALL WRONG.
ワドルナドク
ハンバーガー
WOW- THAT'S SAKURA.
THERE HE IS...
HUH. SO YOU'RE THE ONE.
ARE THEY KOMATSU'S SPONSORS?
!?
HMMM...

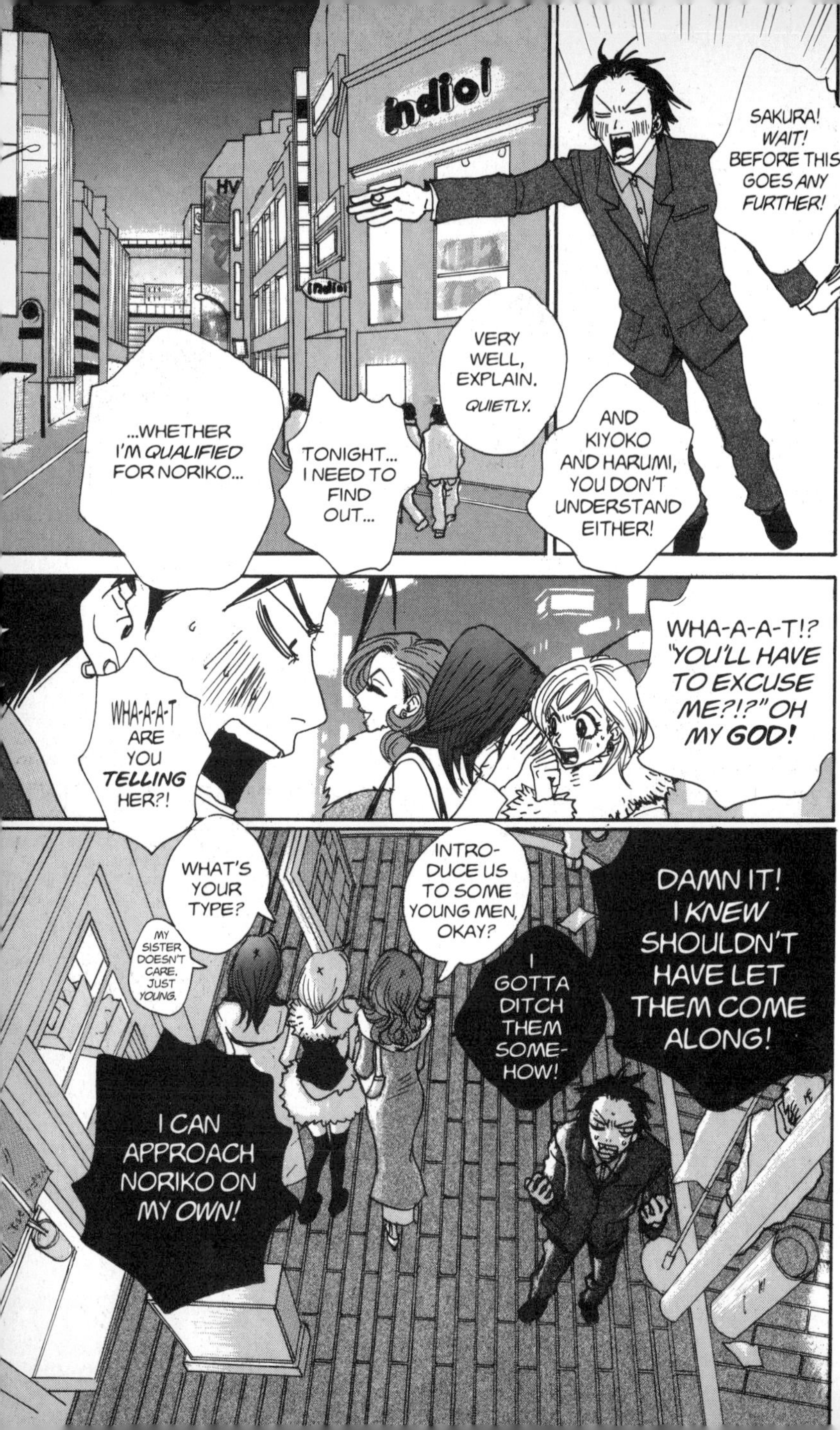
SAKURA! WAIT! BEFORE THIS GOES ANY FURTHER!
AND KIYOKO AND HARUMI, YOU DON'T UNDERSTAND EITHER!
indio
VERY WELL, EXPLAIN. QUIETLY.
TONIGHT... I NEED TO FIND OUT...
...WHETHER I'M QUALIFIED FOR NORIKO...
WHA-A-A-T!? "YOU'LL HAVE TO EXCUSE ME?!?" OH MY GOD!
WHA-A-A-T ARE YOU TELLING HER?!
DAMN IT! I KNEW SHOULDN'T HAVE LET THEM COME ALONG!
I GOTTA DITCH THEM SOME-HOW!
INTRO-DUCE US TO SOME YOUNG MEN, OKAY?
WHAT'S YOUR TYPE?
MY SISTER DOESN'T CARE. JUST YOUNG.
I CAN APPROACH NORIKO ON MY OWN!

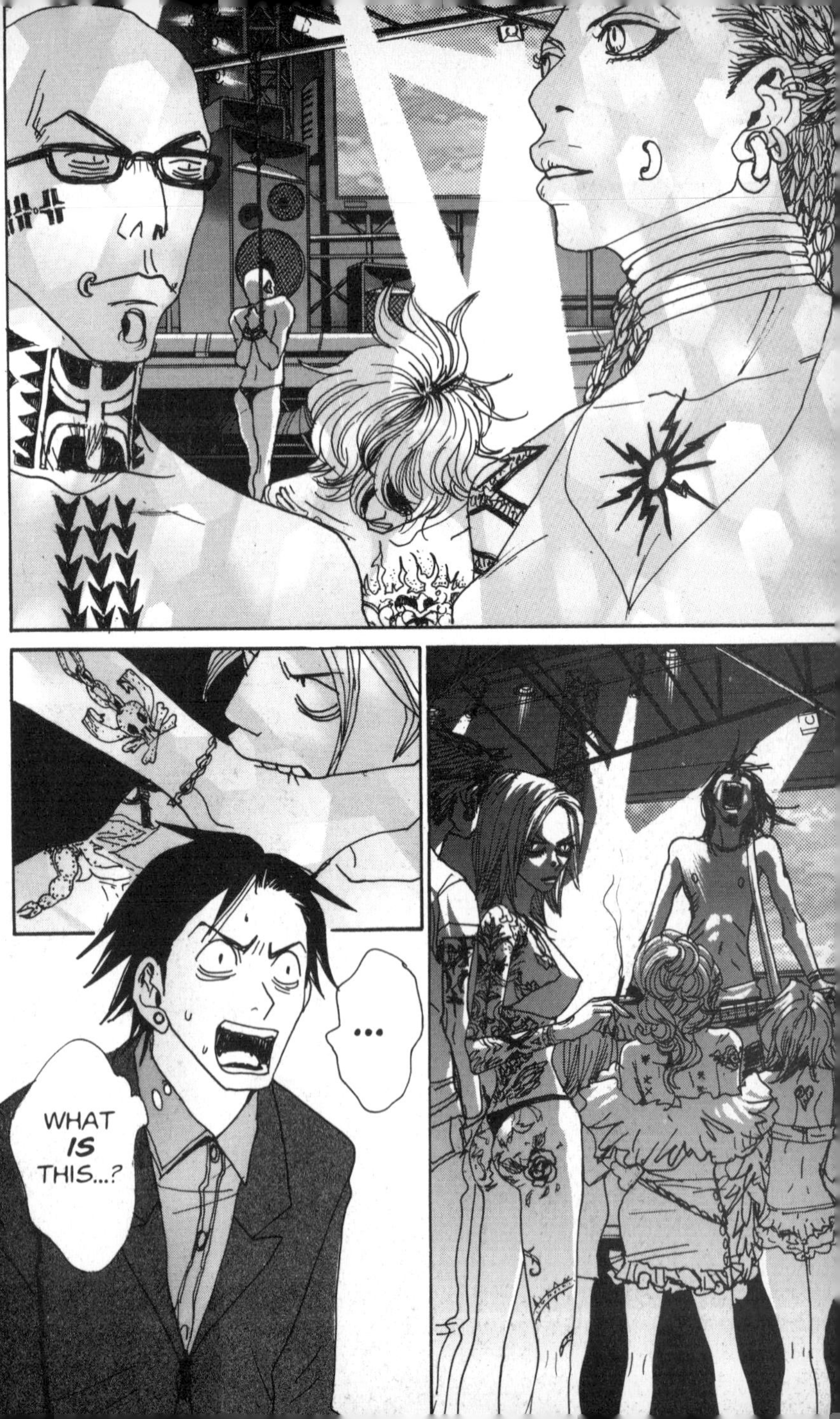
...
WHAT *IS* THIS...?

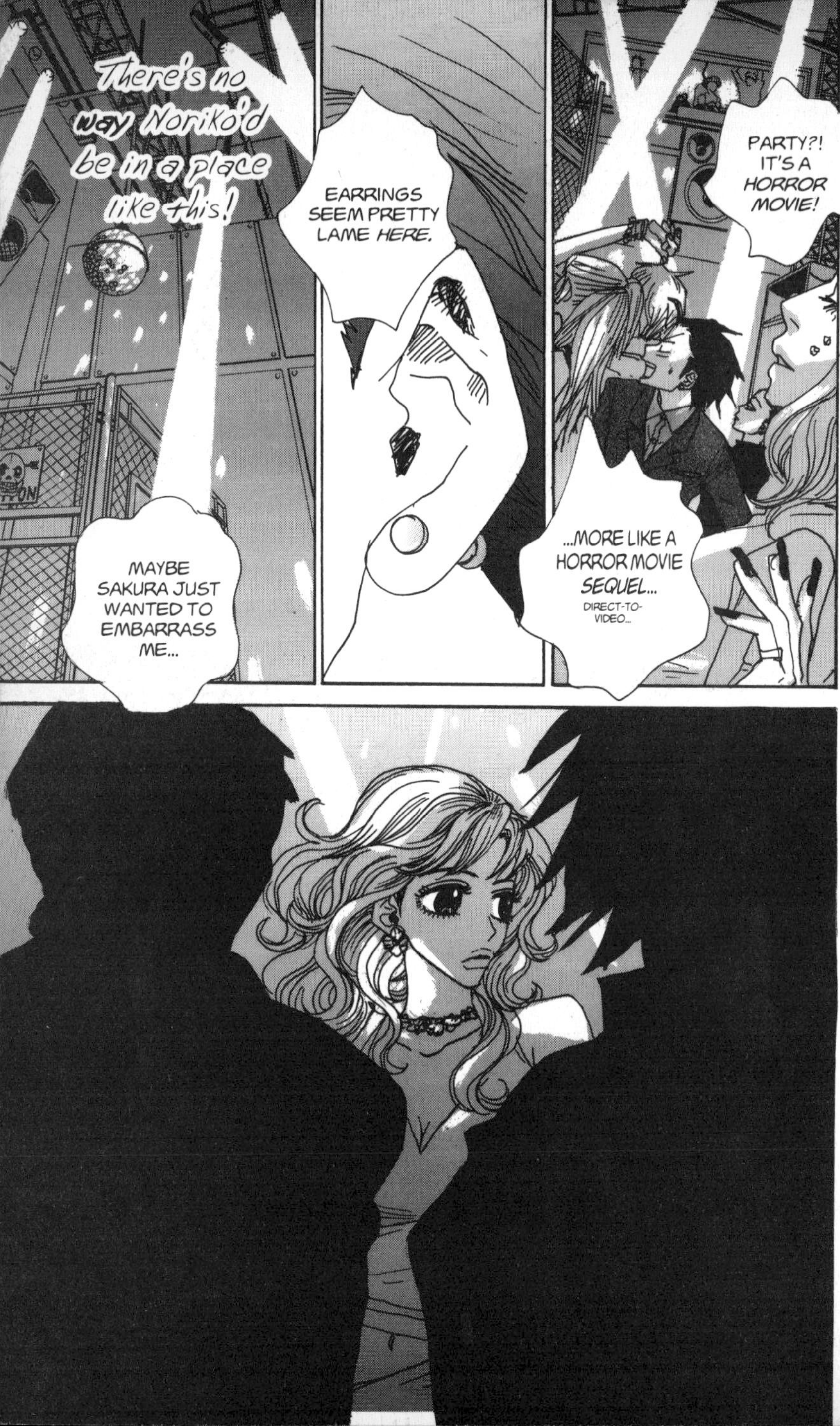
PARTY?! IT'S A HORROR MOVIE!
...MORE LIKE A HORROR MOVIE SEQUEL...
DIRECT-TO-VIDEO...
EARRINGS SEEM PRETTY LAME HERE.
There's no way Noriko'd be in a place like this!
MAYBE SAKURA JUST WANTED TO EMBARRASS ME...

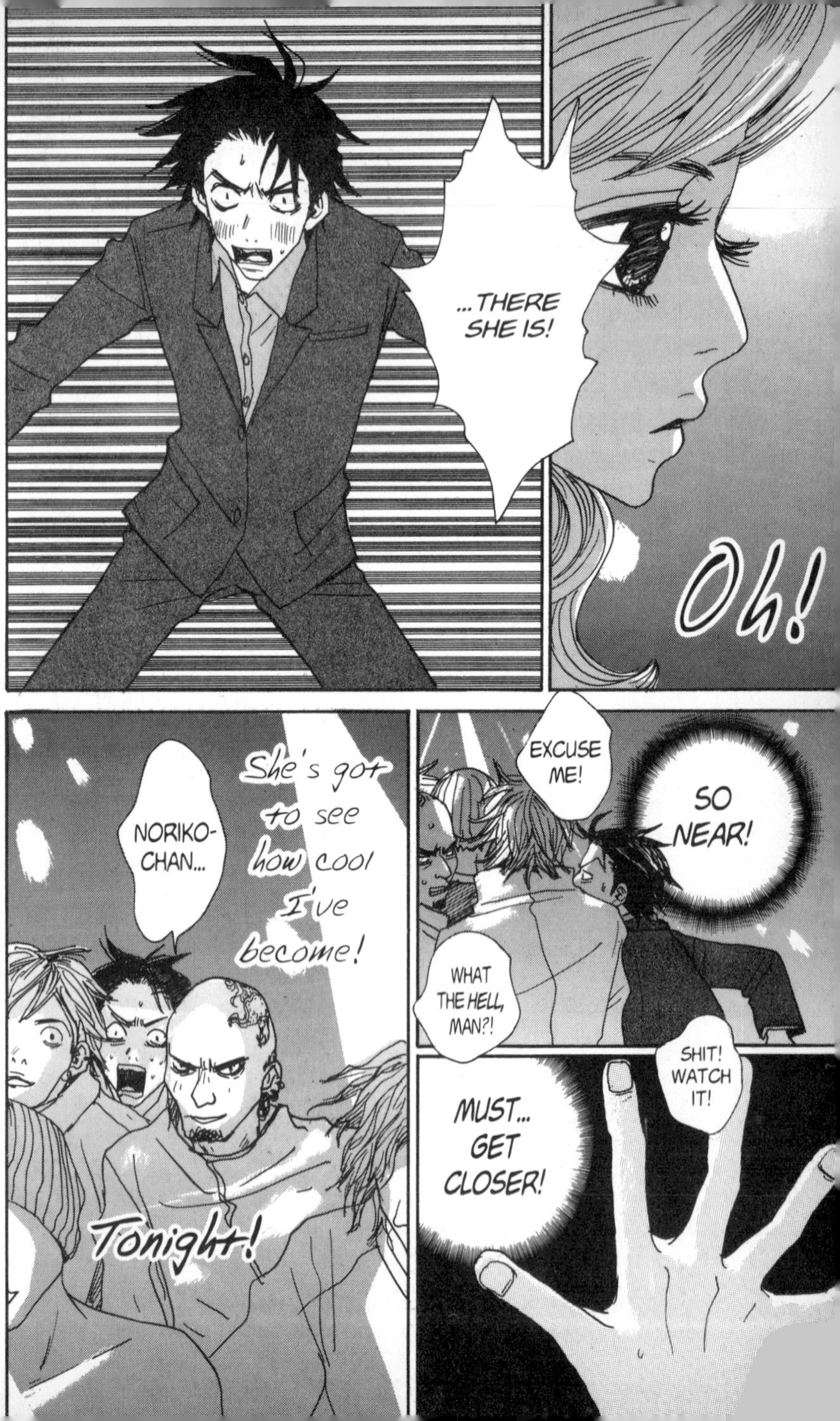
Oh!
...THERE SHE IS!
EXCUSE ME!
SO NEAR!
WHAT THE HELL, MAN?!
SHIT! WATCH IT!
MUST... GET CLOSER!
She's got to see how cool I've become!
NORIKO-CHAN...
Tonight!

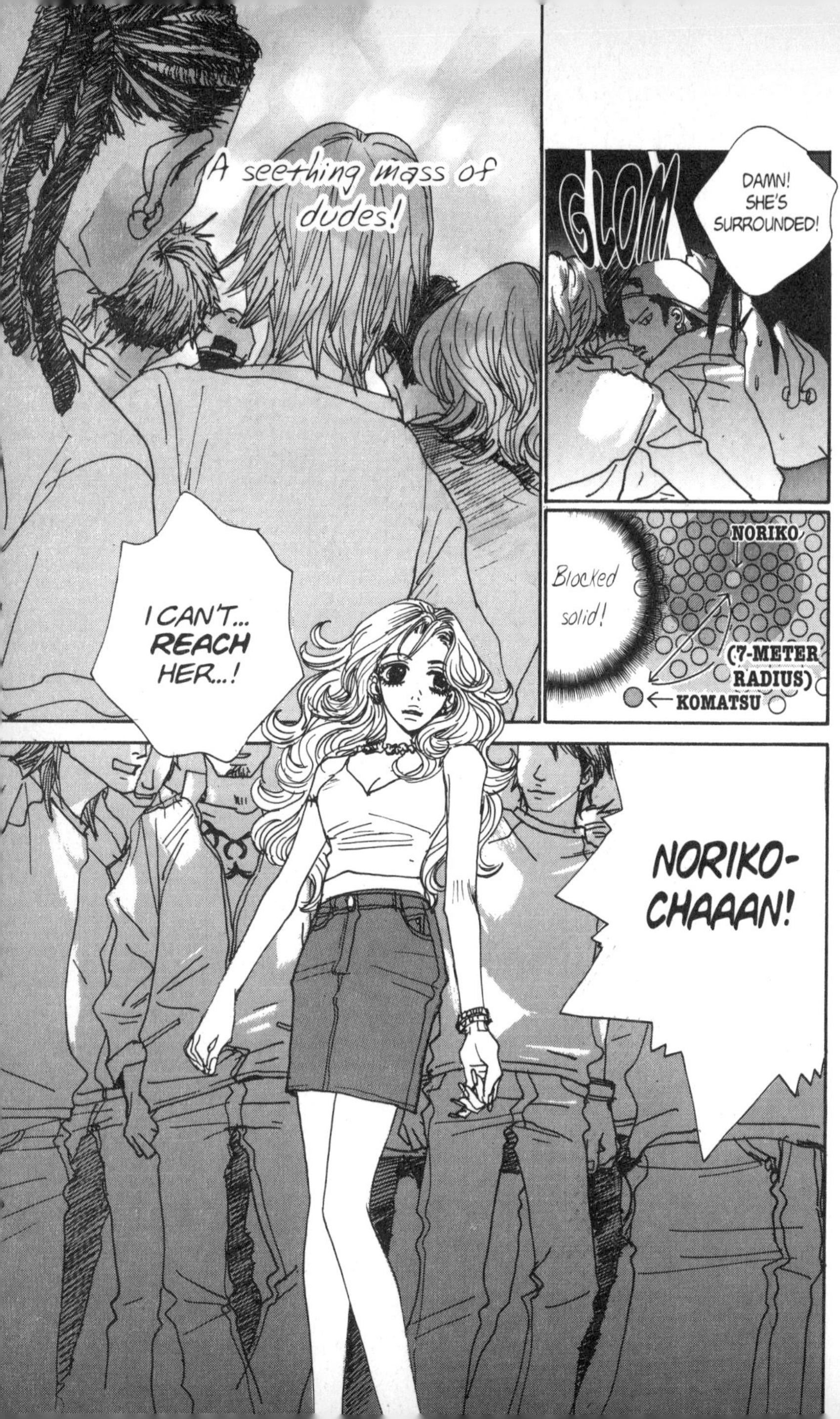
GLOM
DAMN! SHE'S SURROUNDED!
Blocked solid!
NORIKO
(7-METER RADIUS)
KOMATSU
A seething mass of dudes!
I CAN'T... REACH HER...!
NORIKO-CHAAAN!

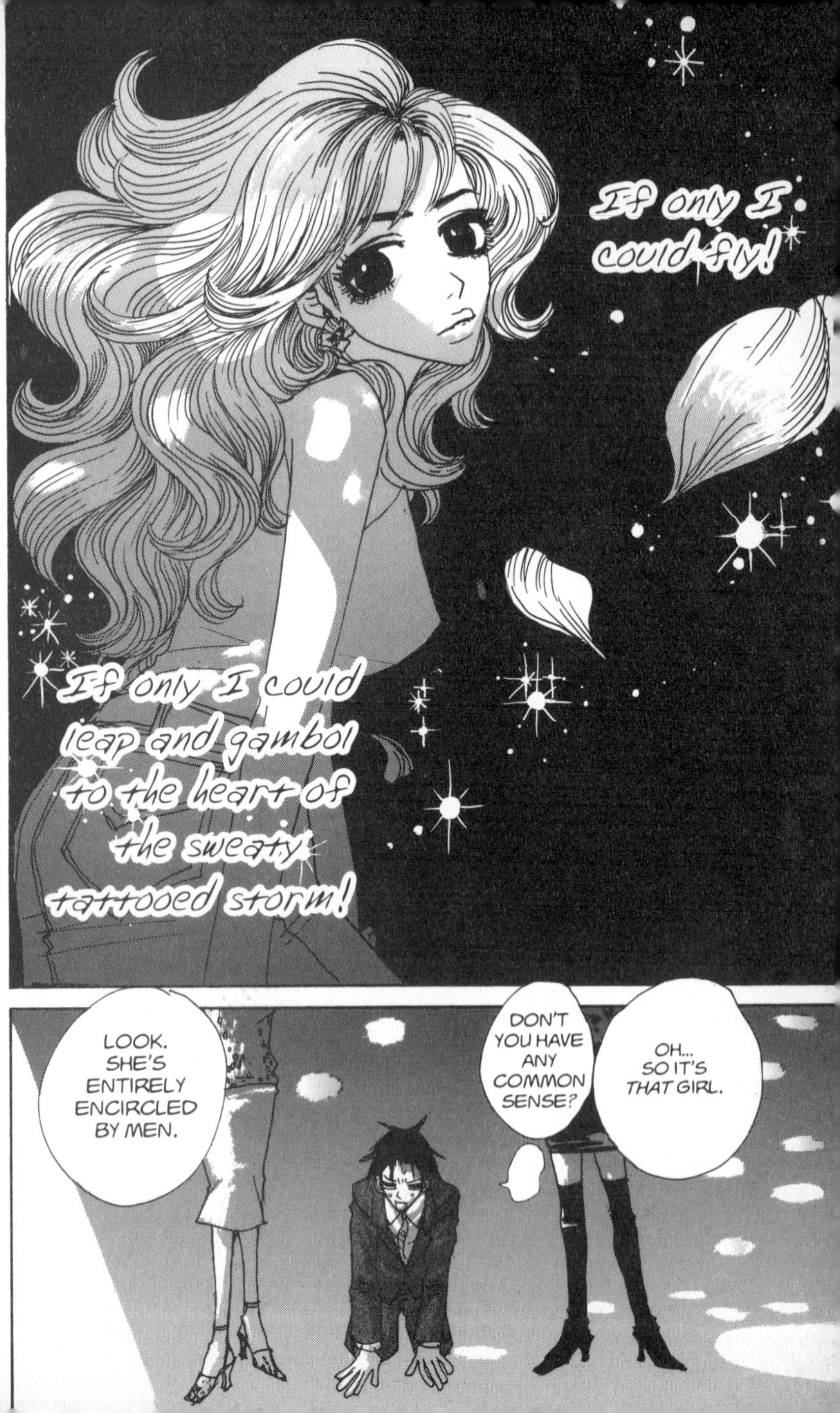
If only I could fly!
If only I could leap and gambol to the heart of the sweaty tattooed storm!
OH... SO IT'S THAT GIRL.
DON'T YOU HAVE ANY COMMON SENSE?
LOOK. SHE'S ENTIRELY ENCIRCLED BY MEN.

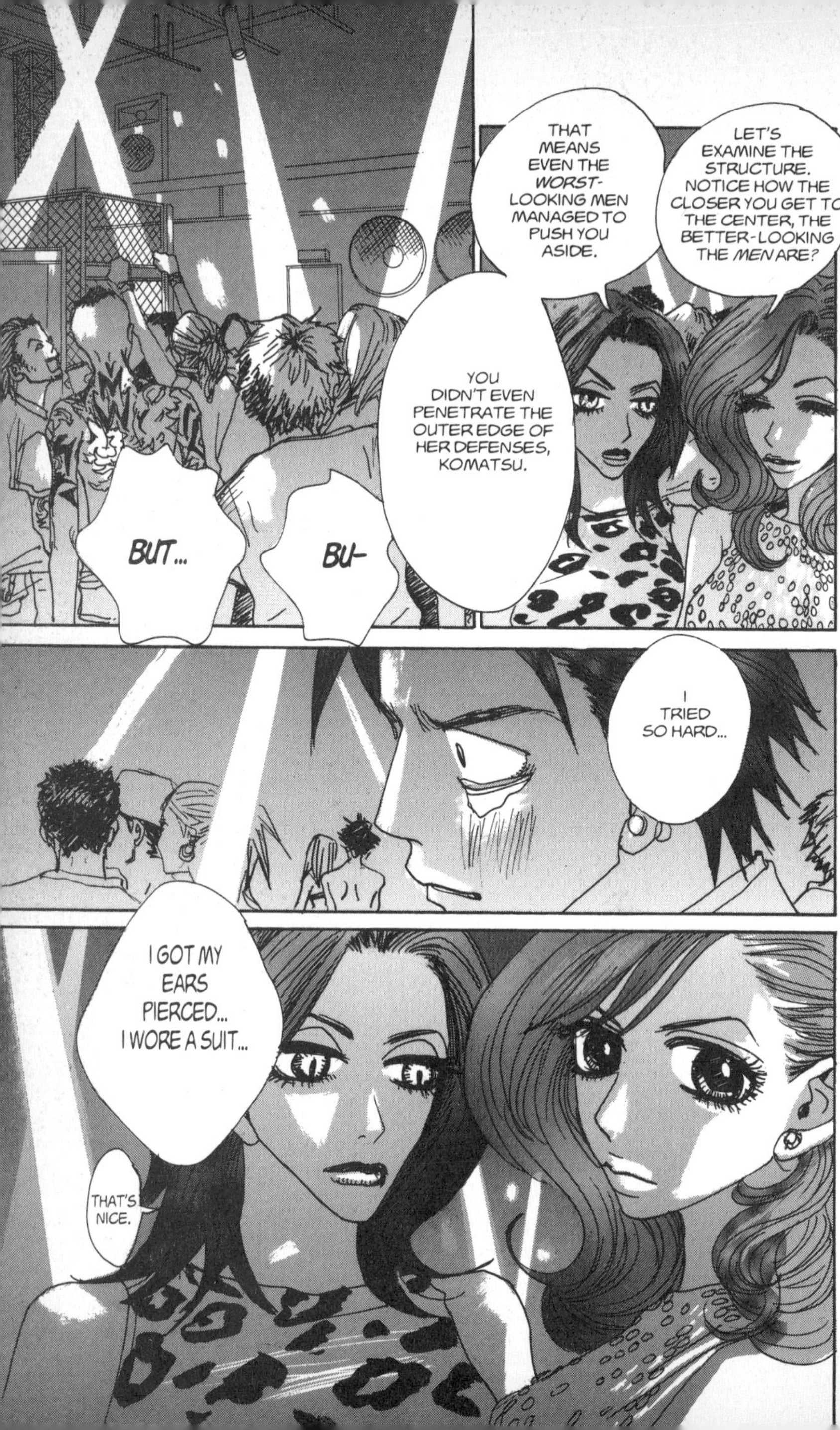
LET'S EXAMINE THE STRUCTURE. NOTICE HOW THE CLOSER YOU GET TO THE CENTER, THE BETTER-LOOKING THE *MEN* ARE?
THAT MEANS EVEN THE *WORST*-LOOKING MEN MANAGED TO PUSH YOU ASIDE.
YOU DIDN'T EVEN PENETRATE THE OUTER EDGE OF HER DEFENSES, KOMATSU.
BU-
BUT...
I TRIED SO HARD...
I GOT MY EARS PIERCED... I WORE A SUIT...
THAT'S NICE.

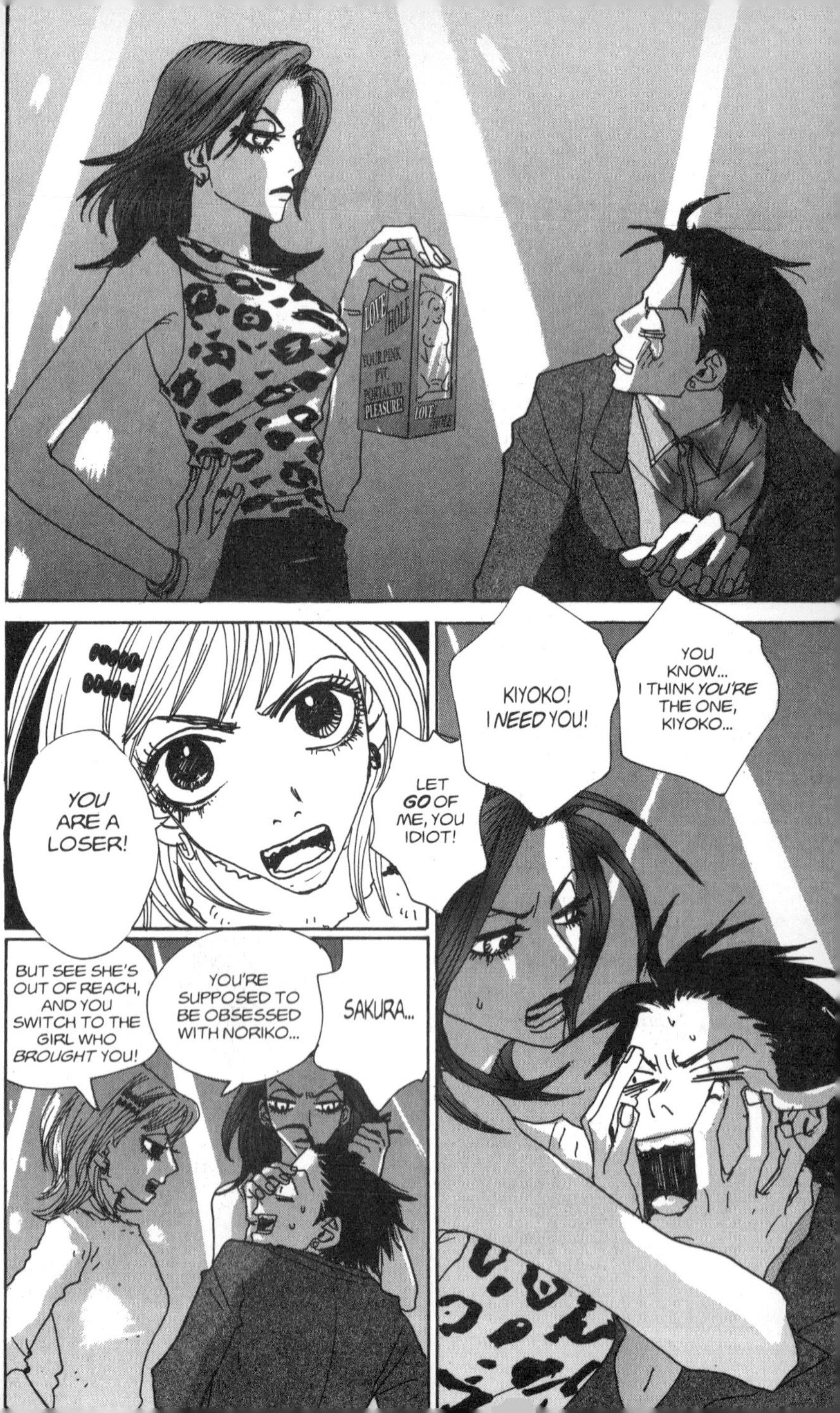
LOVE HOLE
YOUR PINK PVC PORTAL TO PLEASURE!
LOVE HOLE
YOU KNOW... I THINK *YOU'RE* THE ONE, KIYOKO...
KIYOKO! I *NEED* YOU!
LET ***GO*** OF ME, YOU IDIOT!
YOU ARE A LOSER!
SAKURA...
YOU'RE SUPPOSED TO BE OBSESSED WITH NORIKO...
BUT SEE SHE'S OUT OF REACH, AND YOU SWITCH TO THE GIRL WHO *BROUGHT* YOU!

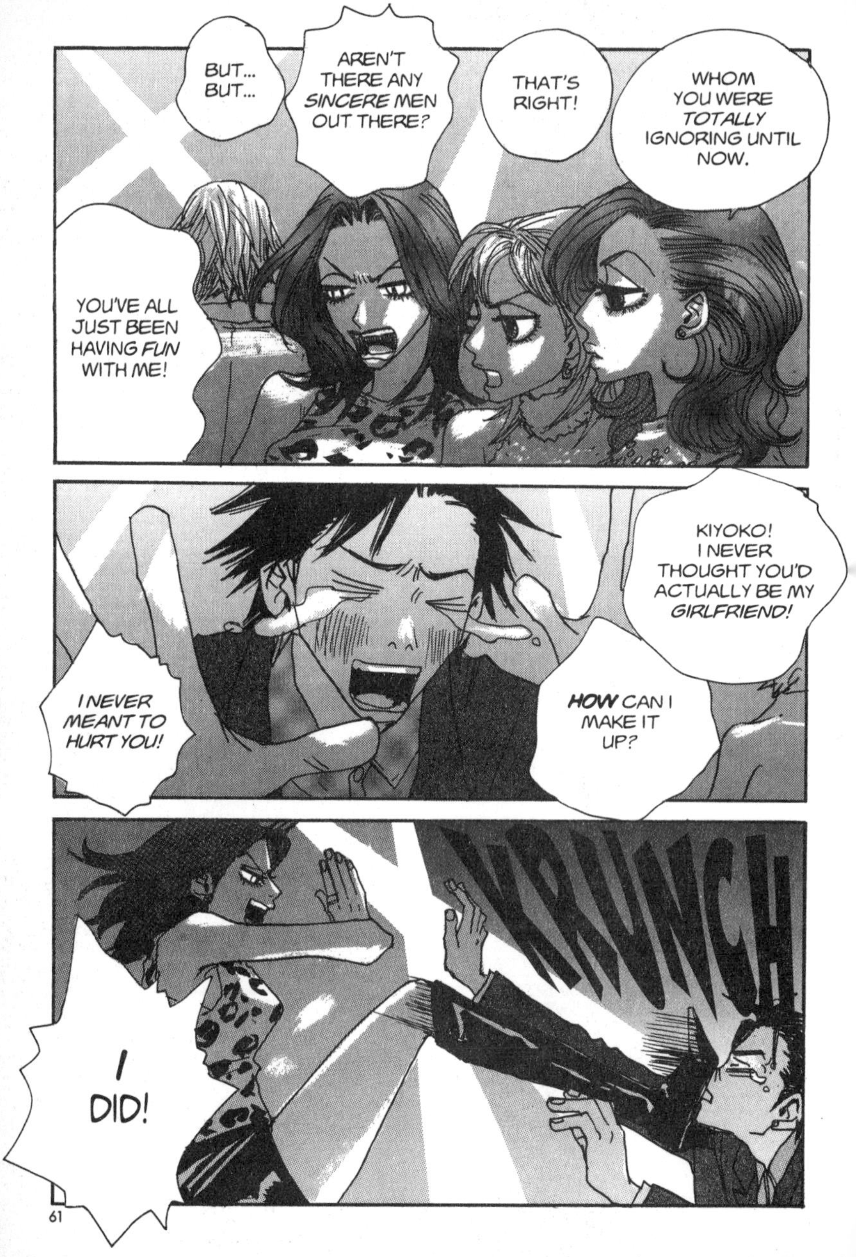
WHOM YOU WERE *TOTALLY* IGNORING UNTIL NOW.
THAT'S RIGHT!
AREN'T THERE ANY *SINCERE* MEN OUT THERE?
BUT... BUT...
YOU'VE ALL JUST BEEN HAVING *FUN* WITH ME!
KIYOKO! I NEVER THOUGHT YOU'D ACTUALLY BE MY *GIRLFRIEND!*
HOW CAN I MAKE IT UP?
I NEVER MEANT TO HURT YOU!
KRUNCH
I DID!

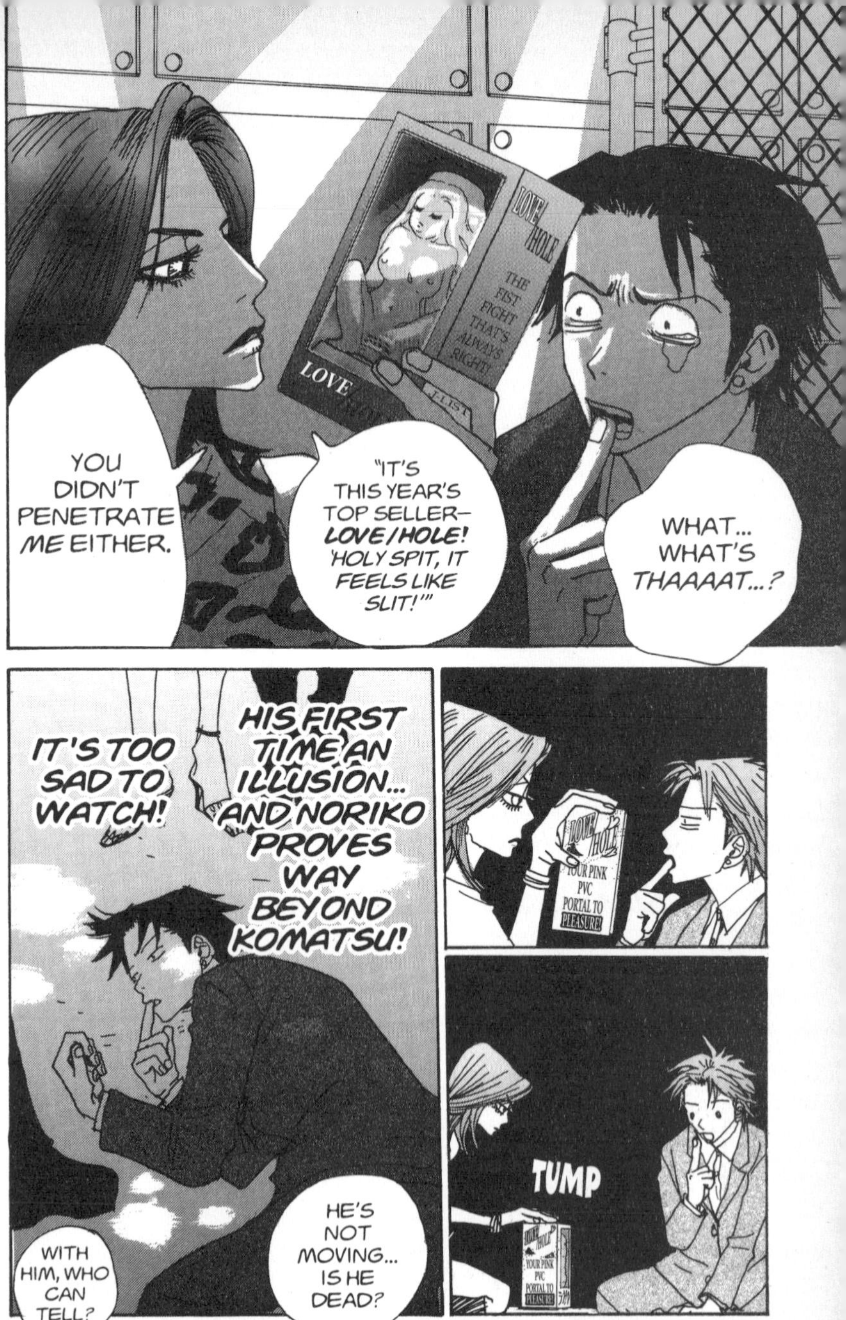
LOVE/HOLE
THE FIST FIGHT THAT'S ALWAYS RIGHT!
LOVE
J-LIST
WHAT... WHAT'S THAAAAT...?
"IT'S THIS YEAR'S TOP SELLER– LOVE/HOLE! 'HOLY SPIT, IT FEELS LIKE SLIT!'"
YOU DIDN'T PENETRATE ME EITHER.
LOVE/HOLE
YOUR PINK PVC PORTAL TO PLEASURE!
TUMP
LOVE/HOLE
YOUR PINK PVC PORTAL TO PLEASURE!
HIS FIRST TIME AN ILLUSION... AND NORIKO PROVES WAY BEYOND KOMATSU!
IT'S TOO SAD TO WATCH!
HE'S NOT MOVING... IS HE DEAD?
WITH HIM, WHO CAN TELL?

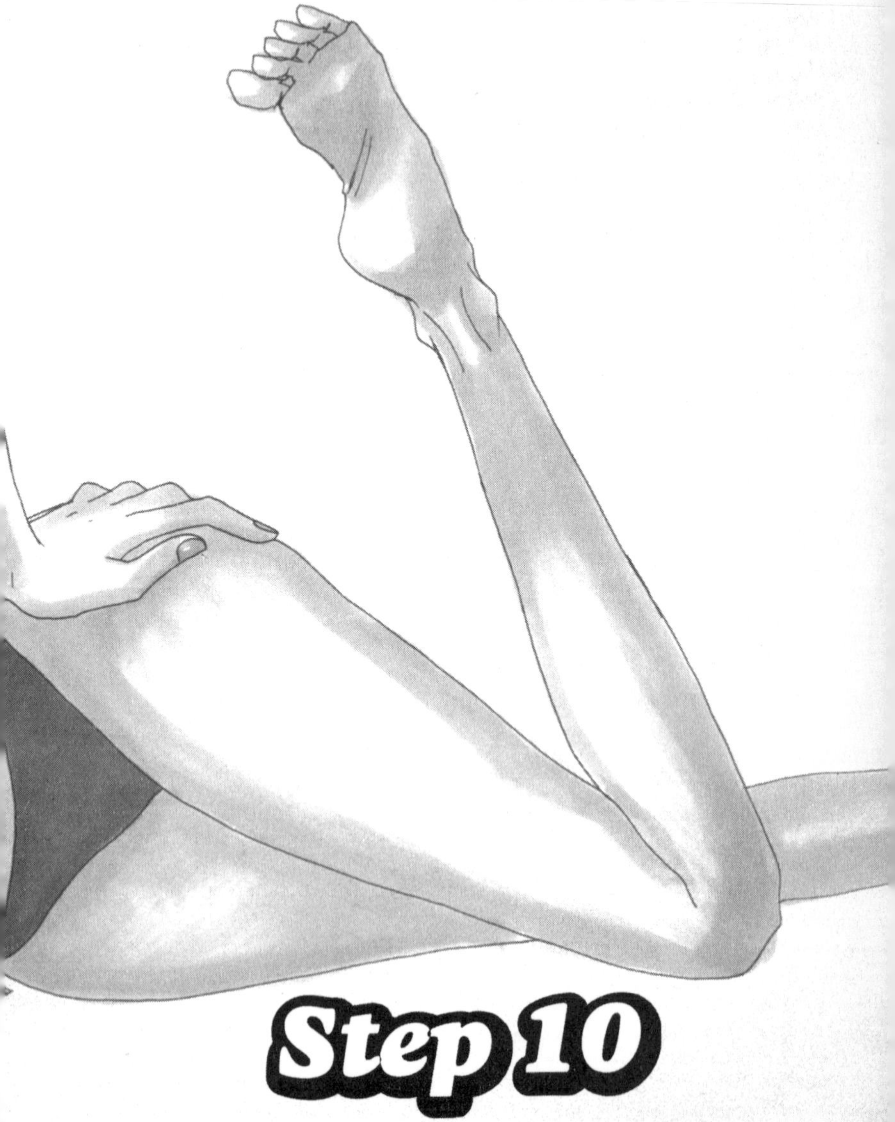

Step 10

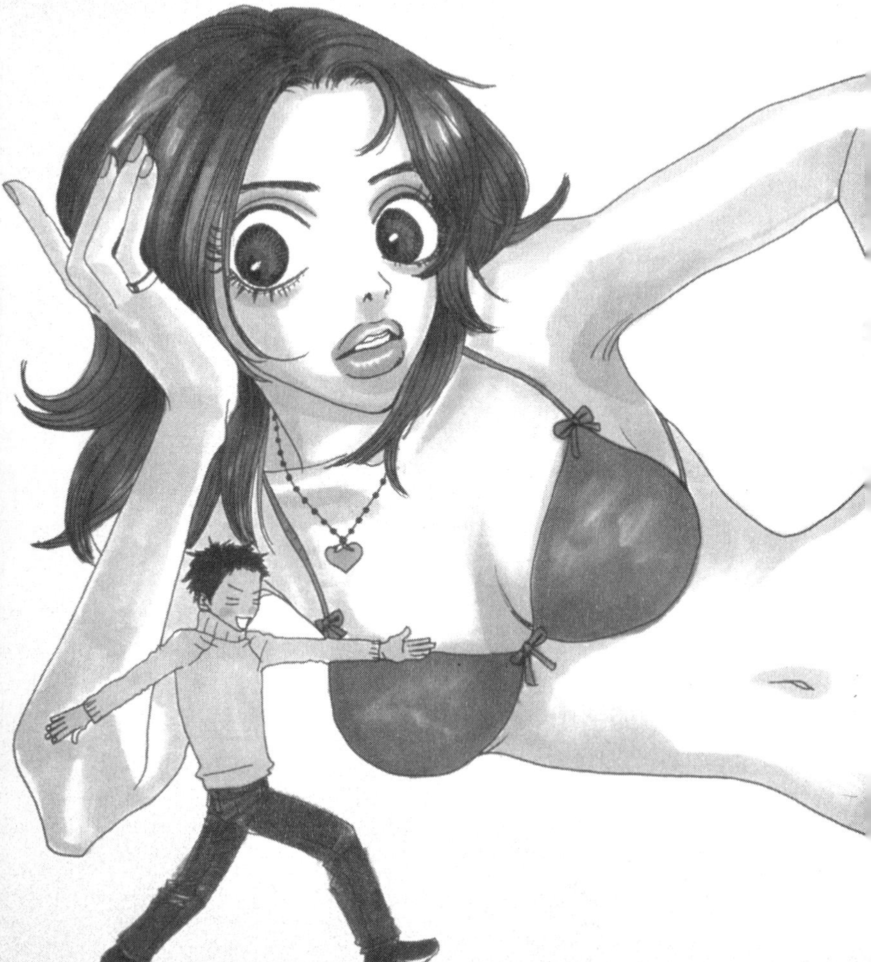

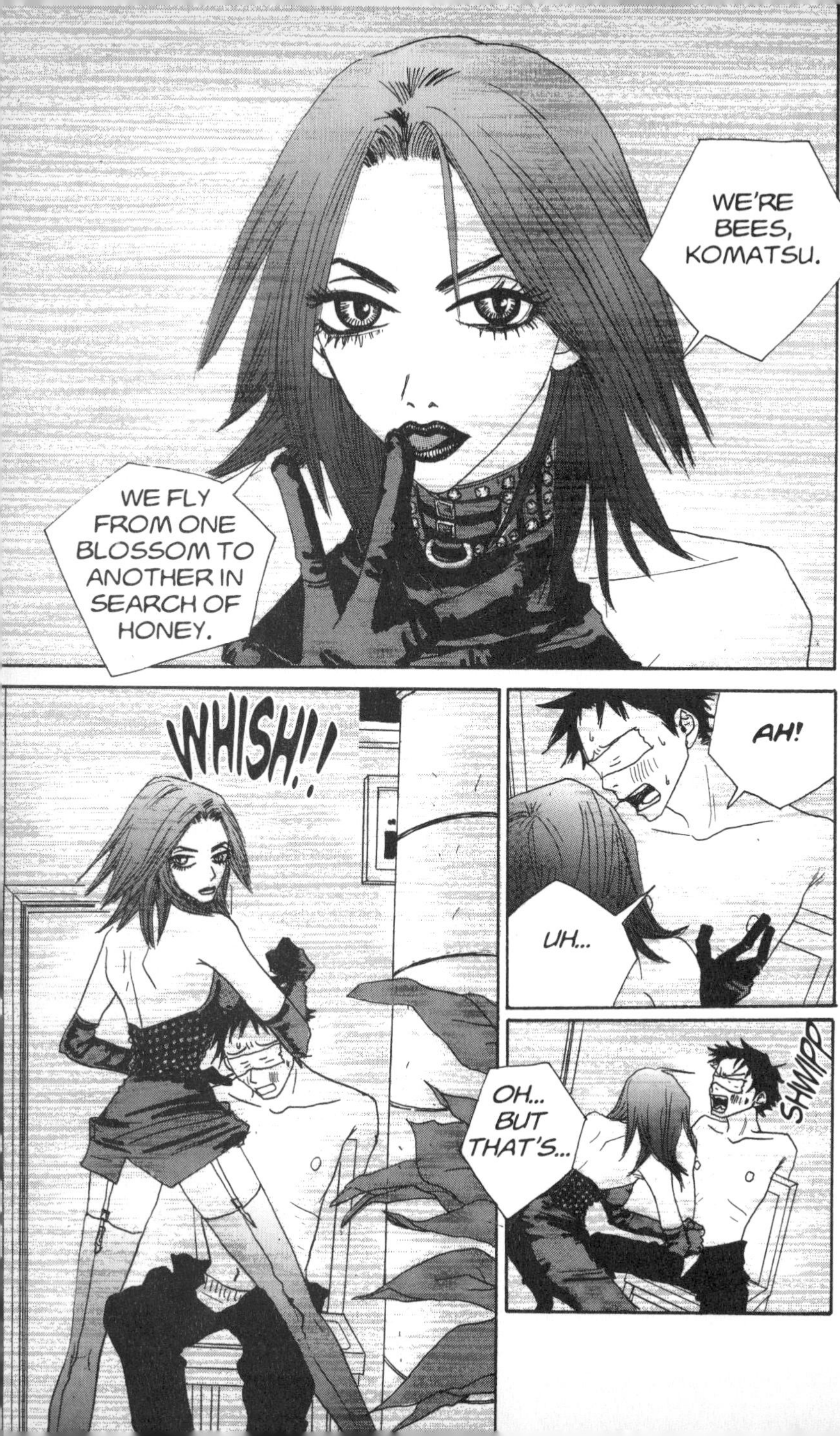
WE'RE BEES, KOMATSU.
WE FLY FROM ONE BLOSSOM TO ANOTHER IN SEARCH OF HONEY.
AH!
UH...
OH... BUT THAT'S...
SHWIPP
WHISH!!

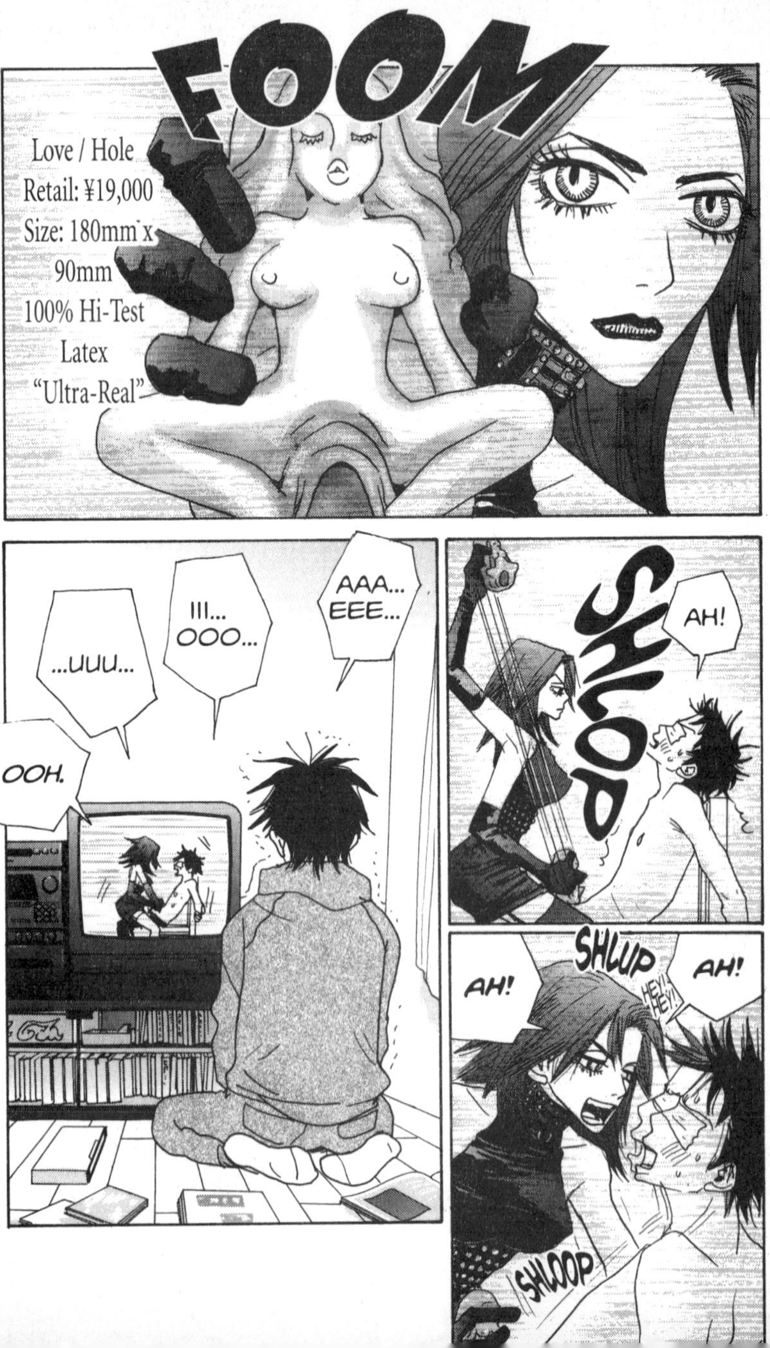
FOOM
Love / Hole
Retail: ¥19,000
Size: 180mm x 90mm
100% Hi-Test Latex
"Ultra-Real"
SHLOOP
AH!
SHLUP
AH!
HEY! HEY!
AH!
SHLOOP
AAA... EEE...
III... OOO...
...uuu...
OOH.

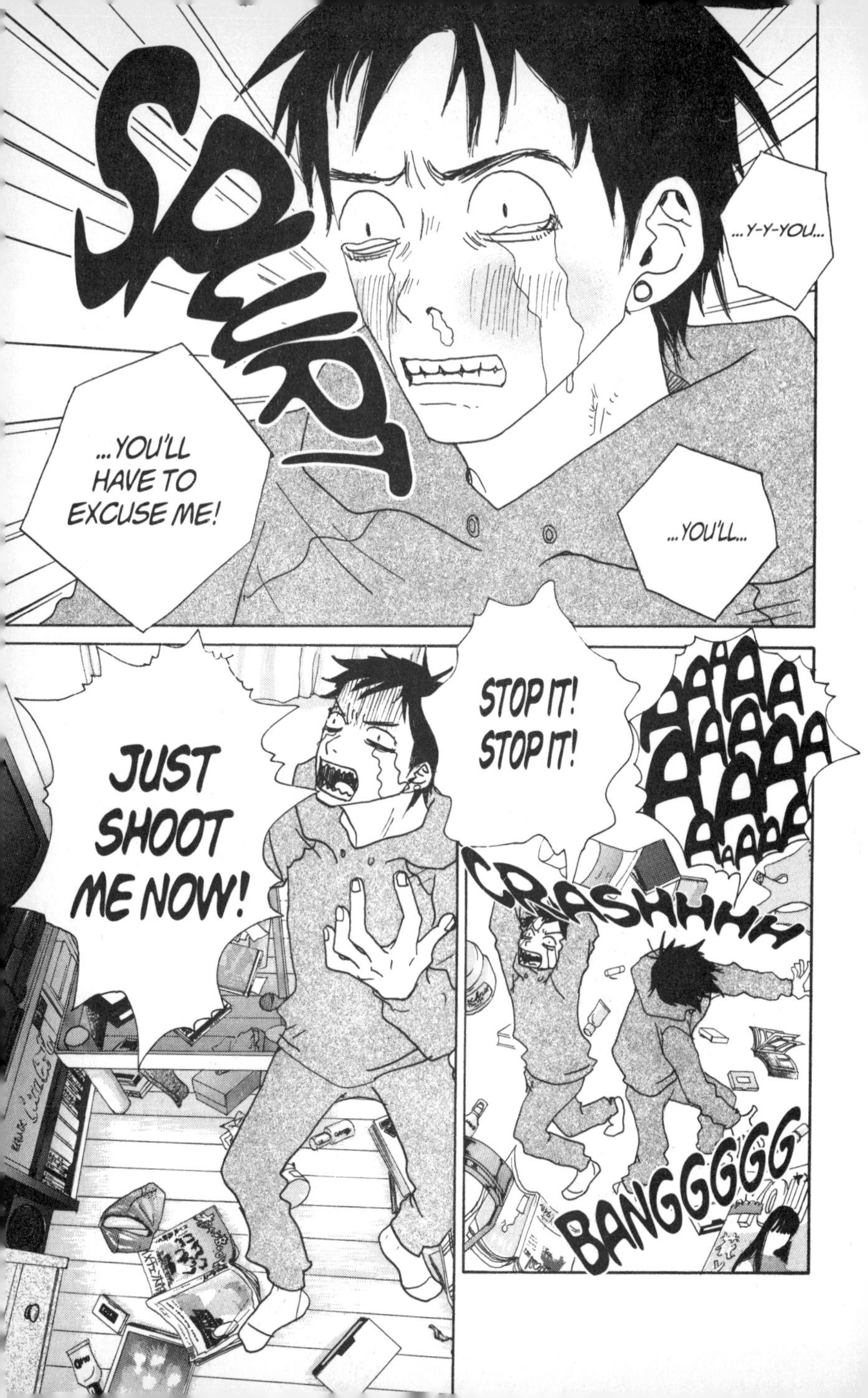
...Y-Y-YOU...
...YOU'LL...
SPLURT
...YOU'LL HAVE TO EXCUSE ME!
AAAAAAAAAAAAAAAAAAA
STOP IT! STOP IT!
CRASHHHH
BANGGGGGG
JUST SHOOT ME NOW!

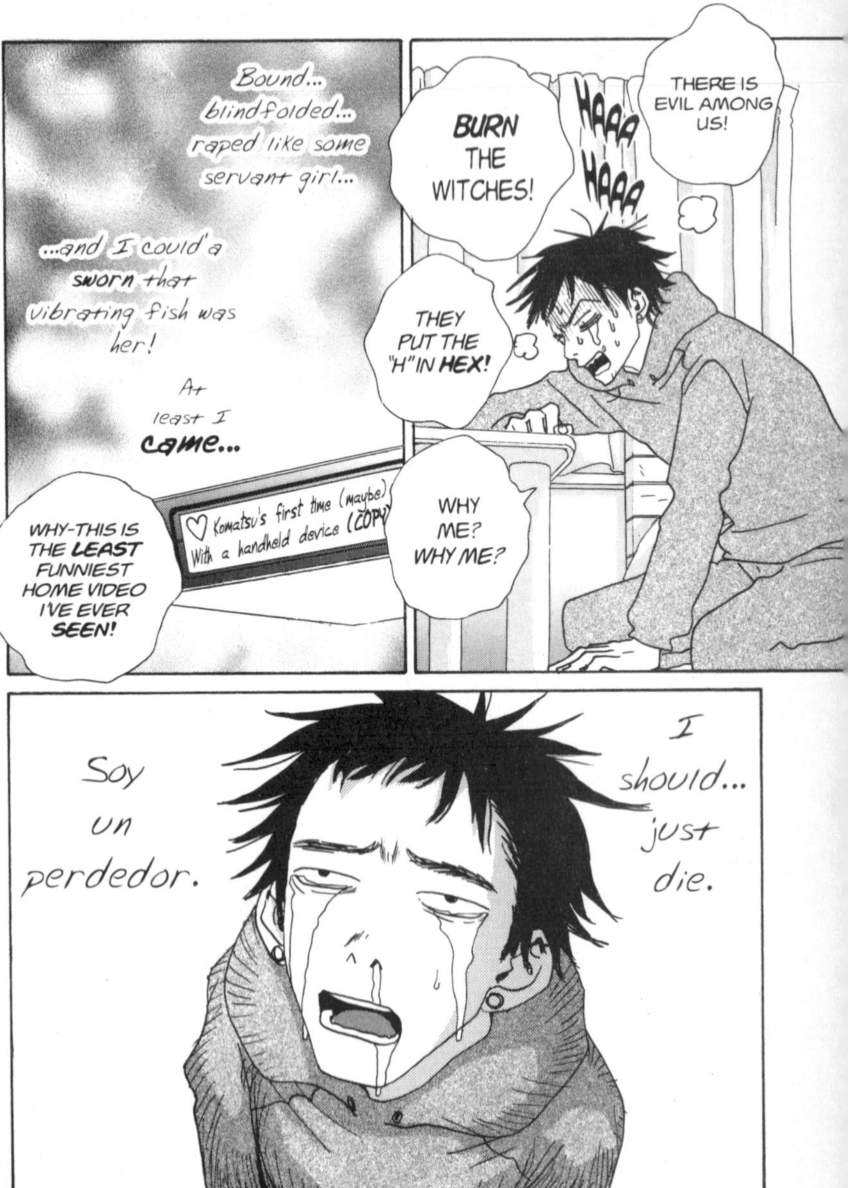
THERE IS EVIL AMONG US!
HAAA HAAA
BURN THE WITCHES!
THEY PUT THE "H" IN HEX!
WHY ME? WHY ME?
Bound... blindfolded... raped like some servant girl...
...and I could'a sworn that vibrating fish was her!
At least I came...
♡ Komatsu's first time (maybe) With a handheld device (COPY)
WHY-THIS IS THE LEAST FUNNIEST HOME VIDEO I'VE EVER SEEN!
I should... just die.
Soy un perdedor.

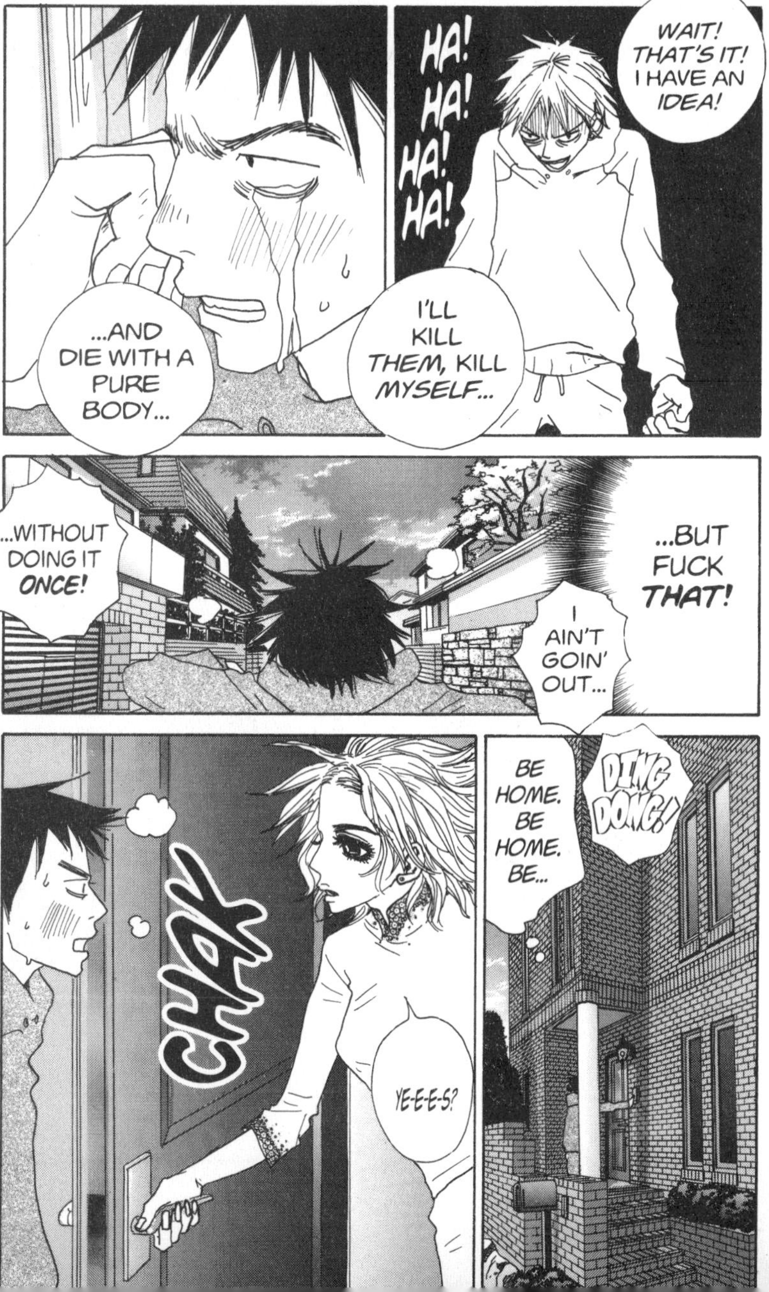
WAIT! THAT'S IT! I HAVE AN IDEA!
HA! HA! HA! HA!
I'LL KILL THEM, KILL MYSELF...
...AND DIE WITH A PURE BODY...
...BUT FUCK THAT!
I AIN'T GOIN' OUT...
...WITHOUT DOING IT ONCE!
DING DONG!
BE HOME. BE HOME. BE...
CHAK
YE-E-E-S?

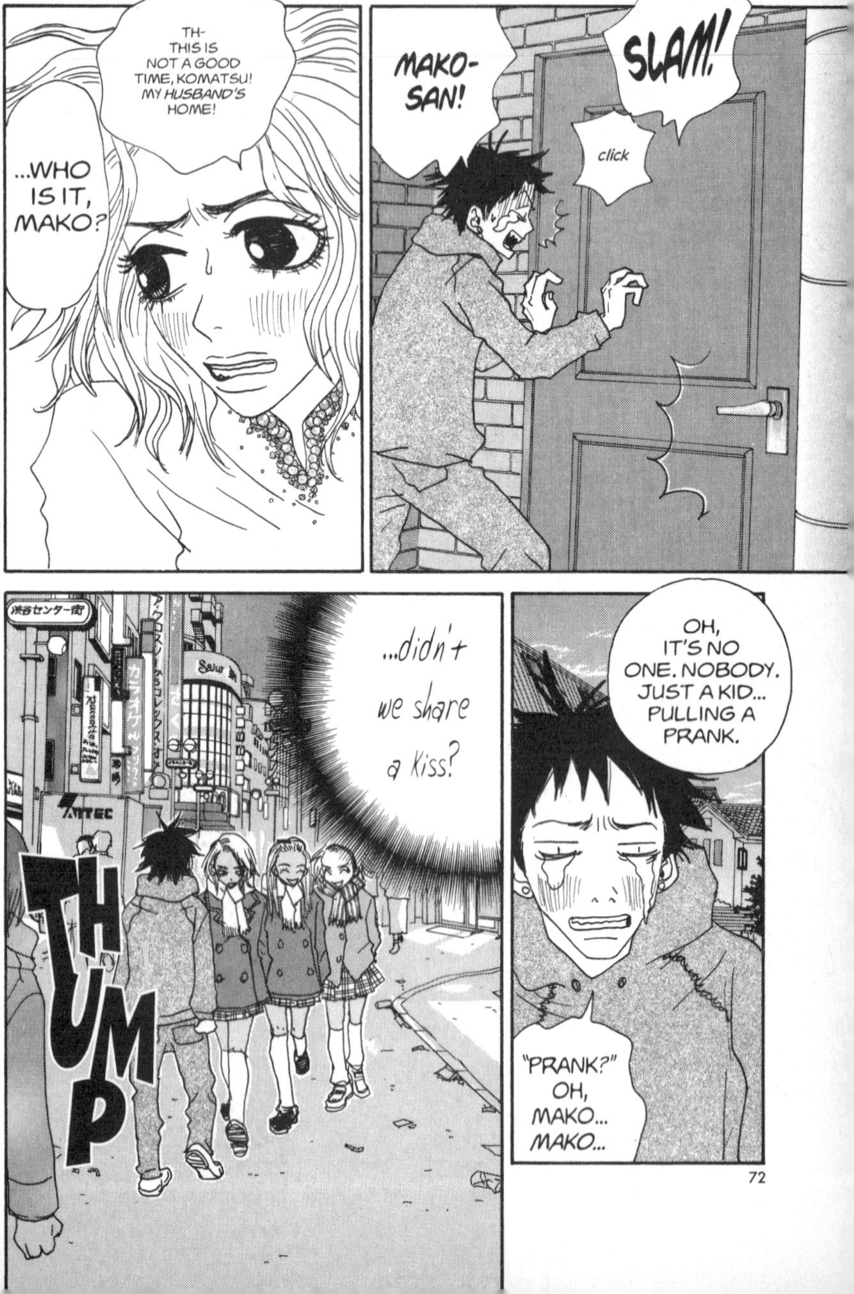
MAKO-SAN!
SLAM!
click
TH- THIS IS NOT A GOOD TIME, KOMATSU! MY HUSBAND'S HOME!
...WHO IS IT, MAKO?
OH, IT'S NO ONE. NOBODY. JUST A KID... PULLING A PRANK.
"PRANK?" OH, MAKO... MAKO...
...didn't we share a kiss?
渋谷センター街
THUMP

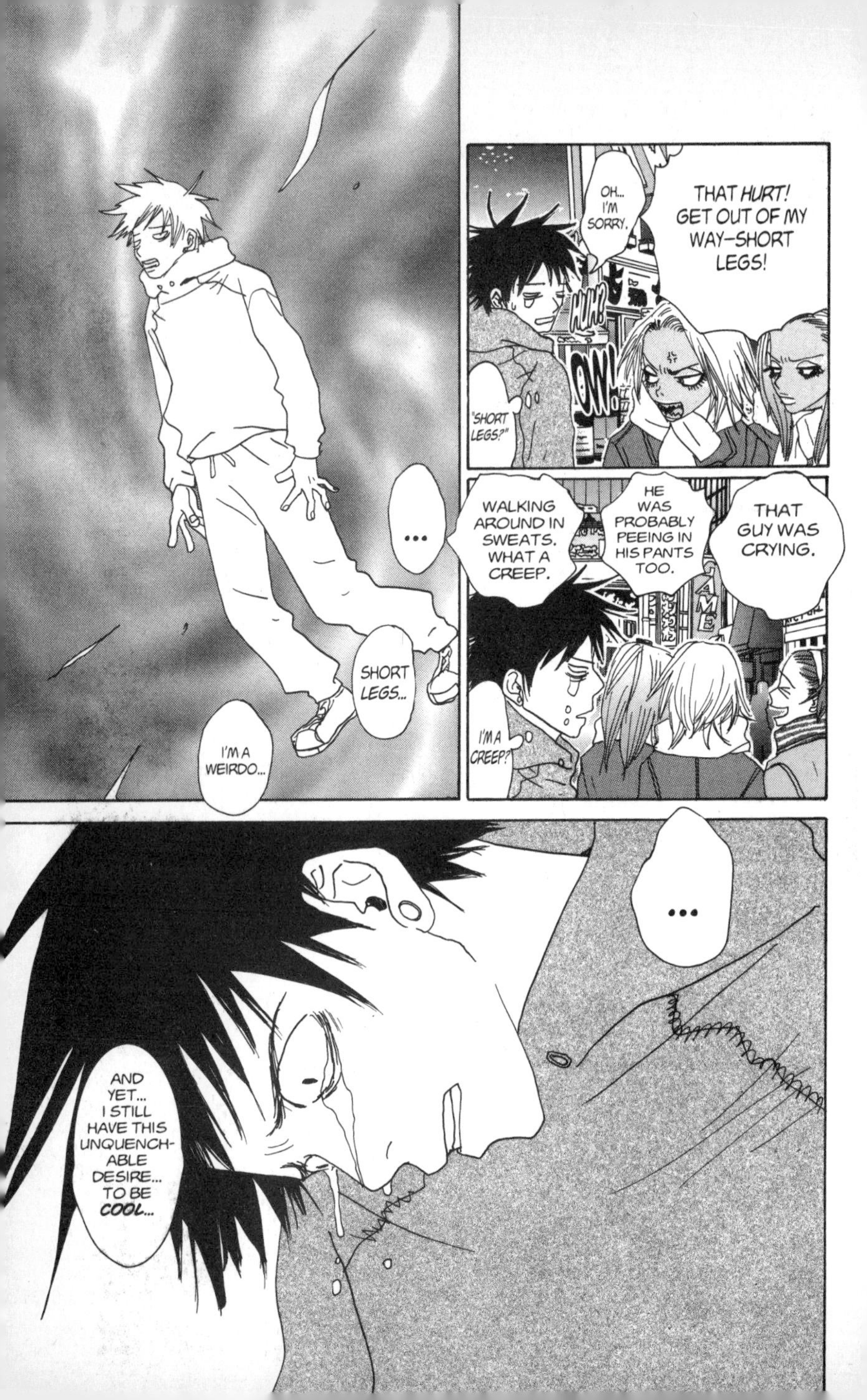
THAT *HURT!* GET OUT OF MY WAY—SHORT LEGS!
OH... I'M SORRY.
OW!
"SHORT LEGS?"
THAT GUY WAS CRYING.
HE WAS PROBABLY PEEING IN HIS PANTS TOO.
WALKING AROUND IN SWEATS. WHAT A CREEP.
I'M A CREEP?
...
SHORT LEGS...
I'M A WEIRDO...
...
AND YET... I STILL HAVE THIS UNQUENCH-ABLE DESIRE... TO BE ***COOL***...

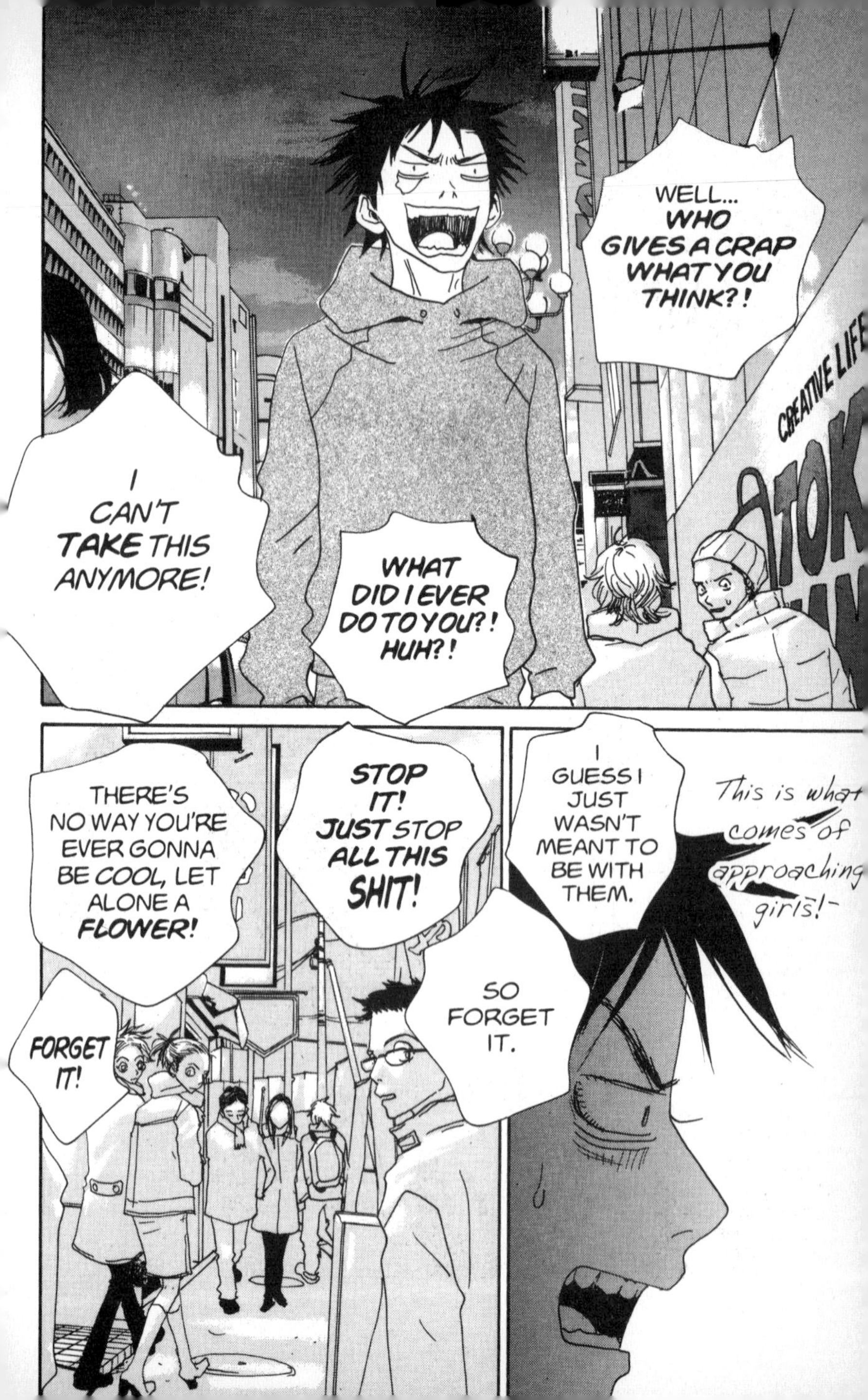
WELL... WHO GIVES A CRAP WHAT YOU THINK?!
WHAT DID I EVER DO TO YOU?! HUH?!
I CAN'T TAKE THIS ANYMORE!
This is what comes of approaching girls!
I GUESS I JUST WASN'T MEANT TO BE WITH THEM.
SO FORGET IT.
STOP IT! JUST STOP ALL THIS SHIT!
THERE'S NO WAY YOU'RE EVER GONNA BE COOL, LET ALONE A FLOWER!
FORGET IT!

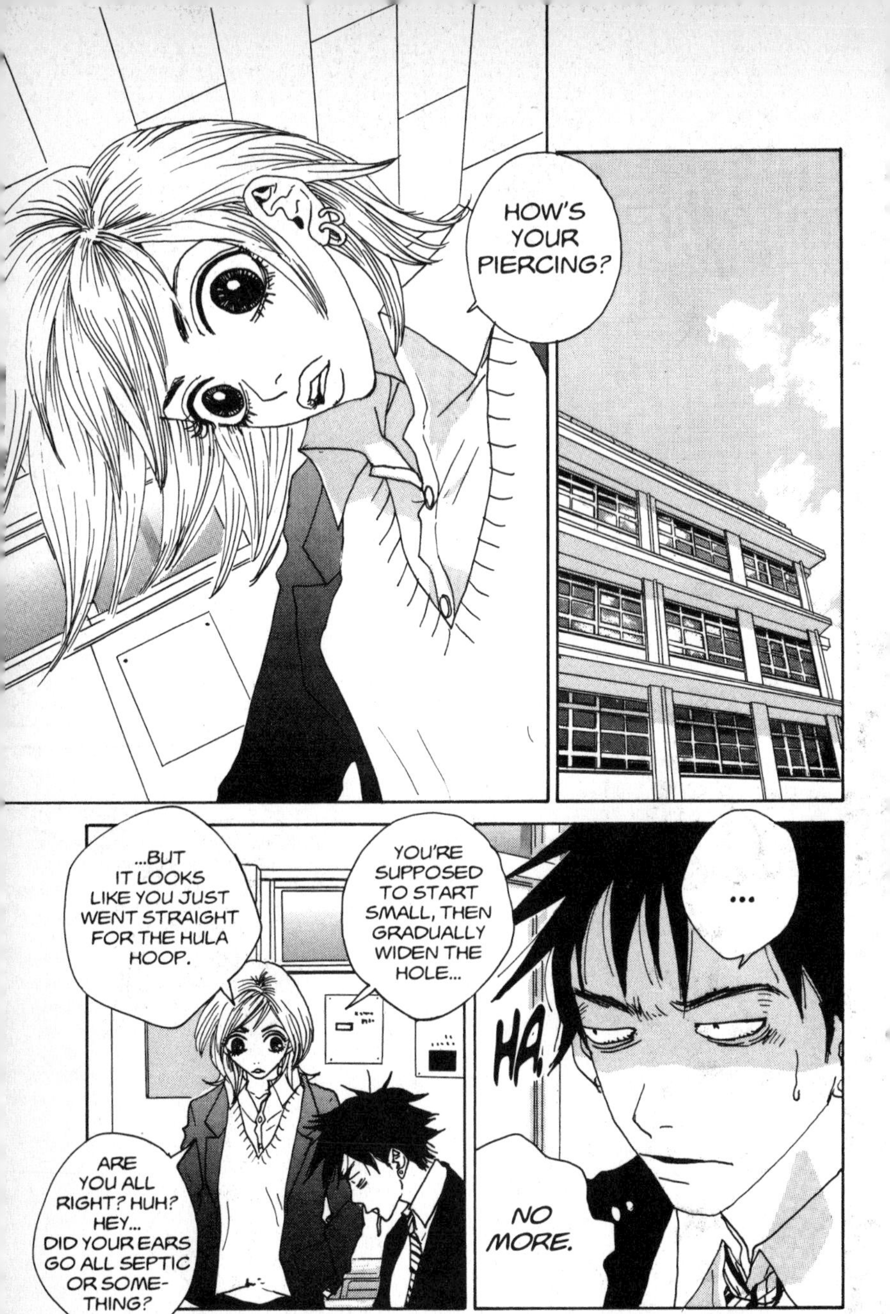
HOW'S YOUR PIERCING?
...
HA
NO MORE.
YOU'RE SUPPOSED TO START SMALL, THEN GRADUALLY WIDEN THE HOLE...
...BUT IT LOOKS LIKE YOU JUST WENT STRAIGHT FOR THE HULA HOOP.
ARE YOU ALL RIGHT? HUH? HEY... DID YOUR EARS GO ALL SEPTIC OR SOME-THING?

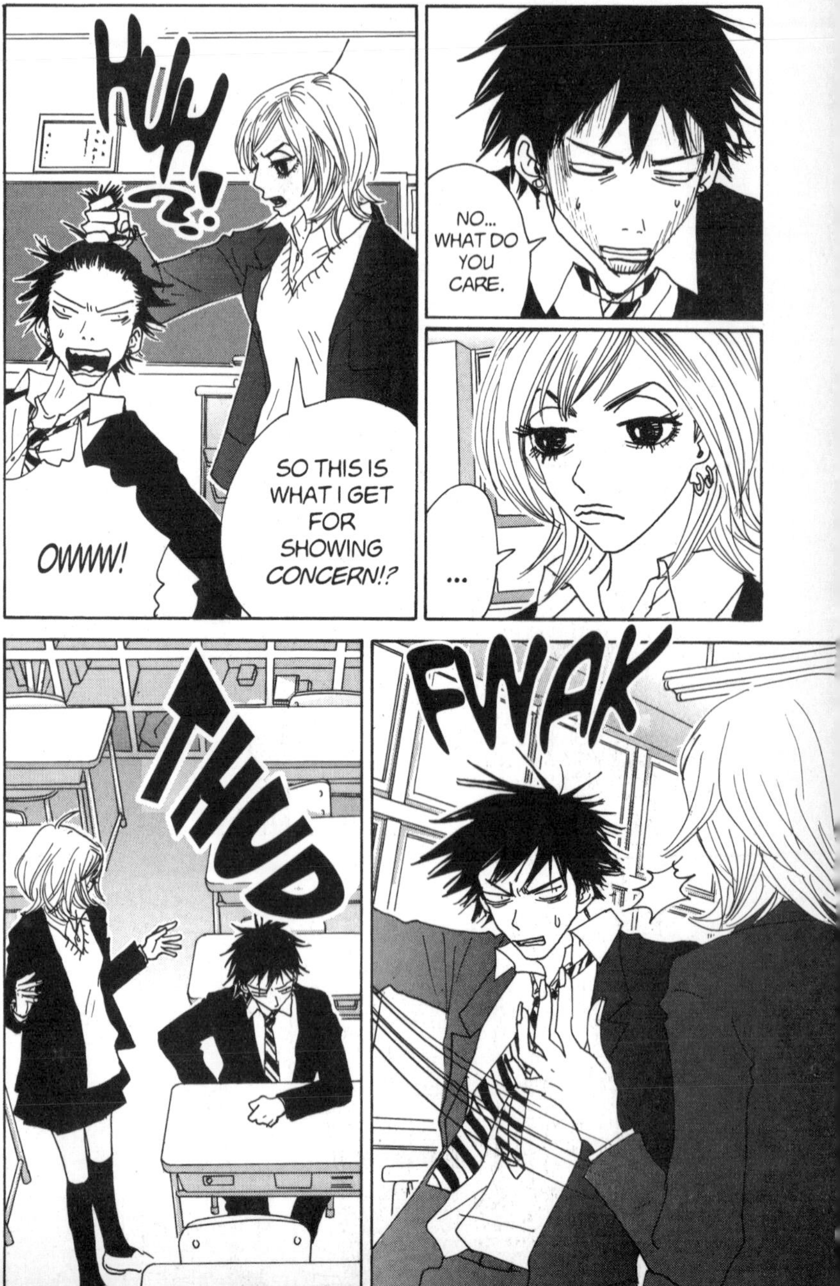
NO... WHAT DO YOU CARE.
...
HUH?!
SO THIS IS WHAT I GET FOR SHOWING CONCERN!?
OWWW!
FWAK
THUD

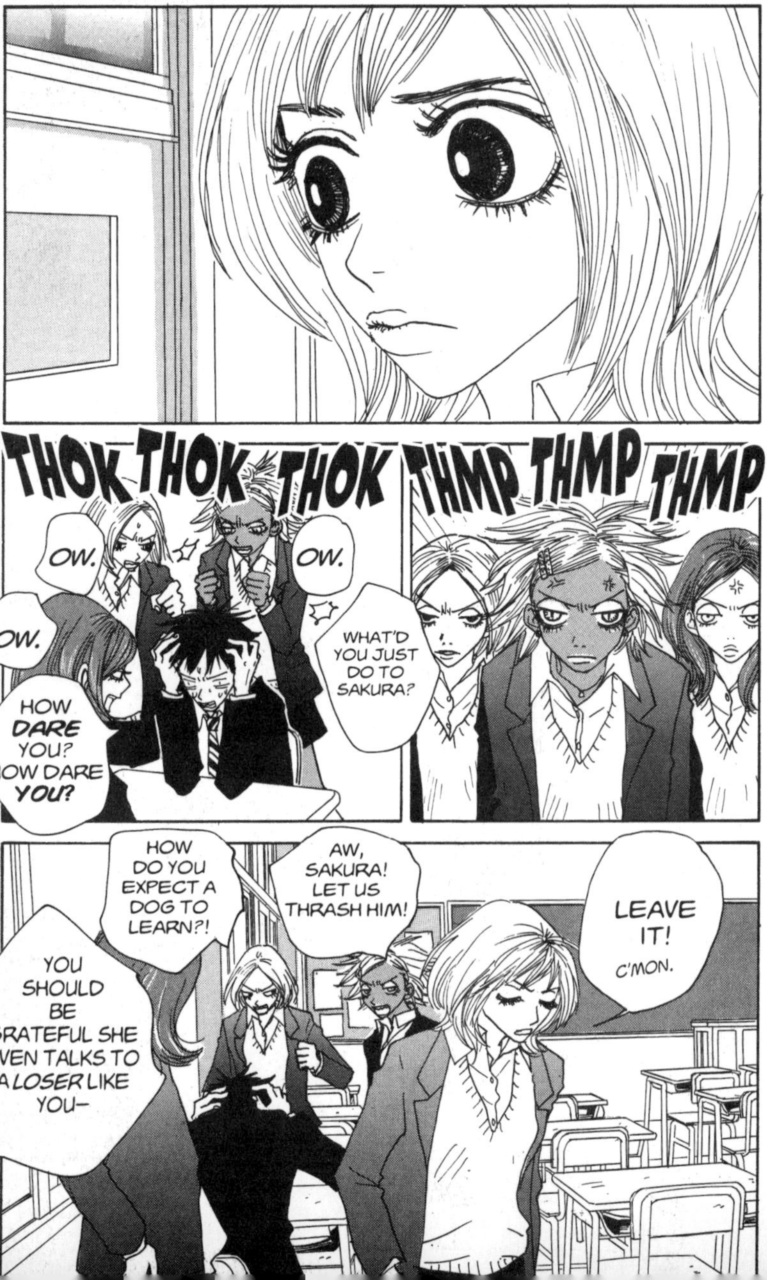
THMP THMP THMP
WHAT'D YOU JUST DO TO SAKURA?
THOK THOK THOK
OW.
OW.
OW.
HOW **DARE** YOU? HOW DARE ***YOU?***
LEAVE IT!
C'MON.
AW, SAKURA! LET US THRASH HIM!
HOW DO YOU EXPECT A DOG TO LEARN?!
YOU SHOULD BE GRATEFUL SHE EVEN TALKS TO A *LOSER* LIKE YOU–

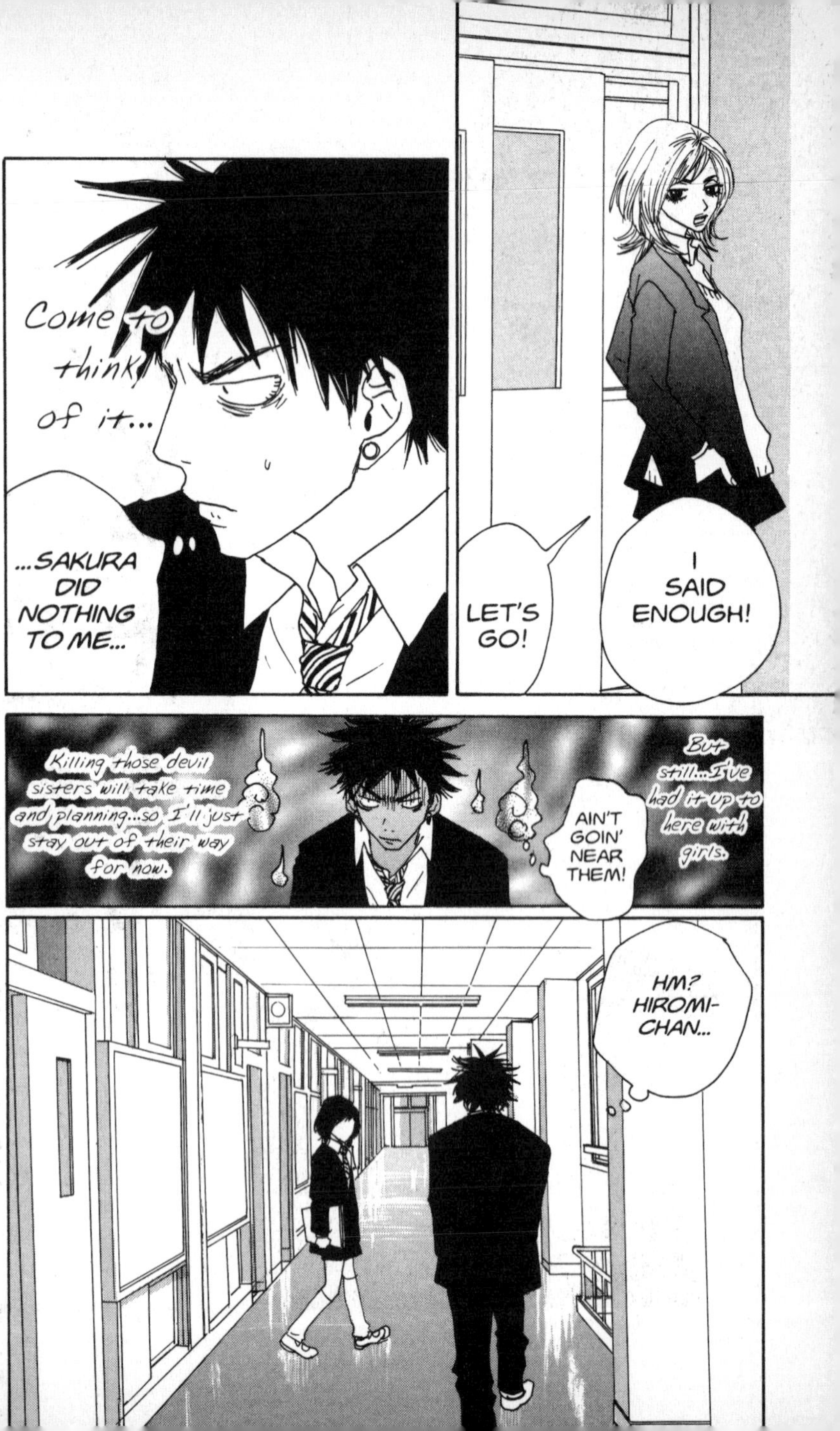
I SAID ENOUGH!
LET'S GO!
Come to think of it...
...SAKURA DID NOTHING TO ME...
But still...I've had it up to here with girls.
AIN'T GOIN' NEAR THEM!
Killing those devil sisters will take time and planning...so I'll just stay out of their way for now.
HM? HIROMI-CHAN...

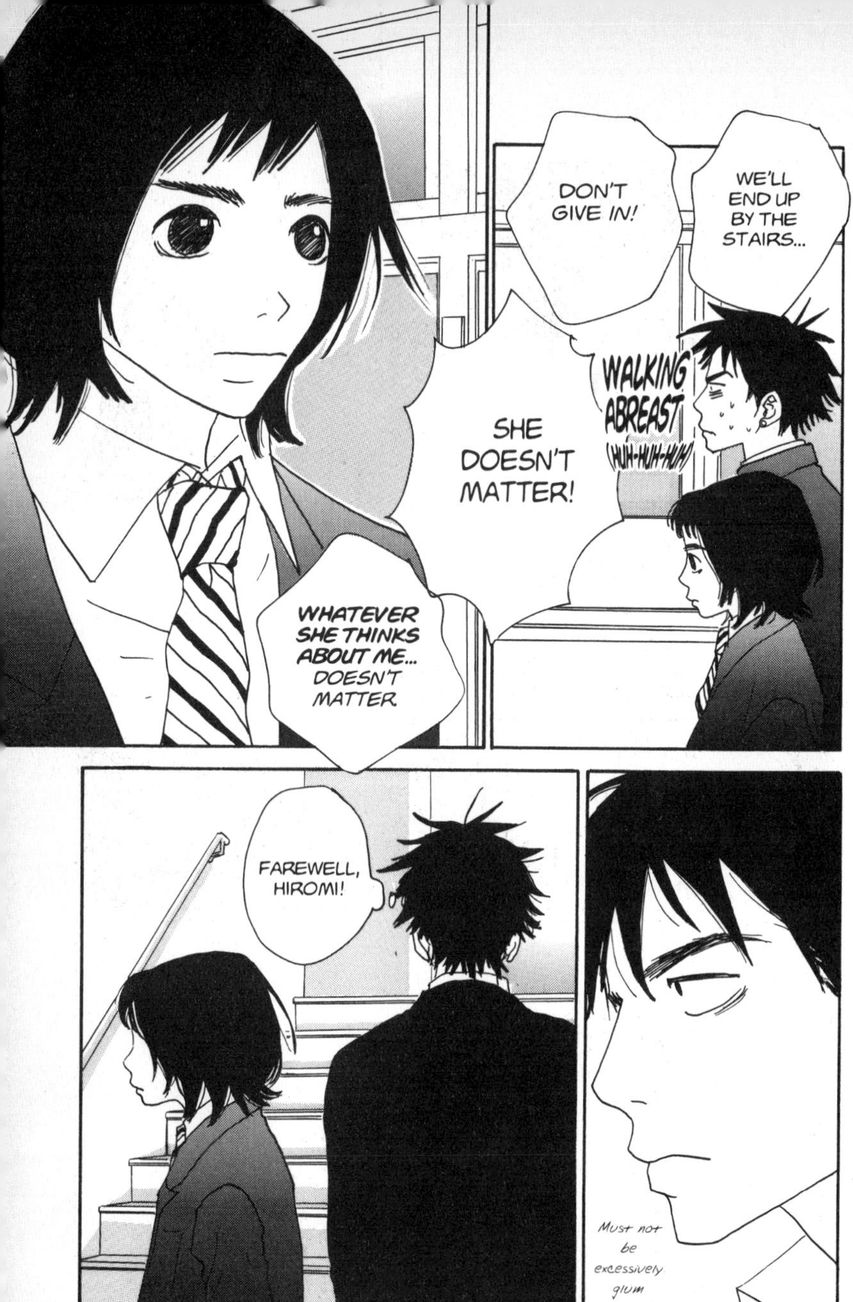
WE'LL END UP BY THE STAIRS...
DON'T GIVE IN!
WALKING ABREAST
(HUH-HUH-HUH)
SHE DOESN'T MATTER!
WHATEVER SHE THINKS ABOUT ME... DOESN'T MATTER.
Must not be excessively glum
FAREWELL, HIROMI!

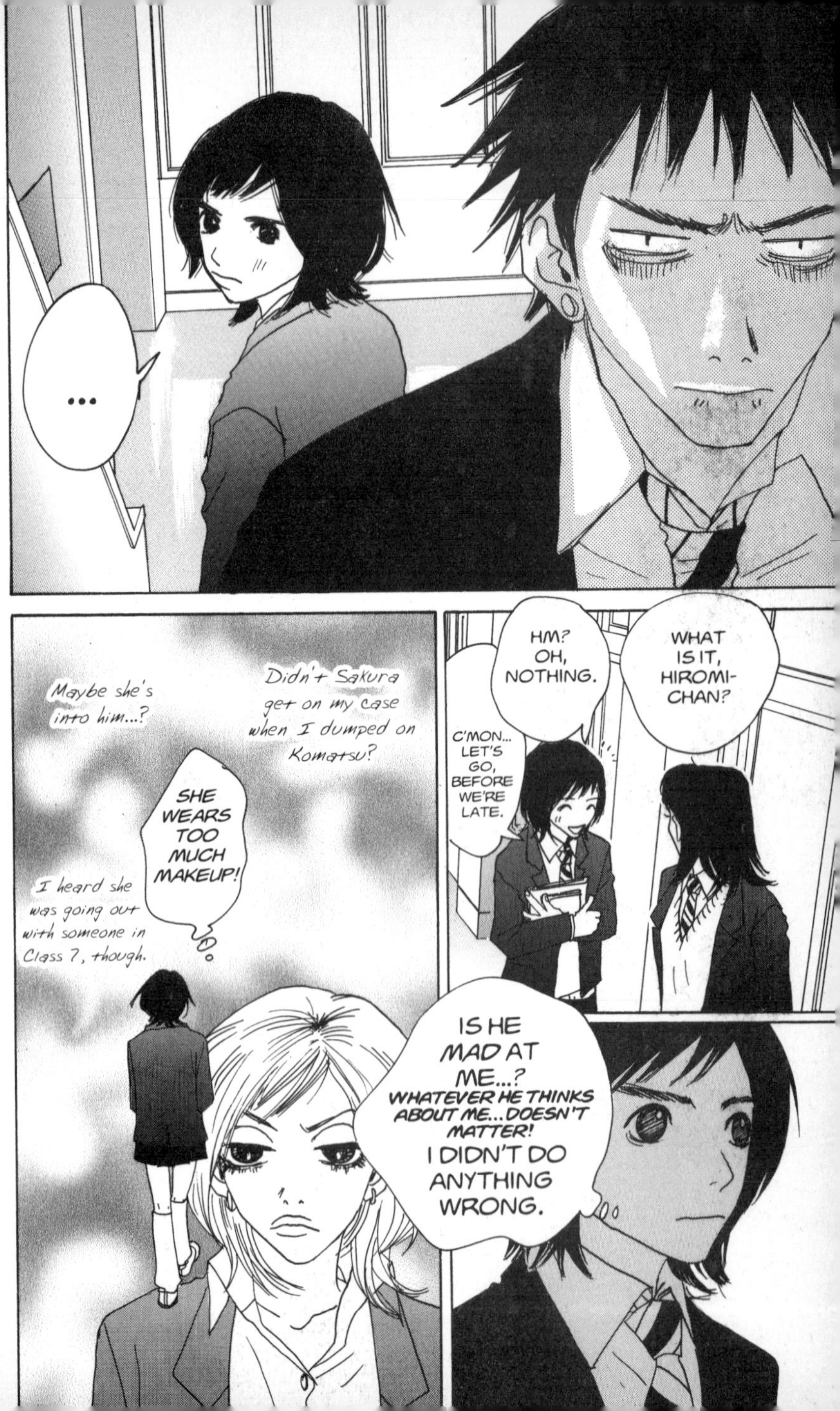
...
WHAT IS IT, HIROMI-CHAN?
HM? OH, NOTHING.
C'MON... LET'S GO, BEFORE WE'RE LATE.
IS HE MAD AT ME...?
WHATEVER HE THINKS ABOUT ME... DOESN'T MATTER!
I DIDN'T DO ANYTHING WRONG.
Didn't Sakura get on my case when I dumped on Komatsu?
Maybe she's into him...?
SHE WEARS TOO MUCH MAKEUP!
I heard she was going out with someone in Class 7, though.

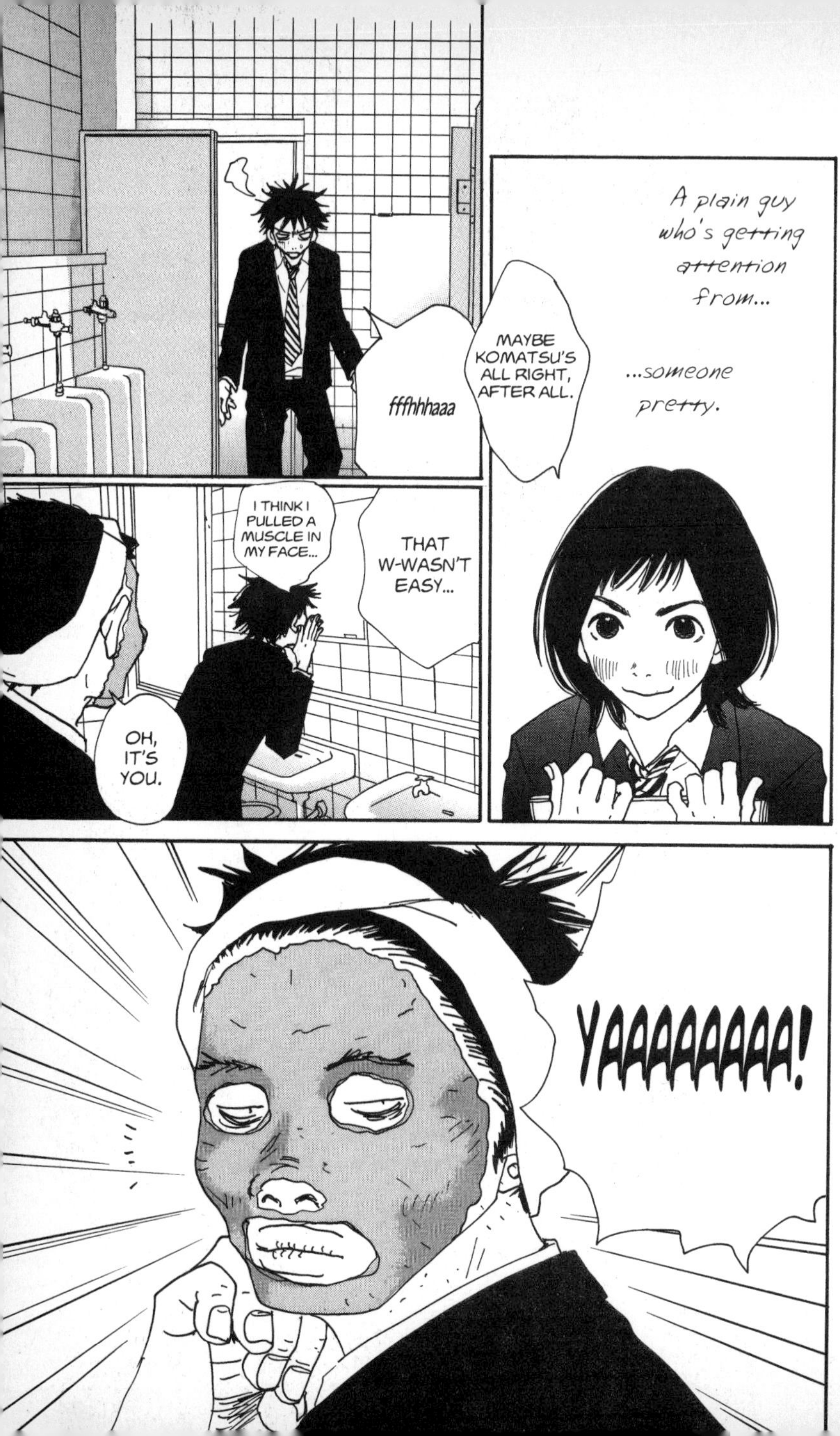
A plain guy who's getting attention from...
...someone pretty.
MAYBE KOMATSU'S ALL RIGHT, AFTER ALL.
fffhhhaaa
THAT W-WASN'T EASY...
I THINK I PULLED A MUSCLE IN MY FACE...
OH, IT'S YOU.
YAAAAAAAA!

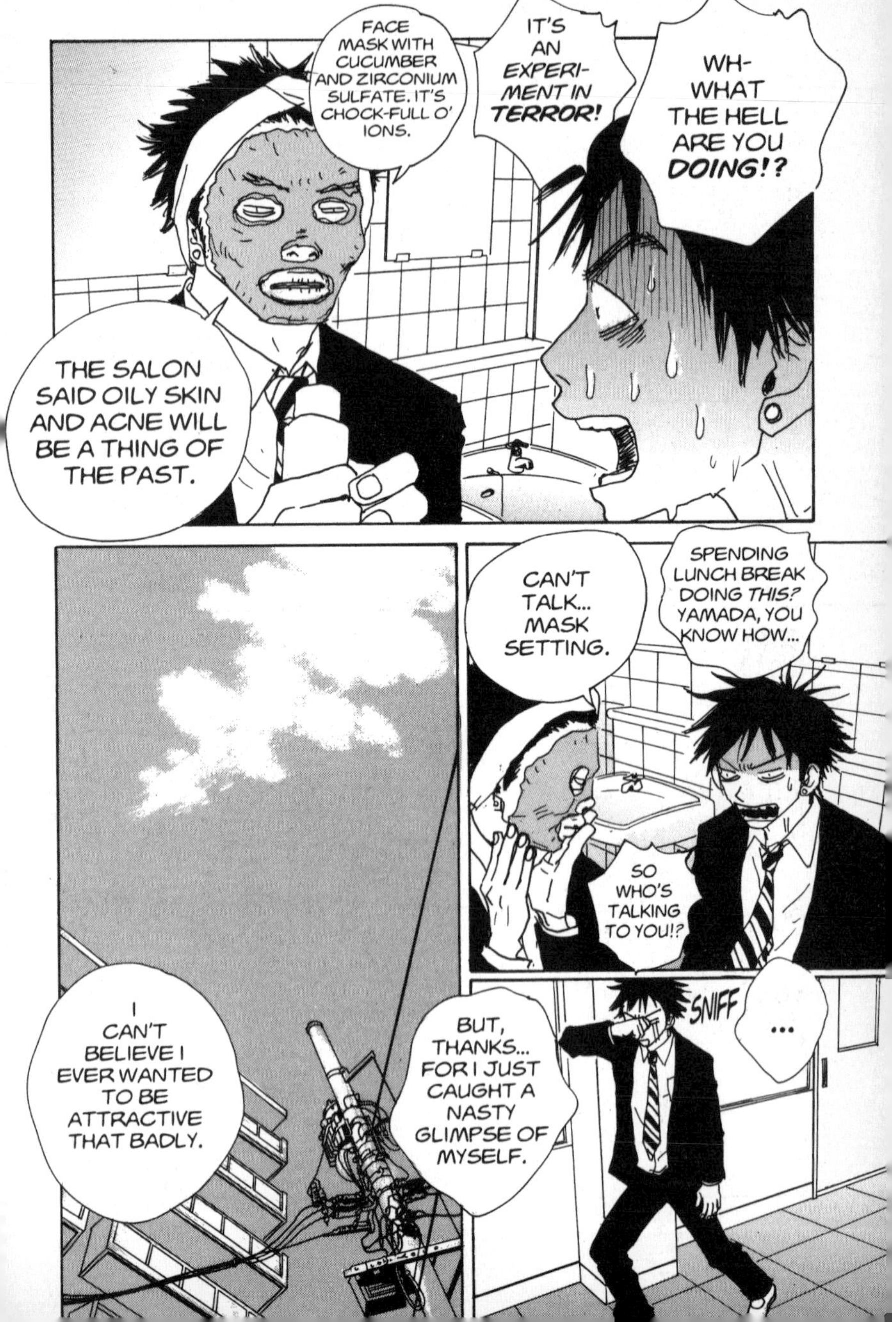
WH- WHAT THE HELL ARE YOU DOING!?
IT'S AN EXPERIMENT IN TERROR!
FACE MASK WITH CUCUMBER AND ZIRCONIUM SULFATE. IT'S CHOCK-FULL O' IONS.
THE SALON SAID OILY SKIN AND ACNE WILL BE A THING OF THE PAST.
SPENDING LUNCH BREAK DOING THIS? YAMADA, YOU KNOW HOW...
CAN'T TALK... MASK SETTING.
SO WHO'S TALKING TO YOU!?
SNIFF
...
BUT, THANKS... FOR I JUST CAUGHT A NASTY GLIMPSE OF MYSELF.
I CAN'T BELIEVE I EVER WANTED TO BE ATTRACTIVE THAT BADLY.

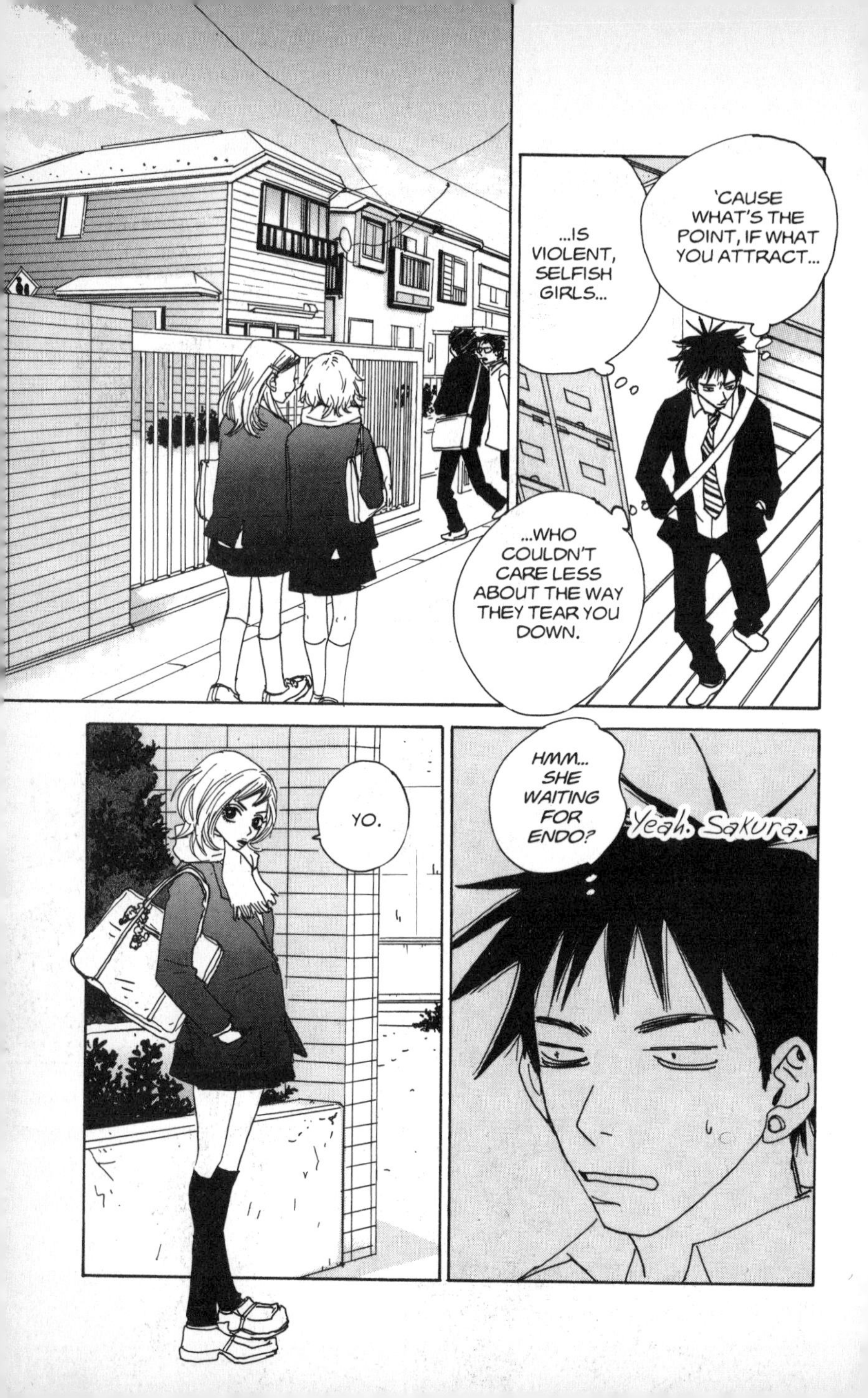
'CAUSE WHAT'S THE POINT, IF WHAT YOU ATTRACT...
...IS VIOLENT, SELFISH GIRLS...
...WHO COULDN'T CARE LESS ABOUT THE WAY THEY TEAR YOU DOWN.
Yeah. Sakura.
HMM... SHE WAITING FOR ENDO?
YO.

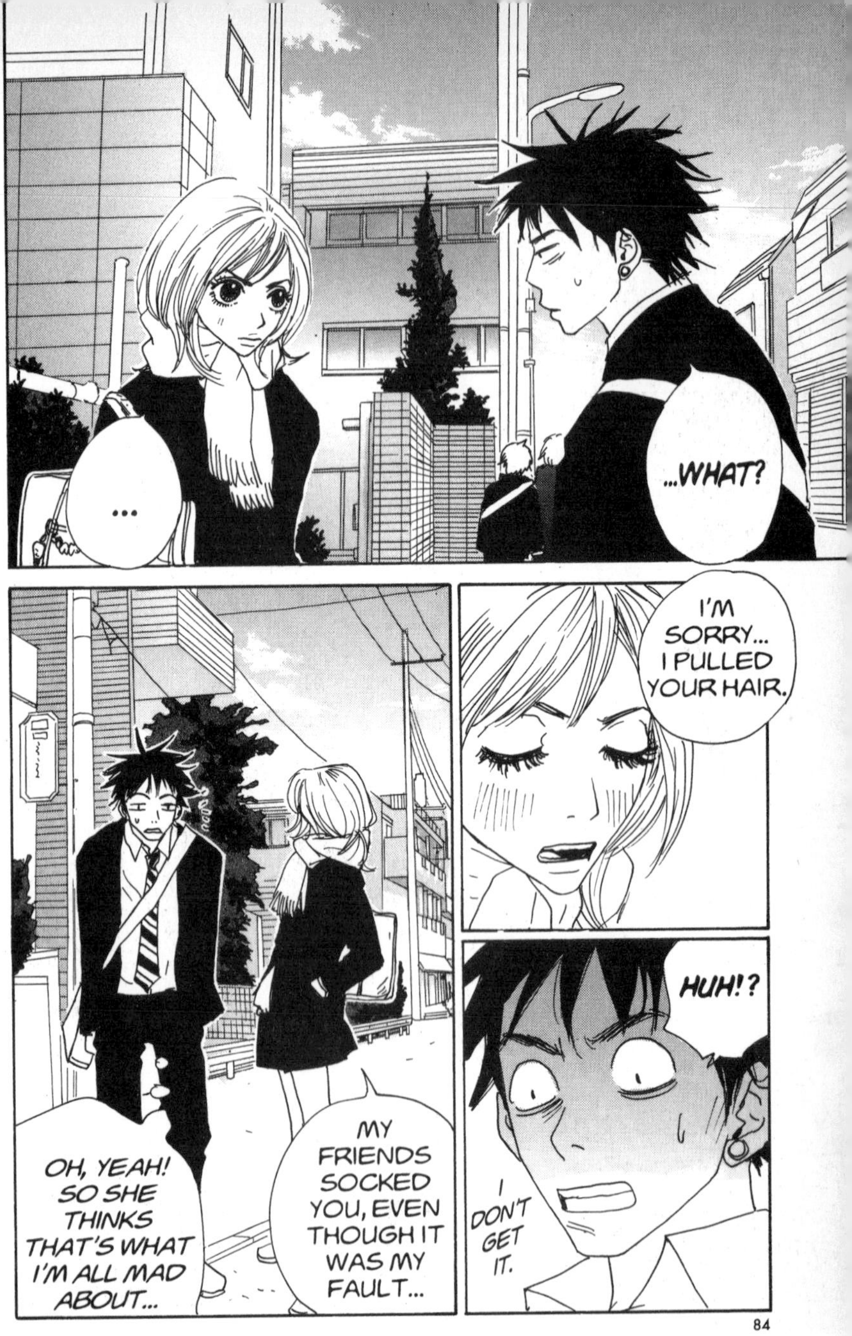
...WHAT?
...
I'M SORRY... I PULLED YOUR HAIR.
HUH!?
I DON'T GET IT.
MY FRIENDS SOCKED YOU, EVEN THOUGH IT WAS MY FAULT...
OH, YEAH! SO SHE THINKS THAT'S WHAT I'M ALL MAD ABOUT...

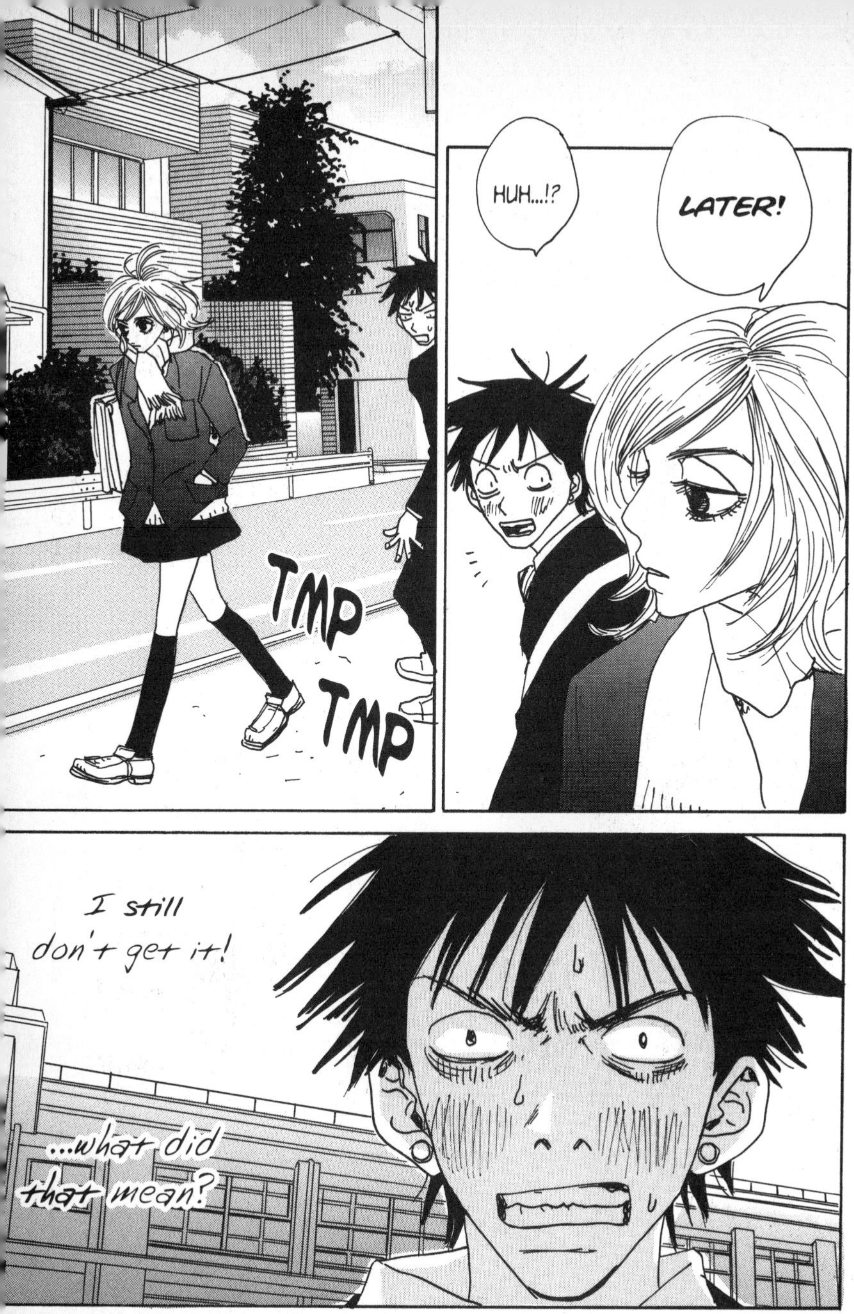
LATER!
HUH...!?
TMP
TMP
I still don't get it!
...what did that mean?

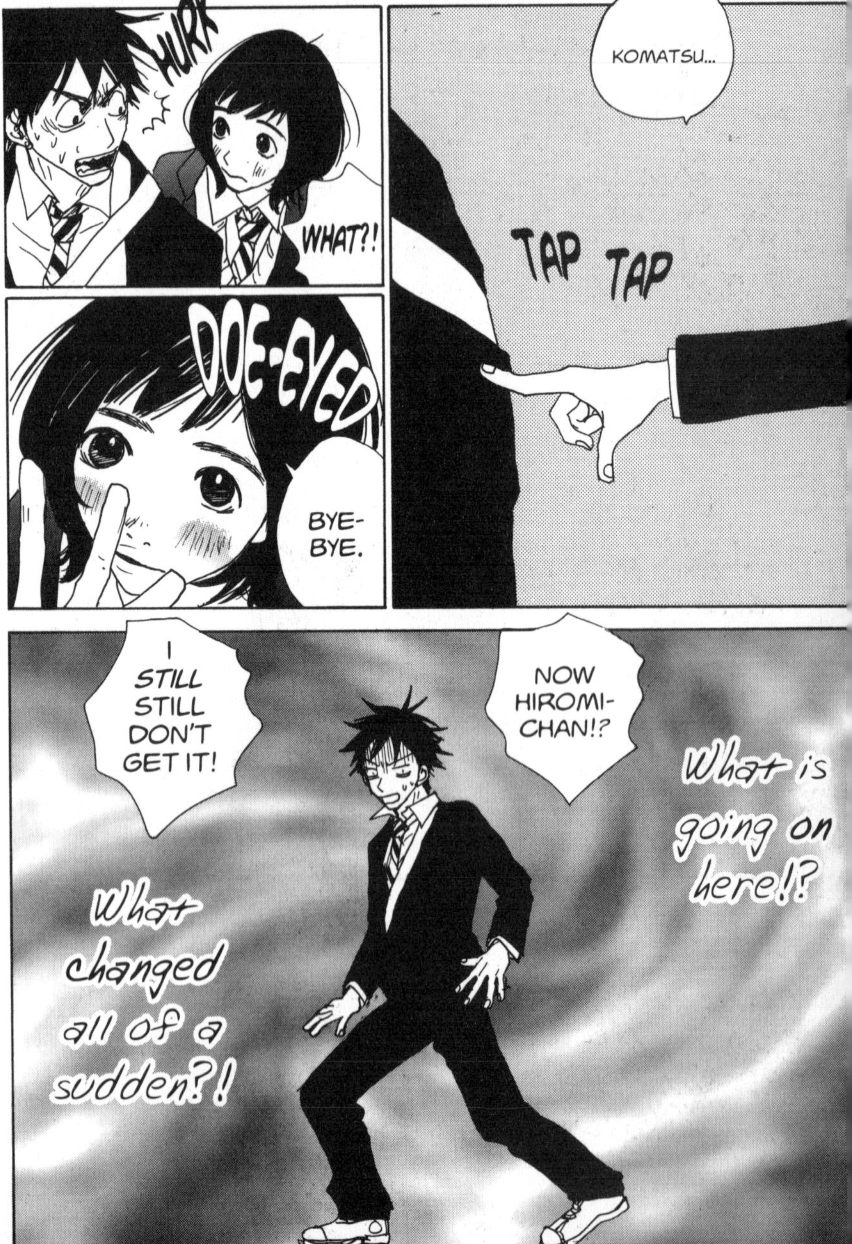
KOMATSU...
TAP TAP
HURK
WHAT?!
DOE-EYED
BYE-BYE.
NOW HIROMI-CHAN!?
I STILL STILL DON'T GET IT!
What is going on here!?
What changed all of a sudden?!

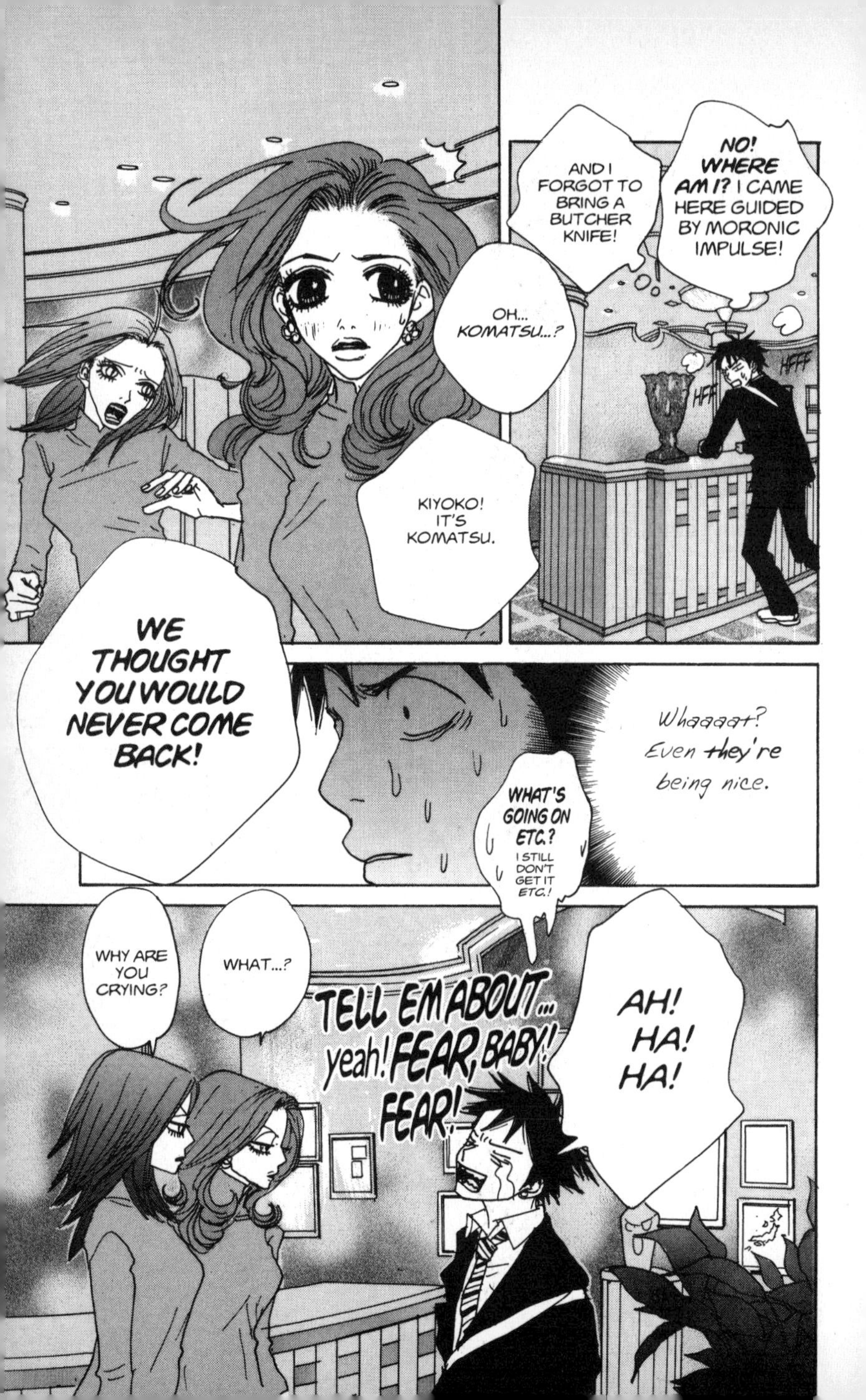
NO! WHERE AM I? I CAME HERE GUIDED BY MORONIC IMPULSE!
AND I FORGOT TO BRING A BUTCHER KNIFE!
HFFF
HFF
OH... KOMATSU...?
KIYOKO! IT'S KOMATSU.
WE THOUGHT YOU WOULD NEVER COME BACK!
Whaaaat? Even they're being nice.
WHAT'S GOING ON ETC.? I STILL DON'T GET IT ETC.!
AH! HA! HA!
TELL EM ABOUT... yeah! FEAR, BABY! FEAR!
WHAT...?
WHY ARE YOU CRYING?

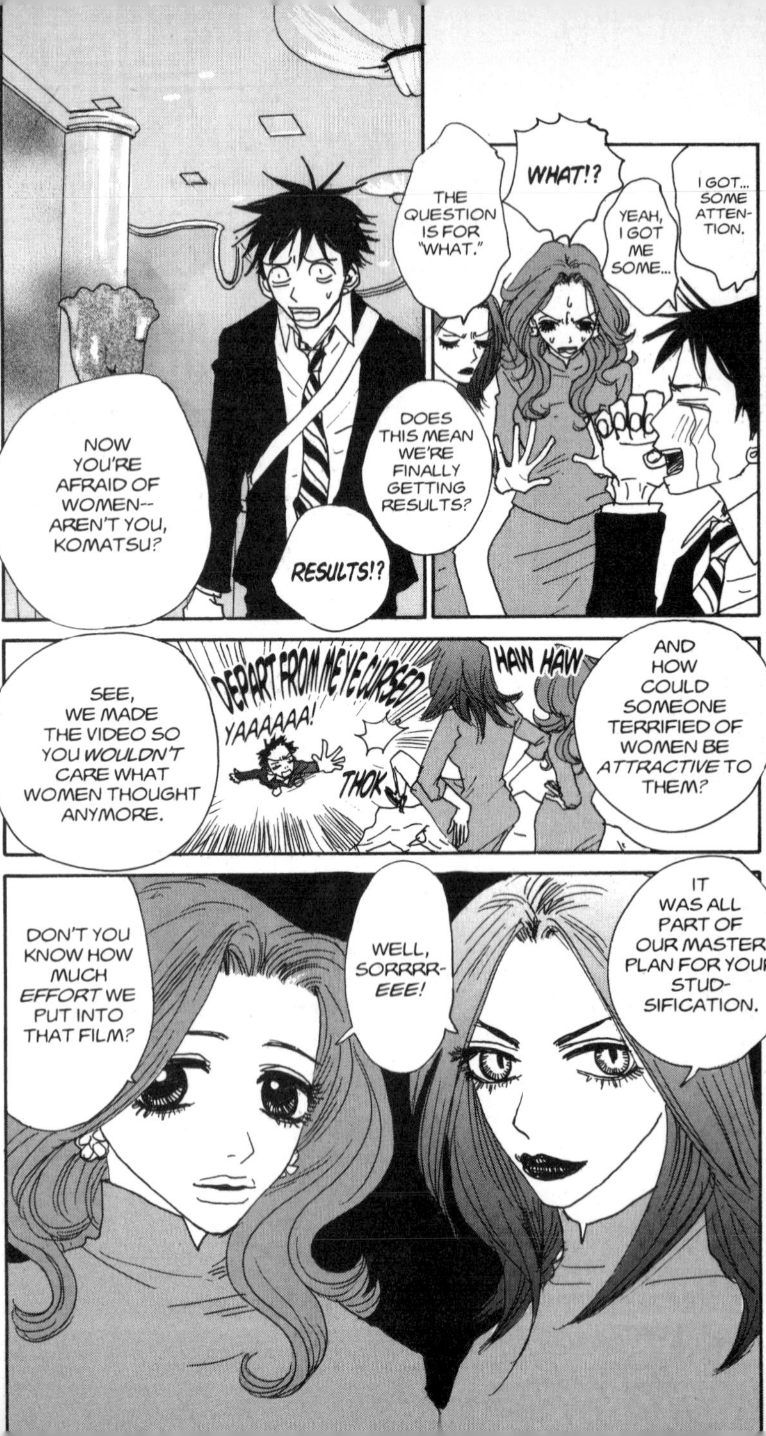
I GOT... SOME ATTENTION.
YEAH, I GOT ME SOME...
WHAT!?
THE QUESTION IS FOR "WHAT."
DOES THIS MEAN WE'RE FINALLY GETTING RESULTS?
RESULTS!?
NOW YOU'RE AFRAID OF WOMEN-- AREN'T YOU, KOMATSU?
AND HOW COULD SOMEONE TERRIFIED OF WOMEN BE ATTRACTIVE TO THEM?
HAW HAW
DEPART FROM ME YE CURSED
YAAAAAA!
THOK
SEE, WE MADE THE VIDEO SO YOU WOULDN'T CARE WHAT WOMEN THOUGHT ANYMORE.
IT WAS ALL PART OF OUR MASTER PLAN FOR YOUR STUD-SIFICATION.
WELL, SORRRR-EEE!
DON'T YOU KNOW HOW MUCH EFFORT WE PUT INTO THAT FILM?

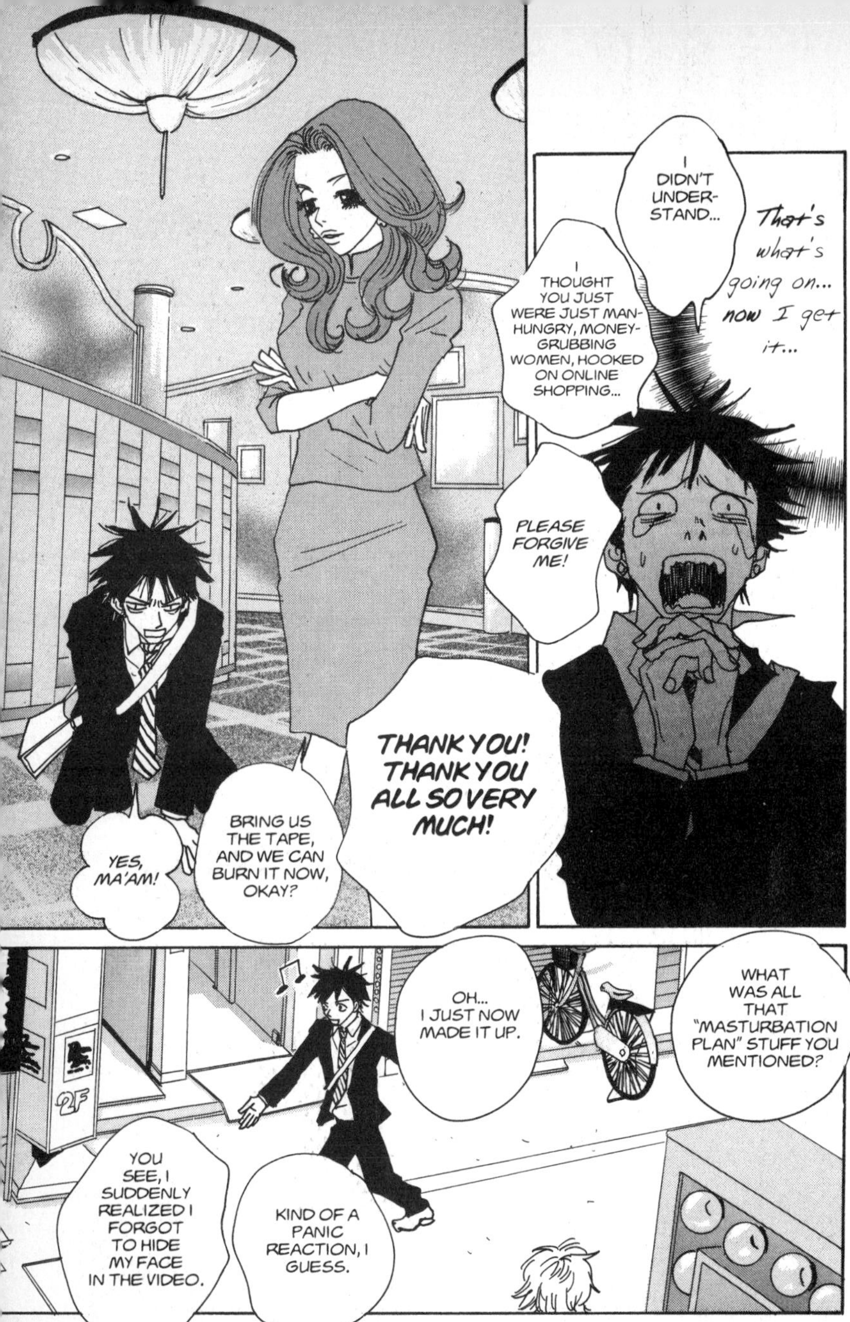
I DIDN'T UNDER-STAND...
That's what's going on... now I get it...
I THOUGHT YOU JUST WERE JUST MAN-HUNGRY, MONEY-GRUBBING WOMEN, HOOKED ON ONLINE SHOPPING...
PLEASE FORGIVE ME!
THANK YOU! THANK YOU ALL SO VERY MUCH!
BRING US THE TAPE, AND WE CAN BURN IT NOW, OKAY?
YES, MA'AM!
WHAT WAS ALL THAT "MASTURBATION PLAN" STUFF YOU MENTIONED?
OH... I JUST NOW MADE IT UP.
KIND OF A PANIC REACTION, I GUESS.
YOU SEE, I SUDDENLY REALIZED I FORGOT TO HIDE MY FACE IN THE VIDEO.
2F

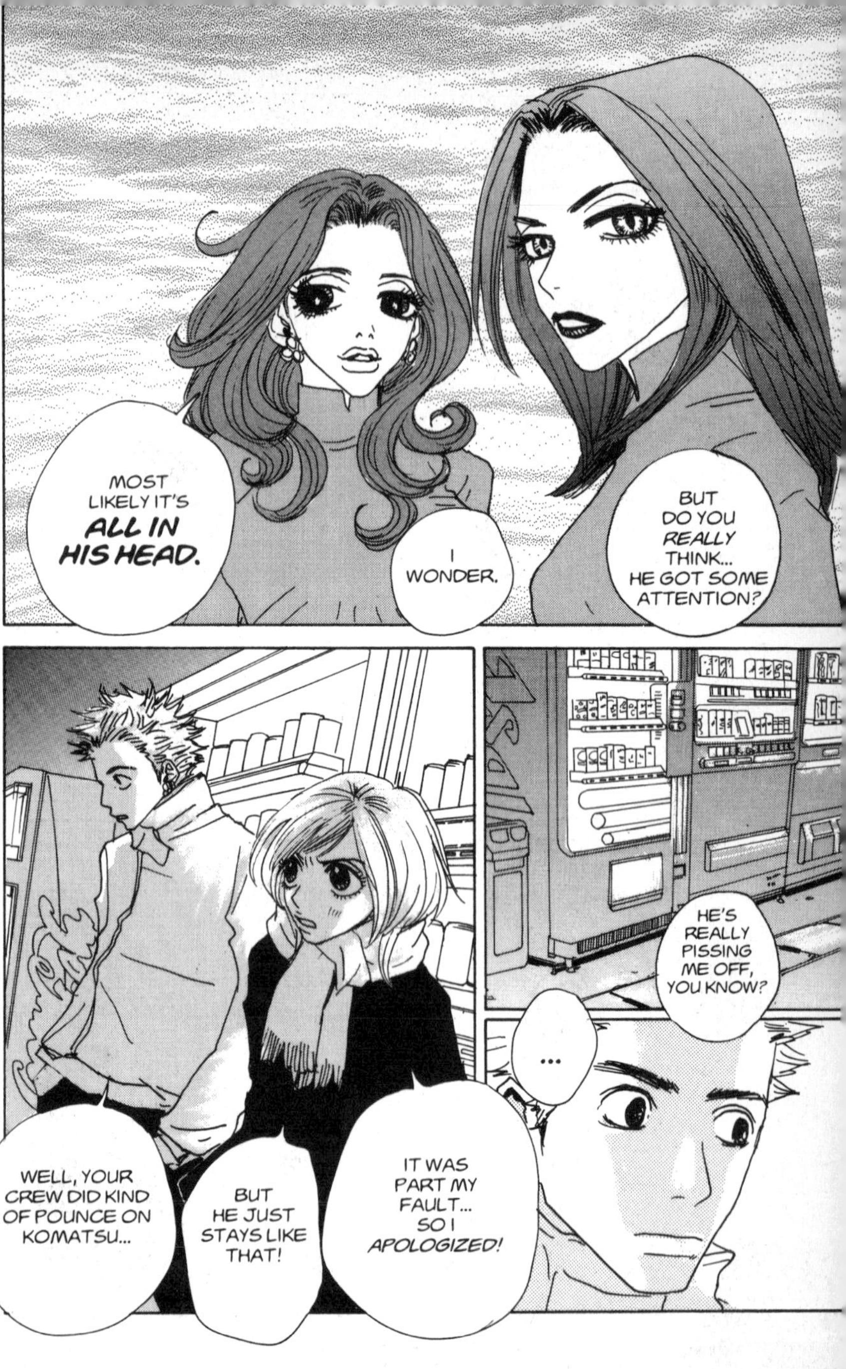
BUT DO YOU *REALLY* THINK... HE GOT SOME ATTENTION?
I WONDER.
MOST LIKELY IT'S **ALL IN HIS HEAD.**
HE'S REALLY PISSING ME OFF, YOU KNOW?
...
IT WAS PART MY FAULT... SO I *APOLOGIZED!*
BUT HE JUST STAYS LIKE THAT!
WELL, YOUR CREW DID KIND OF POUNCE ON KOMATSU...

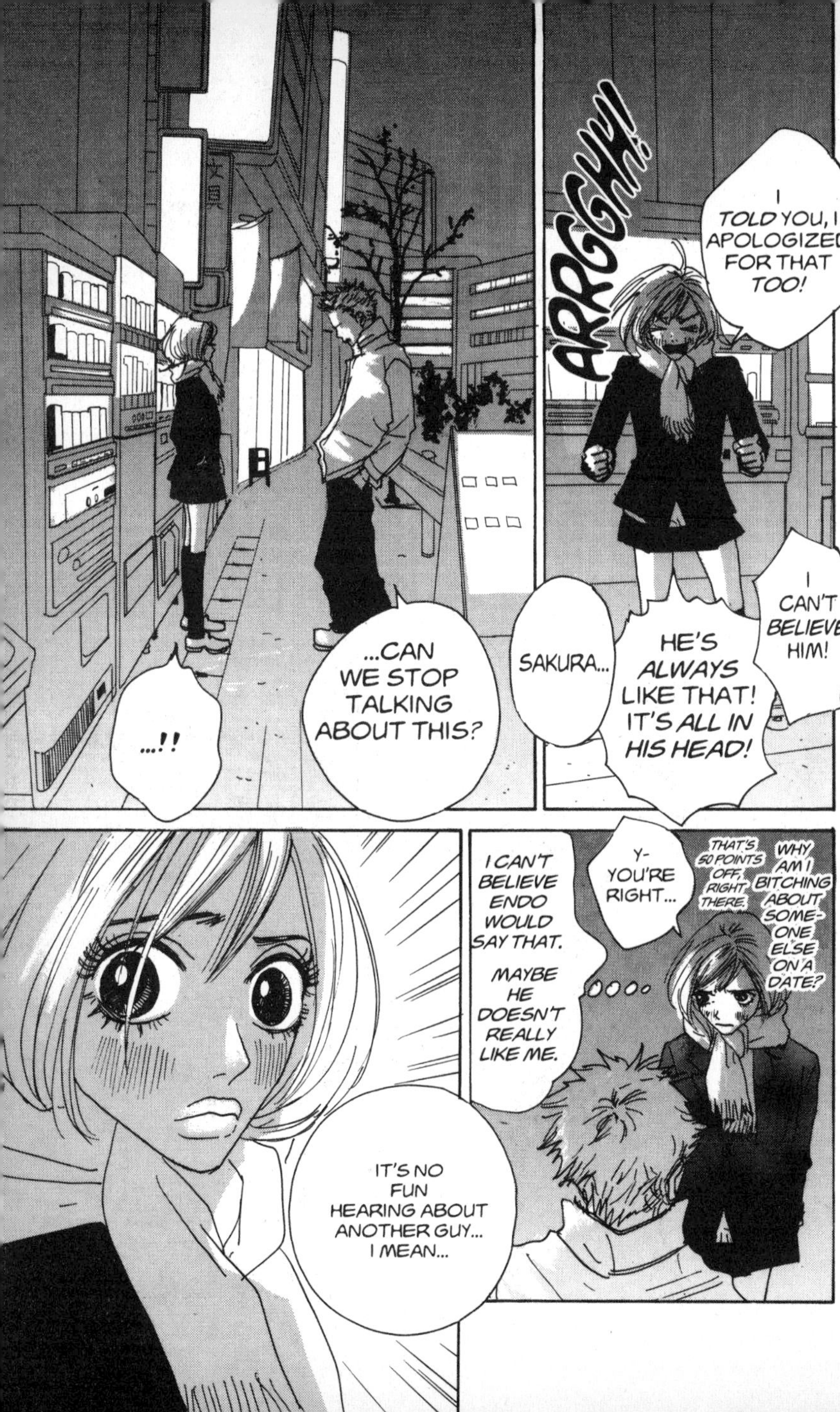
ARRGGHH!!
I TOLD YOU, I APOLOGIZED FOR THAT TOO!
I CAN'T BELIEVE HIM!
HE'S ALWAYS LIKE THAT! IT'S ALL IN HIS HEAD!
SAKURA...
...CAN WE STOP TALKING ABOUT THIS?
...!!
Y-YOU'RE RIGHT...
WHY AM I BITCHING ABOUT SOMEONE ELSE ON A DATE?
THAT'S 50 POINTS OFF, RIGHT THERE.
I CAN'T BELIEVE ENDO WOULD SAY THAT.
MAYBE HE DOESN'T REALLY LIKE ME.
IT'S NO FUN HEARING ABOUT ANOTHER GUY... I MEAN...

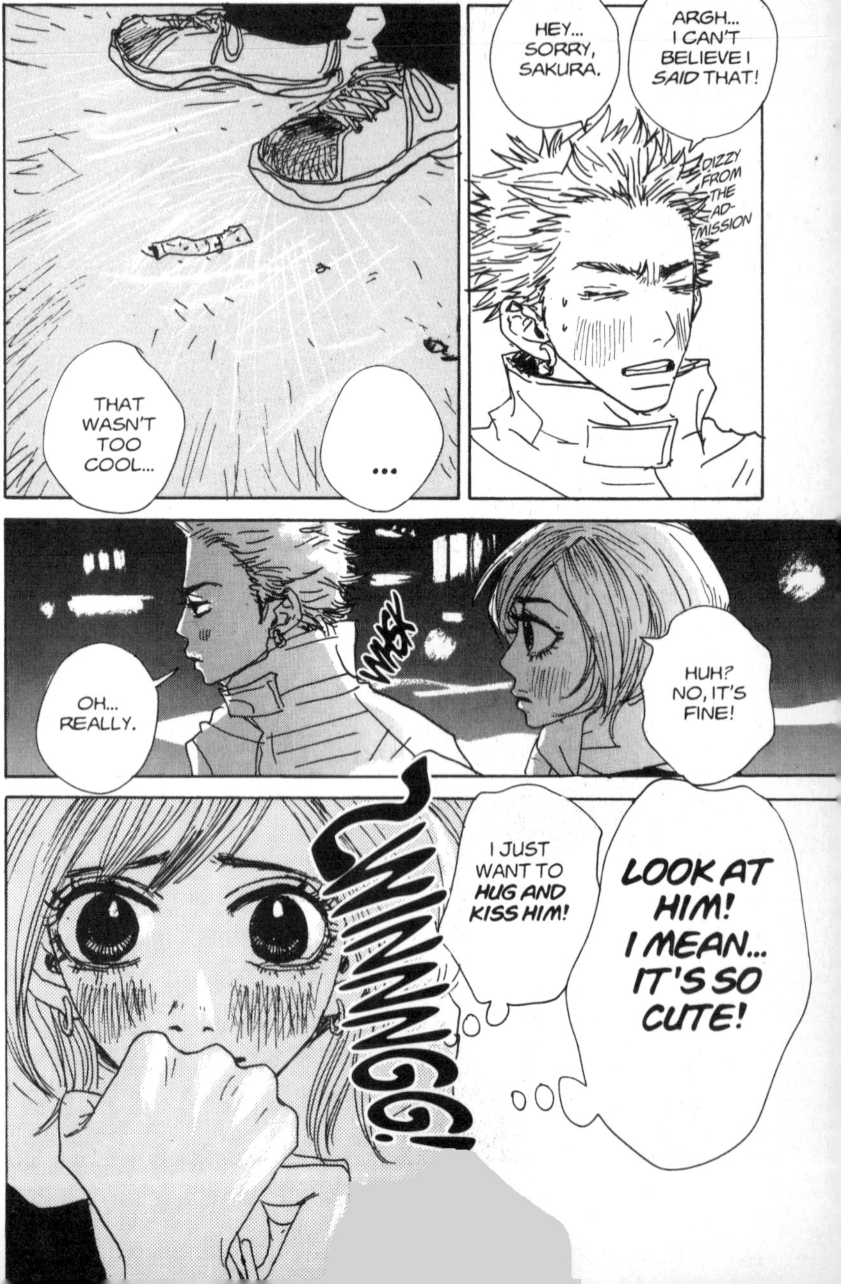
ARGH... I CAN'T BELIEVE I SAID THAT!
HEY... SORRY, SAKURA.
DIZZY FROM THE AD-MISSION
...
THAT WASN'T TOO COOL...
HUH? NO, IT'S FINE!
OH... REALLY.
LOOK AT HIM! I MEAN... IT'S SO CUTE!
I JUST WANT TO HUG AND KISS HIM!
TWINNNGG!

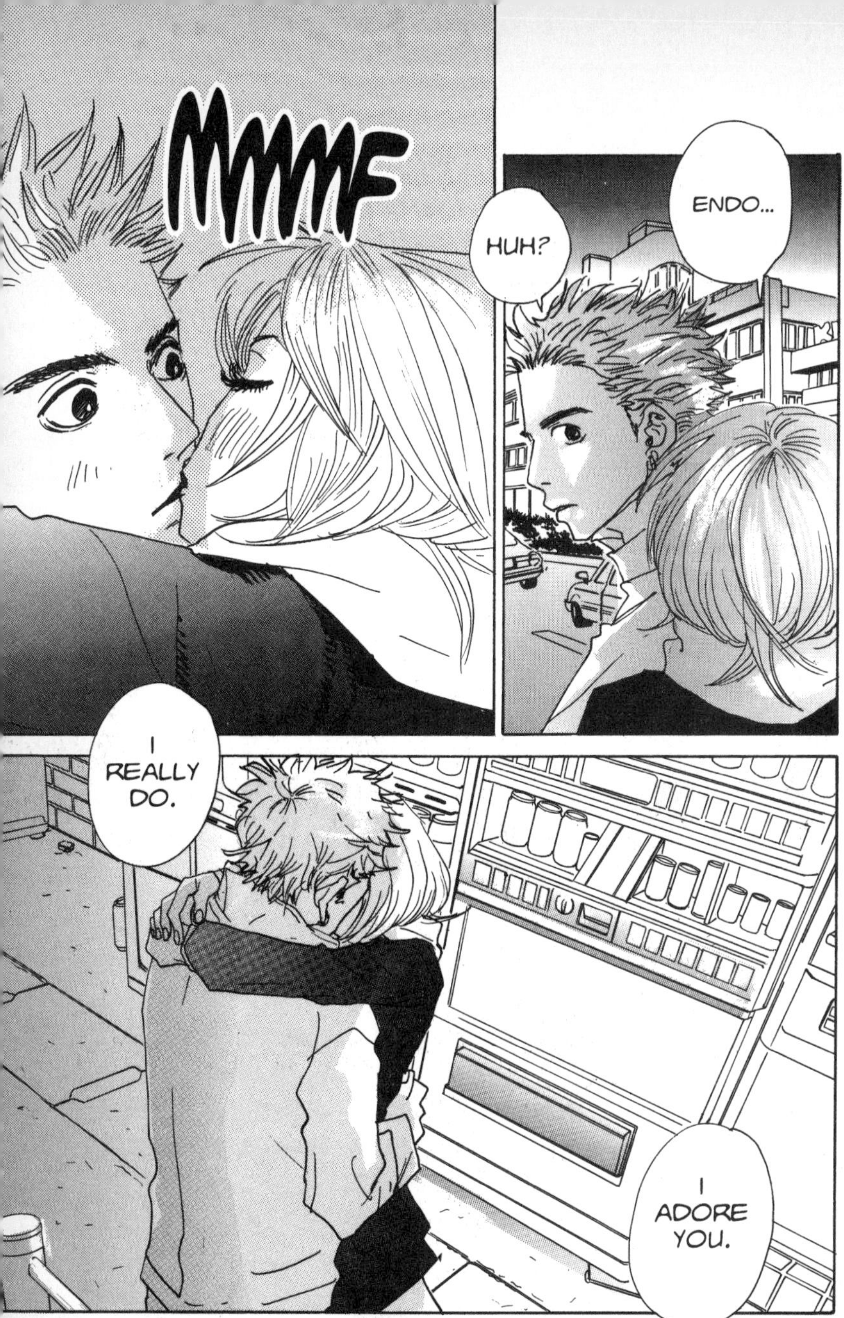
ENDO...
HUH?
MMMF
I ADORE YOU.
I REALLY DO.

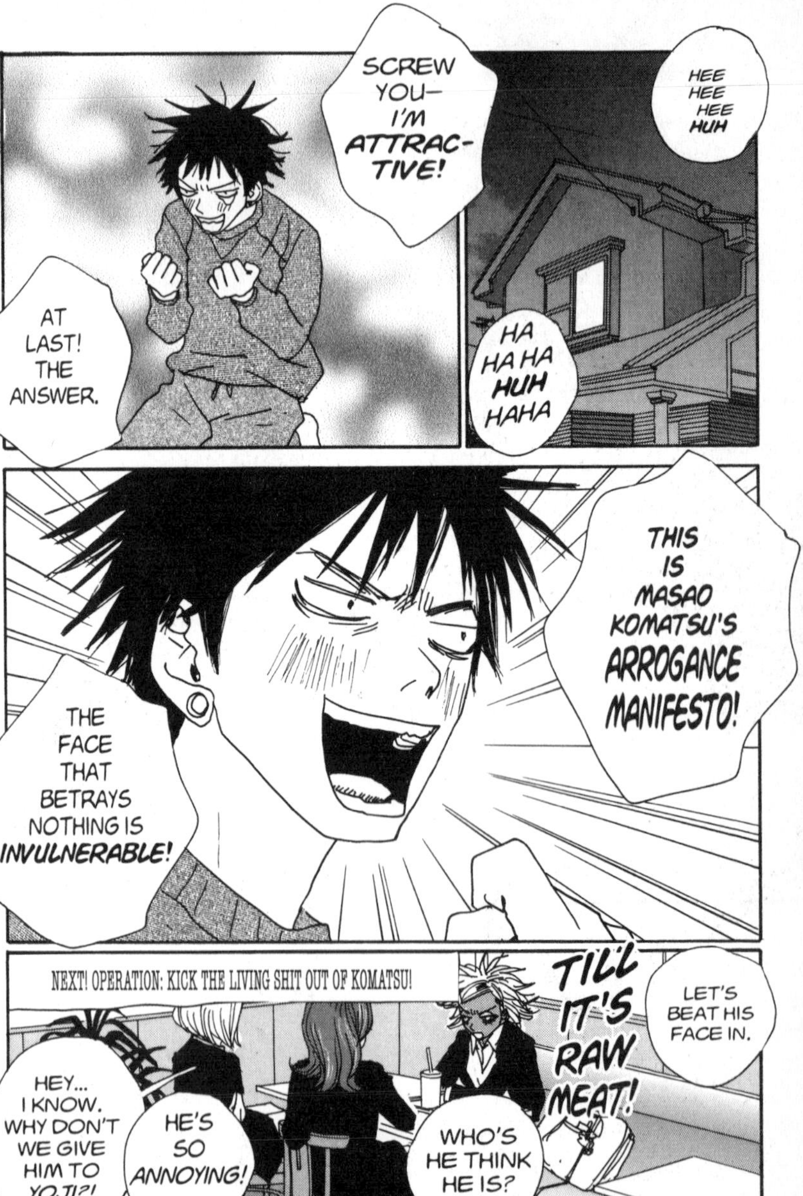
HEE HEE HEE HUH
HA HA HA HUH HAHA
SCREW YOU— I'M ATTRAC- TIVE!
AT LAST! THE ANSWER.
THIS IS MASAO KOMATSU'S ARROGANCE MANIFESTO!
THE FACE THAT BETRAYS NOTHING IS INVULNERABLE!
LET'S BEAT HIS FACE IN.
TILL IT'S RAW MEAT!
NEXT! OPERATION: KICK THE LIVING SHIT OUT OF KOMATSU!
WHO'S HE THINK HE IS?
HE'S SO ANNOYING!
HEY... I KNOW. WHY DON'T WE GIVE HIM TO YOJI?!

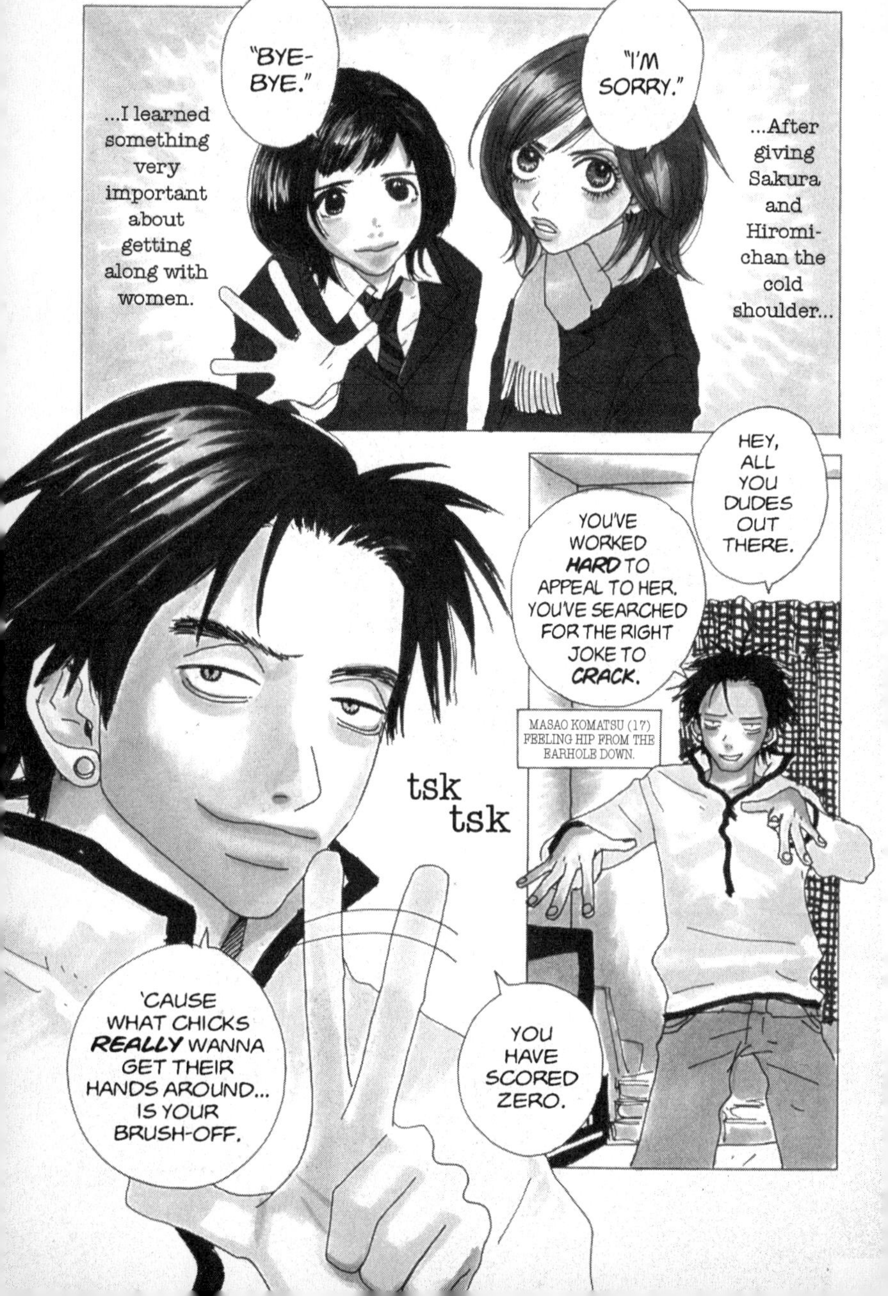
...After giving Sakura and Hiromi-chan the cold shoulder...
"I'M SORRY."
"BYE-BYE."
...I learned something very important about getting along with women.
HEY, ALL YOU DUDES OUT THERE.
YOU'VE WORKED HARD TO APPEAL TO HER. YOU'VE SEARCHED FOR THE RIGHT JOKE TO CRACK.
MASAO KOMATSU (17) FEELING HIP FROM THE EARHOLE DOWN.
tsk tsk
YOU HAVE SCORED ZERO.
'CAUSE WHAT CHICKS REALLY WANNA GET THEIR HANDS AROUND... IS YOUR BRUSH-OFF.

Step 11-1

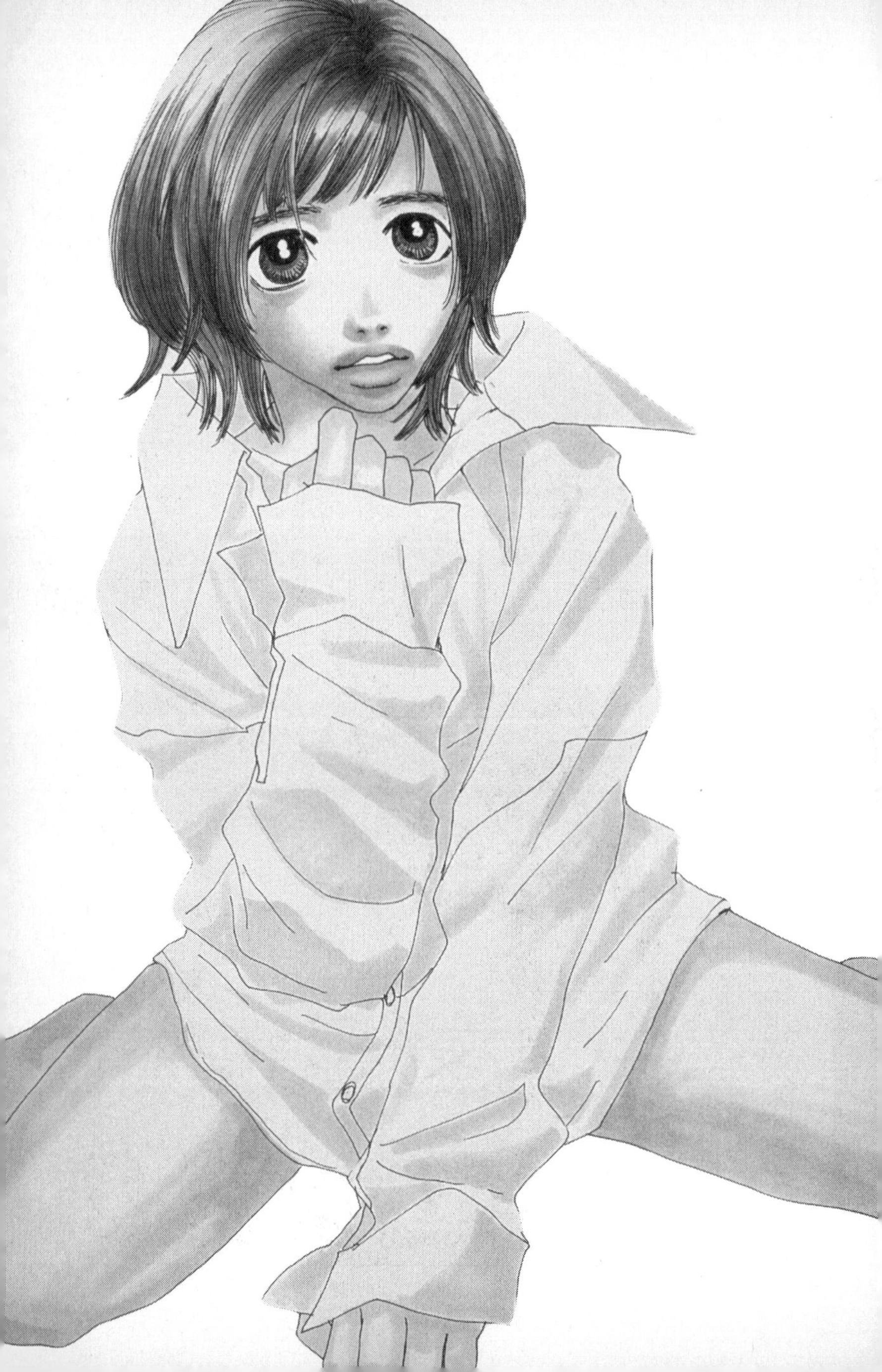

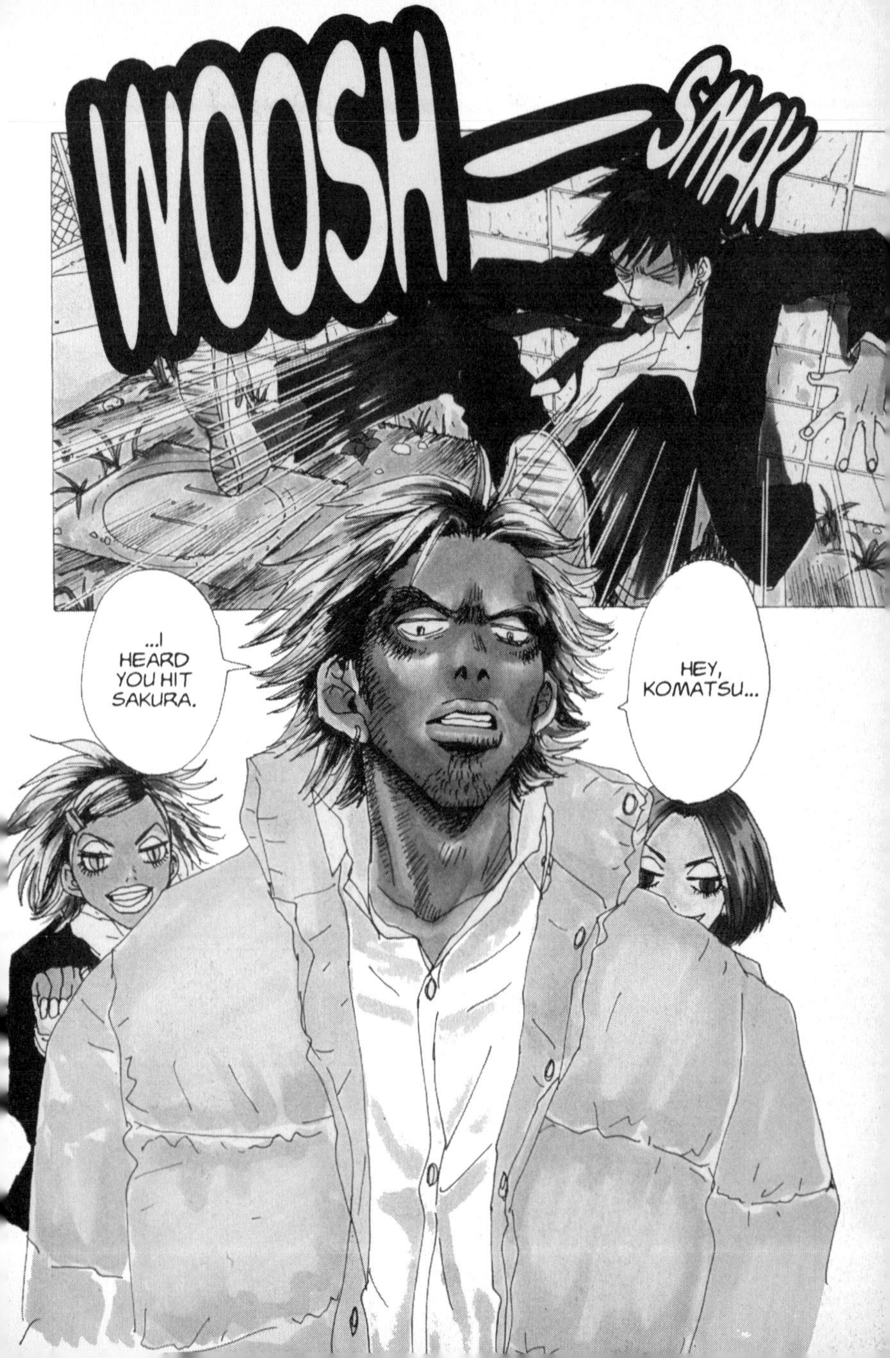
WOOSH
SMAK
HEY, KOMATSU...
...I HEARD YOU HIT SAKURA.

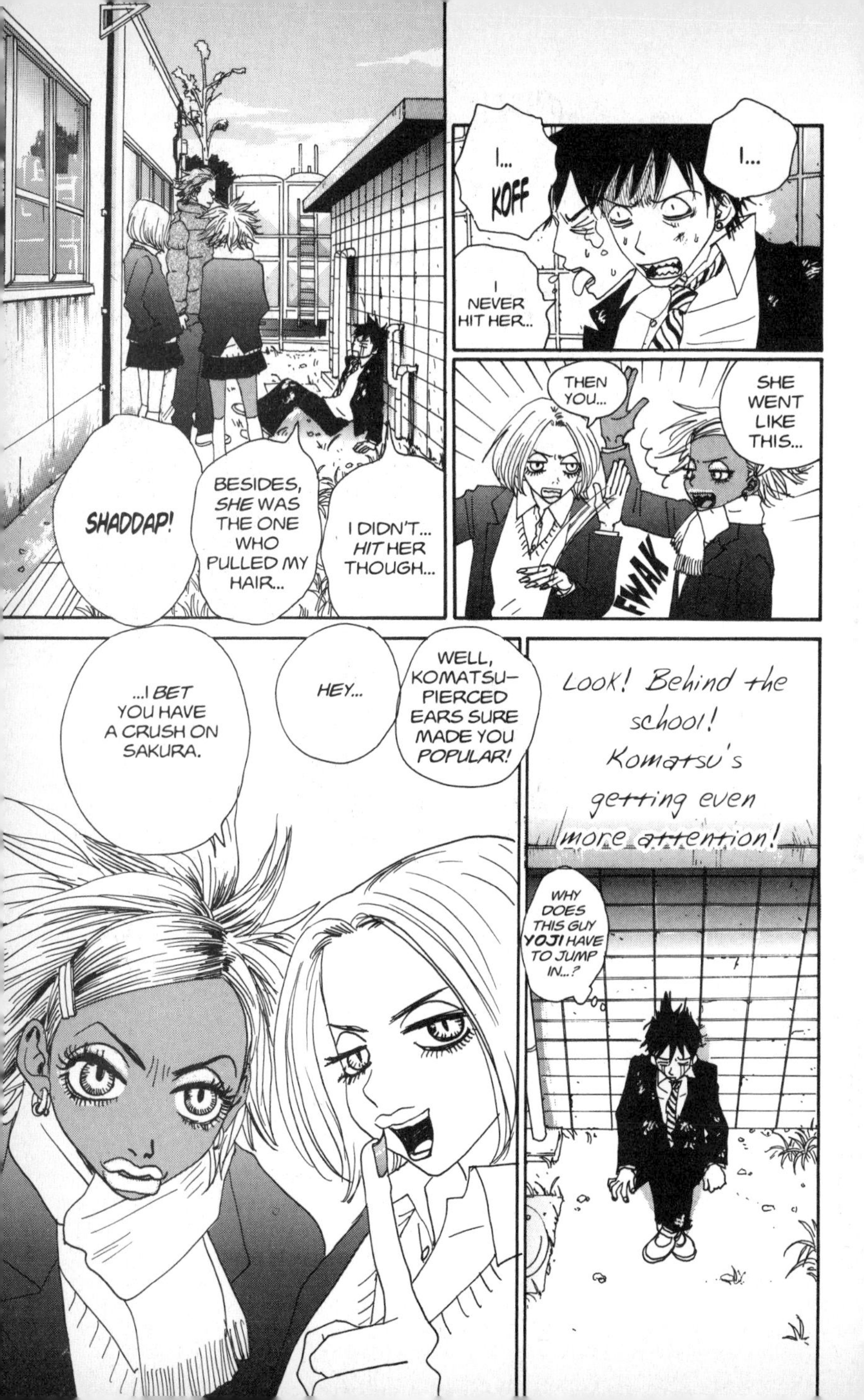
I...
I...
KOFF
I NEVER HIT HER...
SHE WENT LIKE THIS...
THEN YOU...
FWAK
I DIDN'T... HIT HER THOUGH...
BESIDES, SHE WAS THE ONE WHO PULLED MY HAIR...
SHADDAP!
Look! Behind the school! Komatsu's getting even more attention!
WHY DOES THIS GUY YOJI HAVE TO JUMP IN...?
WELL, KOMATSU-PIERCED EARS SURE MADE YOU POPULAR!
HEY...
...I BET YOU HAVE A CRUSH ON SAKURA.

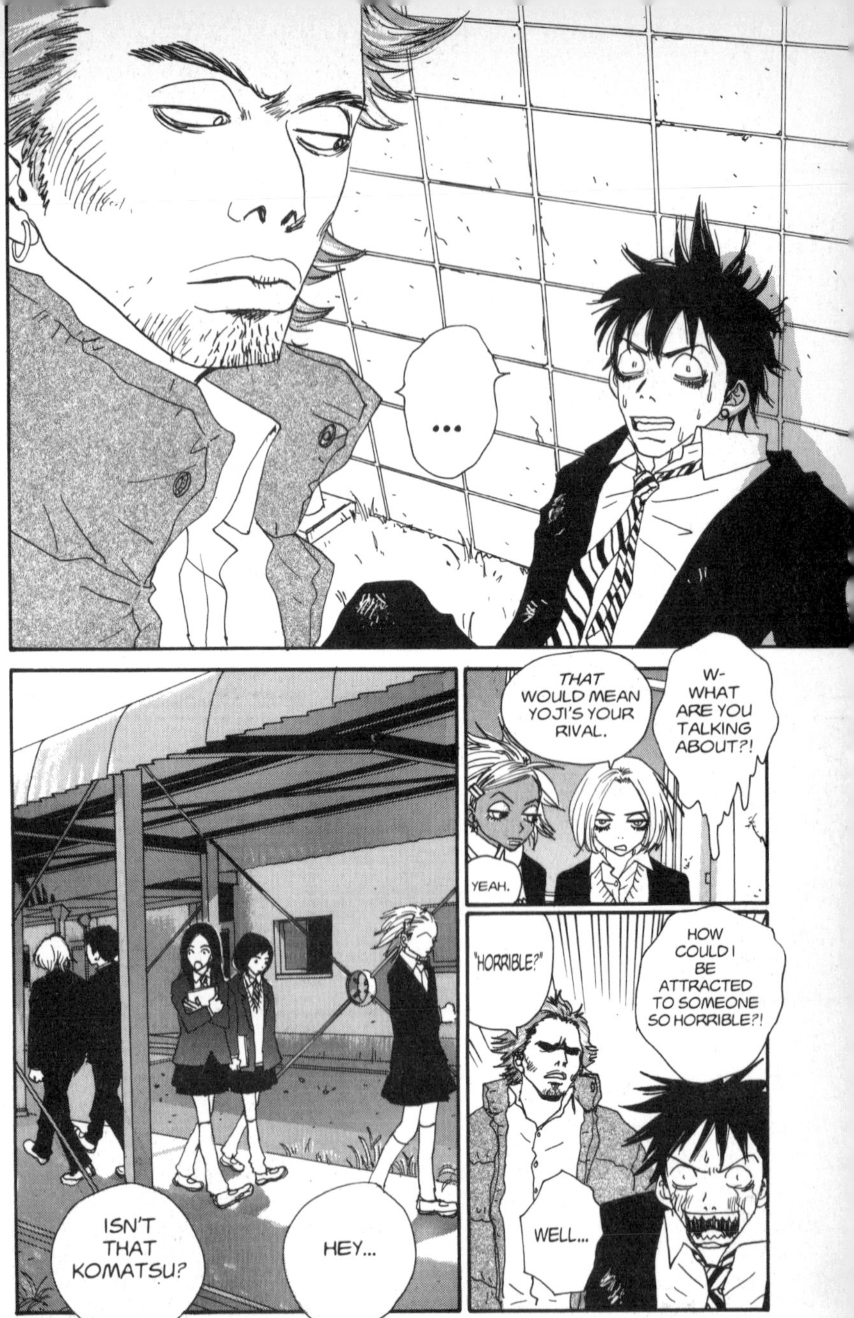
...
W- WHAT ARE YOU TALKING ABOUT?!
THAT WOULD MEAN YOJI'S YOUR RIVAL.
YEAH.
HOW COULD I BE ATTRACTED TO SOMEONE SO HORRIBLE?!
"HORRIBLE?"
WELL...
HEY...
ISN'T THAT KOMATSU?

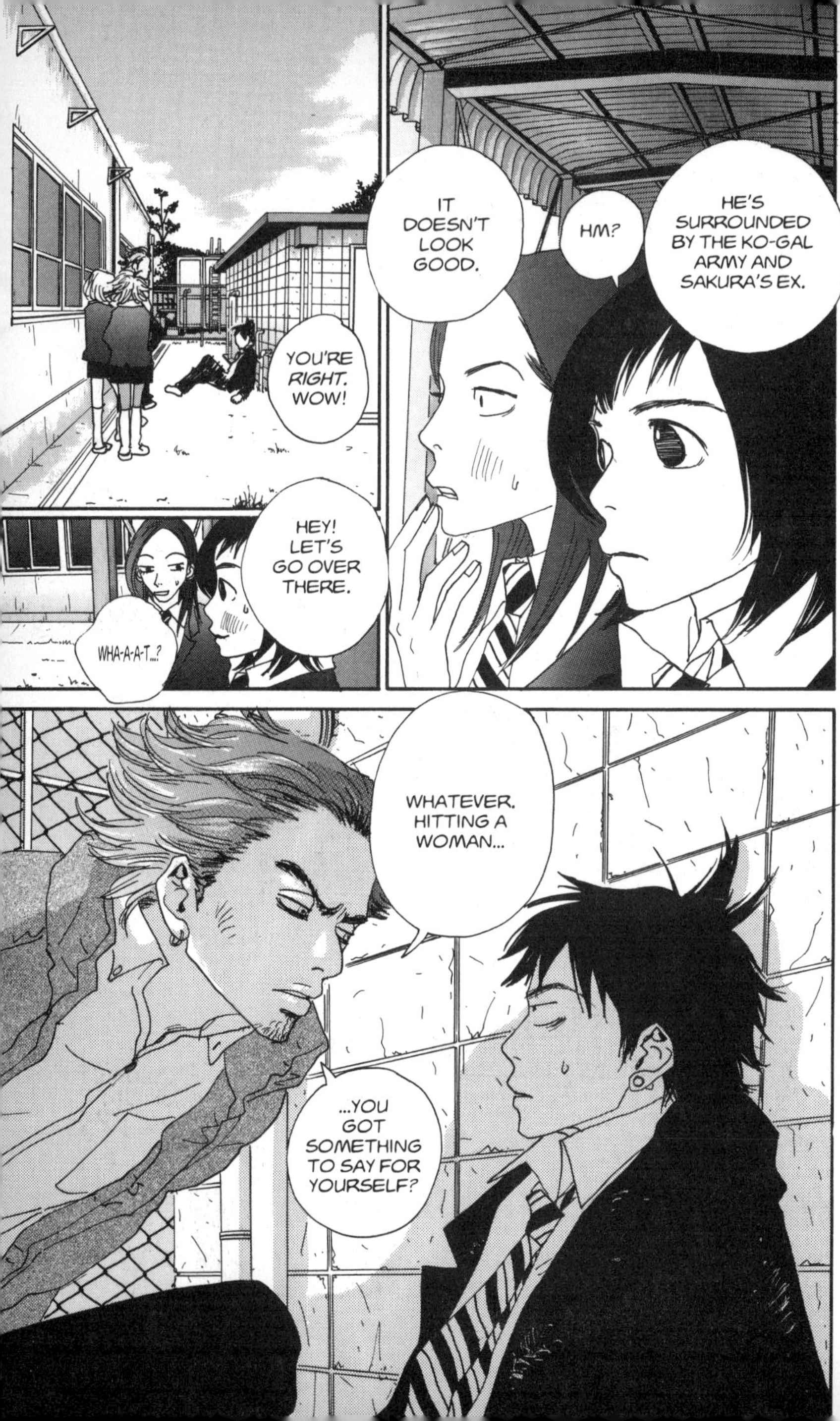
HE'S SURROUNDED BY THE KO-GAL ARMY AND SAKURA'S EX.
HM?
IT DOESN'T LOOK GOOD.
YOU'RE RIGHT. WOW!
HEY! LET'S GO OVER THERE.
WHA-A-A-T...?
WHATEVER. HITTING A WOMAN...
...YOU GOT SOMETHING TO SAY FOR YOURSELF?

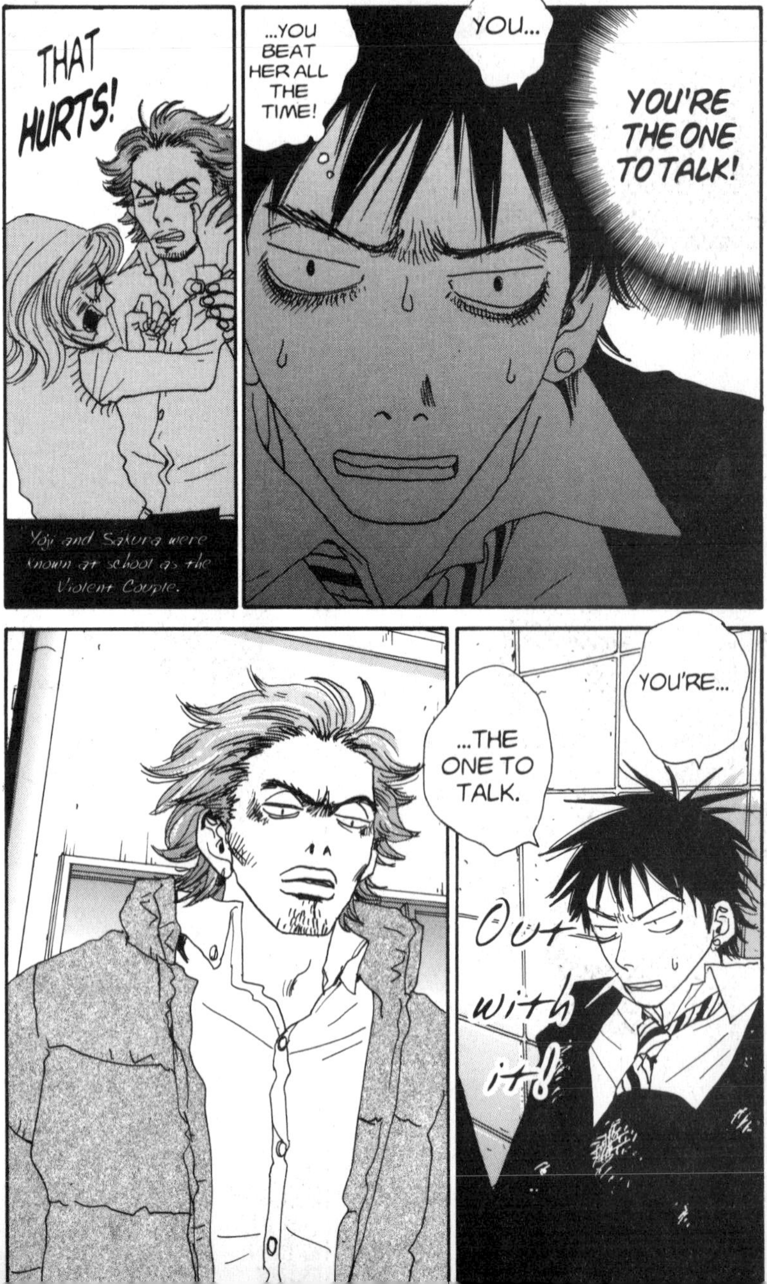
YOU...
YOU'RE THE ONE TO TALK!
...YOU BEAT HER ALL THE TIME!
THAT HURTS!
Yoji and Sakura were known at school as the Violent Couple.
YOU'RE...
...THE ONE TO TALK.
Out with it!

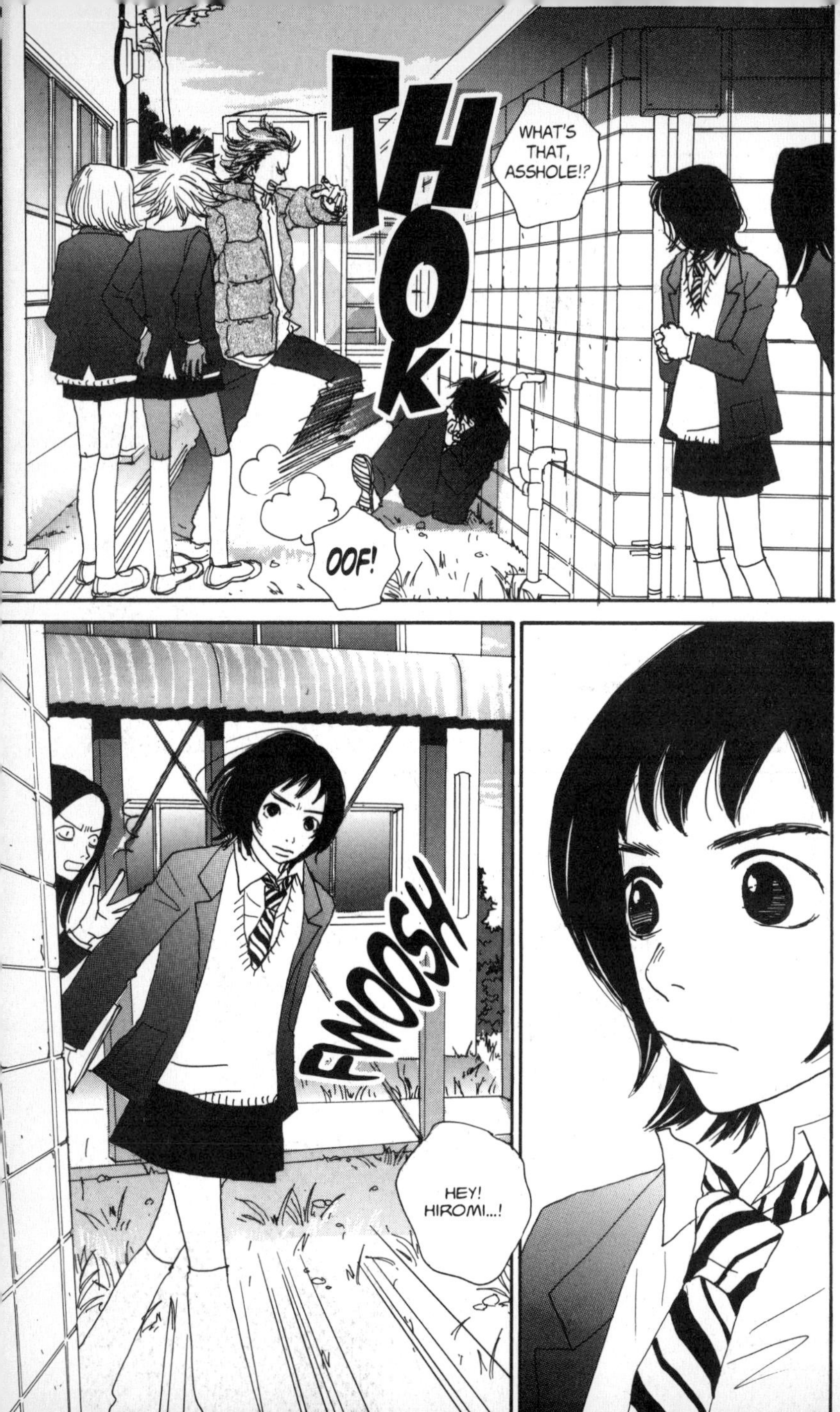
WHAT'S THAT, ASSHOLE!?
THOK
OOF!
FWOOSH
HEY! HIROMI...!

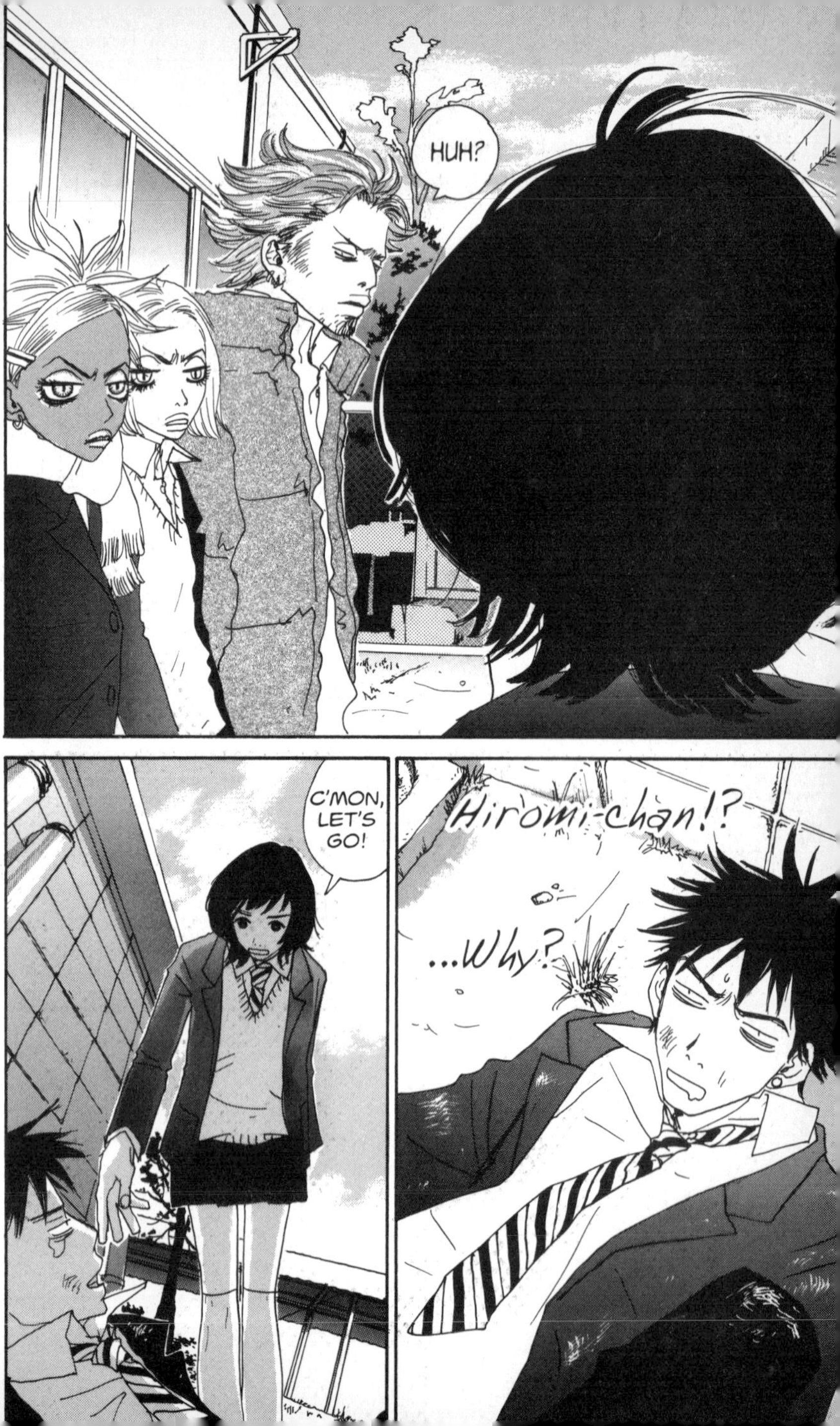
HUH?
Hiromi-chan!?
...Why?
C'MON, LET'S GO!

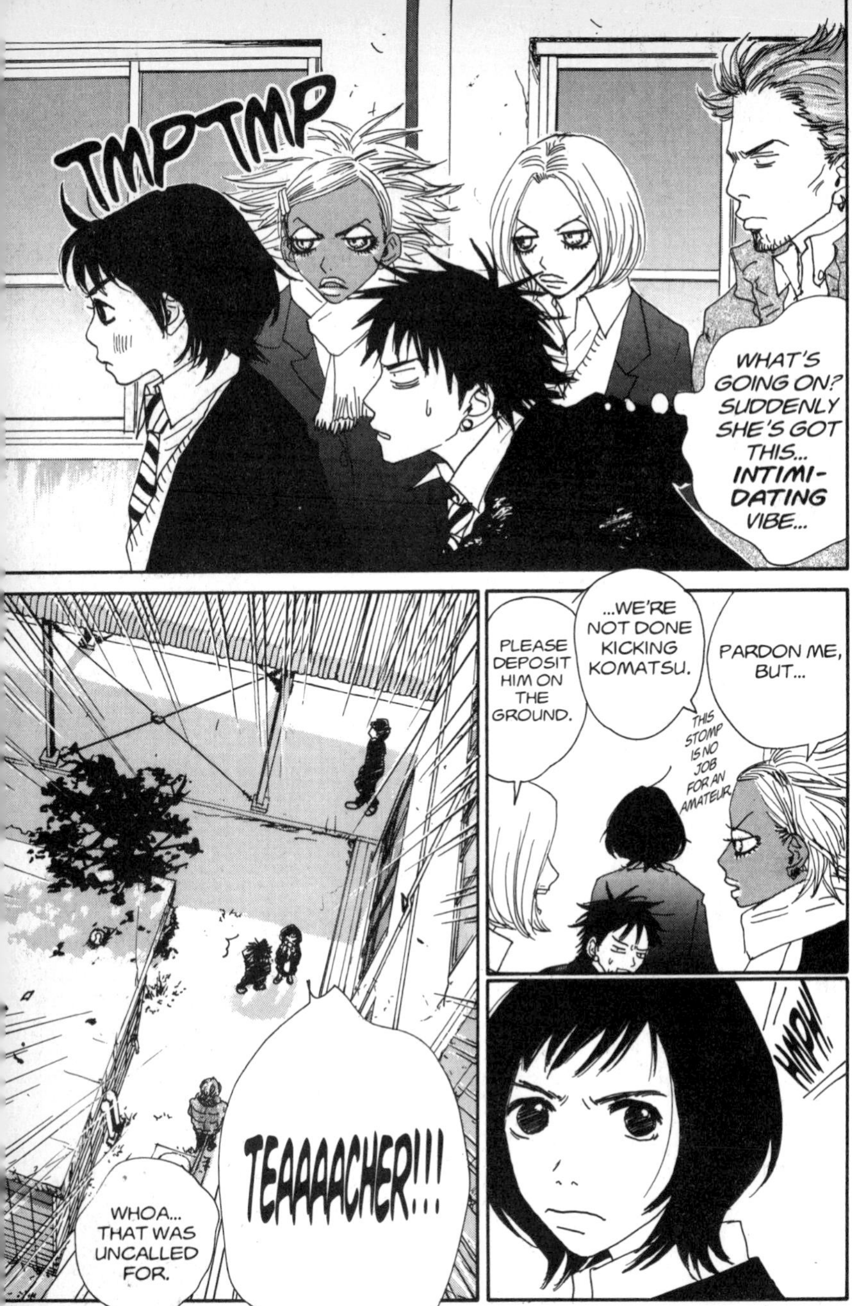

WHAT'S GOING ON? SUDDENLY SHE'S GOT THIS... **INTIMIDATING** VIBE...
TMP TMP
PARDON ME, BUT...
...WE'RE NOT DONE KICKING KOMATSU.
PLEASE DEPOSIT HIM ON THE GROUND.
THIS STOMP IS NO JOB FOR AN AMATEUR.
HMPH!
TEAAAACHER!!!
WHOA... THAT WAS UNCALLED FOR.

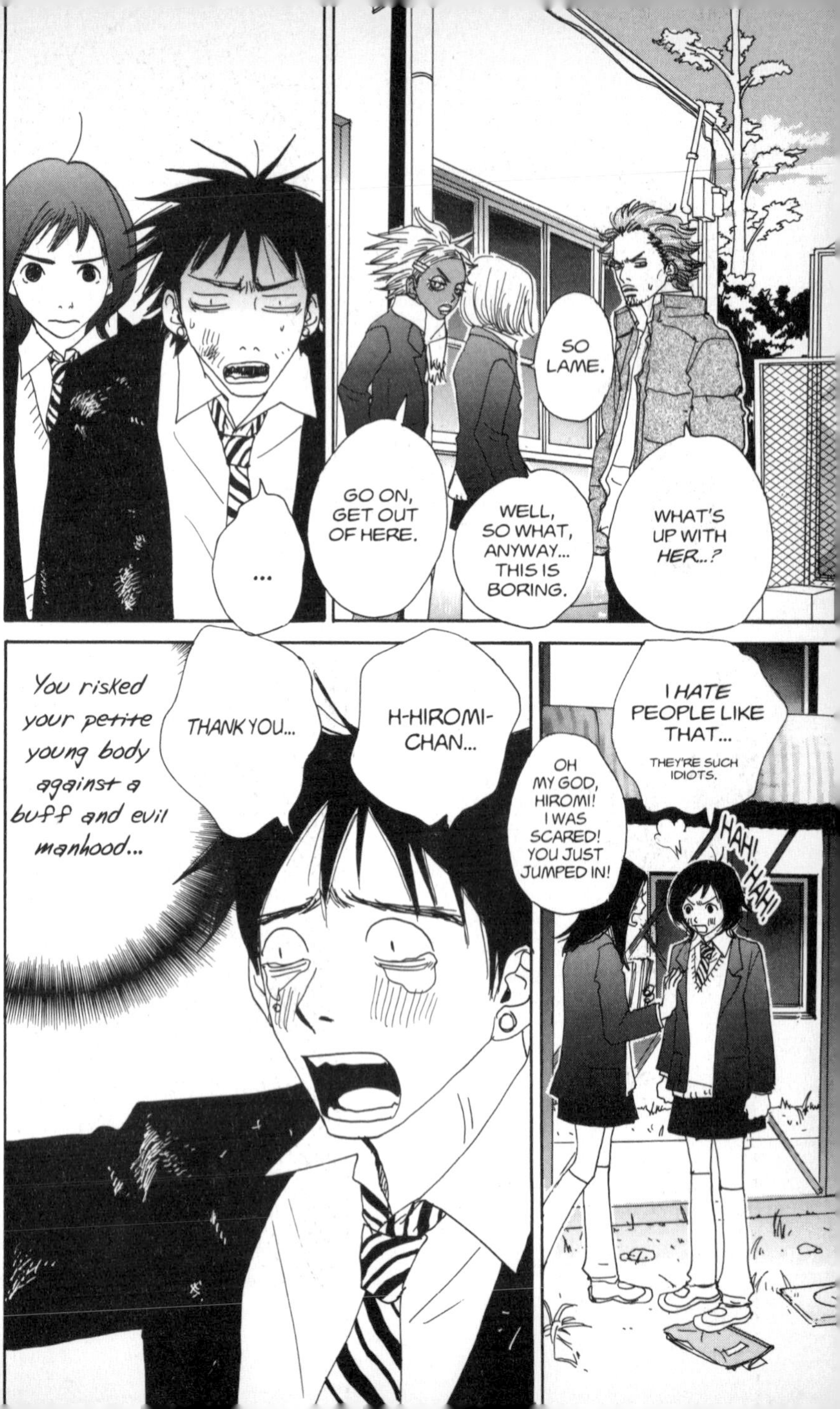
SO LAME.
WHAT'S UP WITH HER...?
WELL, SO WHAT, ANYWAY... THIS IS BORING.
GO ON, GET OUT OF HERE.
...
I HATE PEOPLE LIKE THAT... THEY'RE SUCH IDIOTS.
HAH! HAH!
OH MY GOD, HIROMI! I WAS SCARED! YOU JUST JUMPED IN!
H-HIROMI-CHAN...
THANK YOU...
You risked your petite young body against a buff and evil manhood...

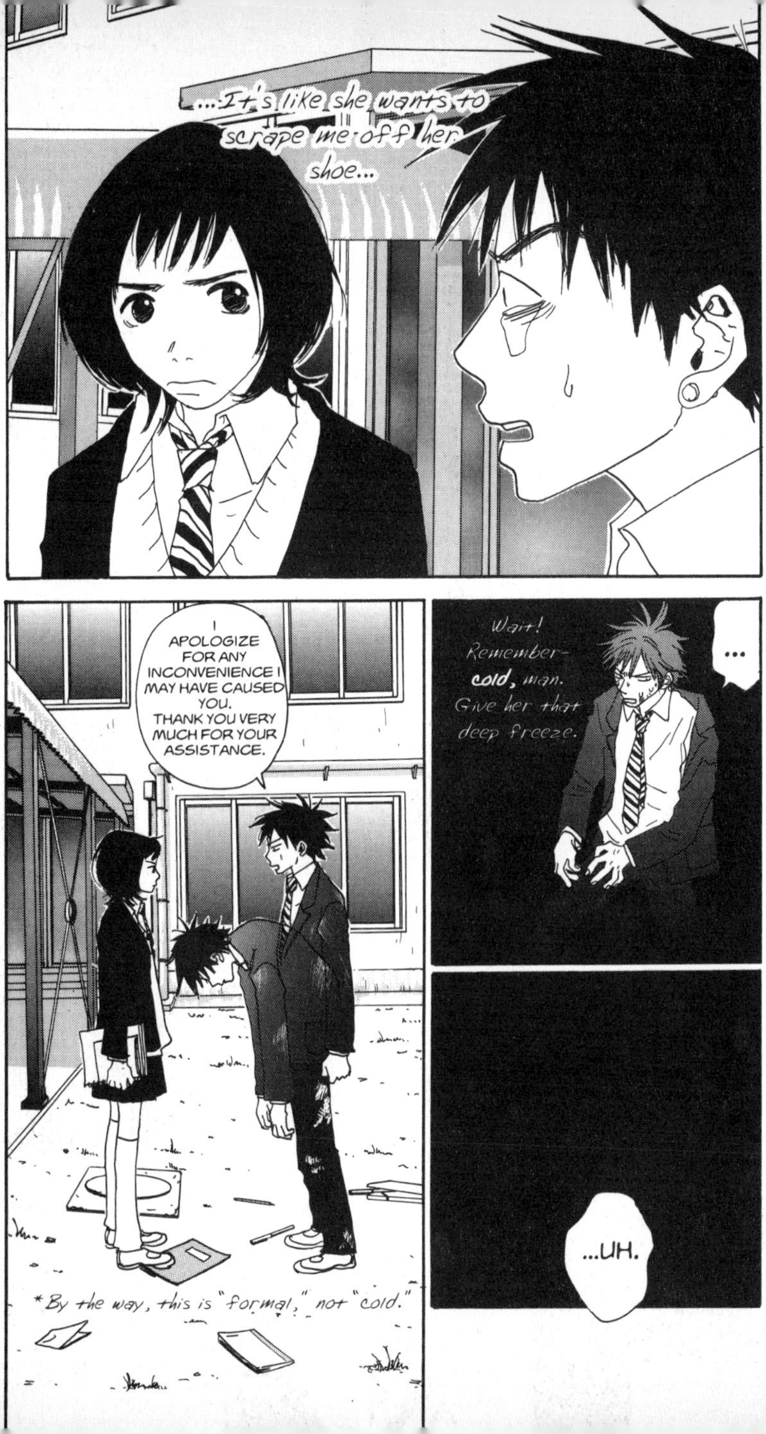
...It's like she wants to scrape me off her shoe...
Wait! Remember- cold, man. Give her that deep freeze.
...
...UH.
I APOLOGIZE FOR ANY INCONVENIENCE I MAY HAVE CAUSED YOU. THANK YOU VERY MUCH FOR YOUR ASSISTANCE.
*By the way, this is "formal," not "cold."

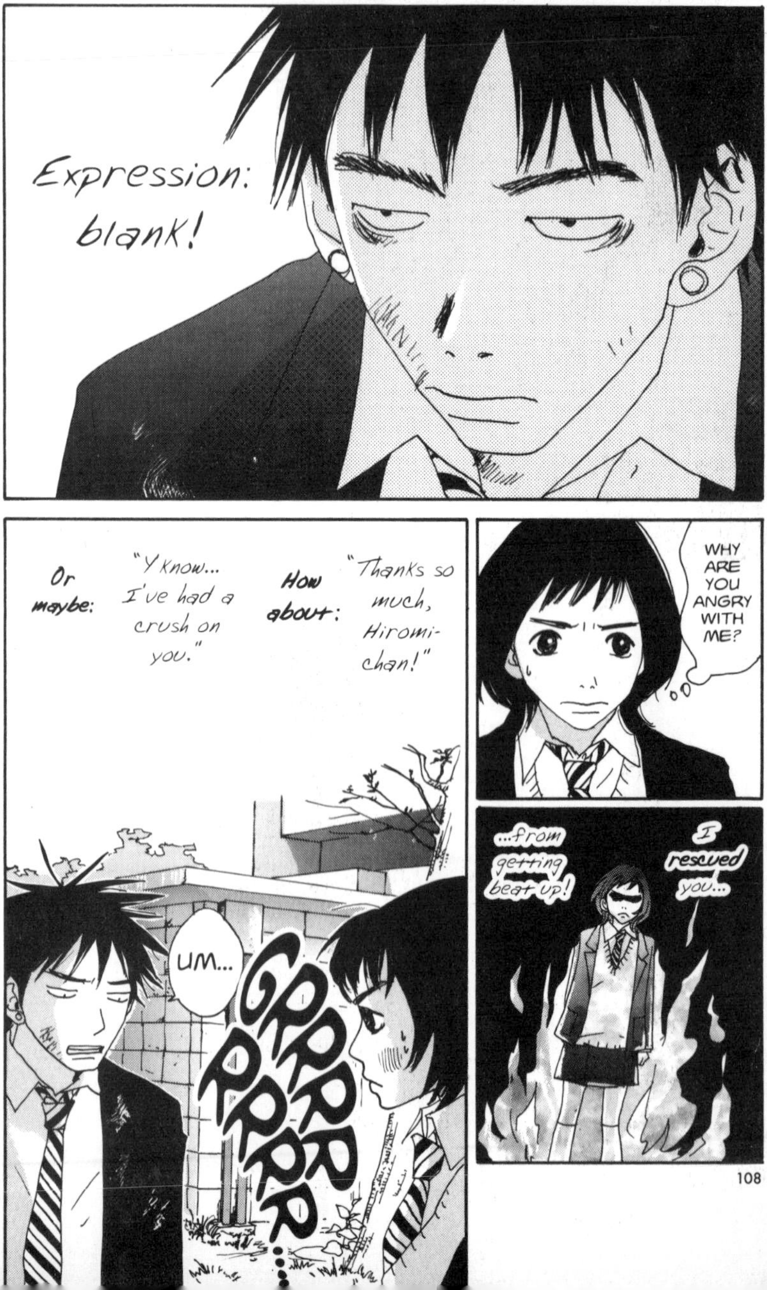
Expression: blank!
WHY ARE YOU ANGRY WITH ME?
I rescued you...
...from getting beat up!
How about: "Thanks so much, Hiromi-chan!"
Or maybe: "Y'know... I've had a crush on you."
UM...
GRRRRRRR...

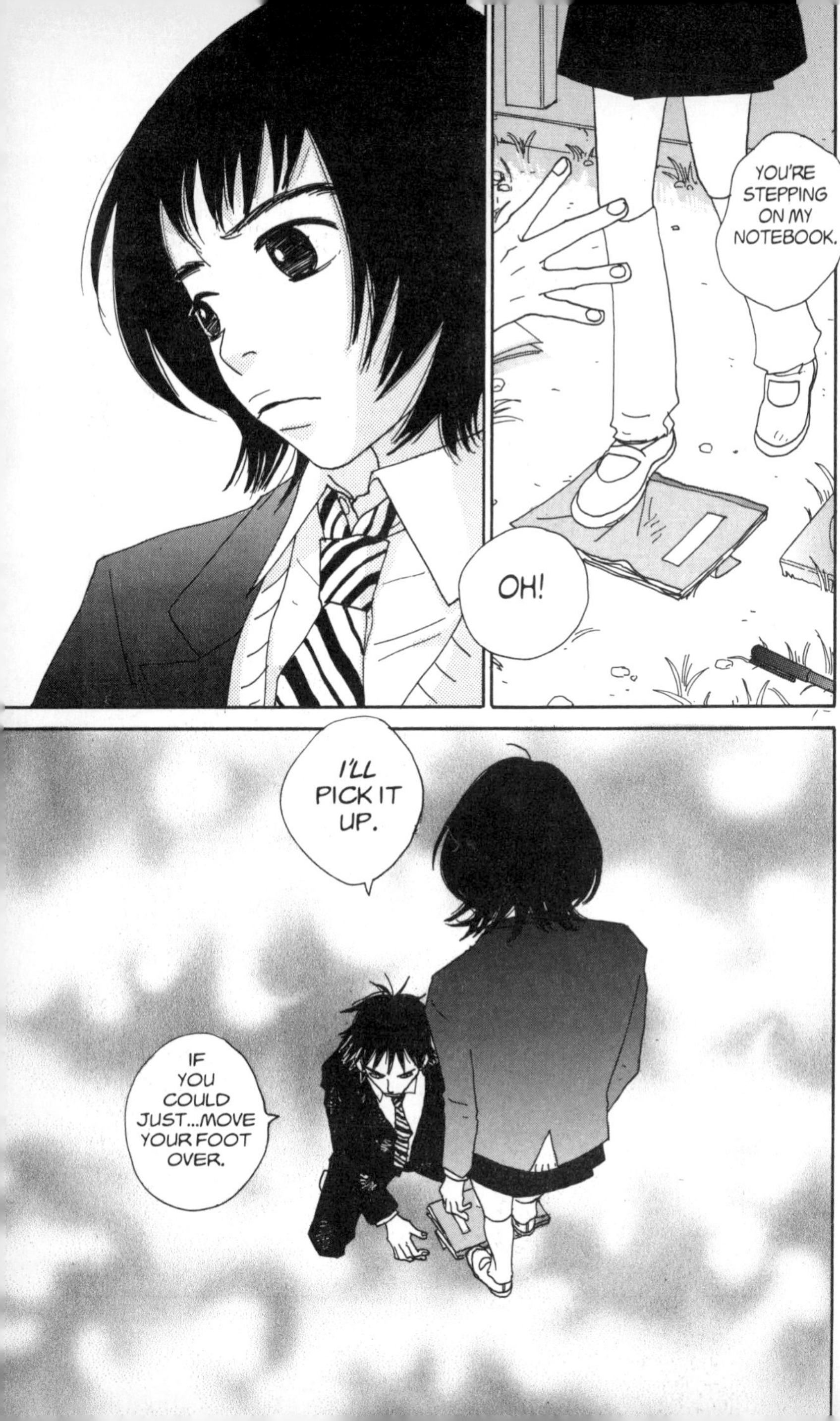
YOU'RE STEPPING ON MY NOTEBOOK.
OH!
I'LL PICK IT UP.
IF YOU COULD JUST...MOVE YOUR FOOT OVER.

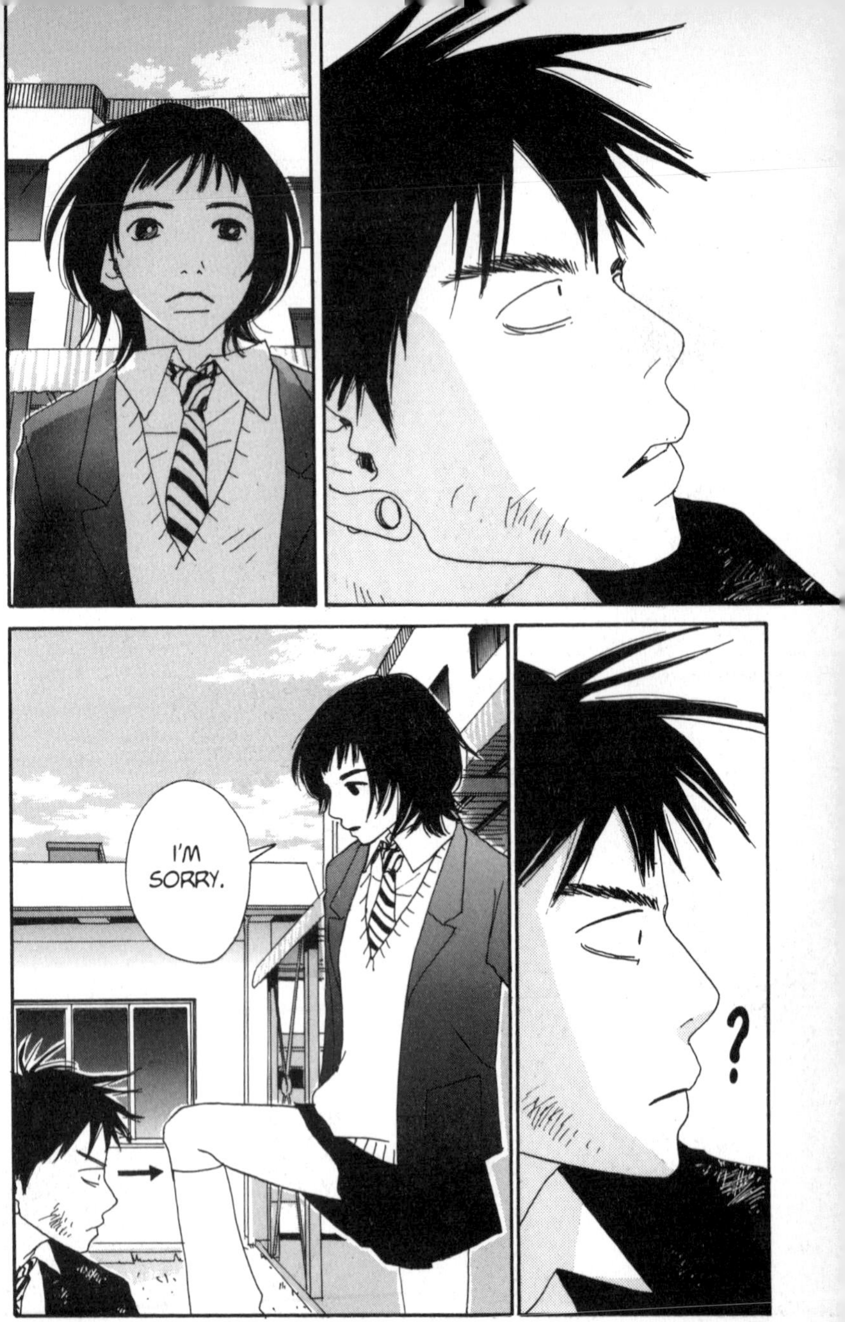
I'M SORRY.
?

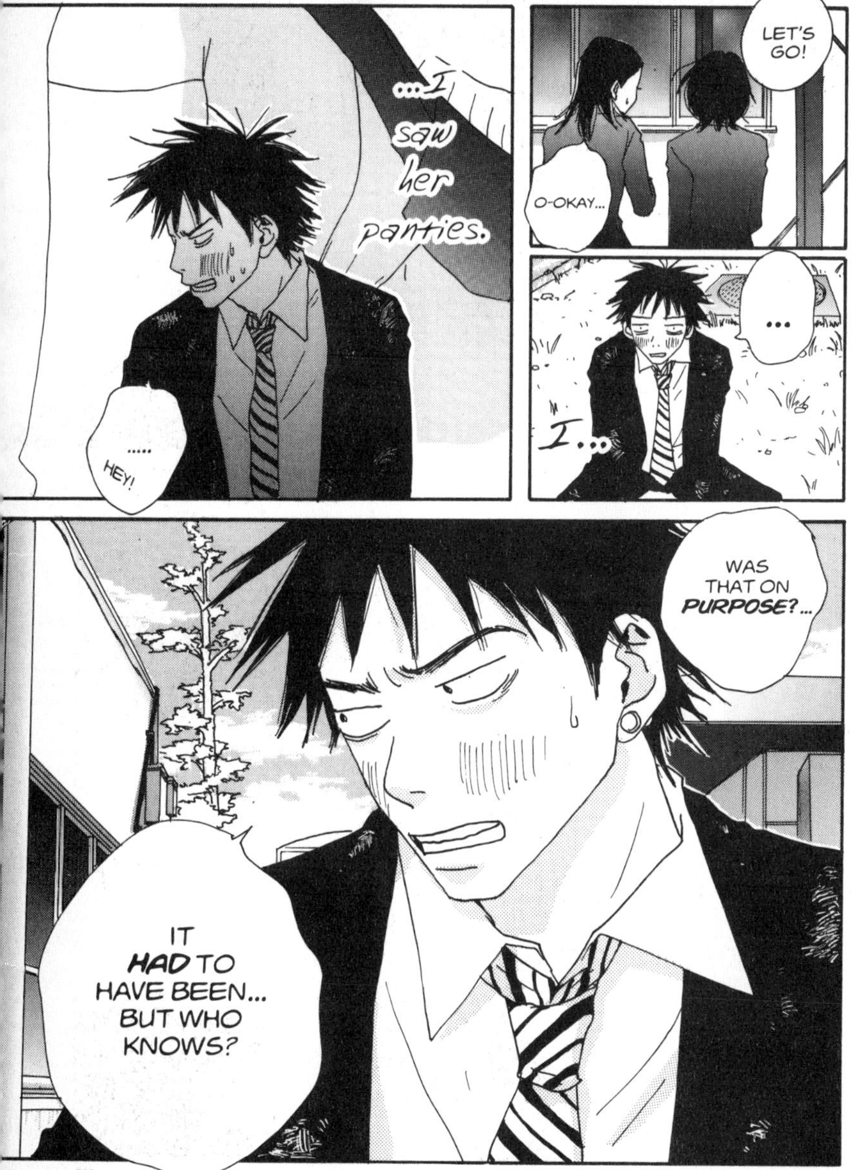
LET'S GO!
O-OKAY...
...
I...
...I saw her panties.
.....
HEY!
WAS THAT ON **PURPOSE?**...
IT **HAD** TO HAVE BEEN... BUT WHO KNOWS?

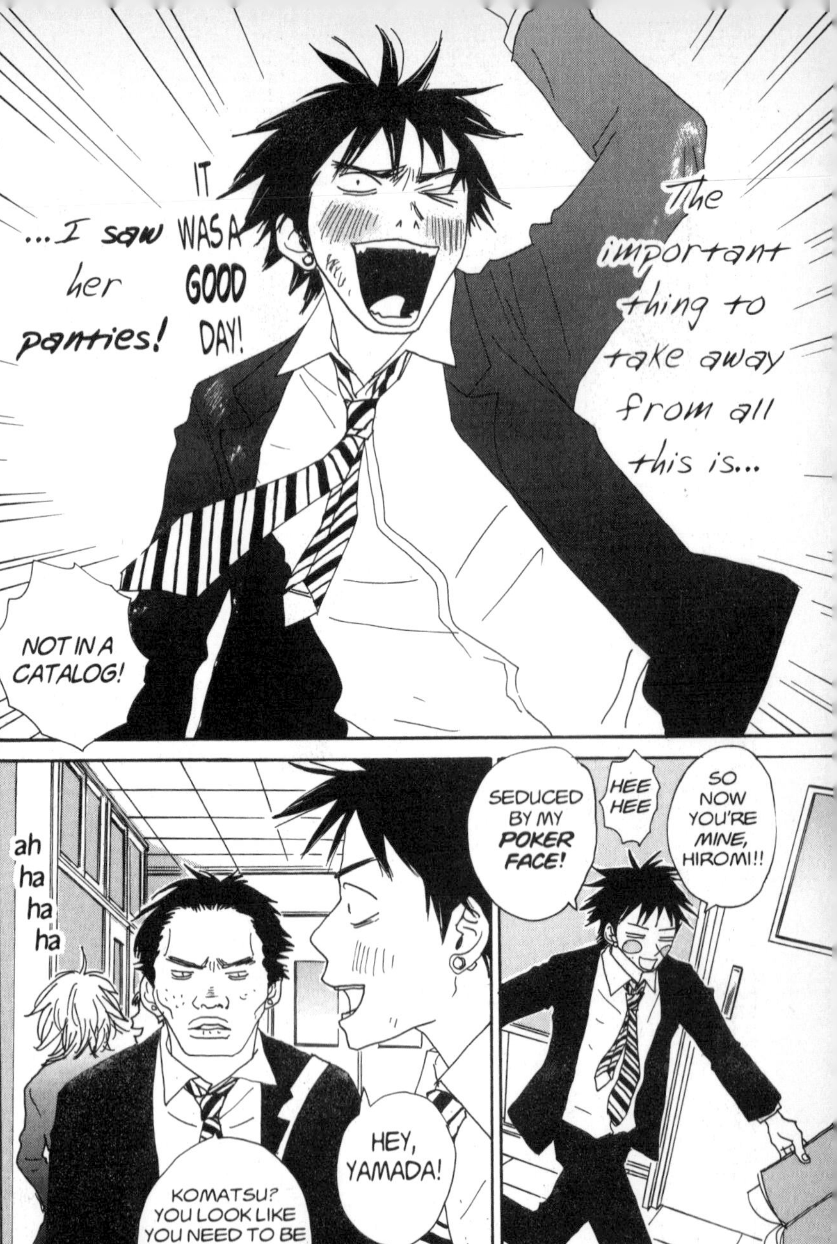
The important thing to take away from all this is...
IT WAS A GOOD DAY!
...I saw her panties!
NOT IN A CATALOG!
SO NOW YOU'RE MINE, HIROMI!!
HEE HEE
SEDUCED BY MY POKER FACE!
HEY, YAMADA!
KOMATSU? YOU LOOK LIKE YOU NEED TO BE DRY-CLEANED IN BACTINE.
ah ha ha ha

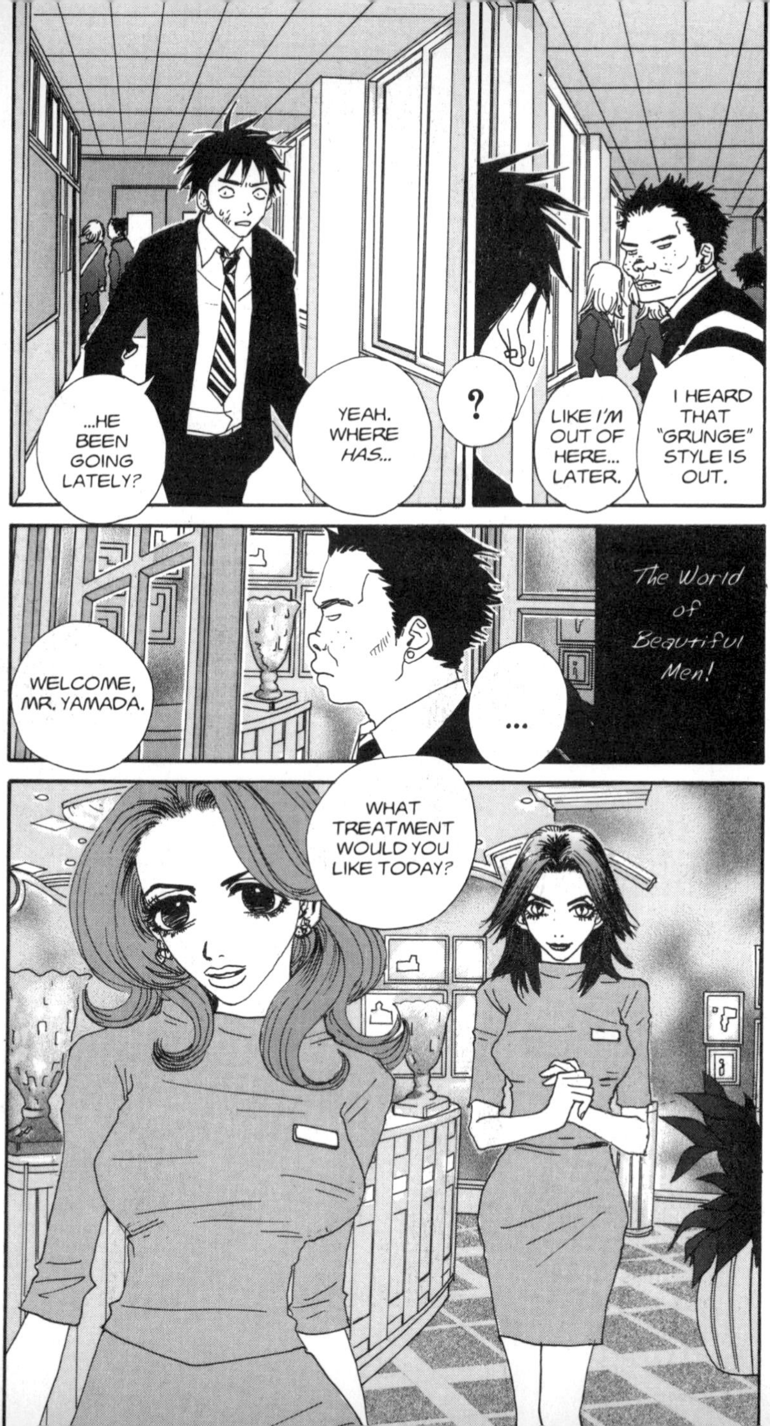
I HEARD THAT "GRUNGE" STYLE IS OUT.
LIKE *I'M* OUT OF HERE... LATER.
?
YEAH. WHERE *HAS*...
...HE BEEN GOING LATELY?
The World of Beautiful Men!
...
WELCOME, MR. YAMADA.
WHAT TREATMENT WOULD YOU LIKE TODAY?

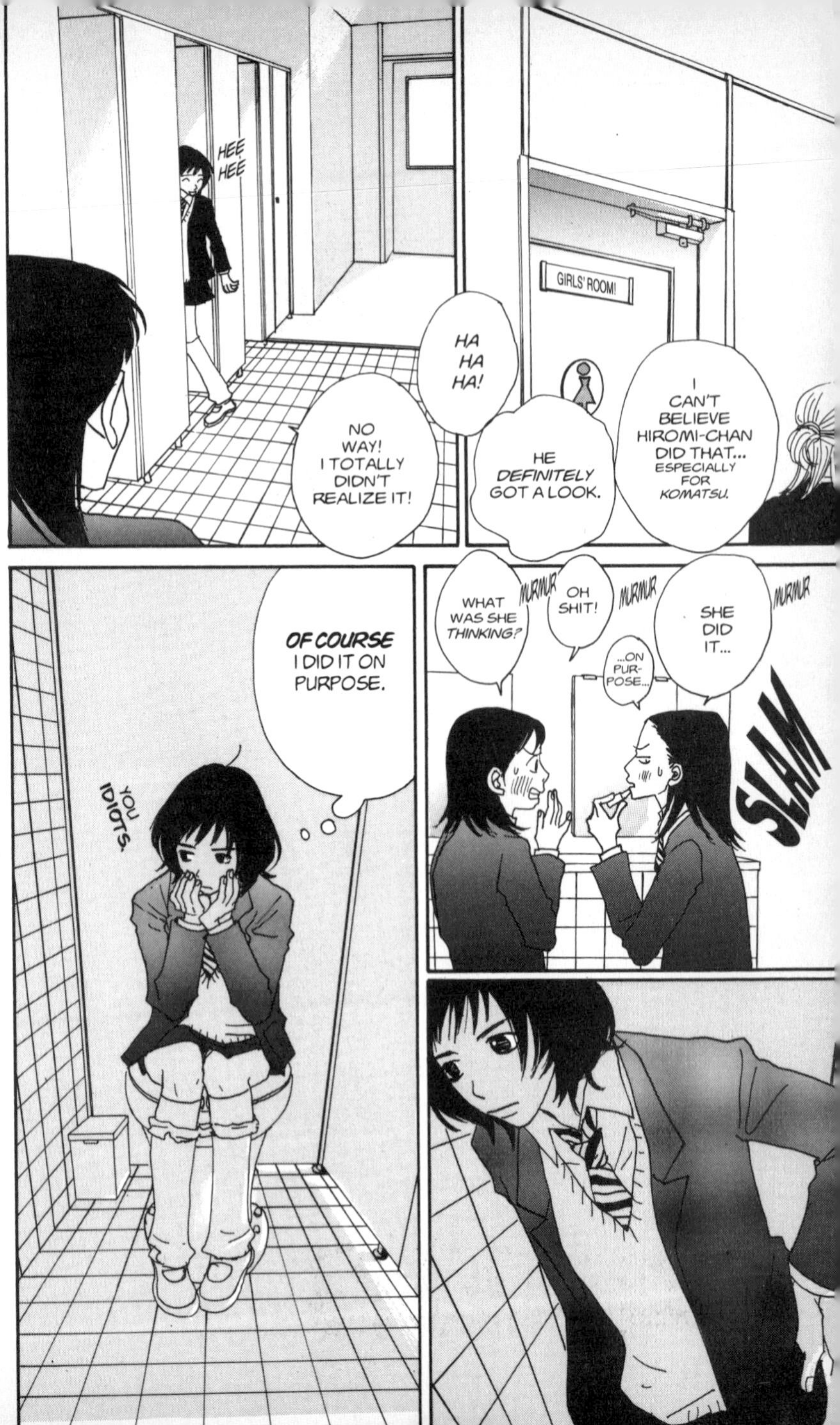
GIRLS' ROOM!
I CAN'T BELIEVE HIROMI-CHAN DID THAT... ESPECIALLY FOR KOMATSU.
HE *DEFINITELY* GOT A LOOK.
HA HA HA!
NO WAY! I TOTALLY DIDN'T REALIZE IT!
HEE HEE
MURMUR
SHE DID IT...
...ON PURPOSE...
MURMUR
OH SHIT!
MURMUR
WHAT WAS SHE *THINKING?*
SLAM
OF COURSE I DID IT ON PURPOSE.
YOU IDIOTS.

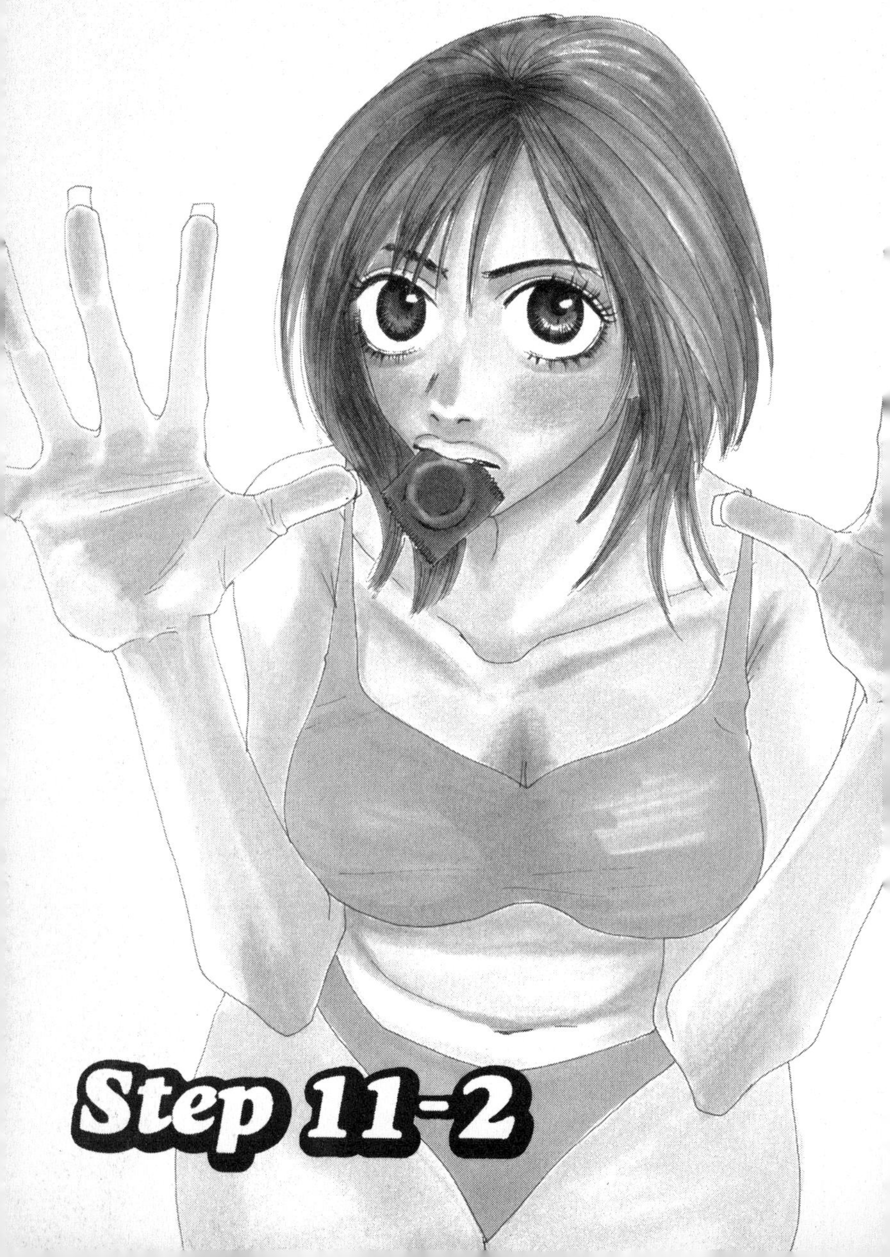
Step 11-2

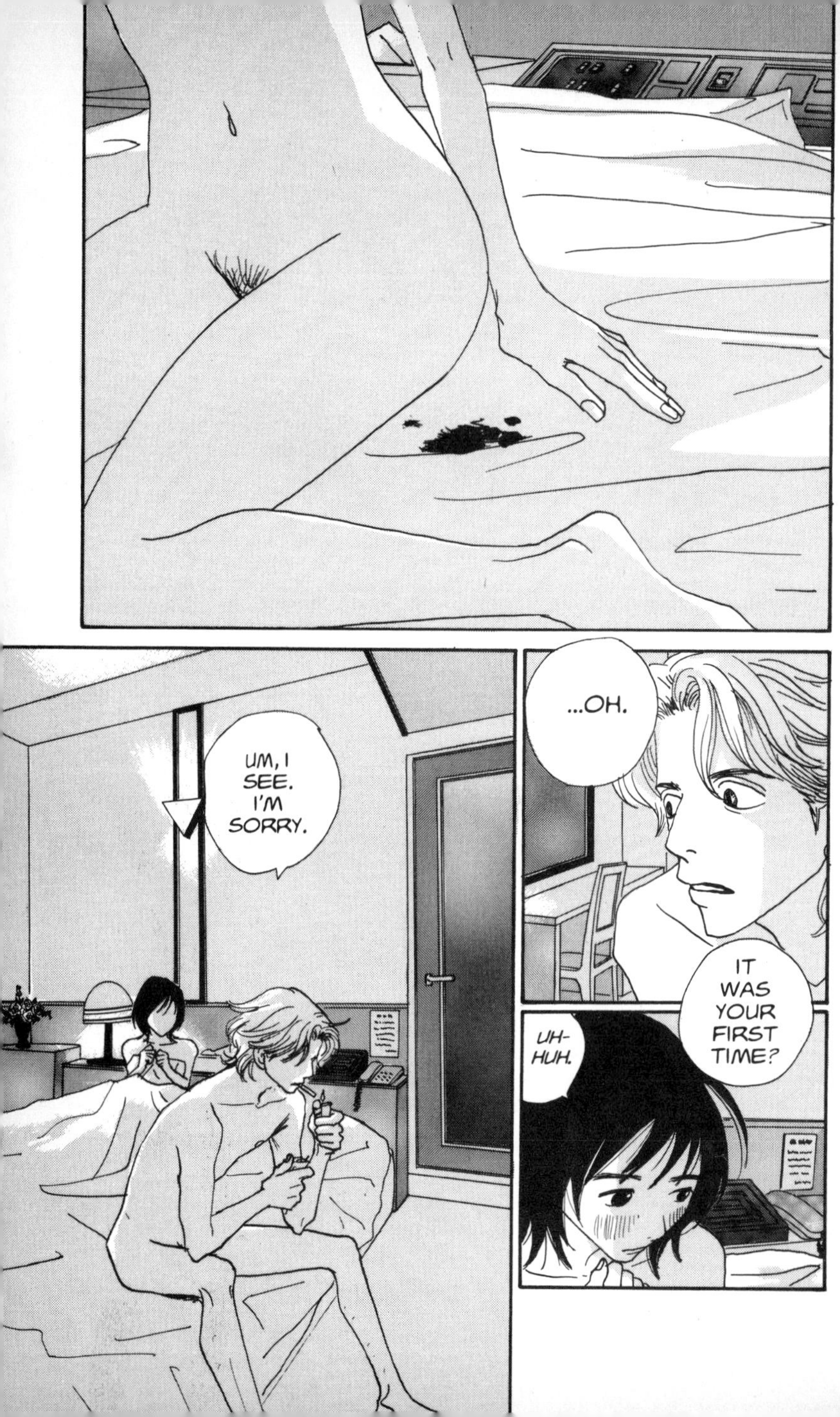
...OH.
IT WAS YOUR FIRST TIME?
UH-HUH.
UM, I SEE. I'M SORRY.

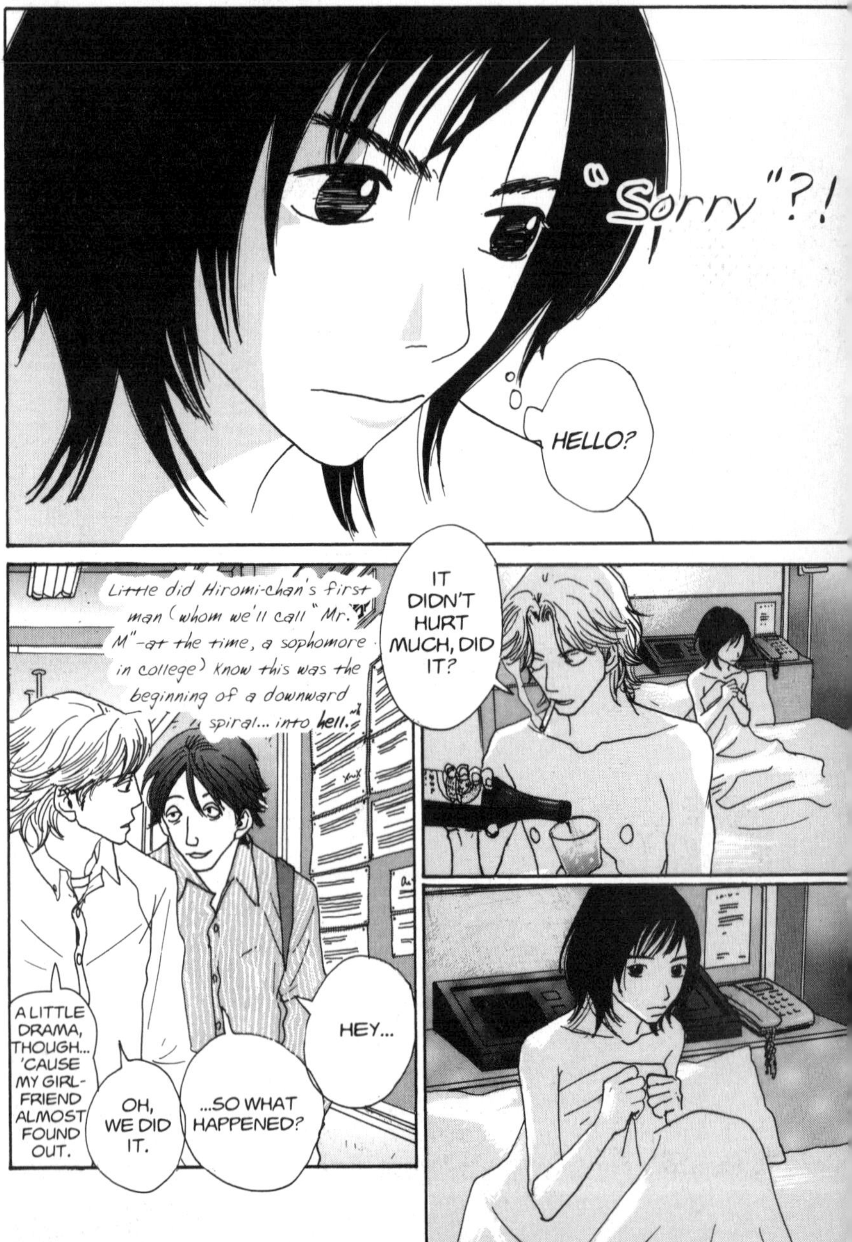
"Sorry"?!
HELLO?
IT DIDN'T HURT MUCH, DID IT?
Little did Hiromi-chan's first man (whom we'll call "Mr. M"-at the time, a sophomore in college) know this was the beginning of a downward spiral... into hell.
HEY...
...SO WHAT HAPPENED?
OH, WE DID IT.
A LITTLE DRAMA, THOUGH... 'CAUSE MY GIRL-FRIEND ALMOST FOUND OUT.

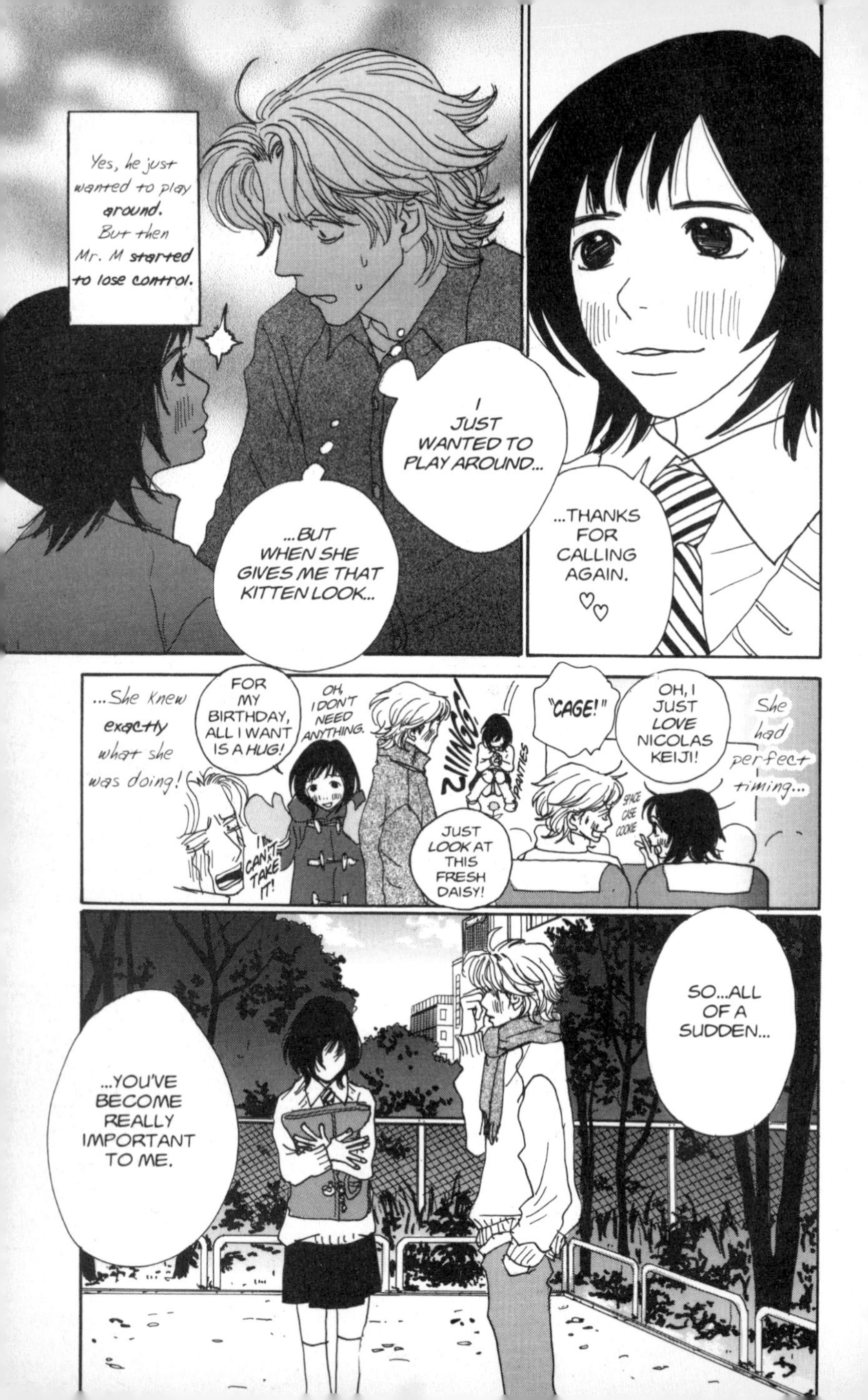
...THANKS FOR CALLING AGAIN. ♡♡
Yes, he just wanted to play around. But then Mr. M started to lose control.
I JUST WANTED TO PLAY AROUND...
...BUT WHEN SHE GIVES ME THAT KITTEN LOOK...
She had perfect timing...
OH, I JUST LOVE NICOLAS KEIJI!
SPACE CASE COOKIE
"CAGE!"
ZIIING!!
PANTIES
JUST LOOK AT THIS FRESH DAISY!
OH, I DON'T NEED ANYTHING.
FOR MY BIRTHDAY, ALL I WANT IS A HUG!
I CAN'T TAKE IT!
...She knew exactly what she was doing!
SO...ALL OF A SUDDEN...
...YOU'VE BECOME REALLY IMPORTANT TO ME.

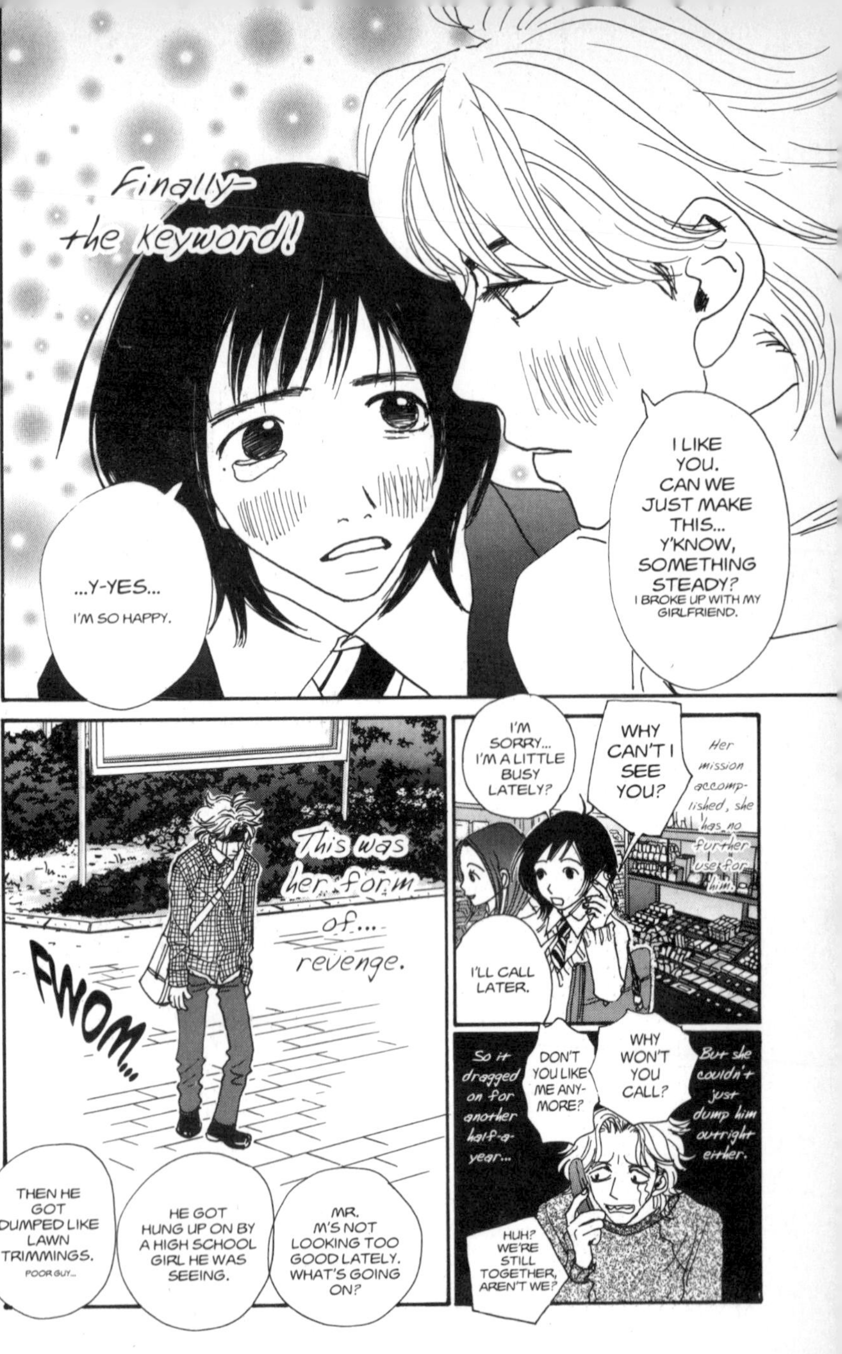
I LIKE YOU. CAN WE JUST MAKE THIS... Y'KNOW, SOMETHING STEADY?
I BROKE UP WITH MY GIRLFRIEND.
Finally— the keyword!
...Y-YES...
I'M SO HAPPY.
Her mission accomplished, she has no further use for him.
WHY CAN'T I SEE YOU?
I'M SORRY... I'M A LITTLE BUSY LATELY?
I'LL CALL LATER.
But she couldn't just dump him outright either.
WHY WON'T YOU CALL?
DON'T YOU LIKE ME ANYMORE?
So it dragged on for another half-a-year...
HUH? WE'RE STILL TOGETHER, AREN'T WE?
This was her form of... revenge.
FWOM...
MR. M'S NOT LOOKING TOO GOOD LATELY. WHAT'S GOING ON?
HE GOT HUNG UP ON BY A HIGH SCHOOL GIRL HE WAS SEEING.
THEN HE GOT DUMPED LIKE LAWN TRIMMINGS.
POOR GUY...

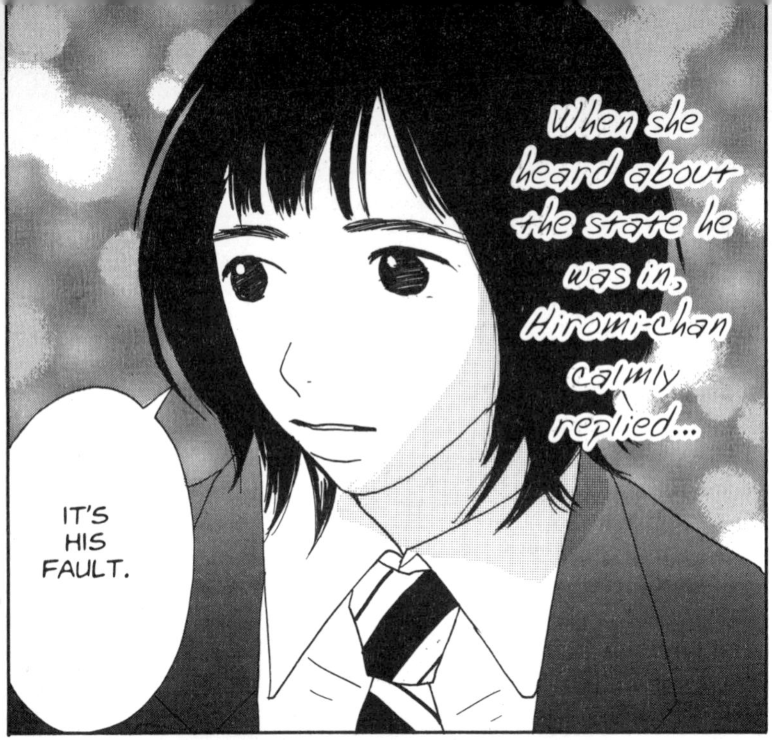
When she heard about the state he was in, Hiromi-chan calmly replied...
IT'S HIS FAULT.
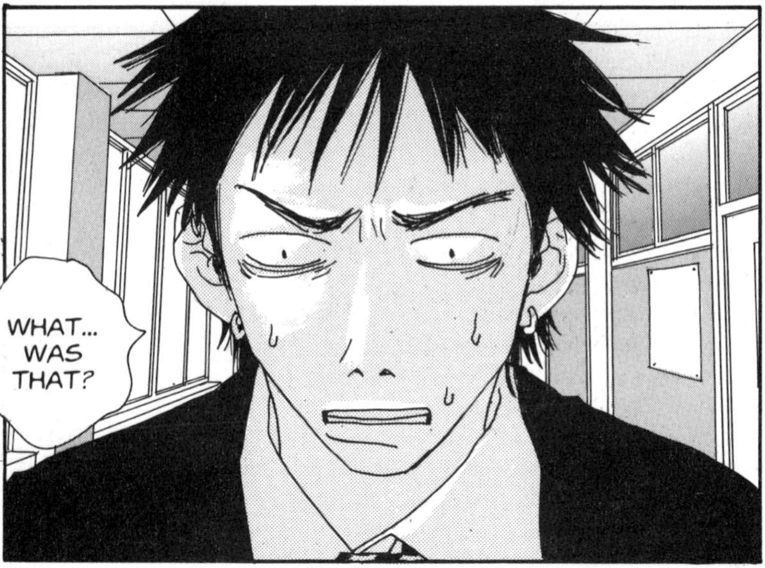
WHAT... WAS THAT?

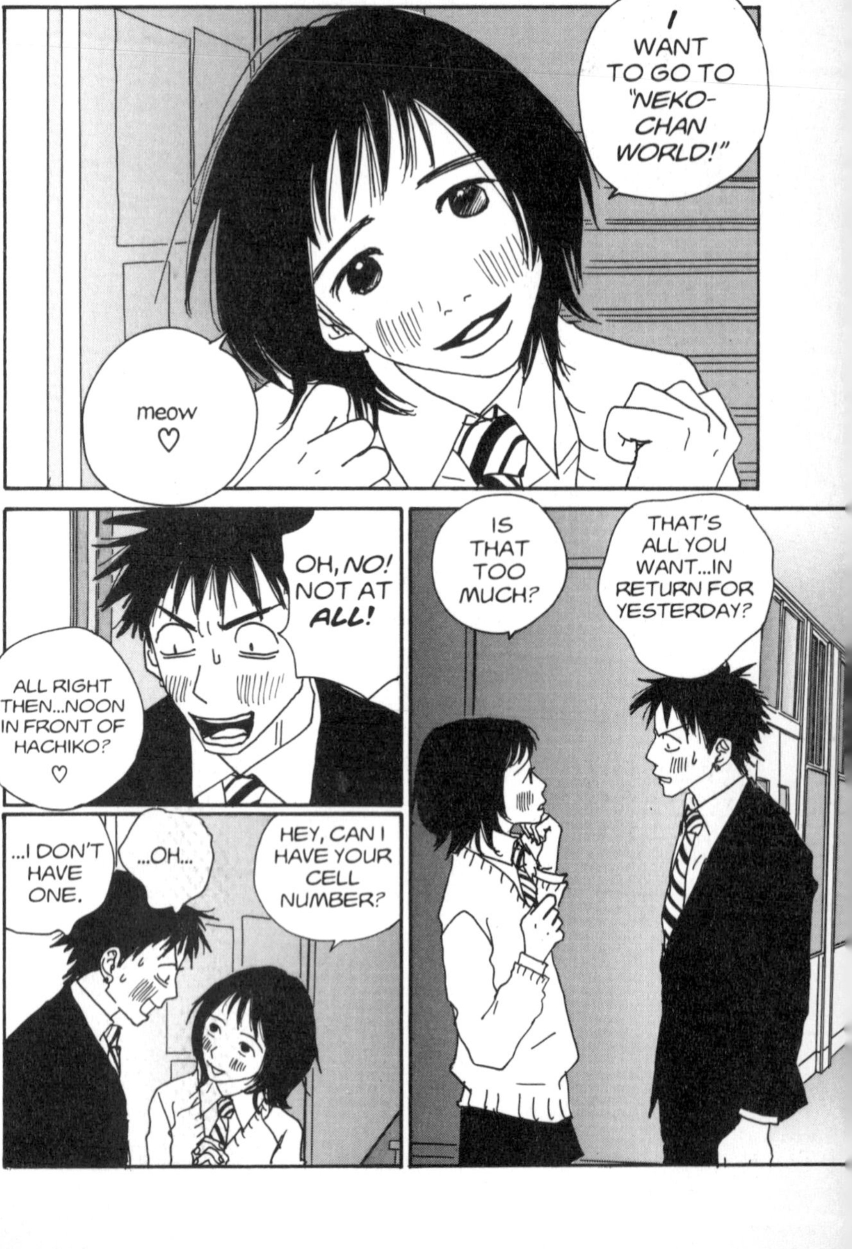
I WANT TO GO TO "NEKO-CHAN WORLD!"
meow ♡
THAT'S ALL YOU WANT...IN RETURN FOR YESTERDAY?
IS THAT TOO MUCH?
OH, NO! NOT AT ALL!
ALL RIGHT THEN...NOON IN FRONT OF HACHIKO? ♡
HEY, CAN I HAVE YOUR CELL NUMBER?
...OH...
...I DON'T HAVE ONE.

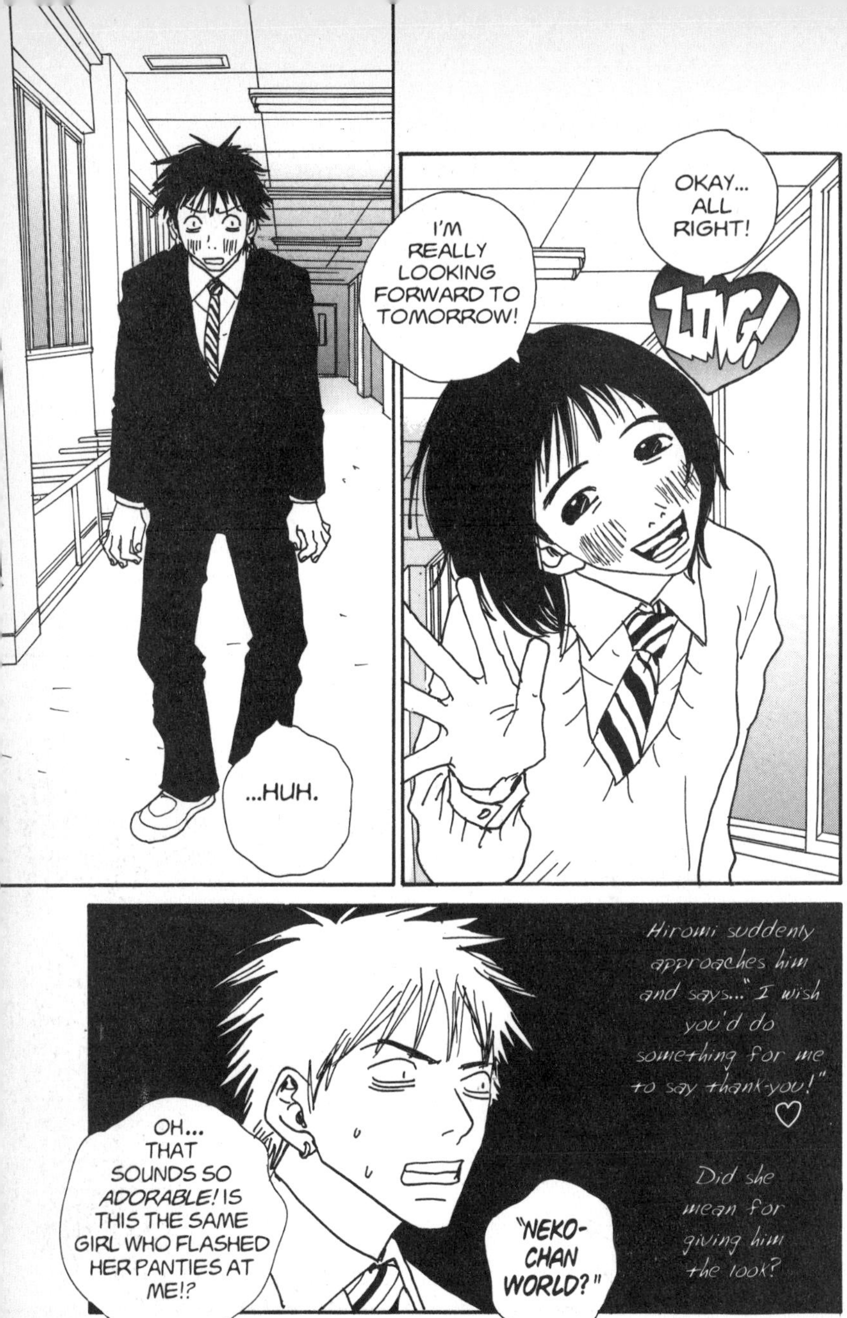
OKAY... ALL RIGHT!
I'M REALLY LOOKING FORWARD TO TOMORROW!
ZING!
...HUH.
Hiromi suddenly approaches him and says..."I wish you'd do something for me to say thank-you!" ♡
Did she mean for giving him the look?
"NEKO-CHAN WORLD?"
OH... THAT SOUNDS SO ADORABLE! IS THIS THE SAME GIRL WHO FLASHED HER PANTIES AT ME!?

REAL PLACE IS CALLED "NEKOTAMA." HTTP://WWW.TCVB.OR.JP/EN/INFOMATION/SMUSEUM/18INUTAMA.HTML

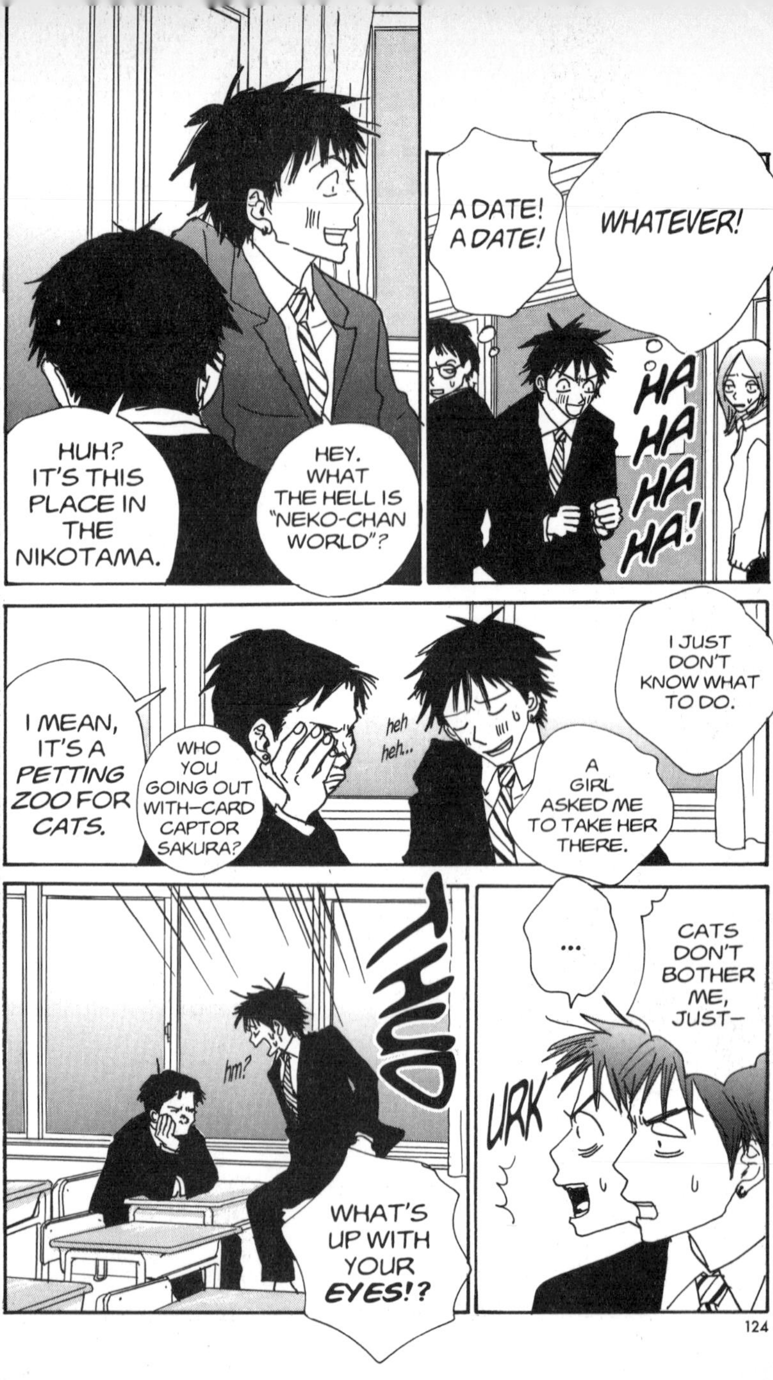

WHATEVER!
A DATE! A DATE!
HA HA HA HA HA!
HEY. WHAT THE HELL IS "NEKO-CHAN WORLD"?
HUH? IT'S THIS PLACE IN THE NIKOTAMA.
I JUST DON'T KNOW WHAT TO DO.
A GIRL ASKED ME TO TAKE HER THERE.
heh heh...
WHO YOU GOING OUT WITH—CARD CAPTOR SAKURA?
I MEAN, IT'S A PETTING ZOO FOR CATS.
CATS DON'T BOTHER ME, JUST—
...
URK
THUD
hm?
WHAT'S UP WITH YOUR EYES!?

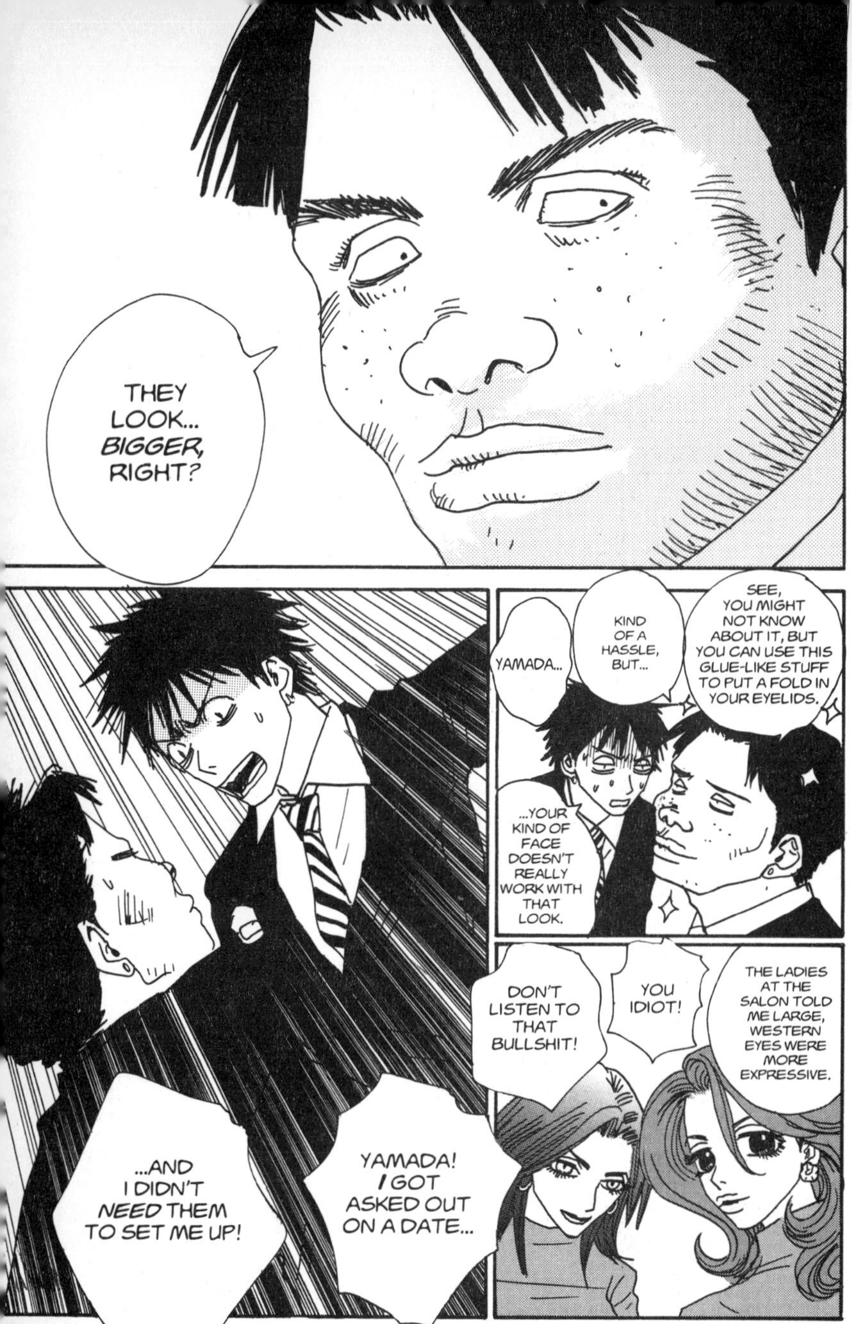
THEY LOOK... *BIGGER,* RIGHT?
SEE, YOU MIGHT NOT KNOW ABOUT IT, BUT YOU CAN USE THIS GLUE-LIKE STUFF TO PUT A FOLD IN YOUR EYELIDS.
KIND OF A HASSLE, BUT...
YAMADA...
...YOUR KIND OF FACE DOESN'T REALLY WORK WITH THAT LOOK.
THE LADIES AT THE SALON TOLD ME LARGE, WESTERN EYES WERE MORE EXPRESSIVE.
YOU IDIOT!
DON'T LISTEN TO THAT BULLSHIT!
YAMADA! *I* GOT ASKED OUT ON A DATE...
...AND I DIDN'T *NEED* THEM TO SET ME UP!

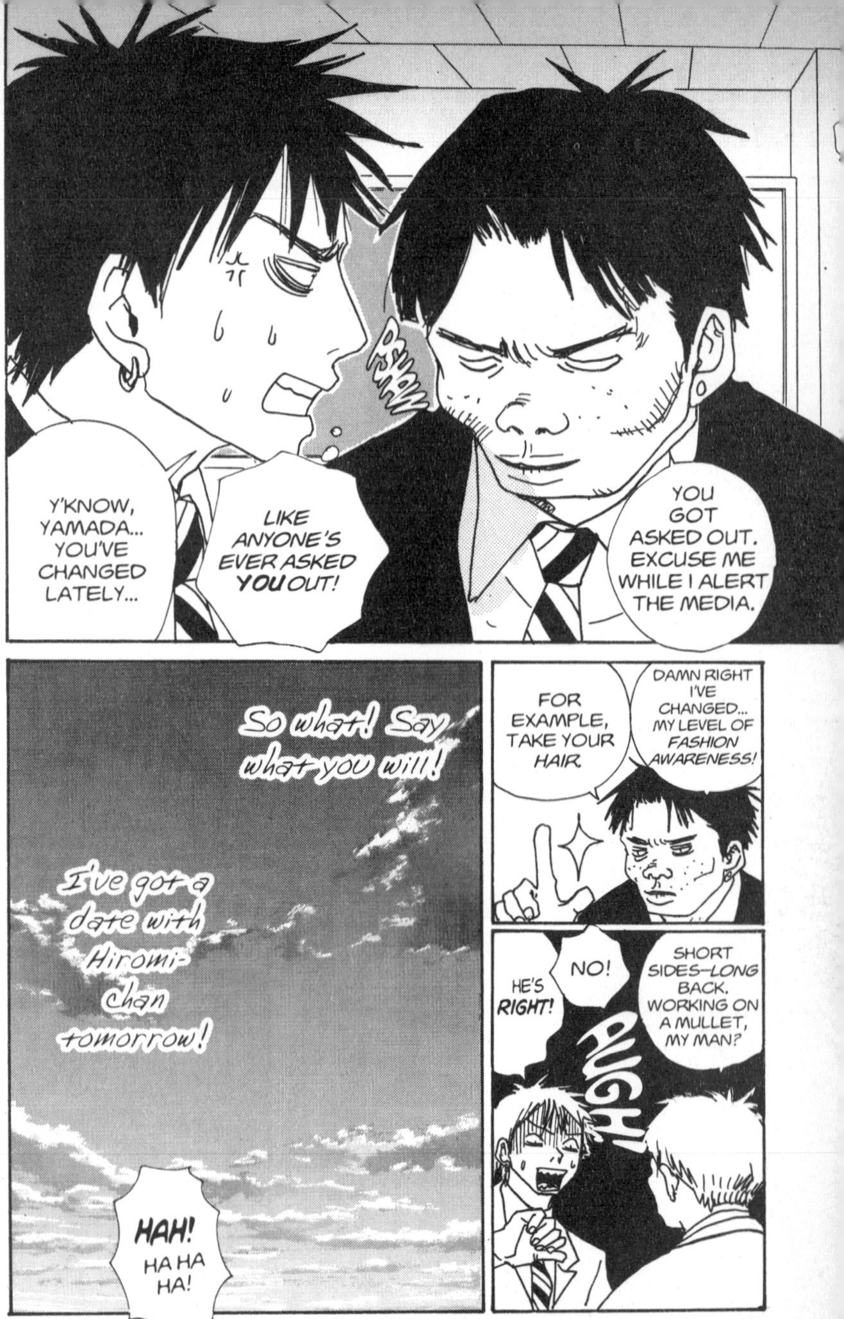
YOU GOT ASKED OUT. EXCUSE ME WHILE I ALERT THE MEDIA.
PSHAW
LIKE ANYONE'S EVER ASKED YOU OUT!
Y'KNOW, YAMADA... YOU'VE CHANGED LATELY...
DAMN RIGHT I'VE CHANGED... MY LEVEL OF FASHION AWARENESS!
FOR EXAMPLE, TAKE YOUR HAIR.
SHORT SIDES—LONG BACK. WORKING ON A MULLET, MY MAN?
NO!
HE'S RIGHT!
AUGH!
So what! Say what you will!
I've got a date with Hiromi-chan tomorrow!
HAH! HA HA HA!

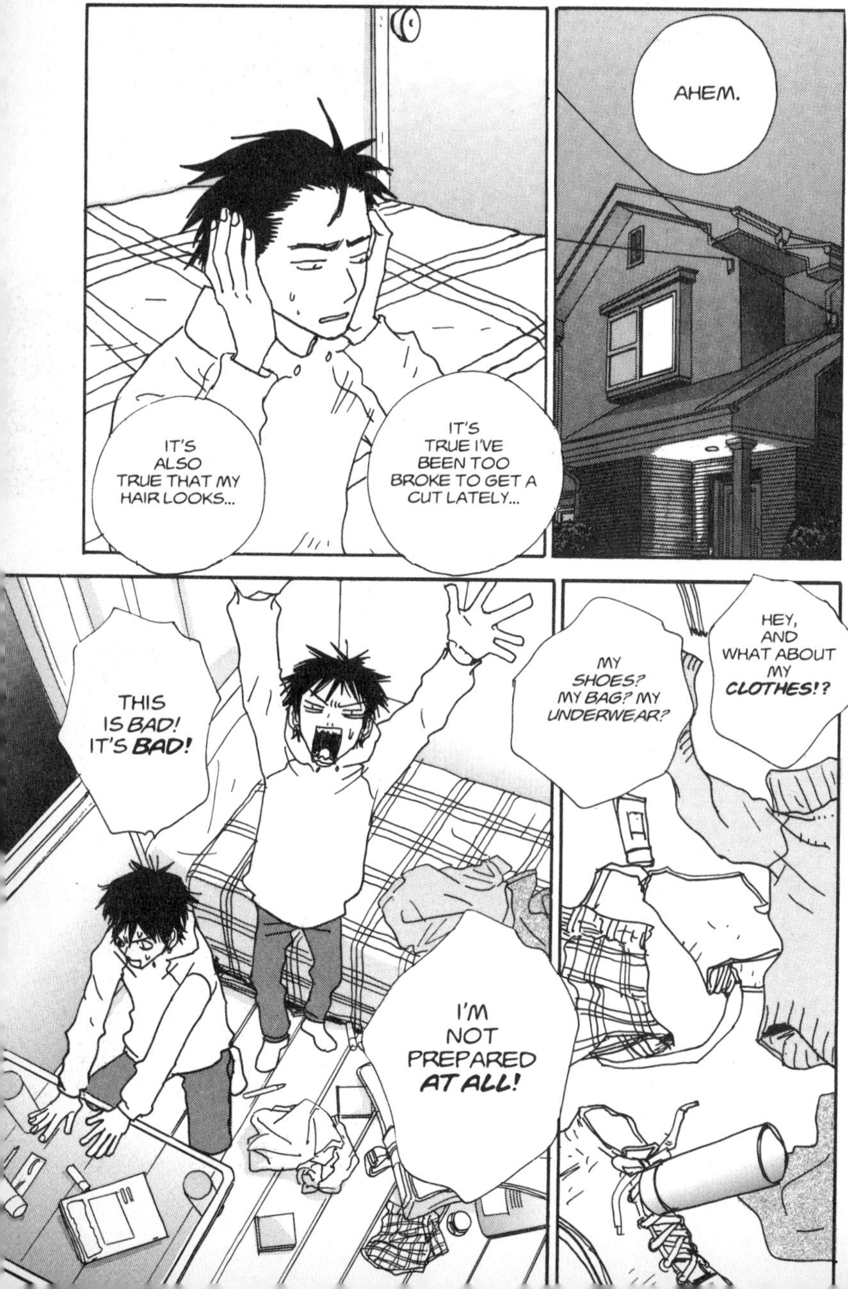
AHEM.
IT'S TRUE I'VE BEEN TOO BROKE TO GET A CUT LATELY...
IT'S ALSO TRUE THAT MY HAIR LOOKS...
HEY, AND WHAT ABOUT MY *CLOTHES!?*
MY *SHOES?* MY BAG? MY *UNDERWEAR?*
THIS IS *BAD!* IT'S *BAD!*
I'M NOT PREPARED *AT ALL!*

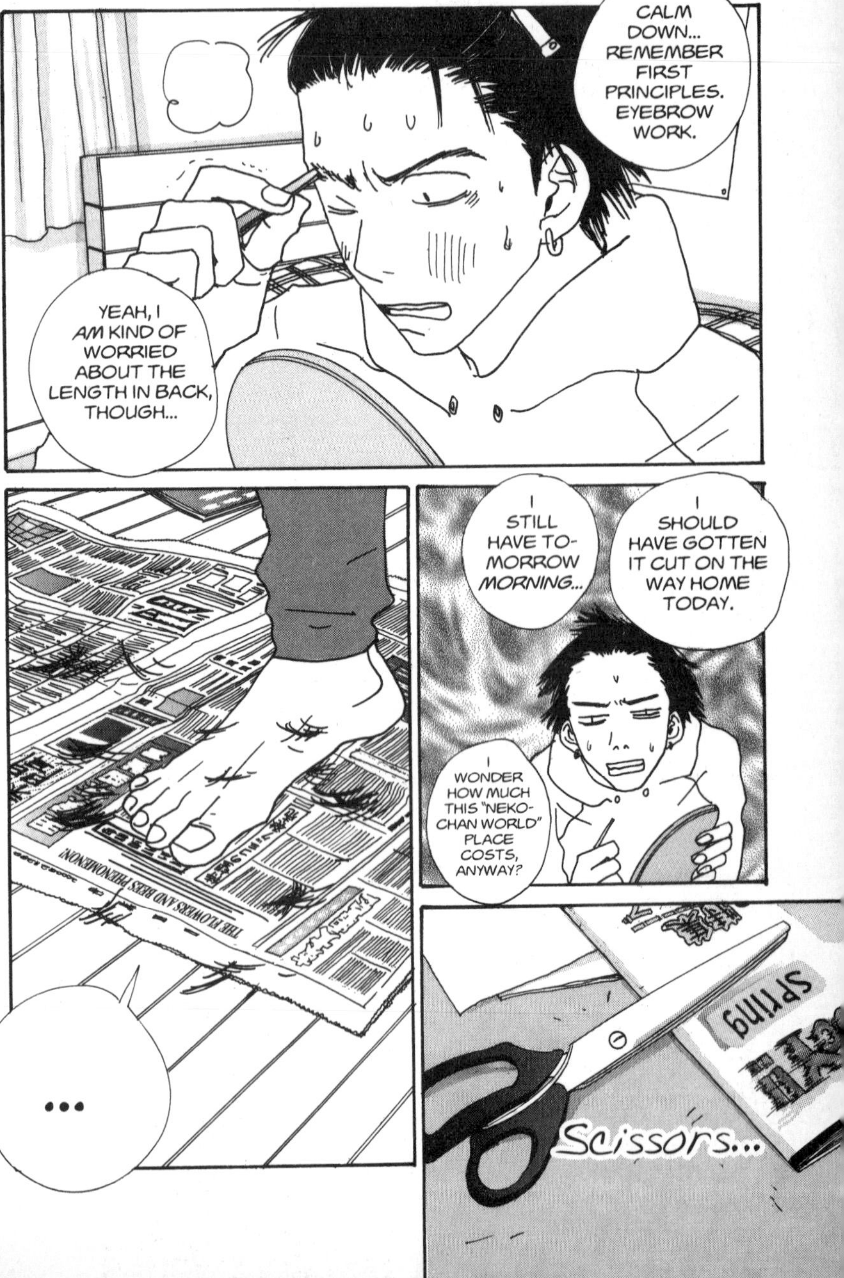
CALM DOWN... REMEMBER FIRST PRINCIPLES. EYEBROW WORK.
YEAH, I AM KIND OF WORRIED ABOUT THE LENGTH IN BACK, THOUGH...
I SHOULD HAVE GOTTEN IT CUT ON THE WAY HOME TODAY.
I STILL HAVE TO-MORROW MORNING...
I WONDER HOW MUCH THIS "NEKO-CHAN WORLD" PLACE COSTS, ANYWAY?
Spring
Scissors...
THE FLOWERS AND BEES PHENOMENON
...

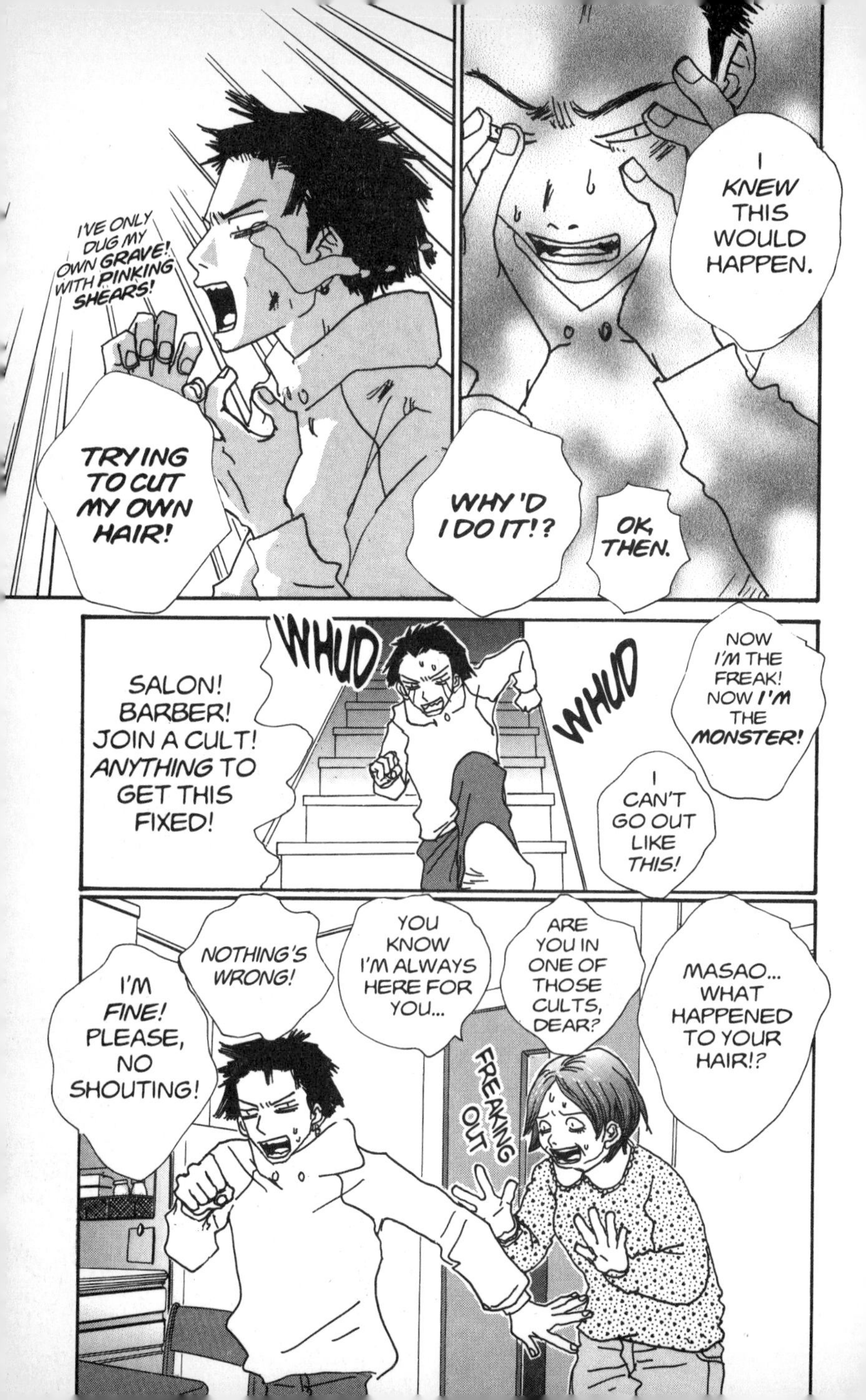
I KNEW THIS WOULD HAPPEN.
OK, THEN.
WHY'D I DO IT!?
I'VE ONLY DUG MY OWN GRAVE! WITH PINKING SHEARS!
TRYING TO CUT MY OWN HAIR!
NOW I'M THE FREAK! NOW I'M THE MONSTER!
I CAN'T GO OUT LIKE THIS!
WHUD
WHUD
SALON! BARBER! JOIN A CULT! ANYTHING TO GET THIS FIXED!
MASAO... WHAT HAPPENED TO YOUR HAIR!?
ARE YOU IN ONE OF THOSE CULTS, DEAR?
YOU KNOW I'M ALWAYS HERE FOR YOU...
FREAKING OUT
NOTHING'S WRONG!
I'M FINE! PLEASE, NO SHOUTING!

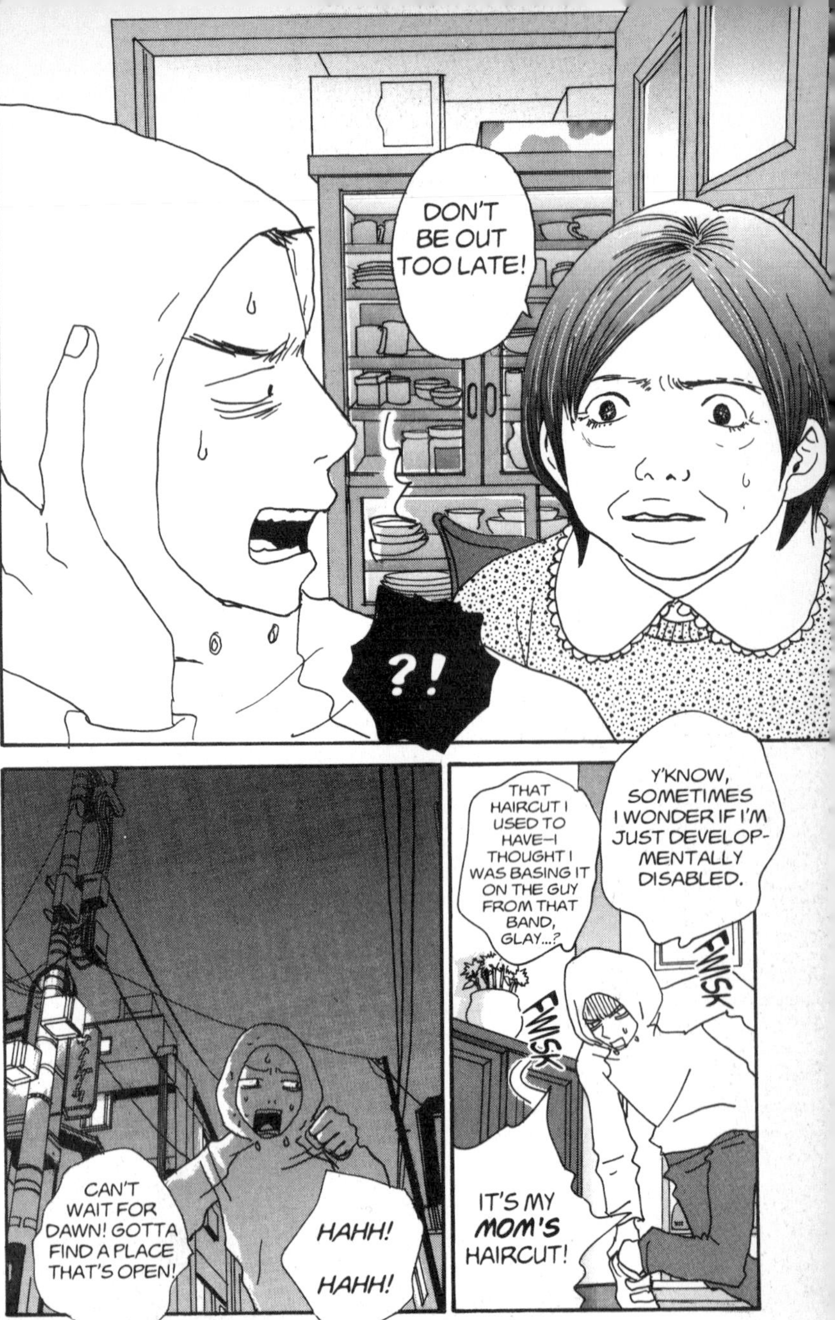
DON'T BE OUT TOO LATE!
?!
Y'KNOW, SOMETIMES I WONDER IF I'M JUST DEVELOP-MENTALLY DISABLED.
THAT HAIRCUT I USED TO HAVE—I THOUGHT I WAS BASING IT ON THE GUY FROM THAT BAND, GLAY...?
FWISK
FWISK
IT'S MY **MOM'S** HAIRCUT!
HAHH! HAHH!
CAN'T WAIT FOR DAWN! GOTTA FIND A PLACE THAT'S OPEN!

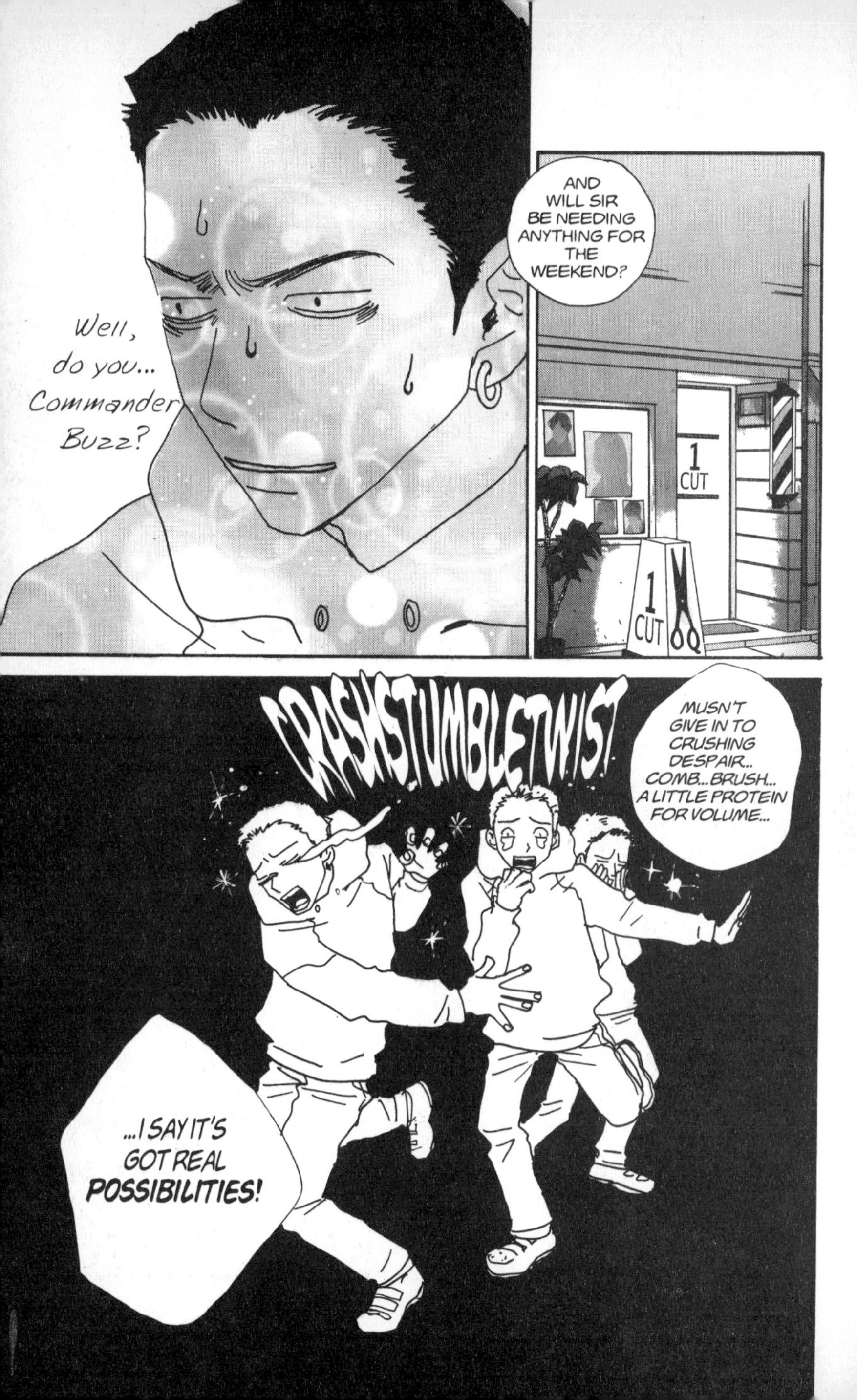
AND WILL SIR BE NEEDING ANYTHING FOR THE WEEKEND?
1 CUT
1 CUT
Well, do you... Commander Buzz?
MUSN'T GIVE IN TO CRUSHING DESPAIR... COMB...BRUSH... A LITTLE PROTEIN FOR VOLUME...
CRASHSTUMBLETWIST
...I SAY IT'S GOT REAL POSSIBILITIES!

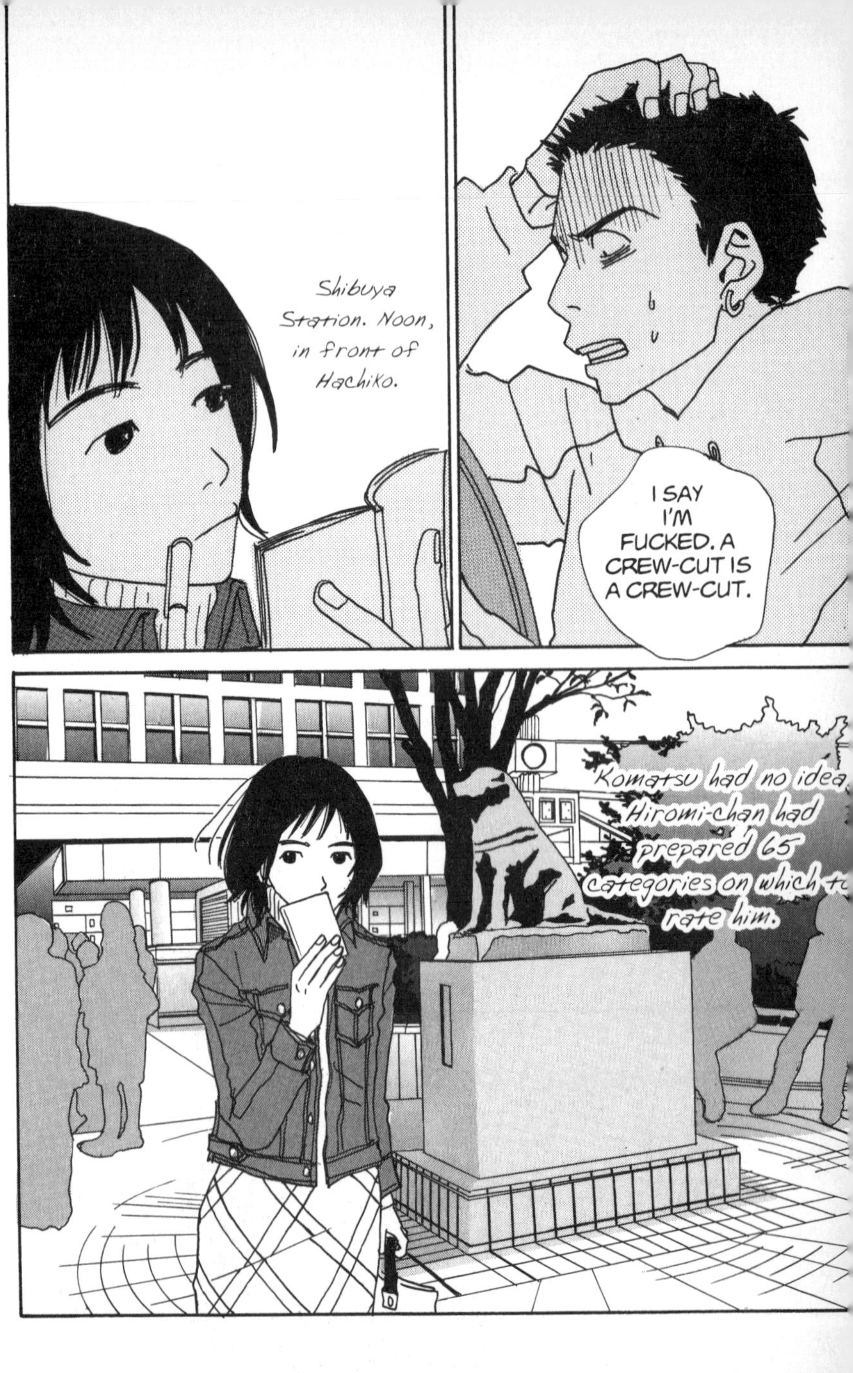
I SAY I'M FUCKED. A CREW-CUT IS A CREW-CUT.
Shibuya Station. Noon, in front of Hachiko.
Komatsu had no idea Hiromi-chan had prepared 65 categories on which t rate him.

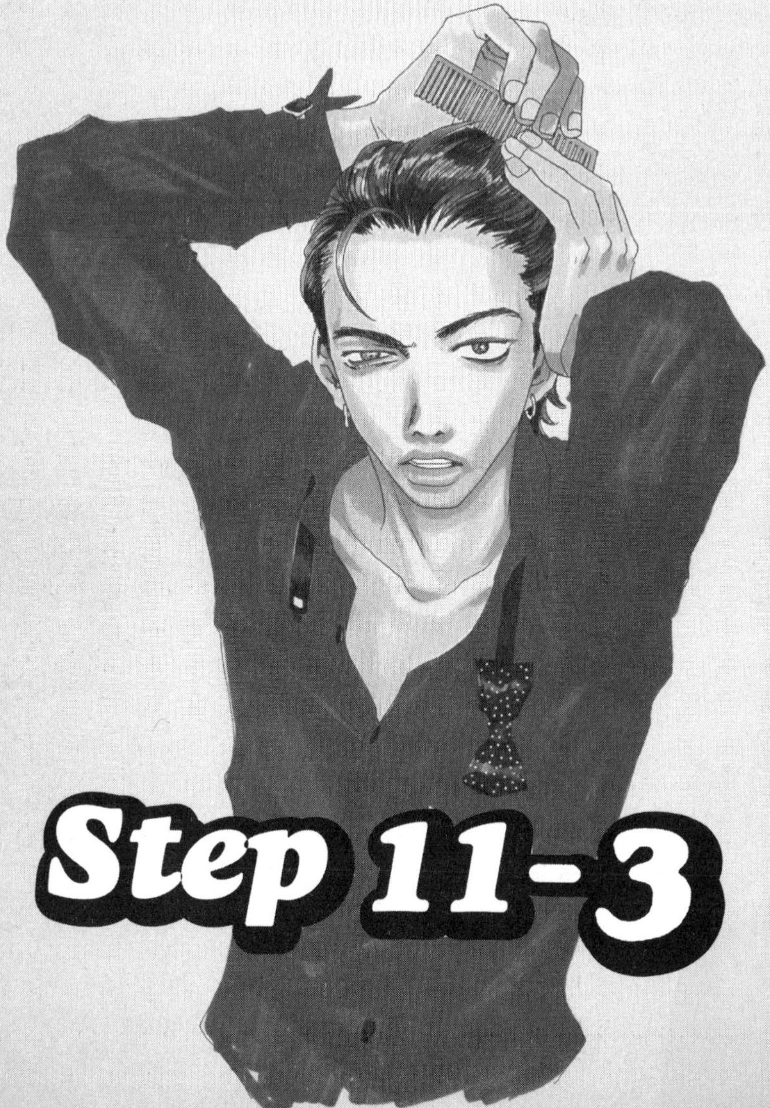

Step 11-3

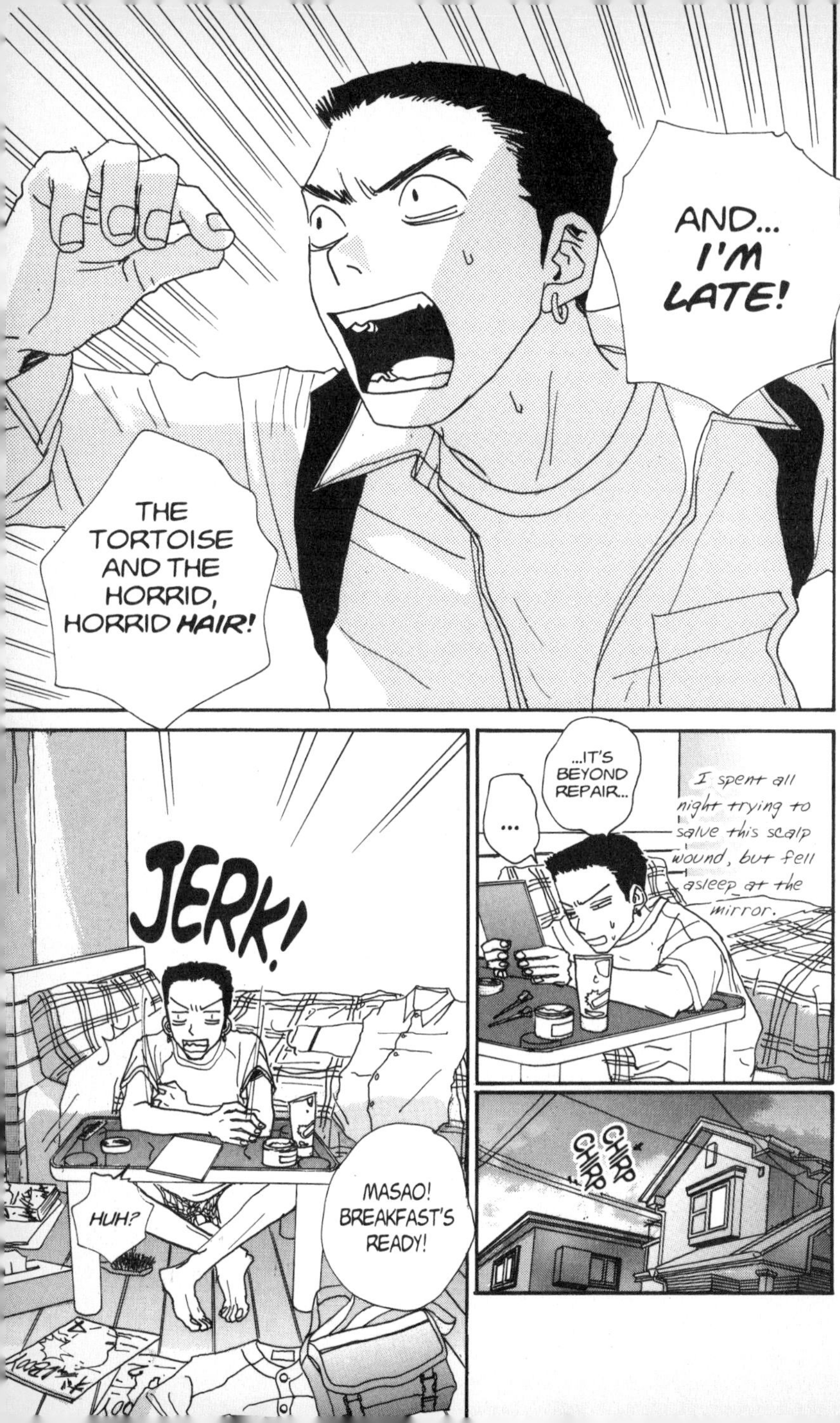
AND... I'M LATE!
THE TORTOISE AND THE HORRID, HORRID HAIR!
...IT'S BEYOND REPAIR...
...
I spent all night trying to salve this scalp wound, but fell asleep at the mirror.
CHIRP CHIRP
MASAO! BREAKFAST'S READY!
HUH?
JERK!

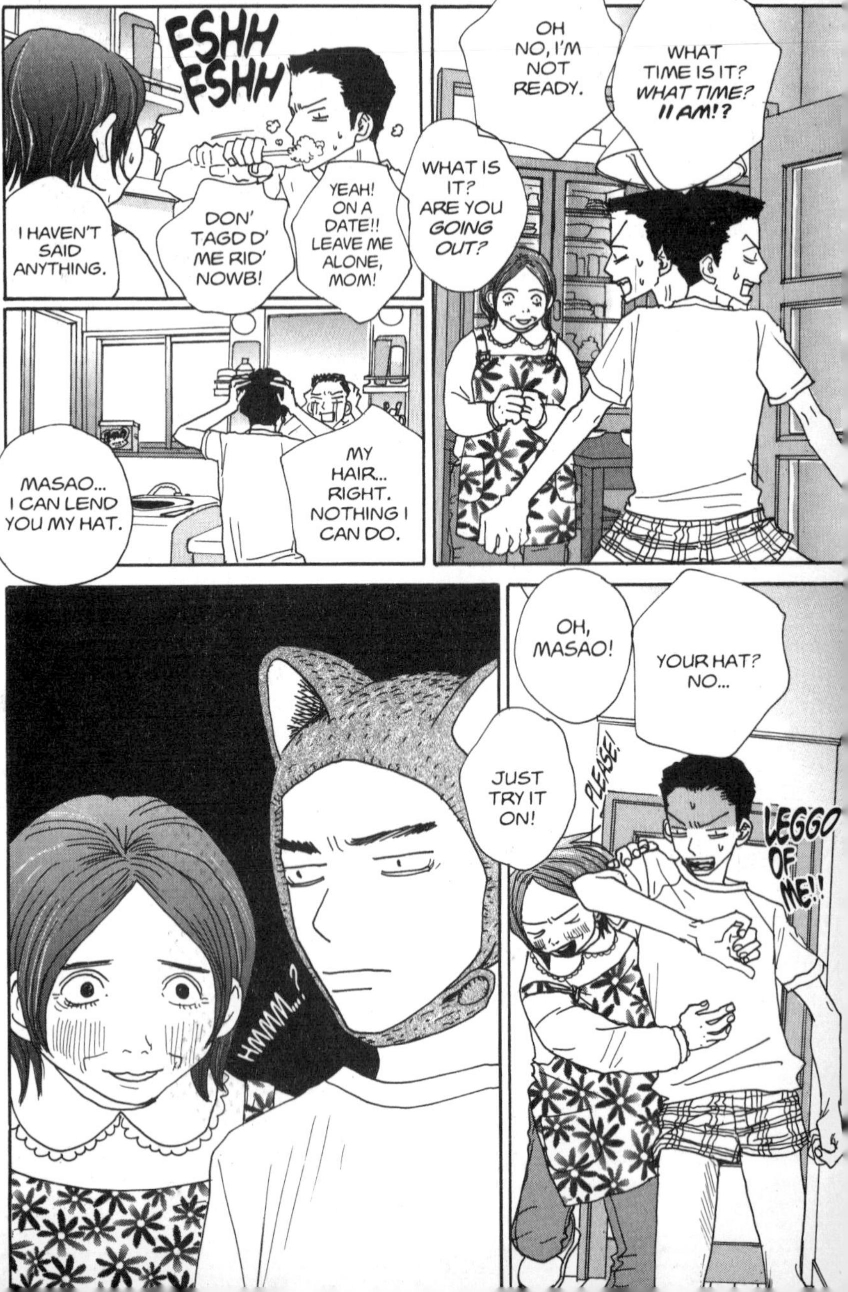
WHAT TIME IS IT? WHAT TIME? 11 AM!?
OH NO, I'M NOT READY.
WHAT IS IT? ARE YOU GOING OUT?
YEAH! ON A DATE!! LEAVE ME ALONE, MOM!
FSHH FSHH
DON' TAGD D' ME RID' NOWB!
I HAVEN'T SAID ANYTHING.
MY HAIR... RIGHT. NOTHING I CAN DO.
MASAO... I CAN LEND YOU MY HAT.
YOUR HAT? NO...
OH, MASAO!
JUST TRY IT ON!
PLEASE!
LEGGO OF ME!!
HMMM...?

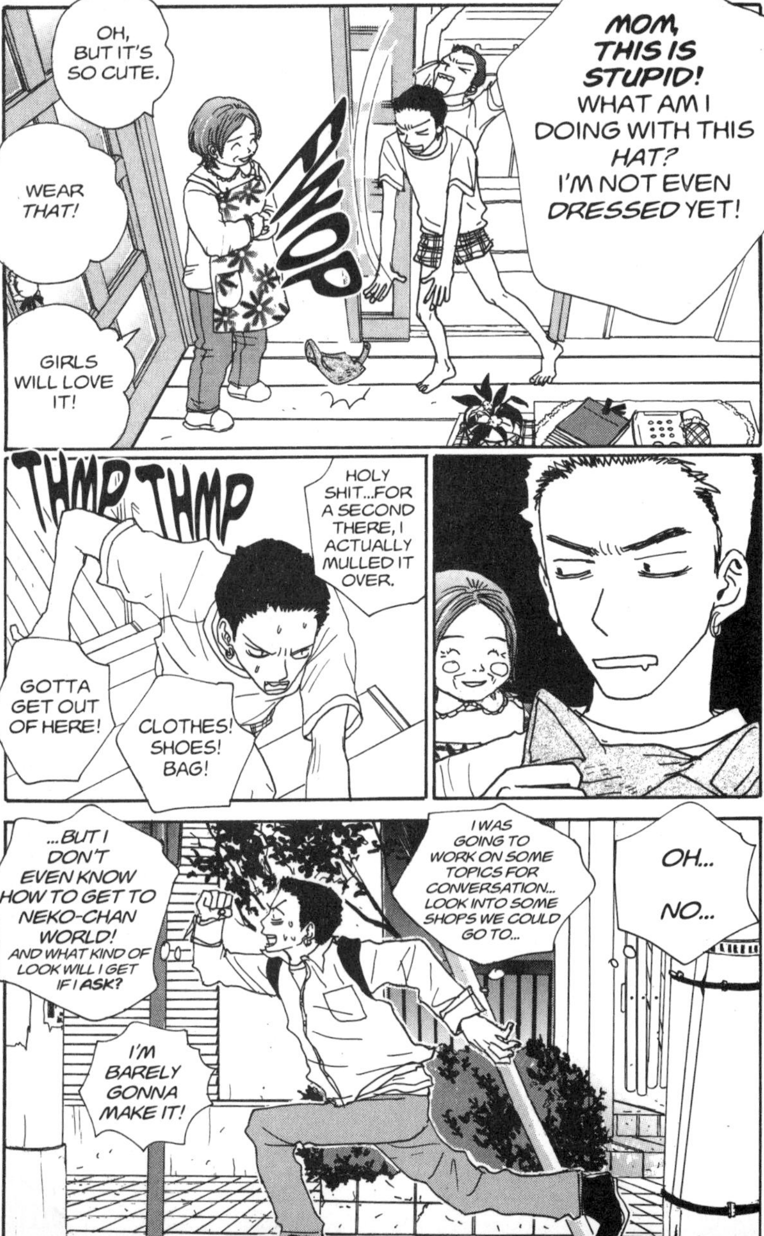
MOM, THIS IS STUPID! WHAT AM I DOING WITH THIS HAT? I'M NOT EVEN DRESSED YET!
SWOP
OH, BUT IT'S SO CUTE.
WEAR THAT!
GIRLS WILL LOVE IT!
HOLY SHIT...FOR A SECOND THERE, I ACTUALLY MULLED IT OVER.
THMP THMP
GOTTA GET OUT OF HERE!
CLOTHES! SHOES! BAG!
OH... NO...
I WAS GOING TO WORK ON SOME TOPICS FOR CONVERSATION... LOOK INTO SOME SHOPS WE COULD GO TO...
...BUT I DON'T EVEN KNOW HOW TO GET TO NEKO-CHAN WORLD! AND WHAT KIND OF LOOK WILL I GET IF I ASK?
I'M BARELY GONNA MAKE IT!

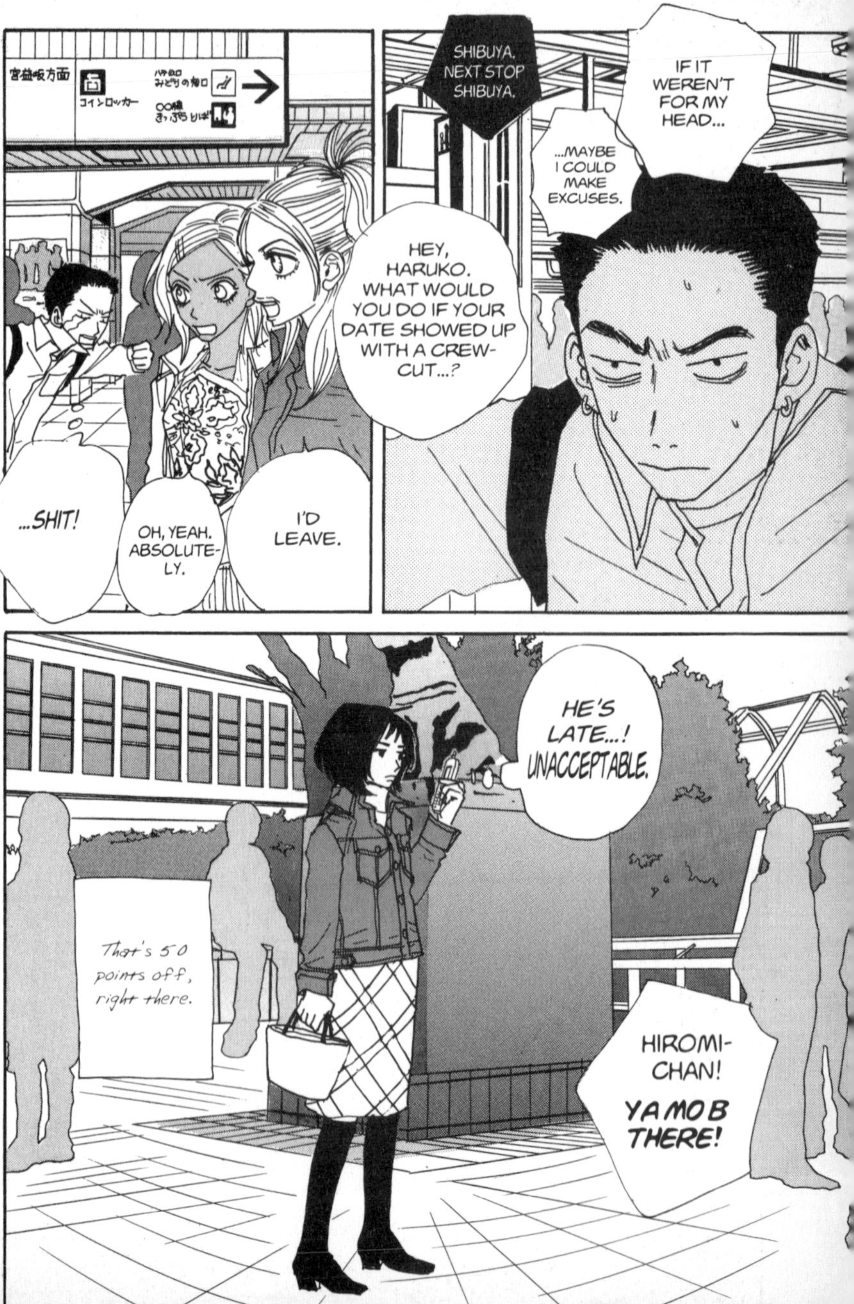
SHIBUYA. NEXT STOP SHIBUYA.
IF IT WEREN'T FOR MY HEAD...
...MAYBE I COULD MAKE EXCUSES.
宮益坂方面
コインロッカー
HEY, HARUKO. WHAT WOULD YOU DO IF YOUR DATE SHOWED UP WITH A CREW-CUT...?
I'D LEAVE.
OH, YEAH. ABSOLUTE-LY.
...SHIT!
HE'S LATE...! UNACCEPTABLE.
That's 50 points off, right there.
HIROMI-CHAN!
YA MO B THERE!

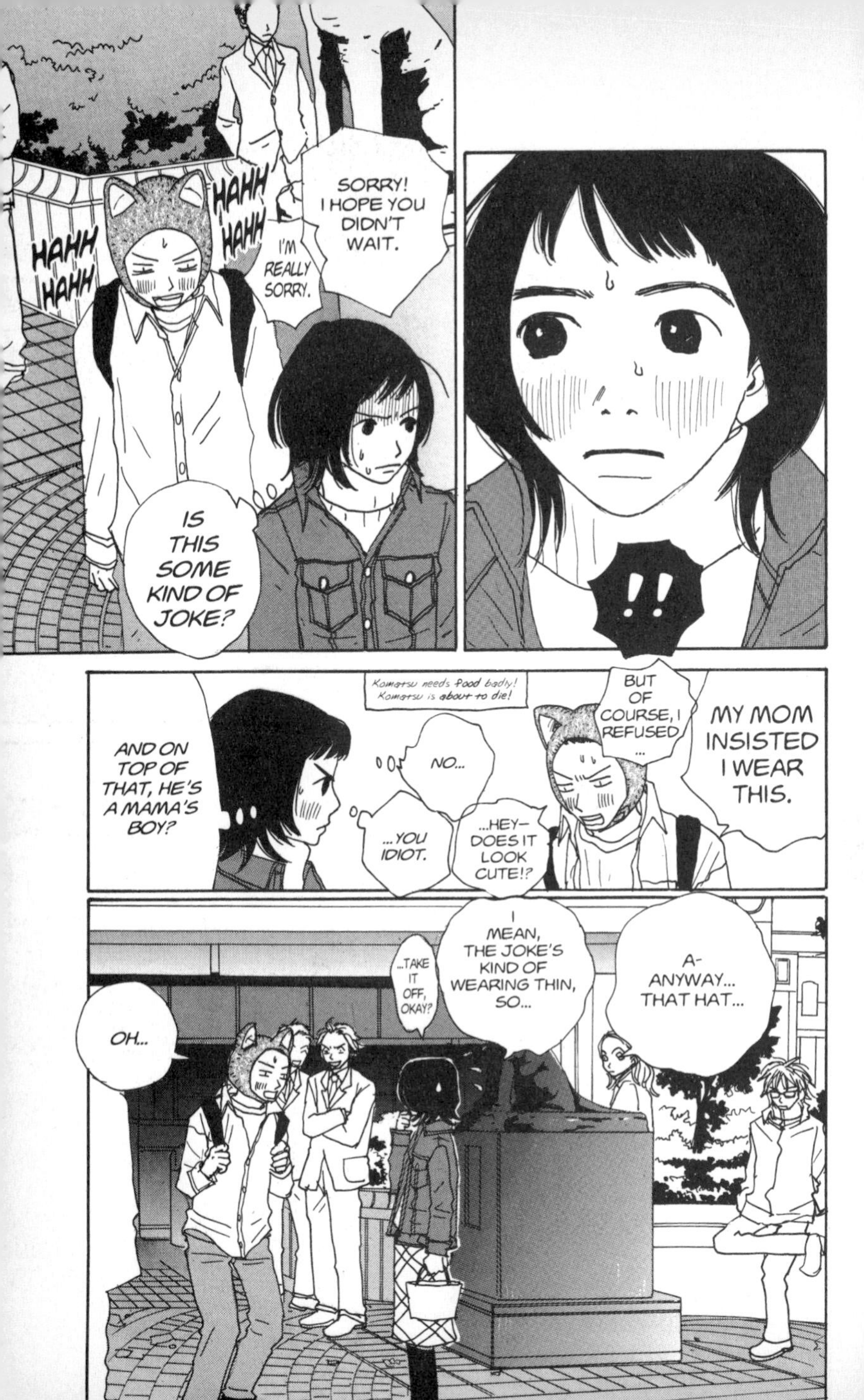
!!
SORRY! I HOPE YOU DIDN'T WAIT.
HAHH HAHH
I'M REALLY SORRY.
HAHH HAHH
IS THIS SOME KIND OF JOKE?
MY MOM INSISTED I WEAR THIS.
BUT OF COURSE, I REFUSED...
...HEY— DOES IT LOOK CUTE!?
NO...
...YOU IDIOT.
Komatsu needs food badly! Komatsu is about to die!
AND ON TOP OF THAT, HE'S A MAMA'S BOY?
A- ANYWAY... THAT HAT...
I MEAN, THE JOKE'S KIND OF WEARING THIN, SO...
...TAKE IT OFF, OKAY?
OH...

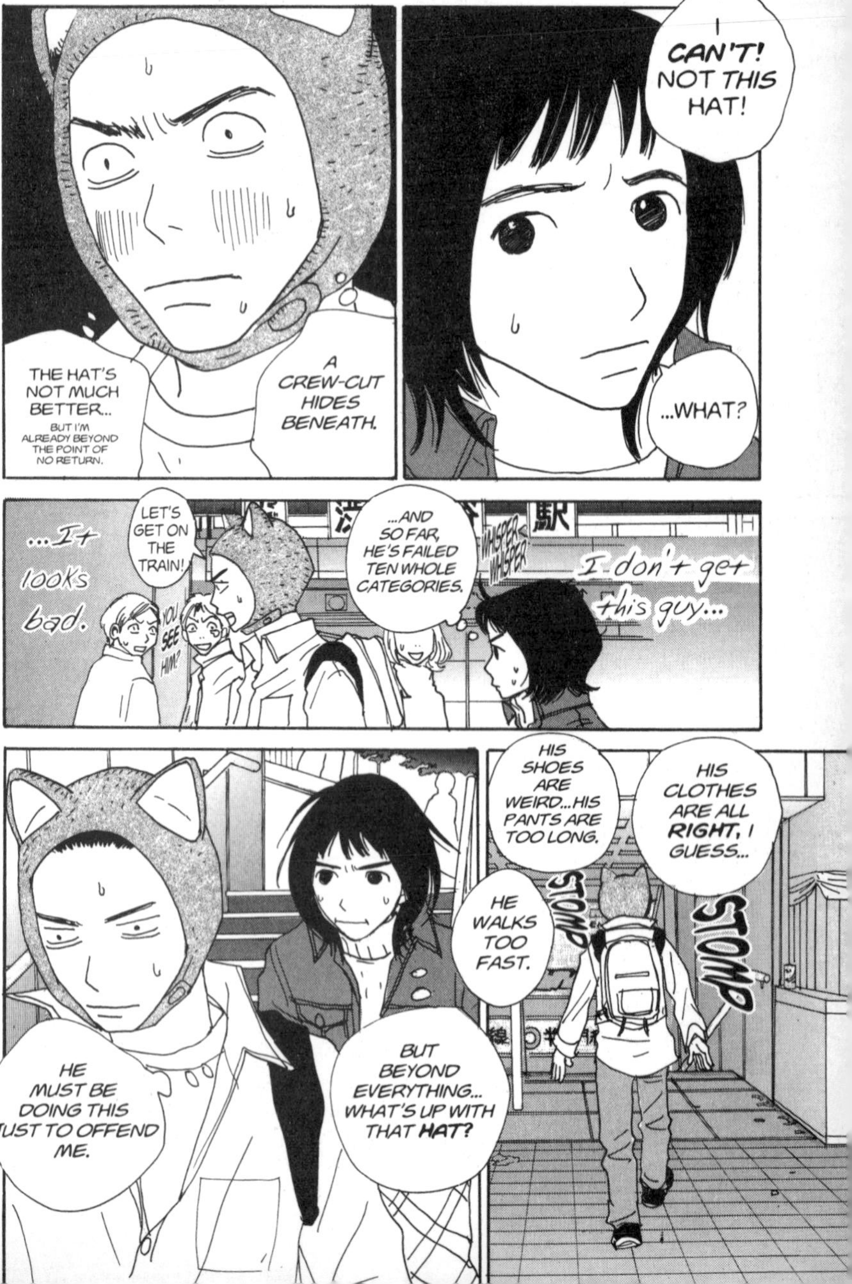
I CAN'T! NOT THIS HAT!
...WHAT?
A CREW-CUT HIDES BENEATH.
THE HAT'S NOT MUCH BETTER...
BUT I'M ALREADY BEYOND THE POINT OF NO RETURN.
I don't get this guy...
WHISPER WHISPER
...AND SO FAR, HE'S FAILED TEN WHOLE CATEGORIES.
LET'S GET ON THE TRAIN!
...It looks bad.
YOU SEE HIM?
HIS CLOTHES ARE ALL RIGHT, I GUESS...
HIS SHOES ARE WEIRD...HIS PANTS ARE TOO LONG.
STOMP
STOMP
HE WALKS TOO FAST.
BUT BEYOND EVERYTHING... WHAT'S UP WITH THAT HAT?
HE MUST BE DOING THIS JUST TO OFFEND ME.

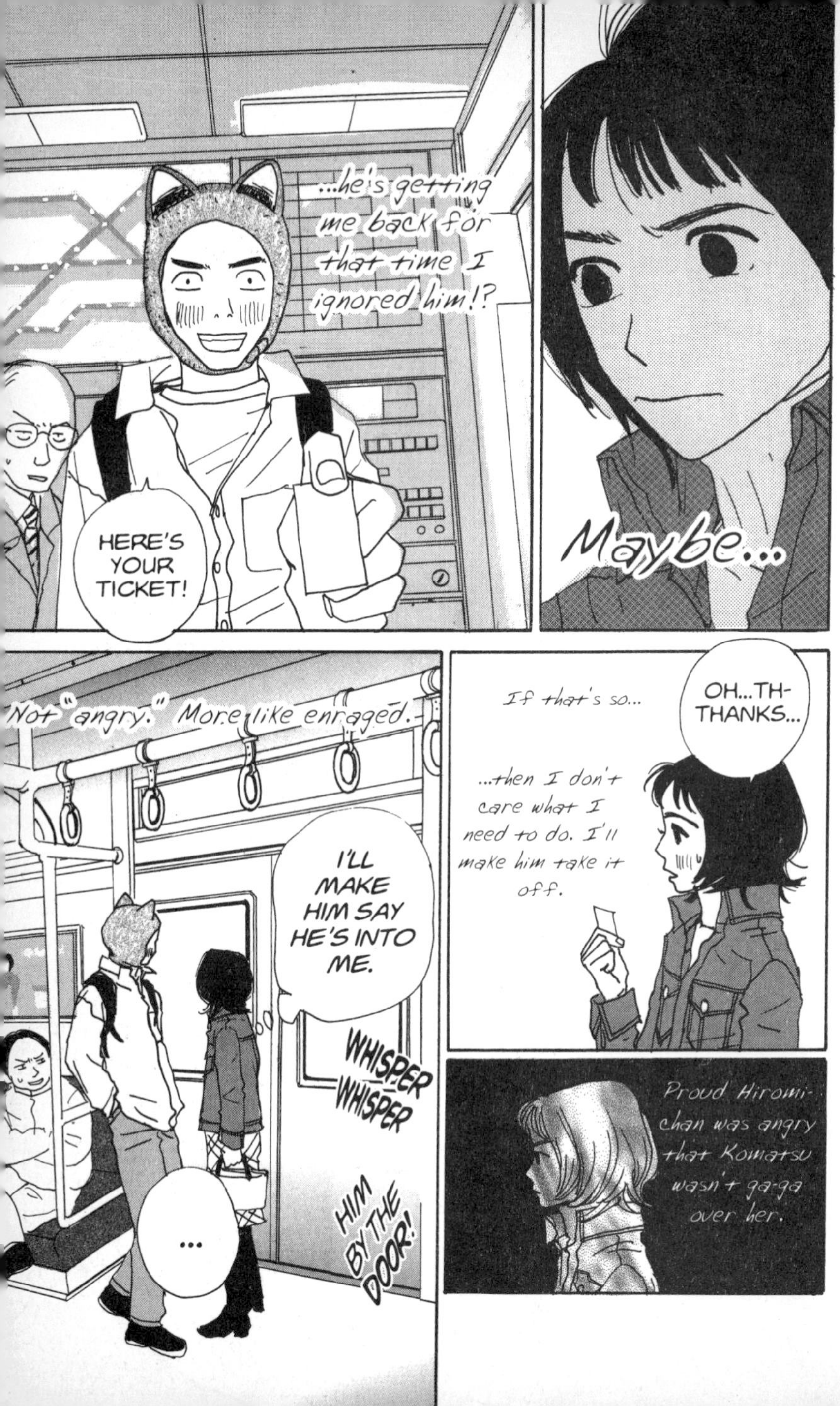
Maybe...
...he's getting me back for that time I ignored him!?
HERE'S YOUR TICKET!
OH...TH-THANKS...
If that's so...
...then I don't care what I need to do. I'll make him take it off.
Proud Hiromi-chan was angry that Komatsu wasn't ga-ga over her.
Not "angry." More like enraged.
I'LL MAKE HIM SAY HE'S INTO ME.
WHISPER WHISPER
HIM BY THE DOOR!
...

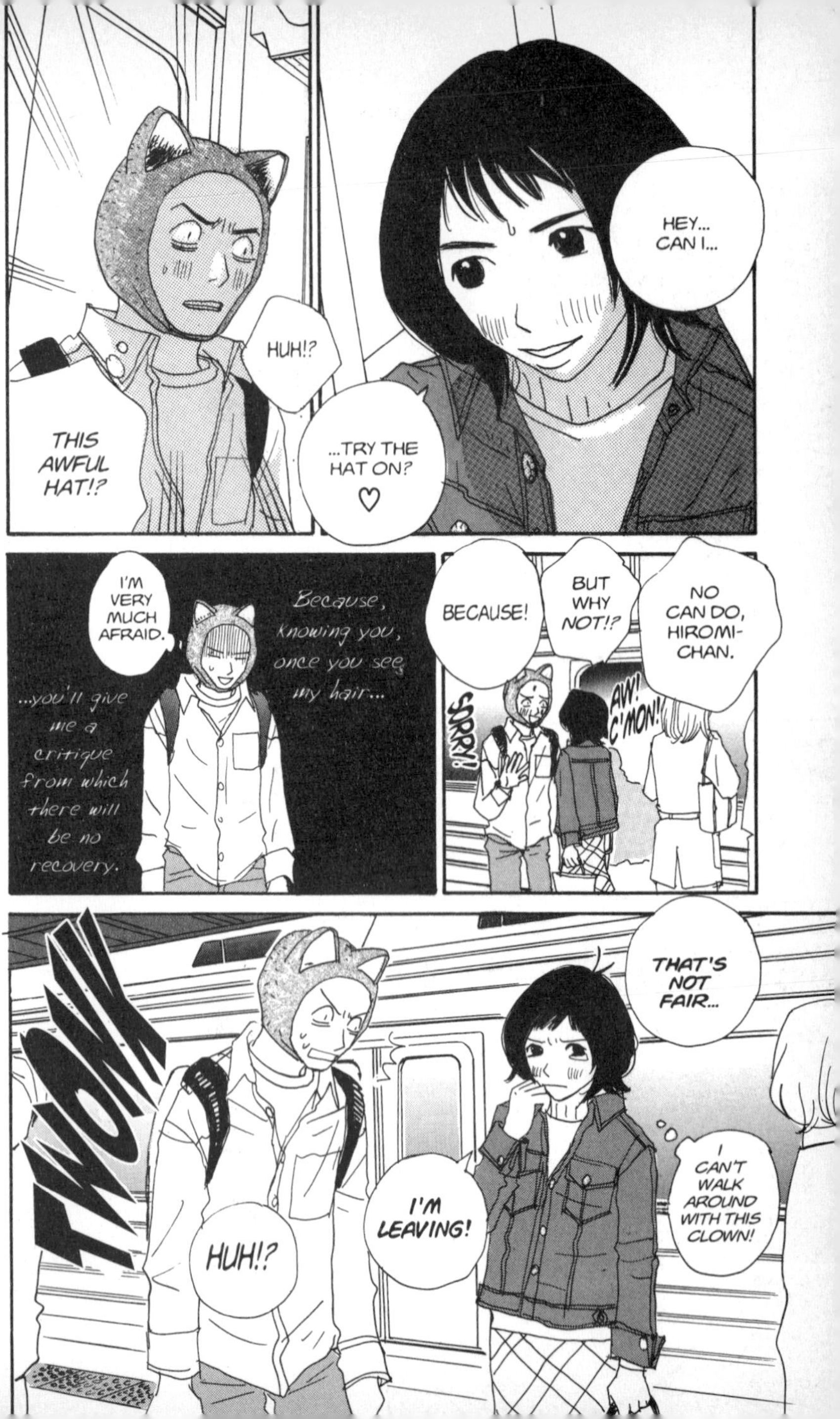
HEY... CAN I...
...TRY THE HAT ON? ♡
HUH!?
THIS AWFUL HAT!?
NO CAN DO, HIROMI-CHAN.
BUT WHY NOT!?
BECAUSE!
AW! C'MON!
SORRY!
Because, knowing you, once you see my hair...
I'M VERY MUCH AFRAID.
...you'll give me a critique from which there will be no recovery.
THAT'S NOT FAIR...
I CAN'T WALK AROUND WITH THIS CLOWN!
I'M LEAVING!
HUH!?
THWOK

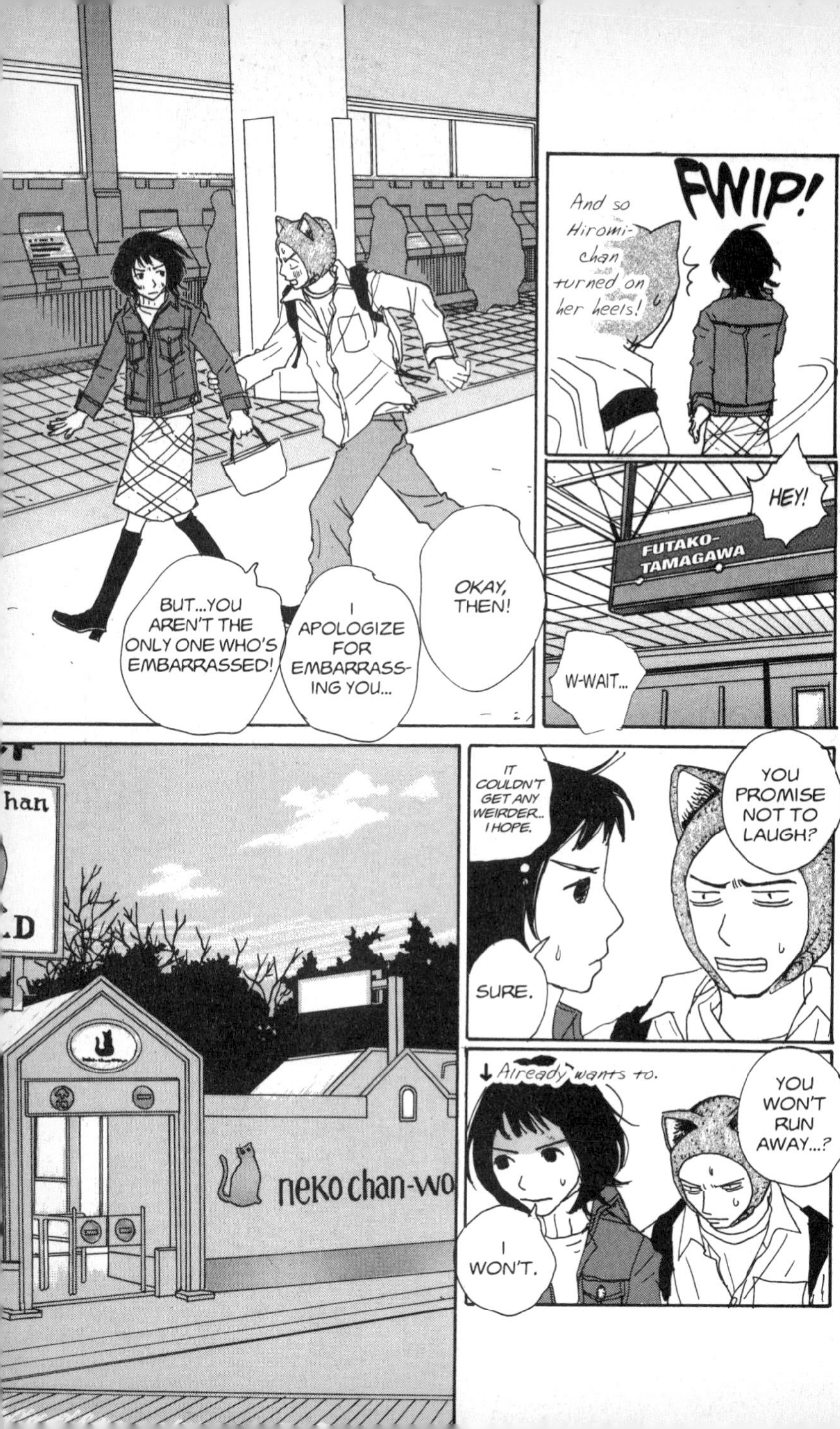
FWIP!
And so Hiromi-chan turned on her heels!
HEY!
FUTAKO-TAMAGAWA
W-WAIT...
OKAY, THEN!
I APOLOGIZE FOR EMBARRASSING YOU...
BUT...YOU AREN'T THE ONLY ONE WHO'S EMBARRASSED!
YOU PROMISE NOT TO LAUGH?
IT COULDN'T GET ANY WEIRDER... I HOPE.
SURE.
YOU WON'T RUN AWAY...?
Already wants to.
I WON'T.
neko chan-wo

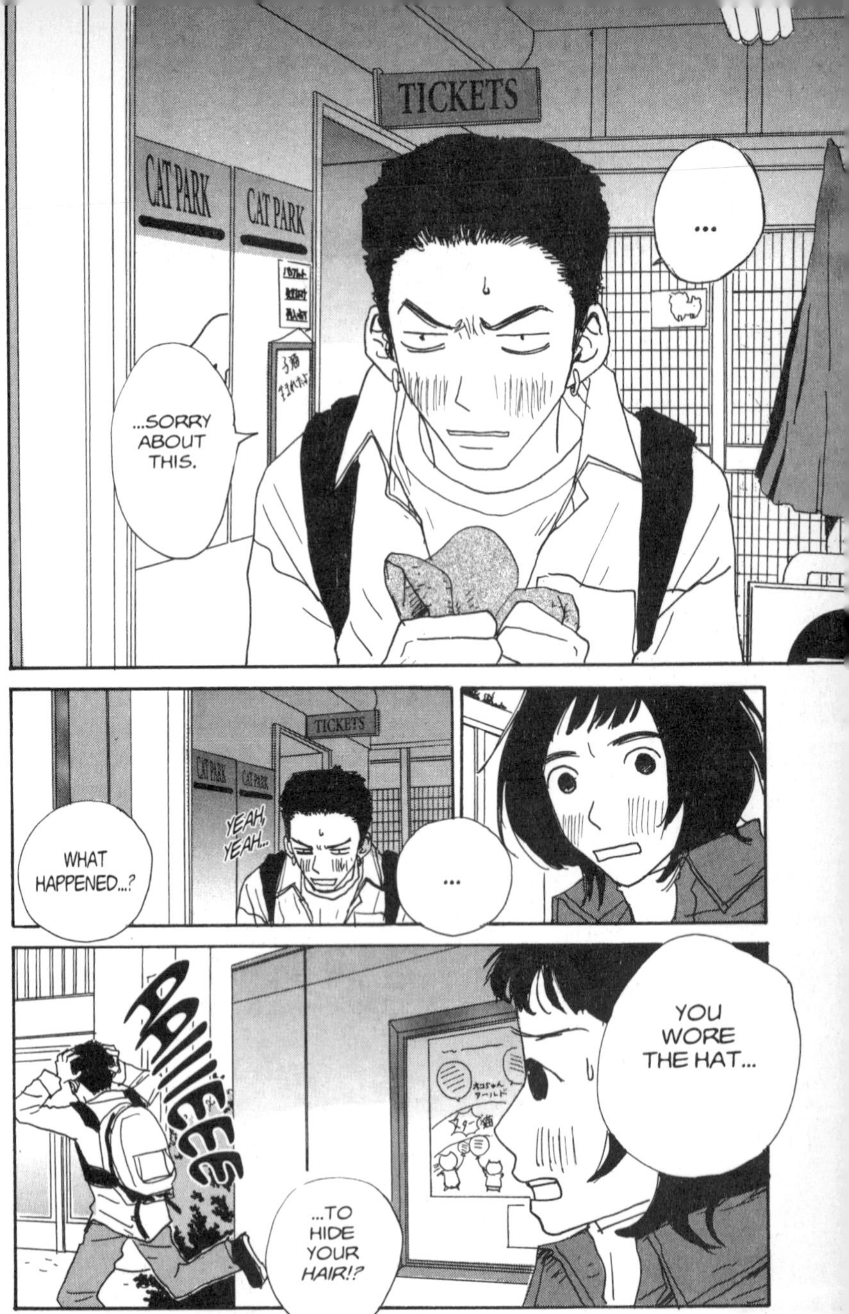
TICKETS
CAT PARK
CAT PARK
...
...SORRY ABOUT THIS.
...
TICKETS
CAT PARK
CAT PARK
YEAH, YEAH...
WHAT HAPPENED...?
YOU WORE THE HAT...
AAIIIEEE
...TO HIDE YOUR HAIR!?

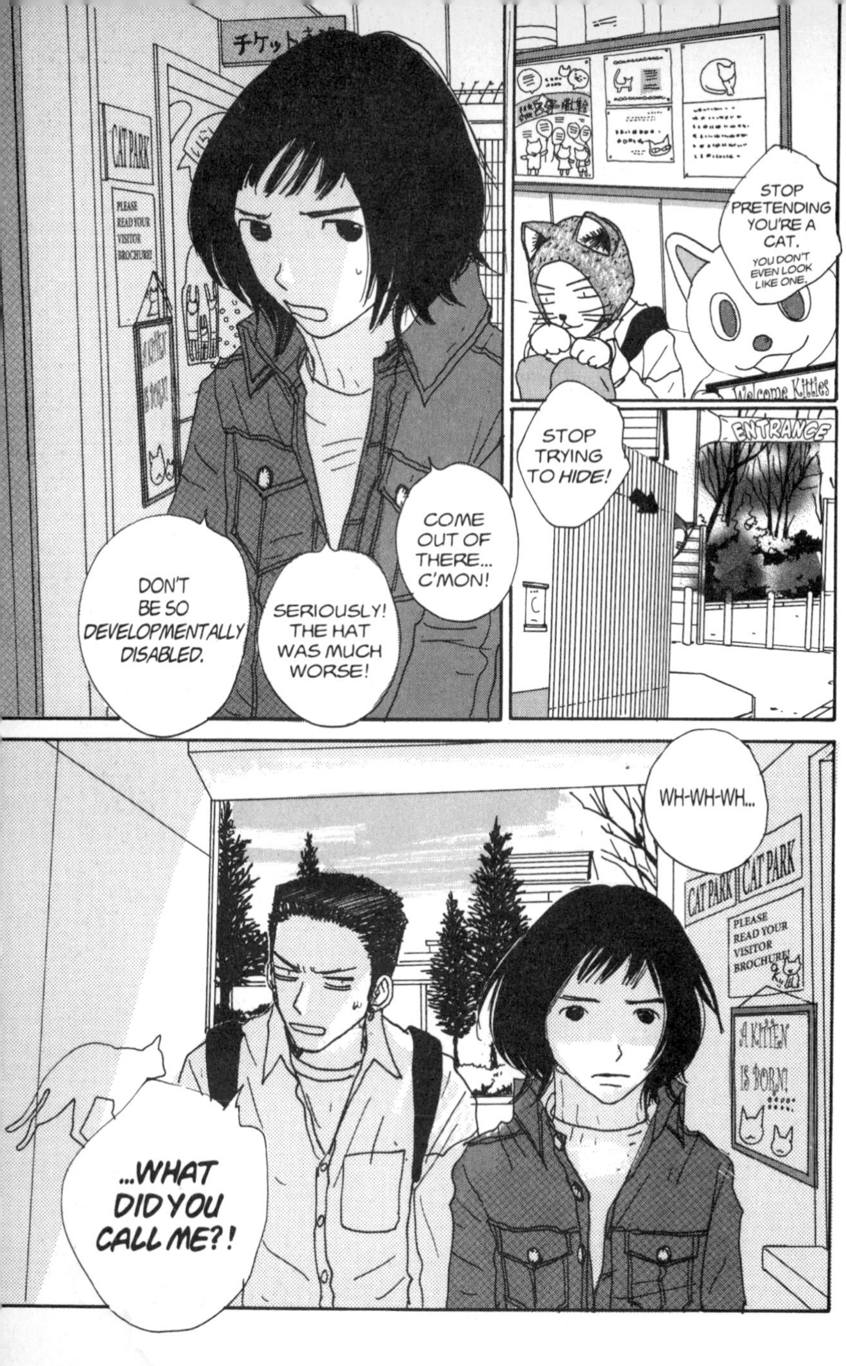
STOP PRETENDING YOU'RE A CAT.
YOU DON'T EVEN LOOK LIKE ONE.
Welcome Kitties
ENTRANCE
STOP TRYING TO HIDE!
CAT PARK
PLEASE READ YOUR VISITOR BROCHURE!
COME OUT OF THERE... C'MON!
SERIOUSLY! THE HAT WAS MUCH WORSE!
DON'T BE SO DEVELOPMENTALLY DISABLED.
WH-WH-WH...
CAT PARK
CAT PARK
PLEASE READ YOUR VISITOR BROCHURE!
A KITTEN IS BORN!
...WHAT DID YOU CALL ME?!

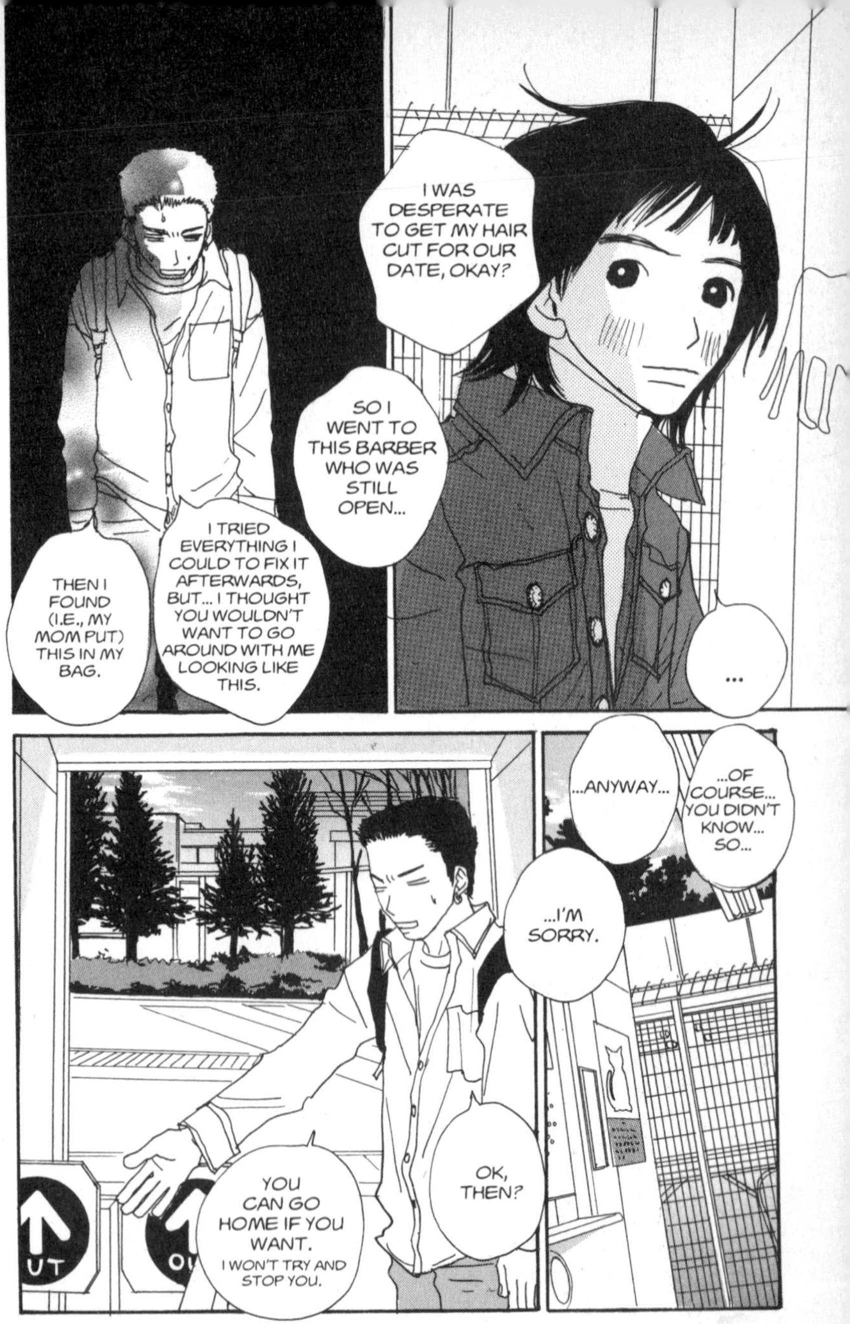
I WAS DESPERATE TO GET MY HAIR CUT FOR OUR DATE, OKAY?
SO I WENT TO THIS BARBER WHO WAS STILL OPEN...
...
I TRIED EVERYTHING I COULD TO FIX IT AFTERWARDS, BUT... I THOUGHT YOU WOULDN'T WANT TO GO AROUND WITH ME LOOKING LIKE THIS.
THEN I FOUND (I.E., MY MOM PUT) THIS IN MY BAG.
...OF COURSE... YOU DIDN'T KNOW... SO...
...ANYWAY...
...I'M SORRY.
OK, THEN?
YOU CAN GO HOME IF YOU WANT.
I WON'T TRY AND STOP YOU.

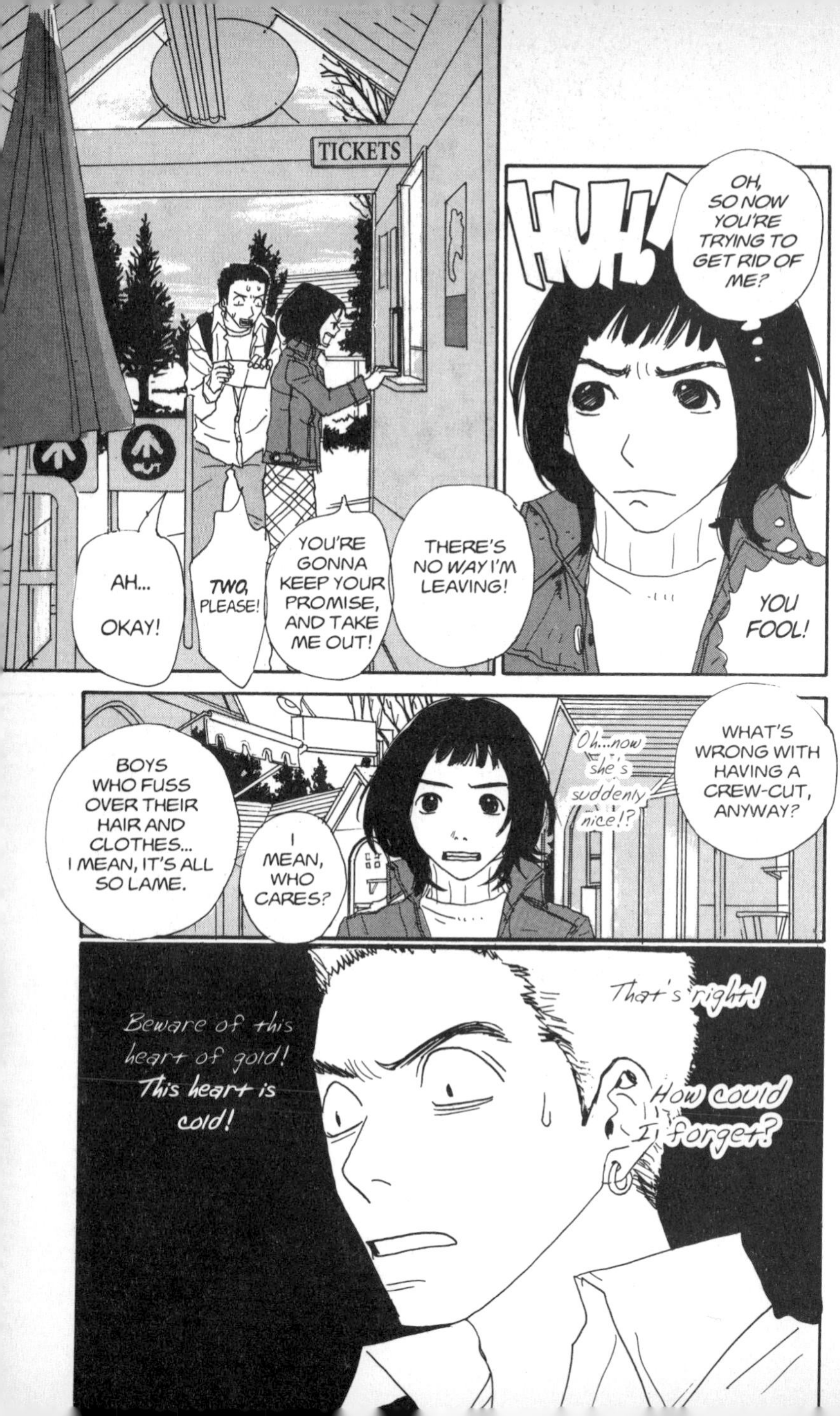
HUH!!
OH, SO NOW YOU'RE TRYING TO GET RID OF ME?
YOU FOOL!
TICKETS
THERE'S NO *WAY* I'M LEAVING!
YOU'RE GONNA KEEP YOUR PROMISE, AND TAKE ME OUT!
TWO, PLEASE!
AH... OKAY!
WHAT'S WRONG WITH HAVING A CREW-CUT, ANYWAY?
Oh...now she's suddenly nice!?
I MEAN, WHO CARES?
BOYS WHO FUSS OVER THEIR HAIR AND CLOTHES... I MEAN, IT'S ALL SO LAME.
That's right!
How could I forget?
Beware of this heart of gold!
This heart is cold!

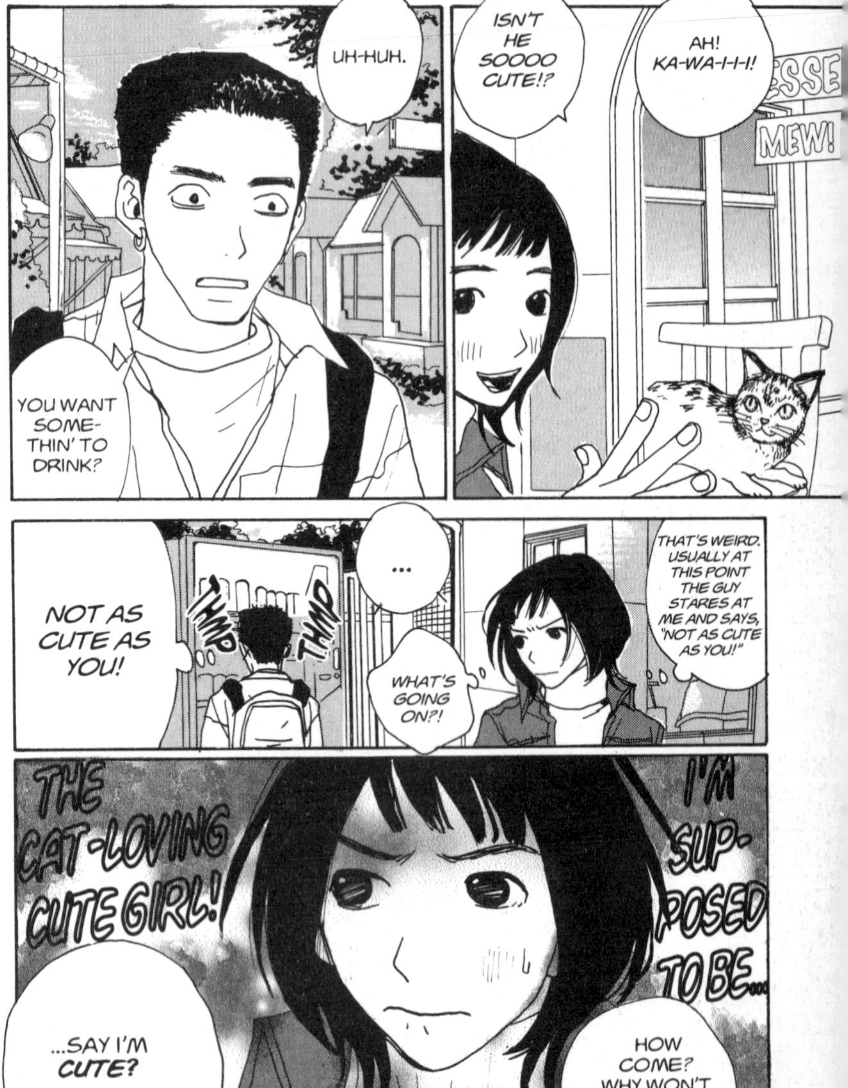
AH! KA-WA-I-I-I!
ISN'T HE SOOOO CUTE!?
ESSE
MEW!
UH-HUH.
YOU WANT SOME-THIN' TO DRINK?
THAT'S WEIRD. USUALLY AT THIS POINT THE GUY STARES AT ME AND SAYS, "NOT AS CUTE AS YOU!"
WHAT'S GOING ON?!
...
THUMP
THUMP
NOT AS CUTE AS YOU!
I'M SUP-POSED TO BE...
THE CAT-LOVING CUTE GIRL!
HOW COME? WHY WON'T KOMATSU...
...SAY I'M CUTE?

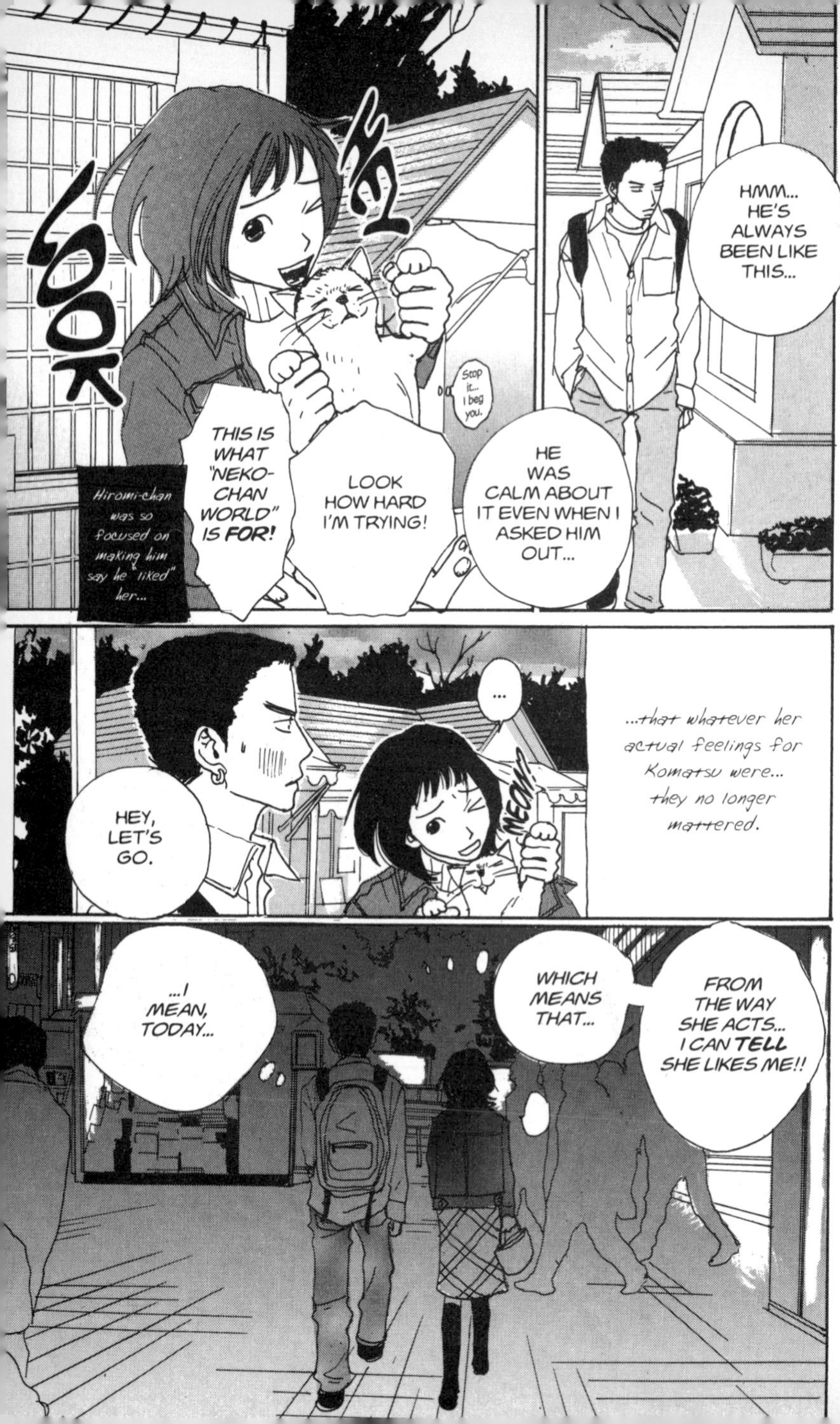
HMM... HE'S ALWAYS BEEN LIKE THIS...
HE WAS CALM ABOUT IT EVEN WHEN I ASKED HIM OUT...
HEY!
LOOK
Stop it... I beg you.
LOOK HOW HARD I'M TRYING!
THIS IS WHAT "NEKO-CHAN WORLD" IS FOR!
Hiromi-chan was so focused on making him say he "liked" her...
...that whatever her actual feelings for Komatsu were... they no longer mattered.
...
MEOW!
HEY, LET'S GO.
FROM THE WAY SHE ACTS... I CAN TELL SHE LIKES ME!!
WHICH MEANS THAT...
...I MEAN, TODAY...

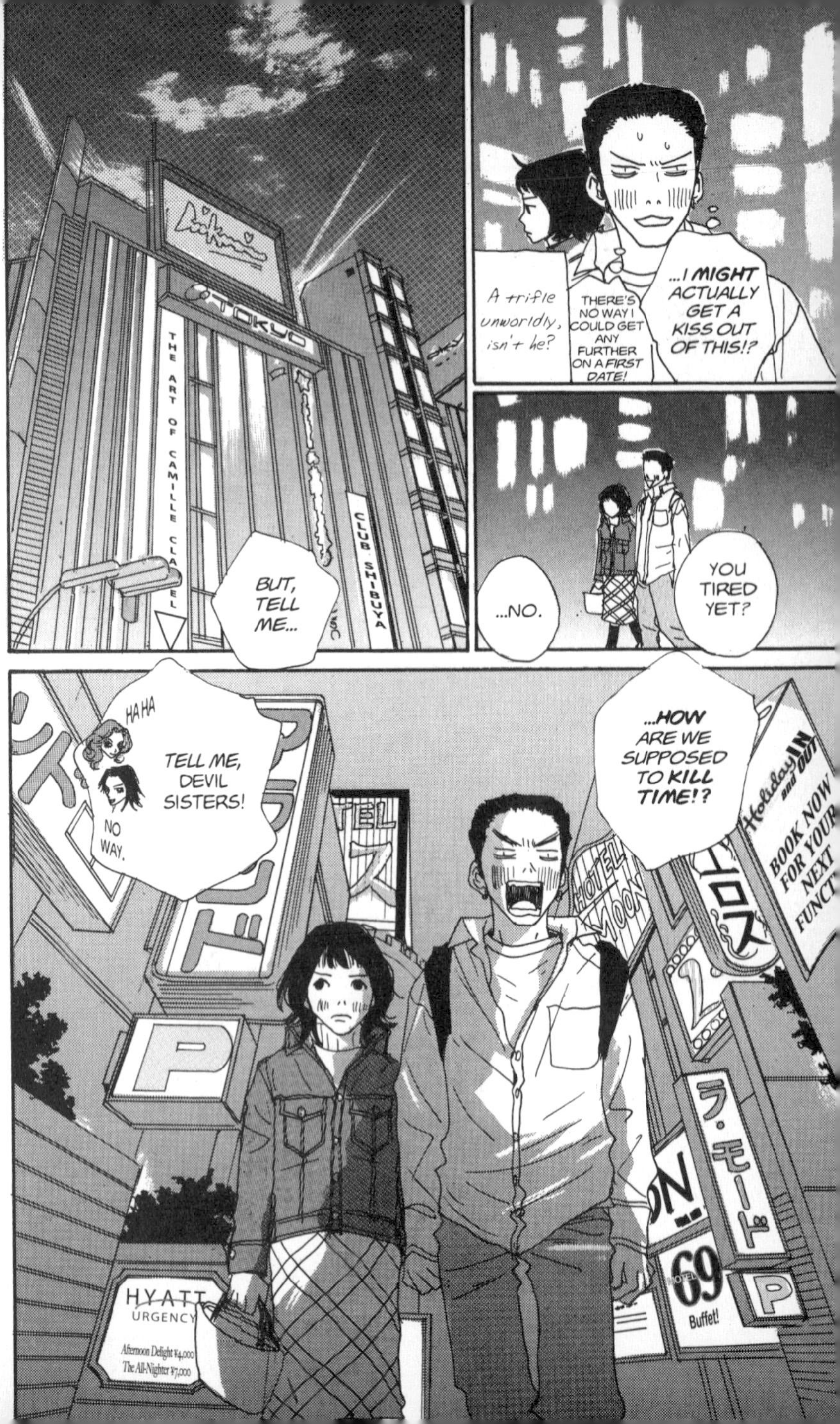
...I MIGHT ACTUALLY GET A KISS OUT OF THIS!?
THERE'S NO WAY I COULD GET ANY FURTHER ON A FIRST DATE!
A trifle unworldly, isn't he?
YOU TIRED YET?
...NO.
TOKYO
THE ART OF CAMILLE CLA EL
CLUB SHIBUYA
BUT, TELL ME...
...HOW ARE WE SUPPOSED TO KILL TIME!?
Holiday IN and OUT
BOOK NOW FOR YOUR NEXT FUNCT
HOTEL MOON
エロス
ラ・モード
HOTEL 69
Buffet!
TELL ME, DEVIL SISTERS!
HA HA
NO WAY.
HYATT URGENCY
Afternoon Delight ¥4,000
The All-Nighter ¥7,000

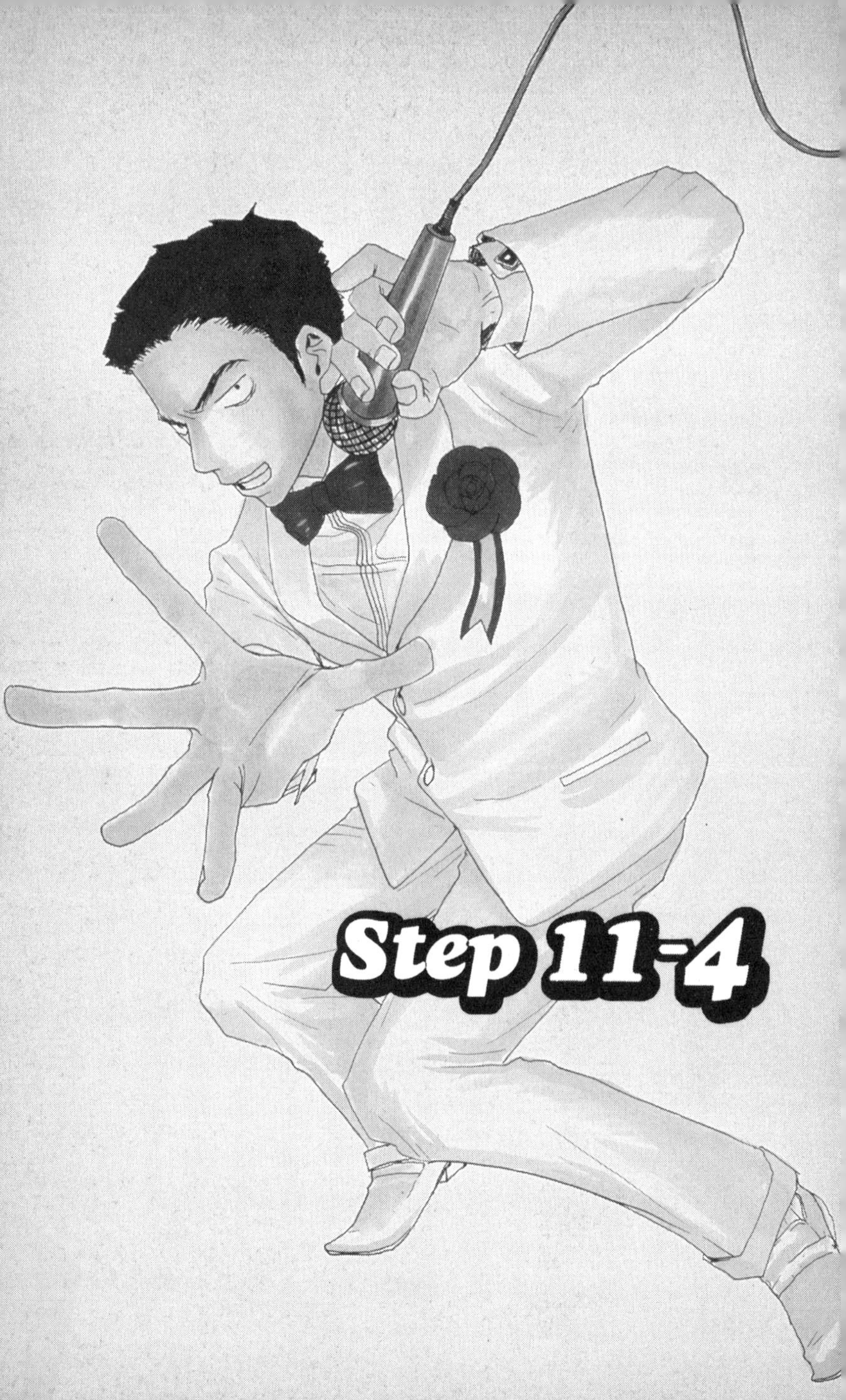
Step 11-4

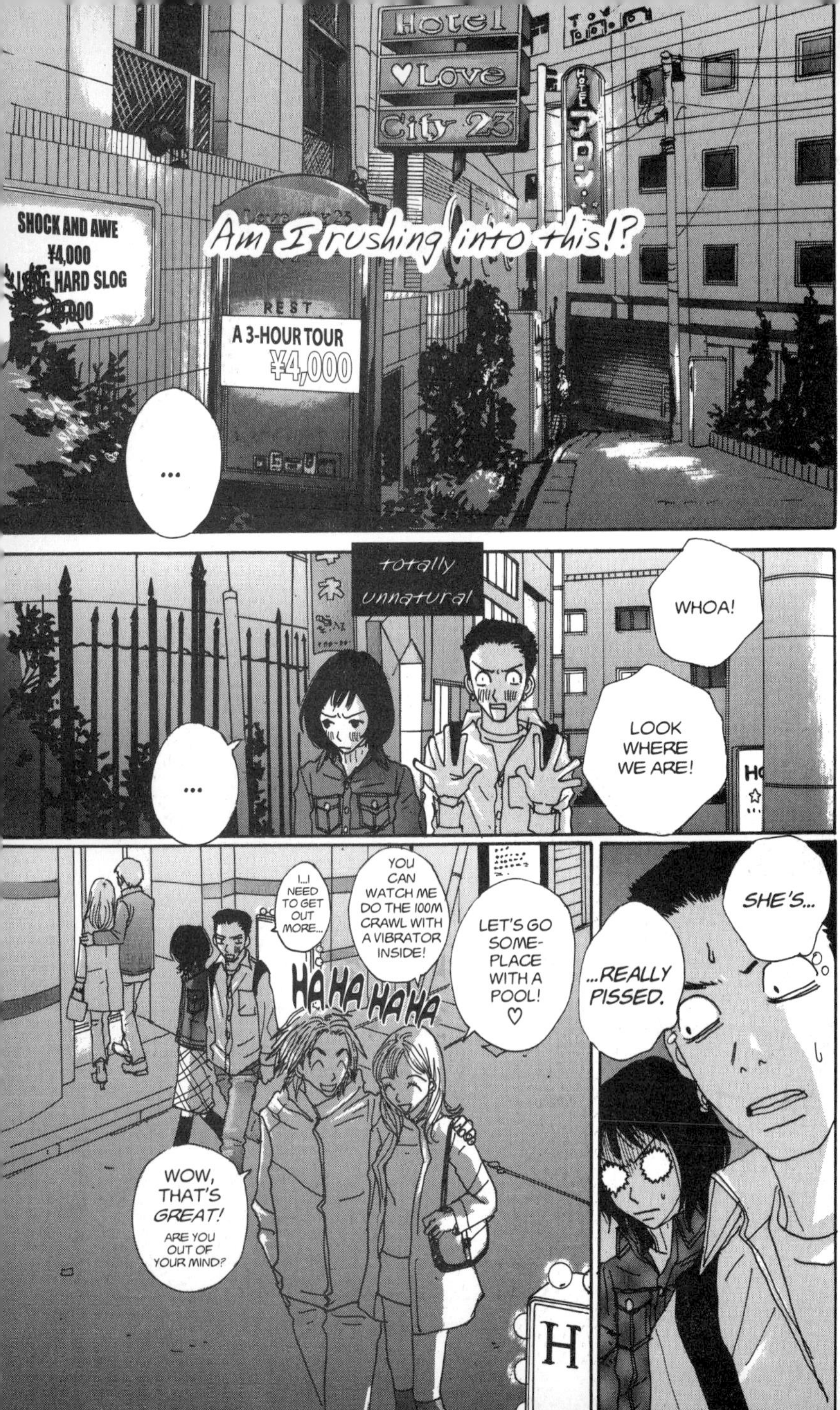
Hotel
♥Love
City 23
Am I rushing into this!?
SHOCK AND AWE
¥4,000
HARD SLOG
REST
A 3-HOUR TOUR
¥4,000
...
WHOA!
LOOK WHERE WE ARE!
totally unnatural
...
SHE'S...
...REALLY PISSED.
LET'S GO SOME-PLACE WITH A POOL! ♡
YOU CAN WATCH ME DO THE 100M CRAWL WITH A VIBRATOR INSIDE!
HA HA HA HA
I...I NEED TO GET OUT MORE...
WOW, THAT'S GREAT!
ARE YOU OUT OF YOUR MIND?
H

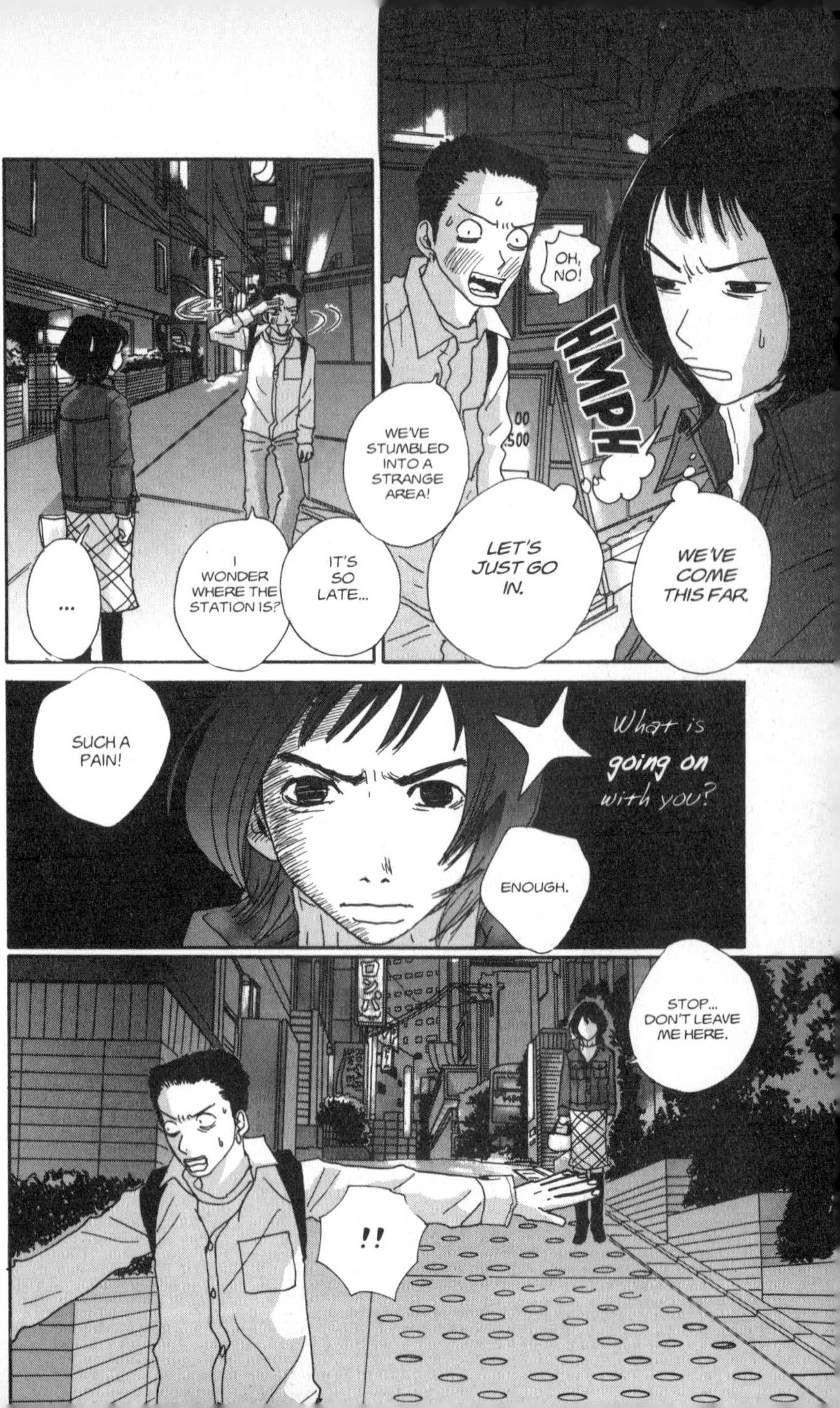
OH, NO!
HMPH
WE'VE COME THIS FAR.
LET'S JUST GO IN.
WE'VE STUMBLED INTO A STRANGE AREA!
IT'S SO LATE...
I WONDER WHERE THE STATION IS?
...
What is going on with you?
SUCH A PAIN!
ENOUGH.
STOP... DON'T LEAVE ME HERE.
!!

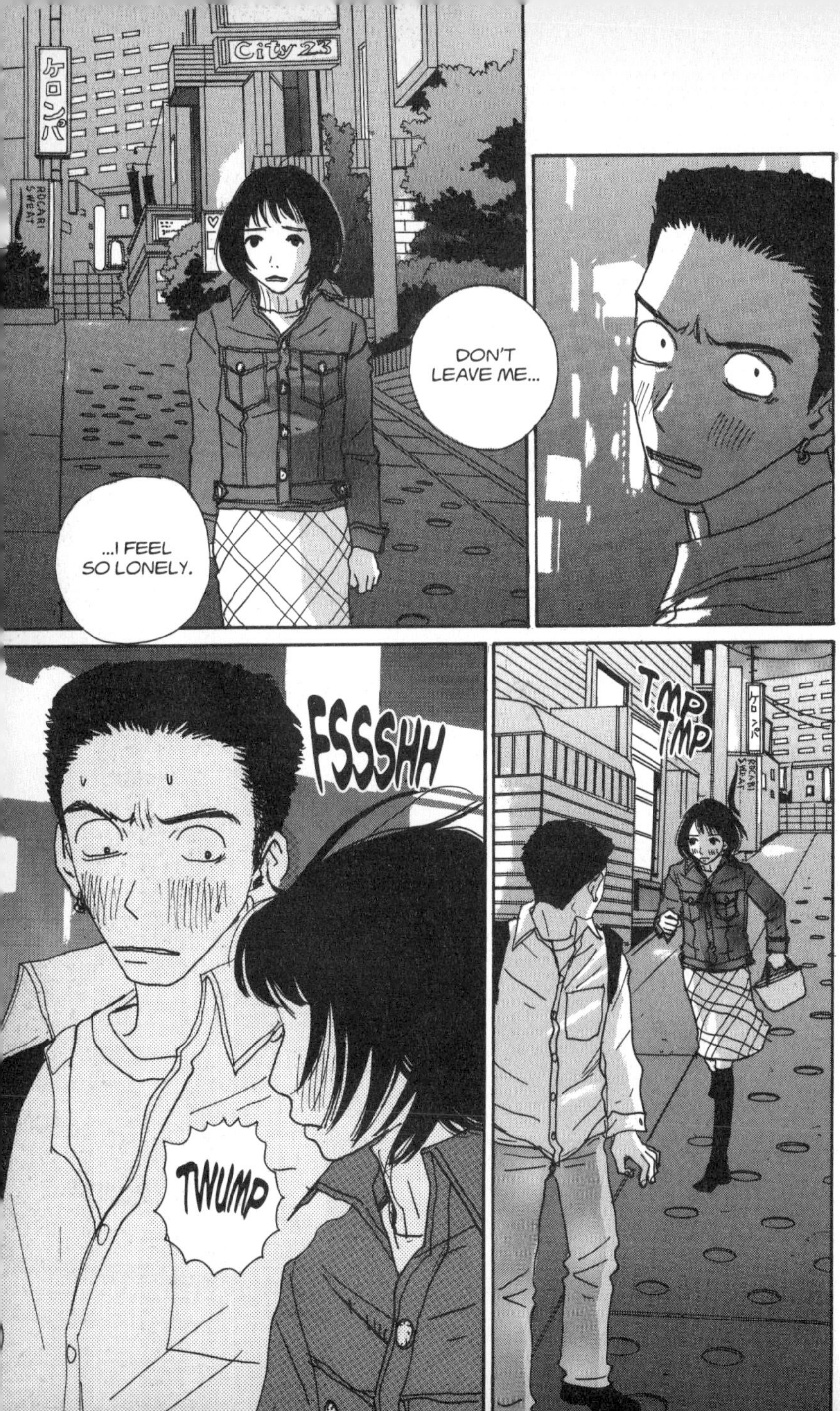
City 23
ケロンパ
DON'T LEAVE ME...
...I FEEL SO LONELY.
TMP TMP
FSSSHH
TWUMP

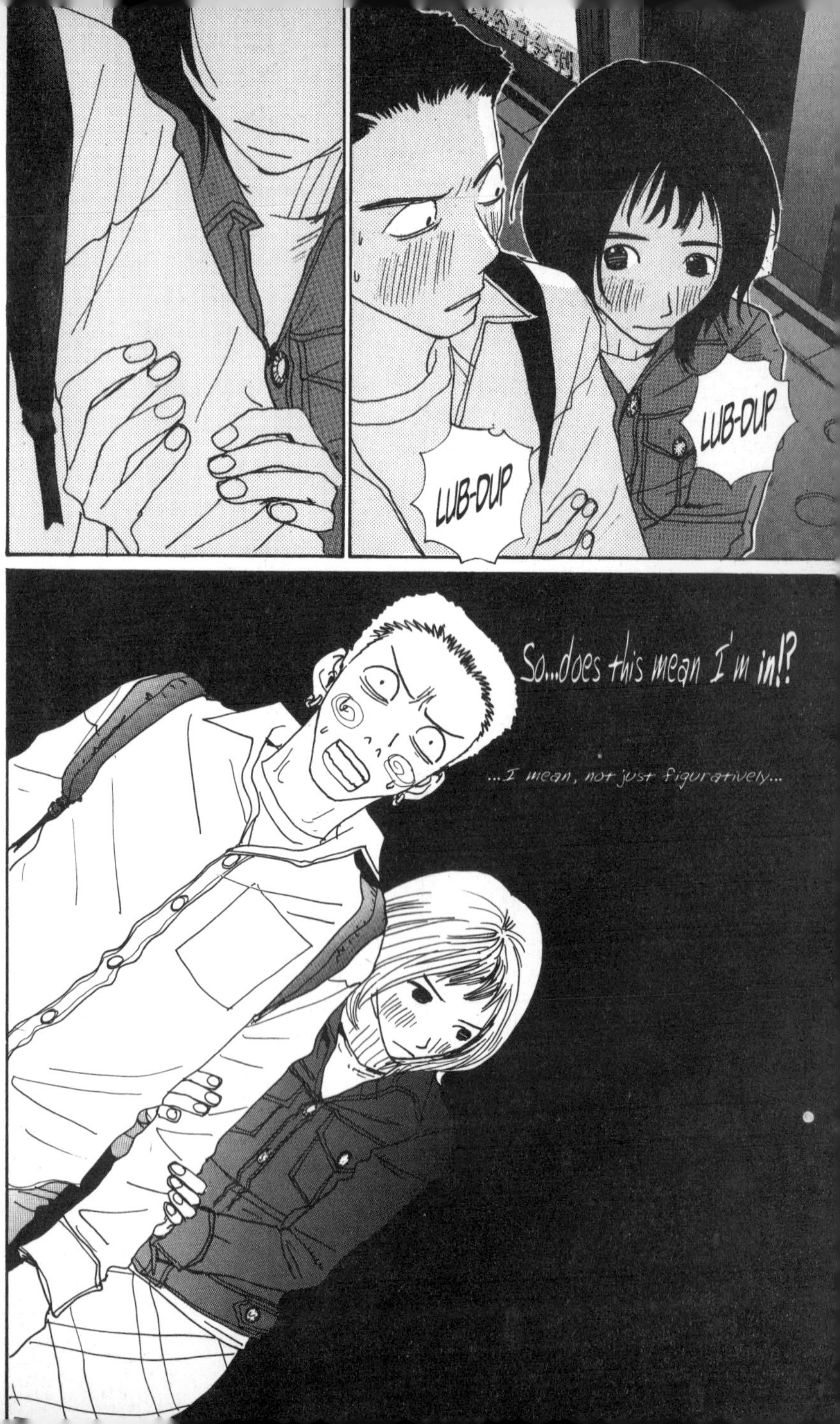
LUB-DUP
LUB-DUP
So...does this mean I'm in!?
...I mean, not just figuratively...

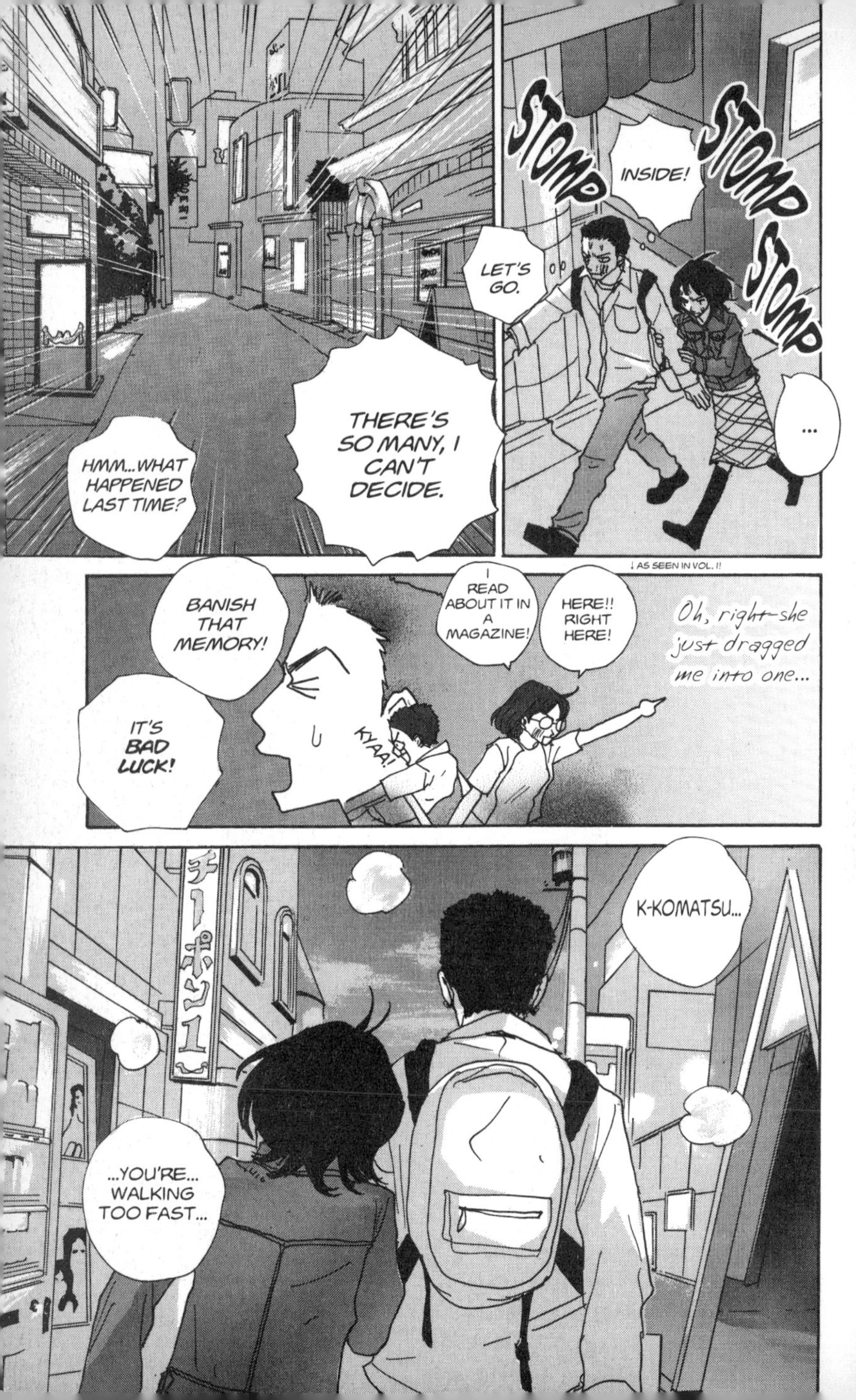
STOMP STOMP
INSIDE!
STOMP
LET'S GO.
...
THERE'S SO MANY, I CAN'T DECIDE.
HMM...WHAT HAPPENED LAST TIME?
↓ AS SEEN IN VOL. 1!
Oh, right—she just dragged me into one...
HERE!! RIGHT HERE!
I READ ABOUT IT IN A MAGAZINE!
KYAA!
BANISH THAT MEMORY!
IT'S BAD LUCK!
K-KOMATSU...
...YOU'RE... WALKING TOO FAST...

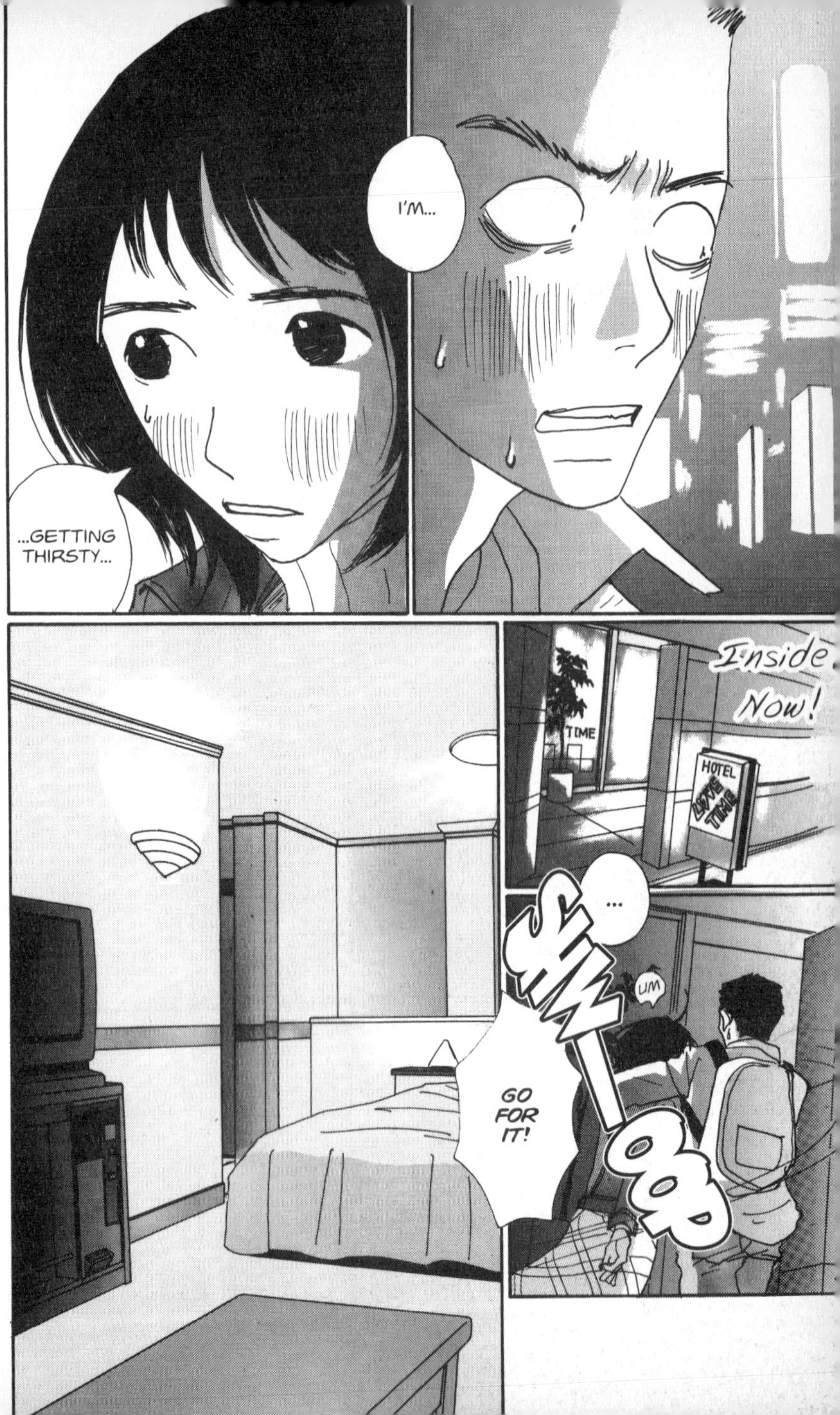
I'M...
...GETTING THIRSTY...
Inside Now!
HOTEL
TIME
...
UM
SHWOOP
GO FOR IT!

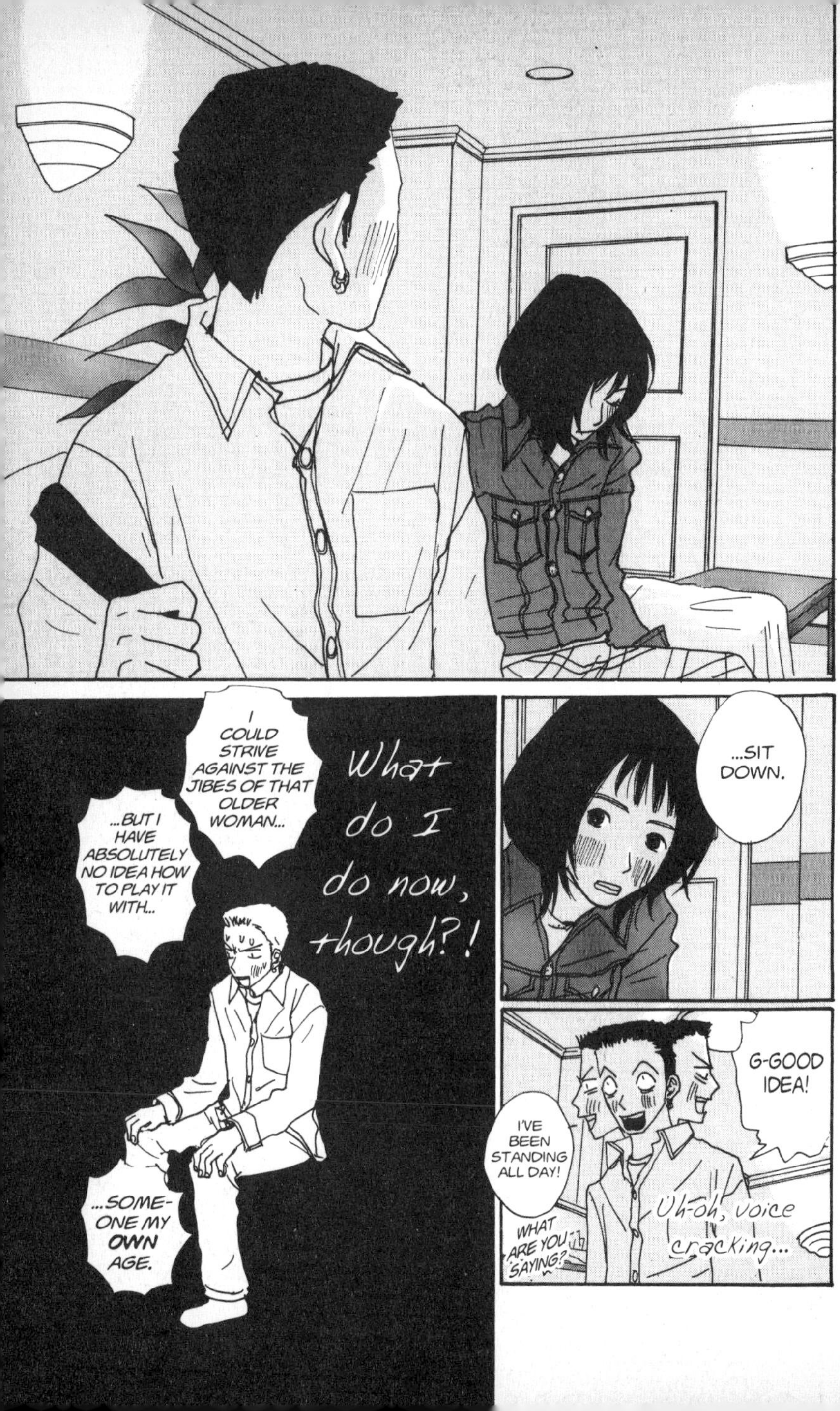
...SIT DOWN.
G-GOOD IDEA!
I'VE BEEN STANDING ALL DAY!
Uh-oh, voice cracking...
WHAT ARE YOU SAYING?
What do I do now, though?!
I COULD STRIVE AGAINST THE JIBES OF THAT OLDER WOMAN...
...BUT I HAVE ABSOLUTELY NO IDEA HOW TO PLAY IT WITH...
...SOME-ONE MY **OWN** AGE.

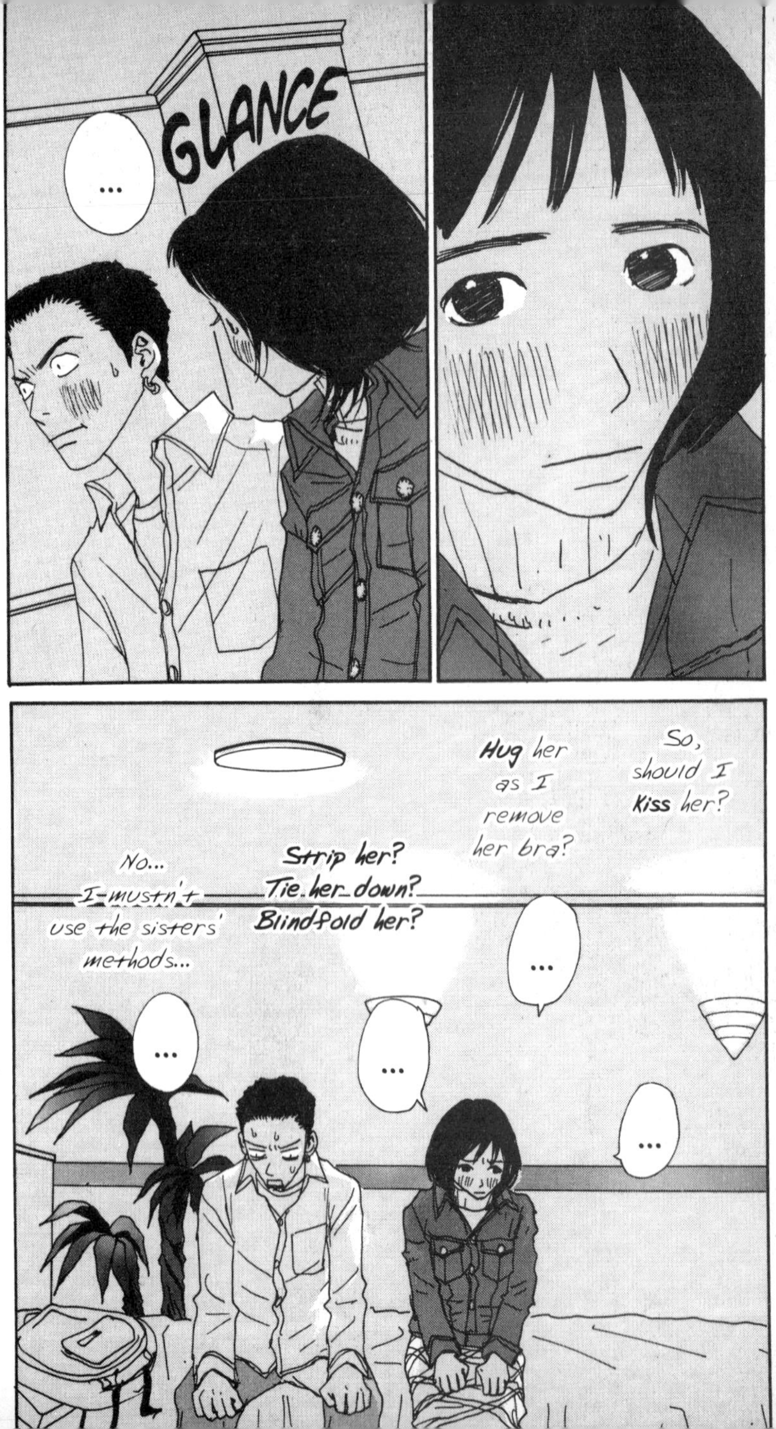
GLANCE
...
So, should I kiss her?
Hug her as I remove her bra?
Strip her? Tie her down? Blindfold her?
No... I mustn't use the sisters' methods...
...
...
...
...

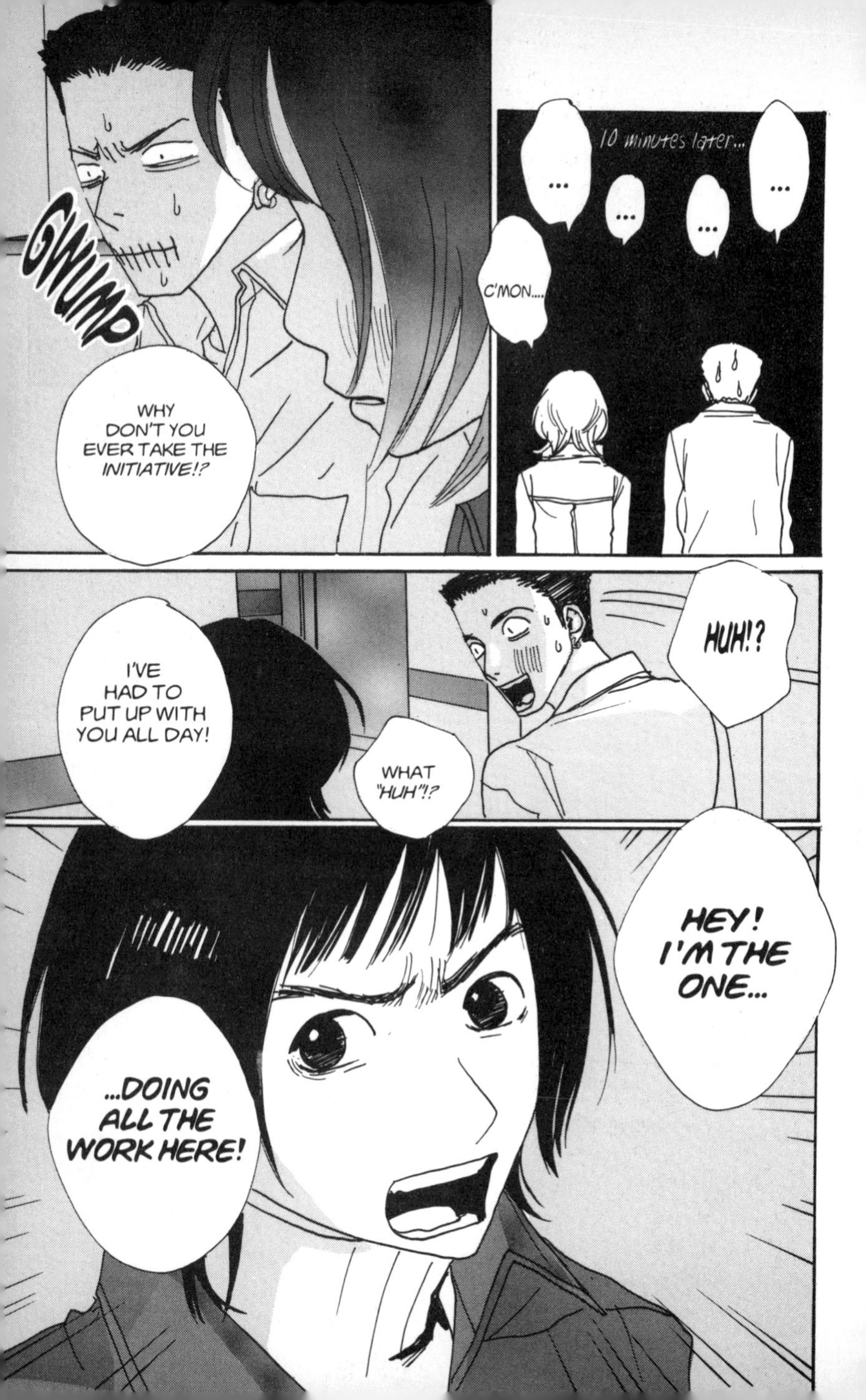
10 minutes later...
...
...
...
...
C'MON....
GWUMP
WHY DON'T YOU EVER TAKE THE INITIATIVE!?
HUH!?
I'VE HAD TO PUT UP WITH YOU ALL DAY!
WHAT "HUH"!?
HEY! I'M THE ONE...
...DOING ALL THE WORK HERE!

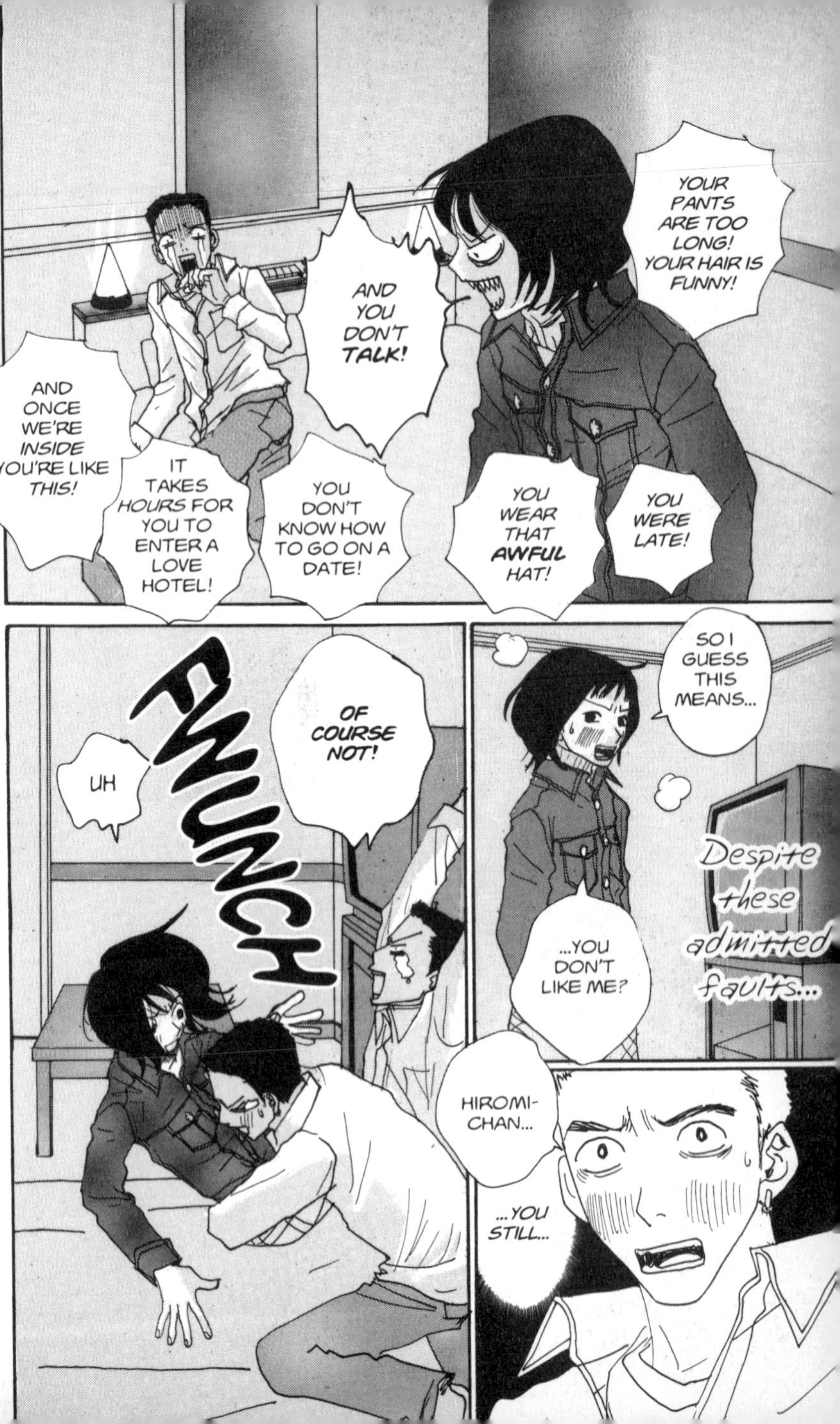
YOUR PANTS ARE TOO LONG! YOUR HAIR IS FUNNY!
AND YOU DON'T TALK!
YOU WERE LATE!
YOU WEAR THAT AWFUL HAT!
YOU DON'T KNOW HOW TO GO ON A DATE!
IT TAKES HOURS FOR YOU TO ENTER A LOVE HOTEL!
AND ONCE WE'RE INSIDE YOU'RE LIKE THIS!
SO I GUESS THIS MEANS...
...YOU DON'T LIKE ME?
Despite these admitted faults...
HIROMI-CHAN...
...YOU STILL...
OF COURSE NOT!
FWUNCH
UH

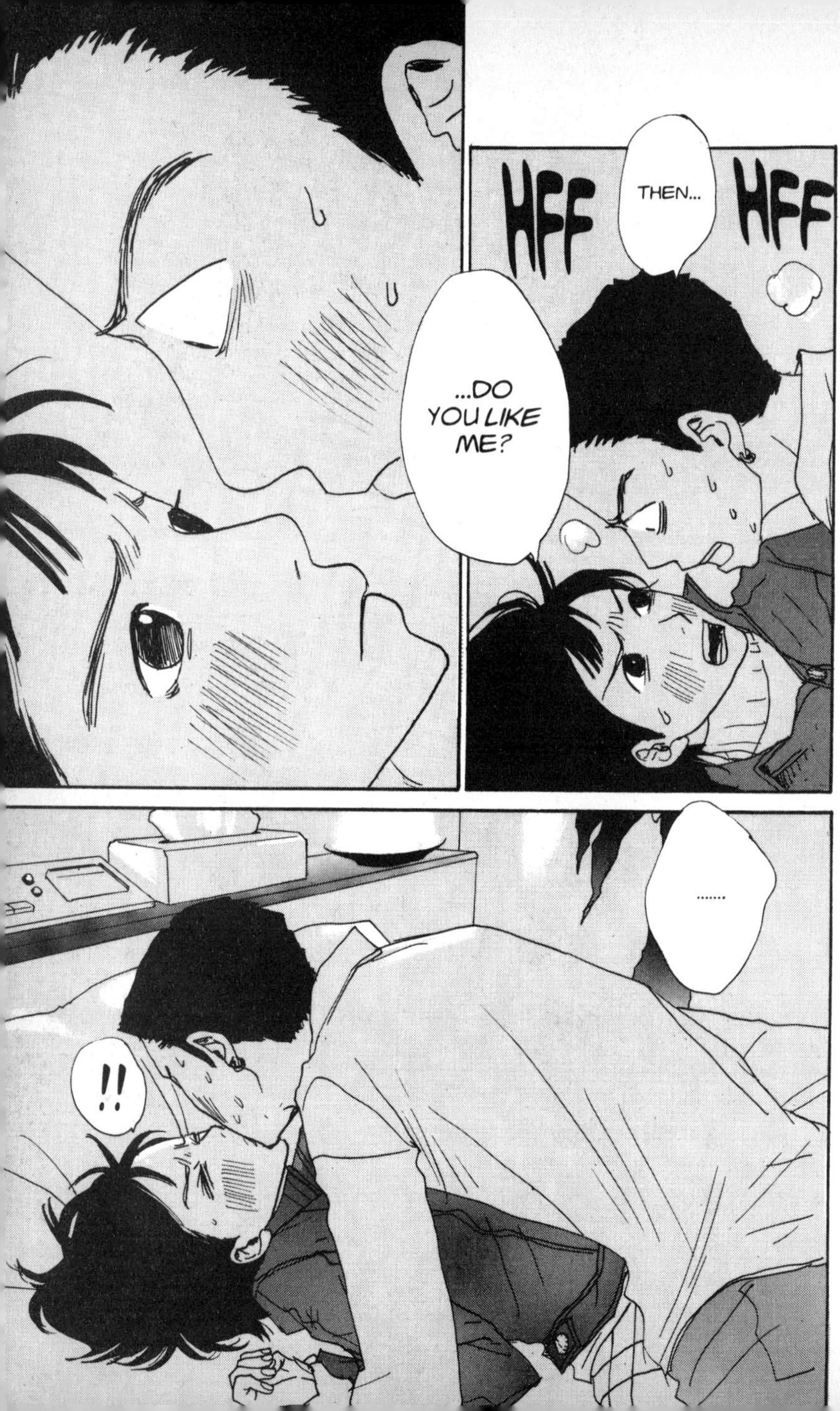
HFF
THEN...
HFF
...DO YOU LIKE ME?
....
!!

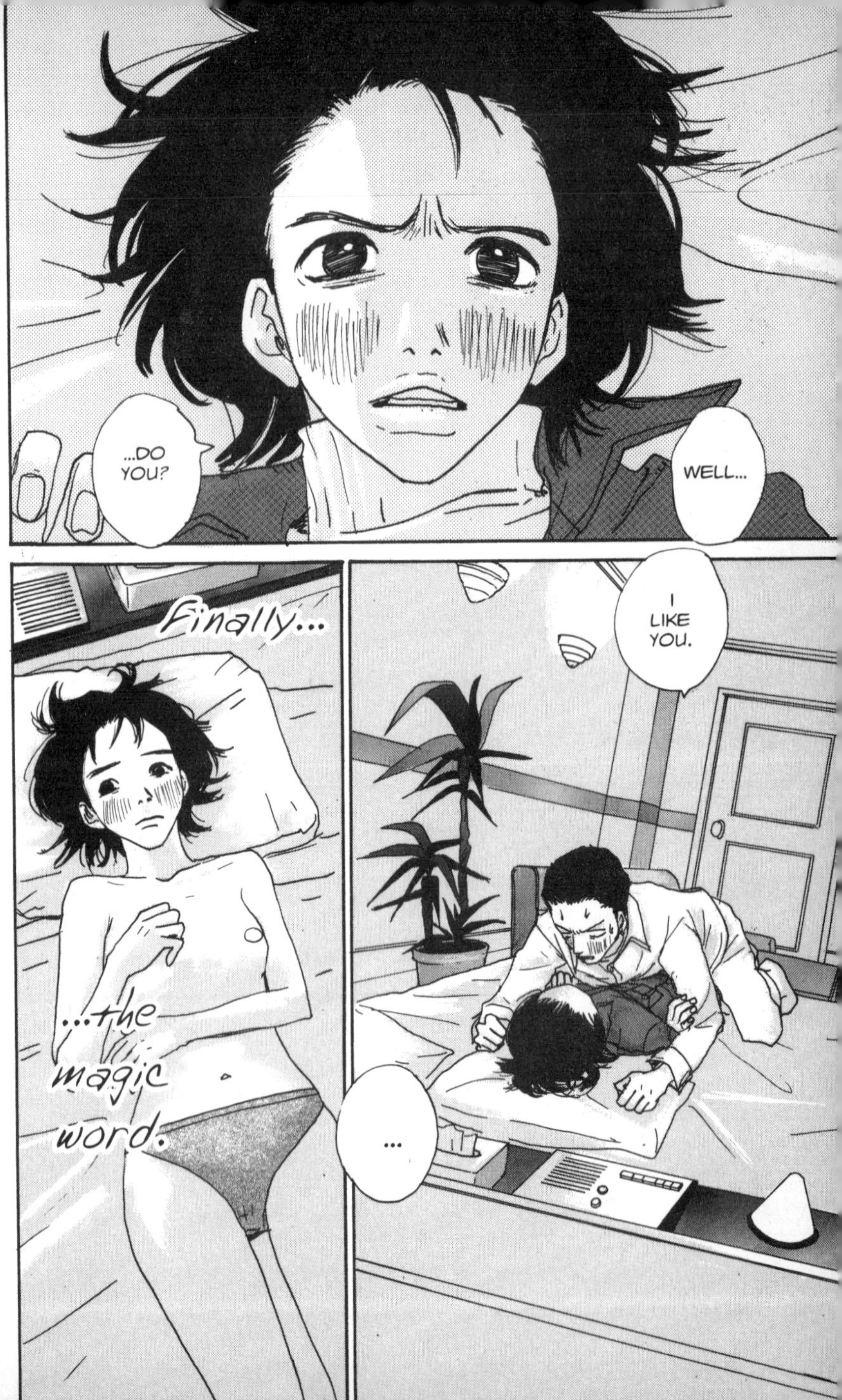
WELL...
...DO YOU?
I LIKE YOU.
...
Finally...
...the magic word.

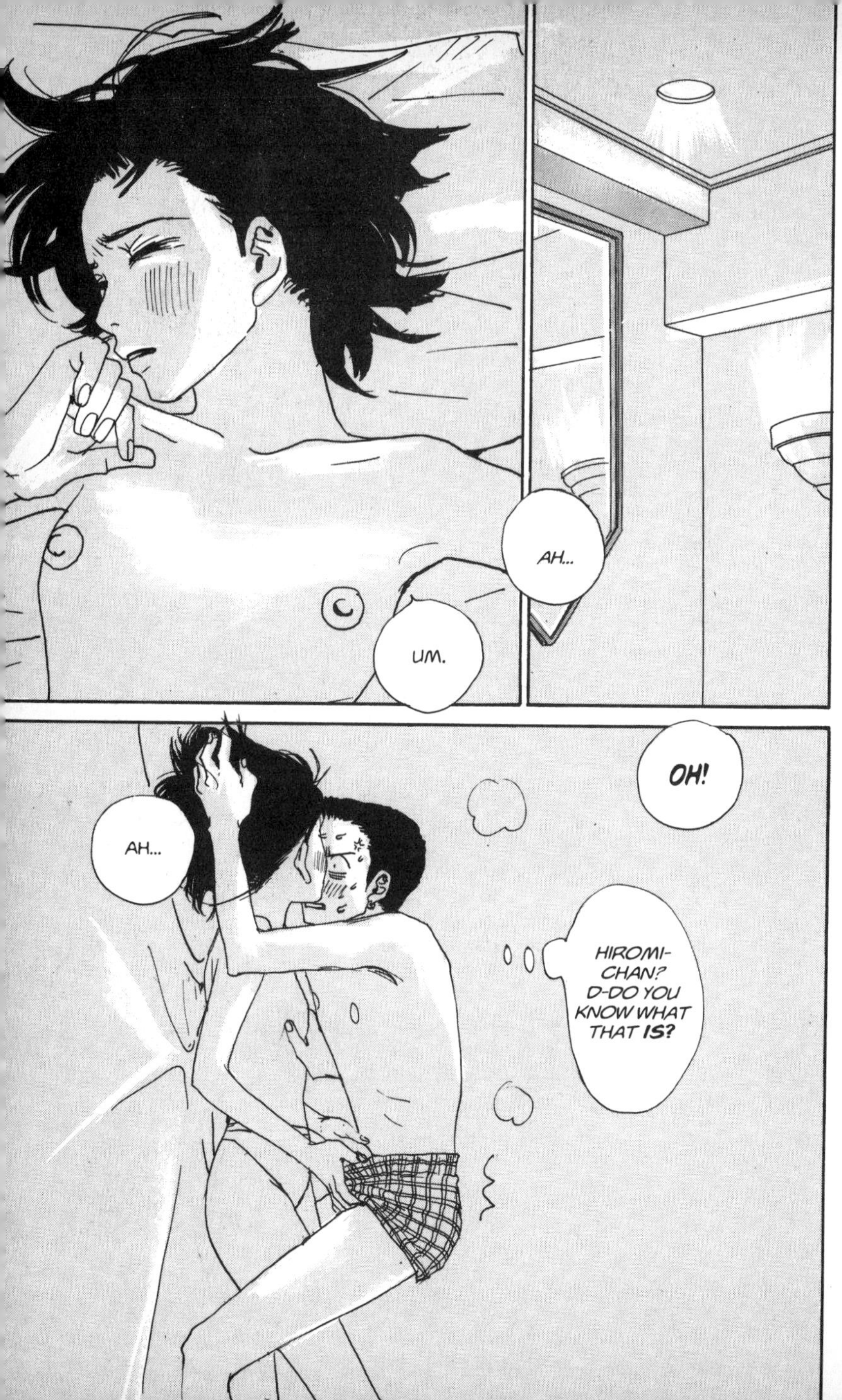
AH...
UM.
OH!
AH...
HIROMI-CHAN? D-DO YOU KNOW WHAT THAT **IS**?

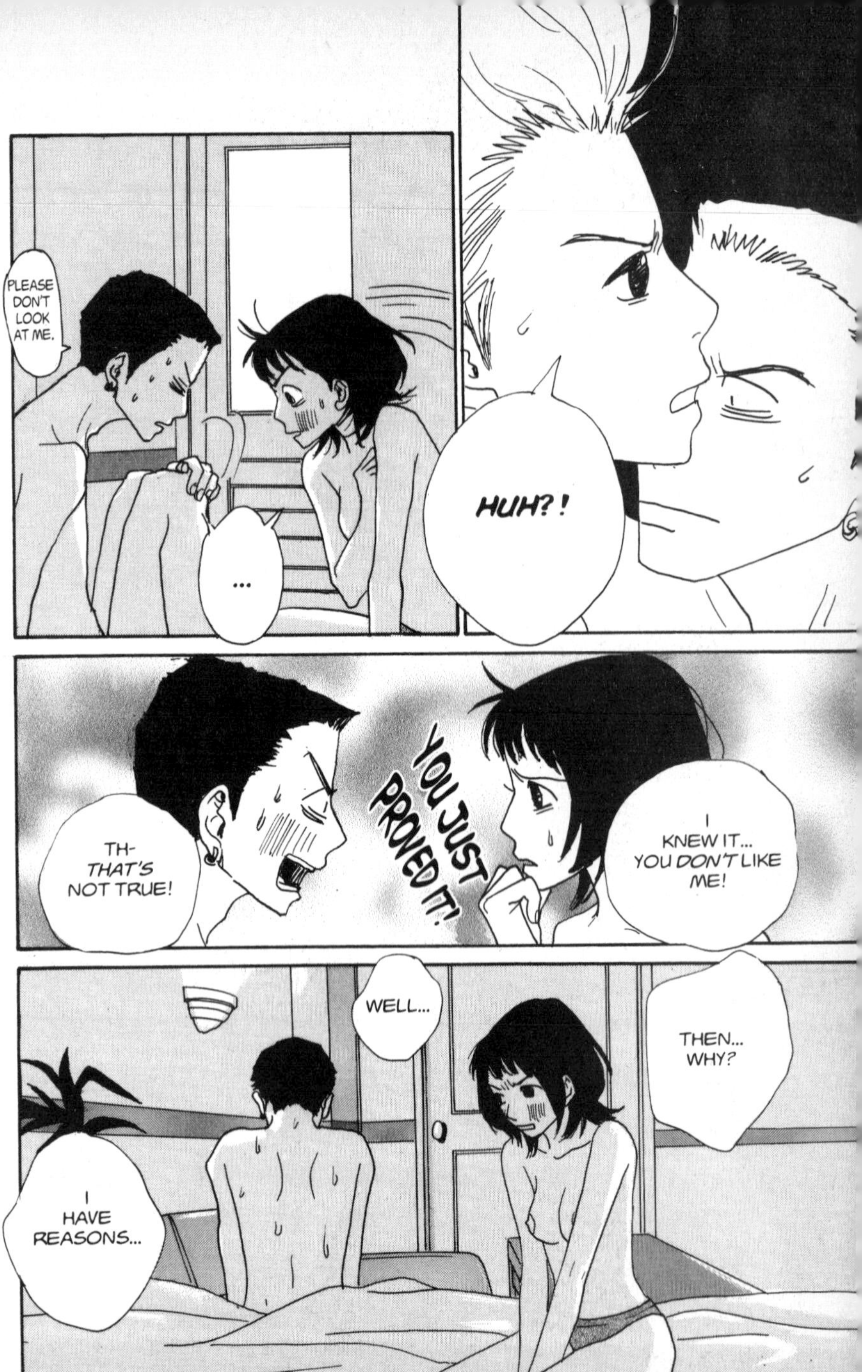
HUH?!
PLEASE DON'T LOOK AT ME.
...
I KNEW IT... YOU *DON'T* LIKE ME!
TH- *THAT'S* NOT TRUE!
YOU JUST PROVED IT!
THEN... WHY?
WELL...
I HAVE REASONS...

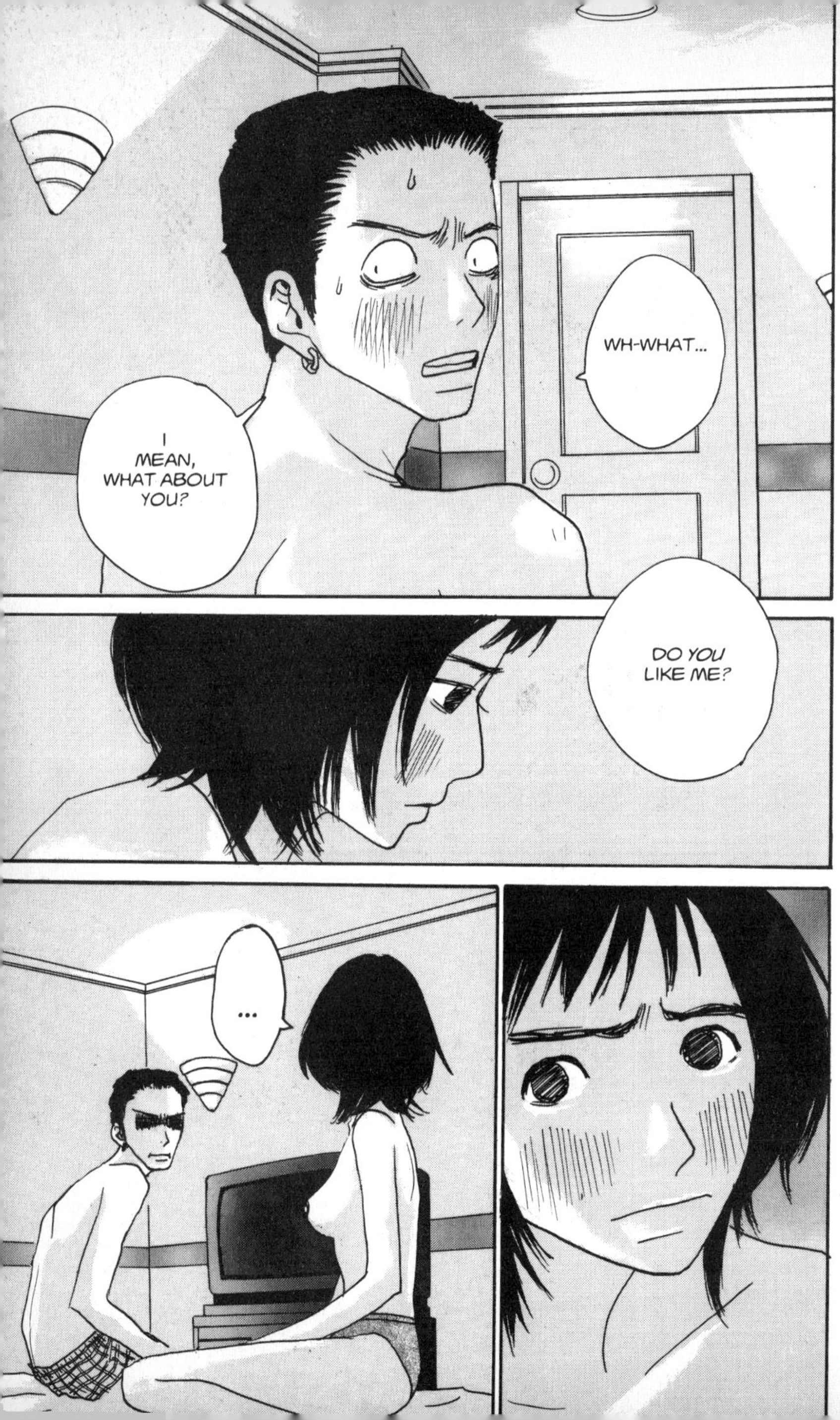
WH-WHAT...
I MEAN, WHAT ABOUT YOU?
DO YOU LIKE ME?
...

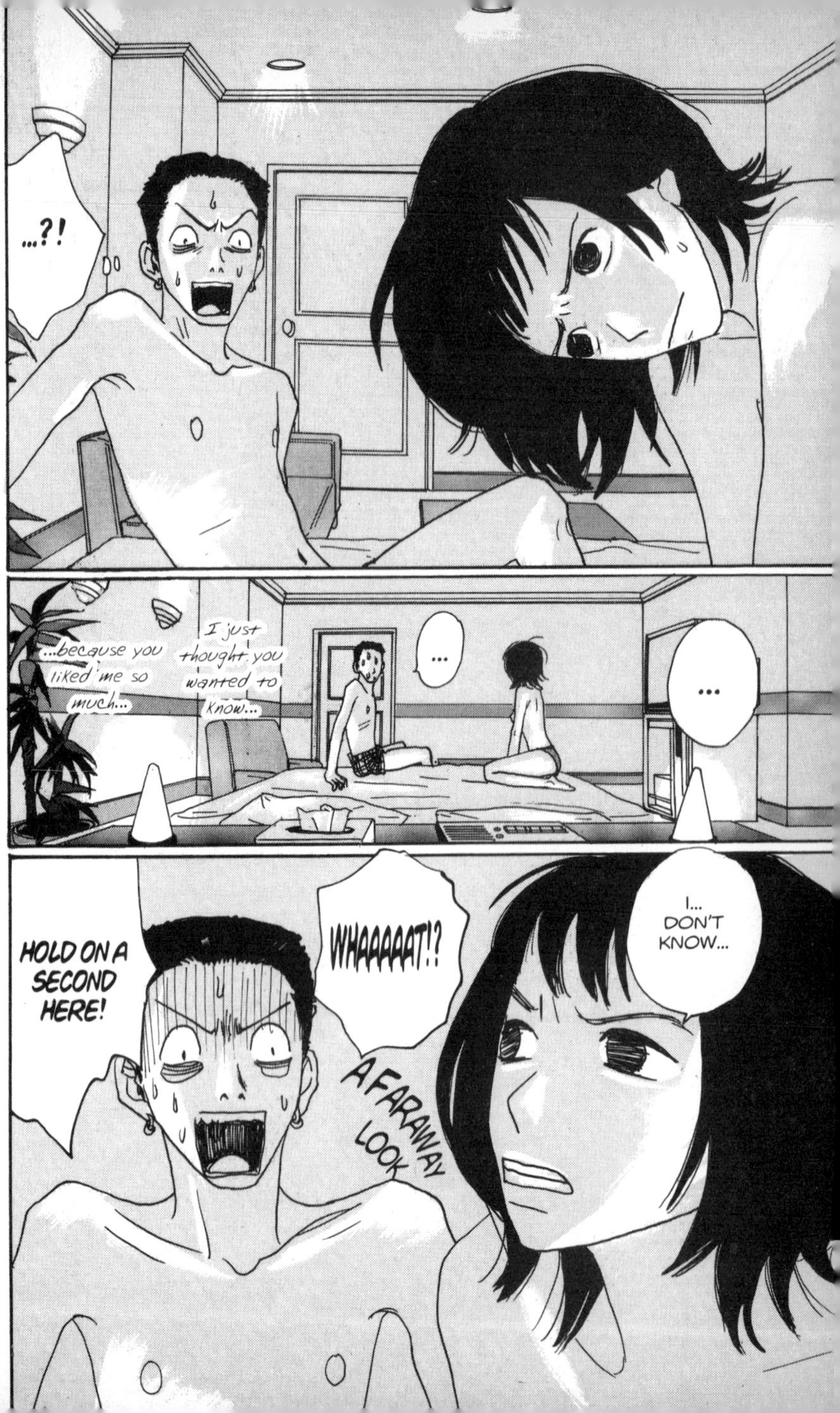
...?!
...
...
I just thought you wanted to know...
...because you liked me so much...
I... DON'T KNOW...
A FARAWAY LOOK
WHAAAAAT!?
HOLD ON A SECOND HERE!

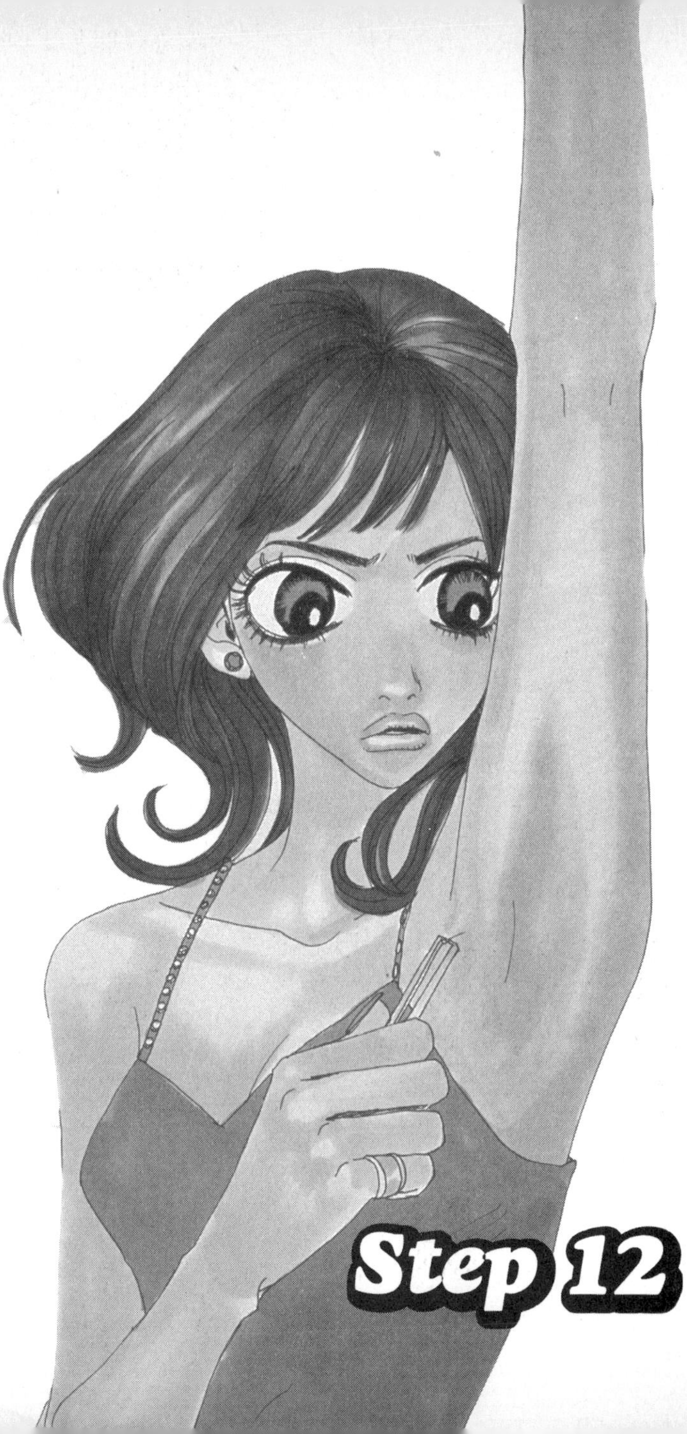
Step 12

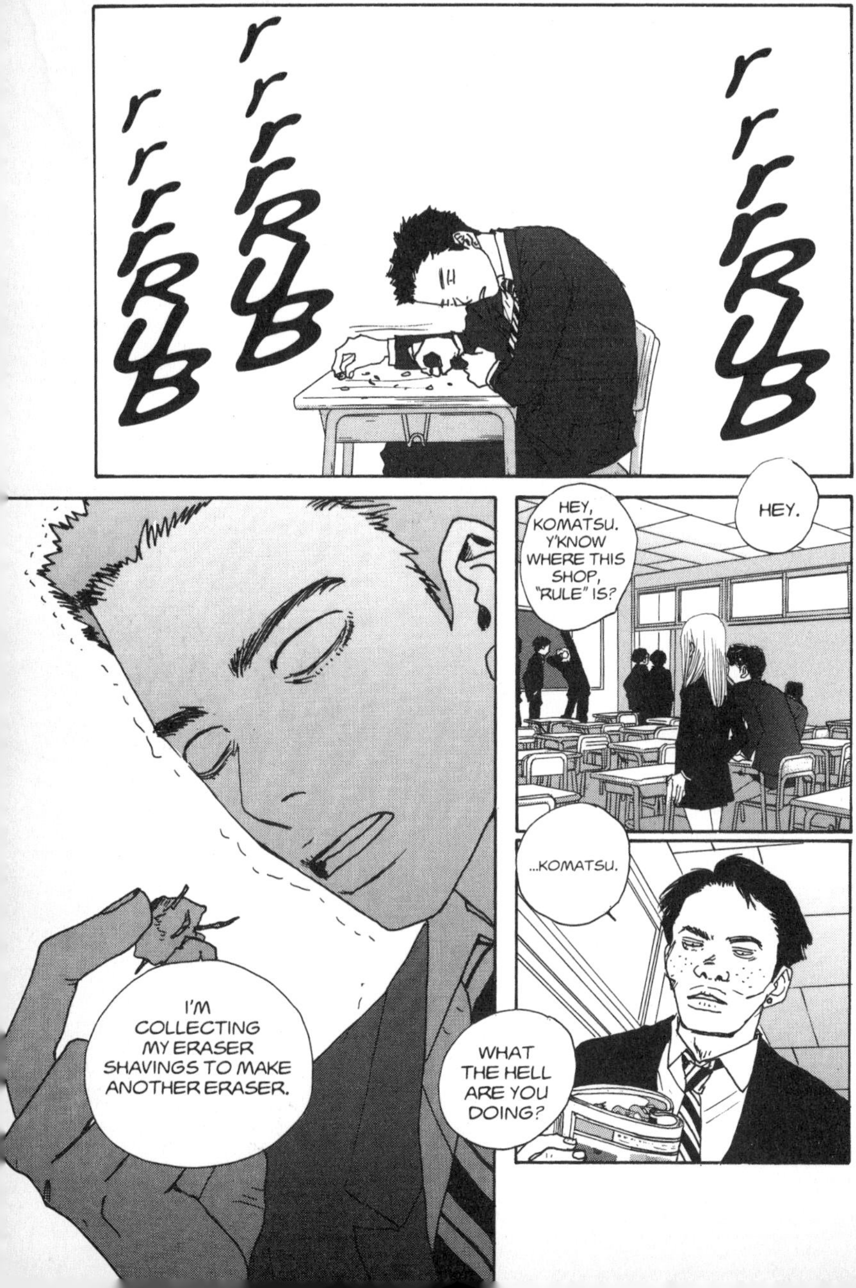
rrrrRUB
rrrRUB
rrrrRUB
HEY.
HEY, KOMATSU. Y'KNOW WHERE THIS SHOP, "RULE" IS?
...KOMATSU.
WHAT THE HELL ARE YOU DOING?
I'M COLLECTING MY ERASER SHAVINGS TO MAKE ANOTHER ERASER.

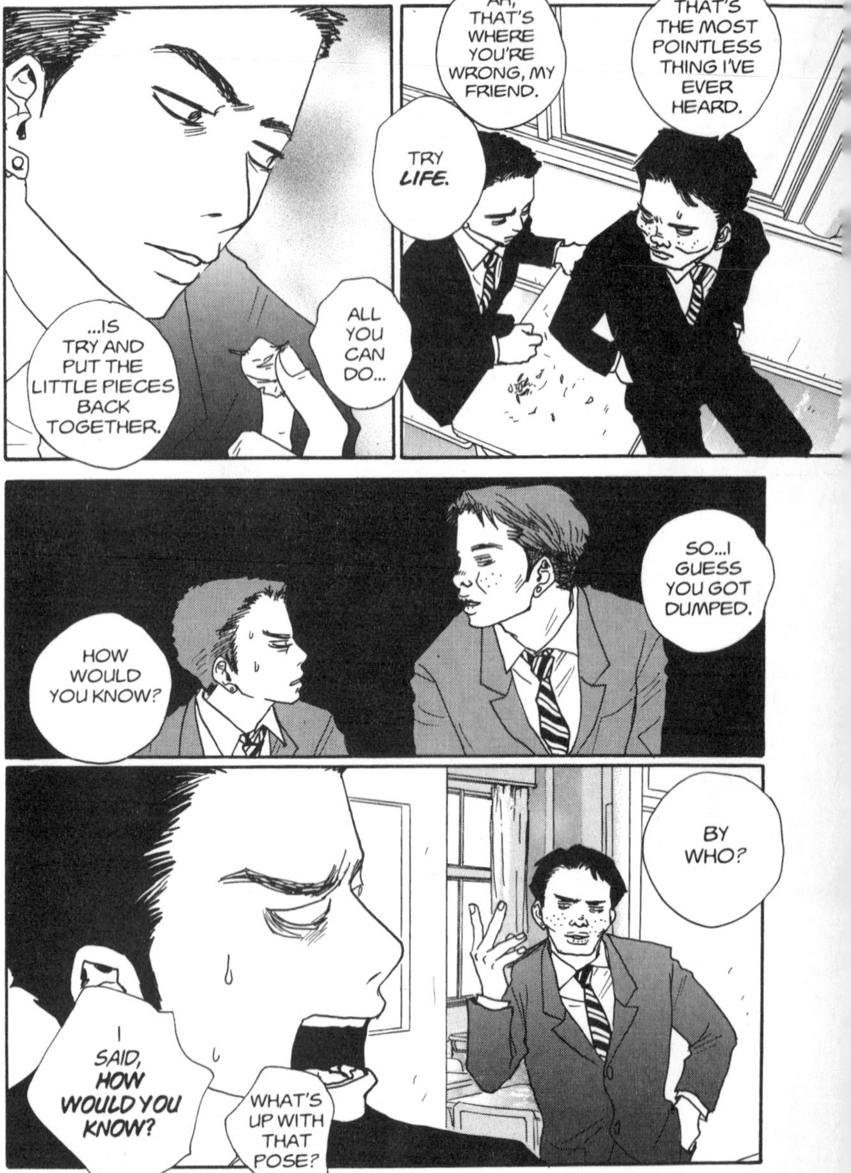
THAT'S THE MOST POINTLESS THING I'VE EVER HEARD.
AH, THAT'S WHERE YOU'RE WRONG, MY FRIEND.
TRY *LIFE*.
ALL YOU CAN DO...
...IS TRY AND PUT THE LITTLE PIECES BACK TOGETHER.
SO...I GUESS YOU GOT DUMPED.
HOW WOULD YOU KNOW?
BY WHO?
I SAID, ***HOW WOULD YOU KNOW?***
WHAT'S UP WITH THAT POSE?

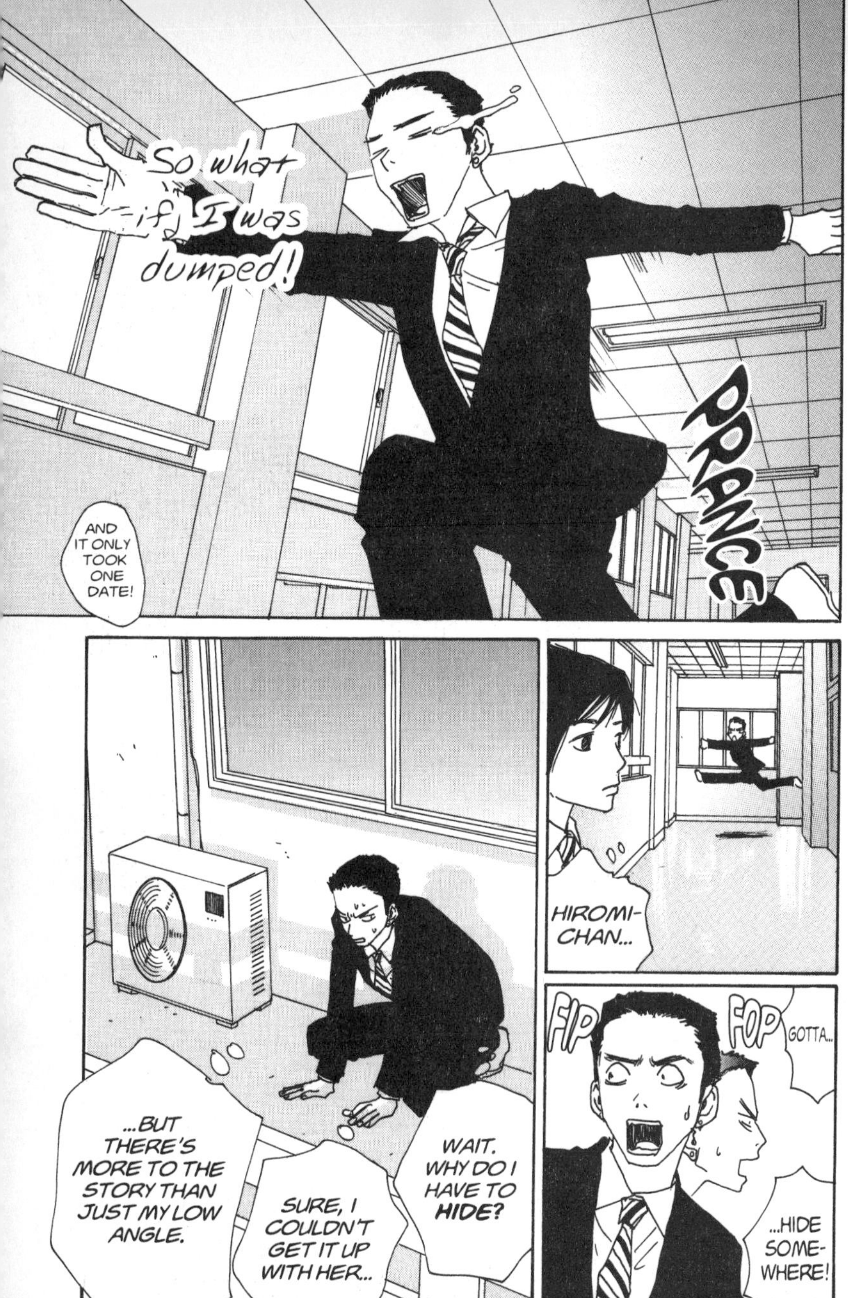
PRANCE
So what if I was dumped!
AND IT ONLY TOOK ONE DATE!
HIROMI-CHAN...
FOP
GOTTA...
FIP
...HIDE SOME-WHERE!
WAIT. WHY DO I HAVE TO HIDE?
SURE, I COULDN'T GET IT UP WITH HER...
...BUT THERE'S MORE TO THE STORY THAN JUST MY LOW ANGLE.

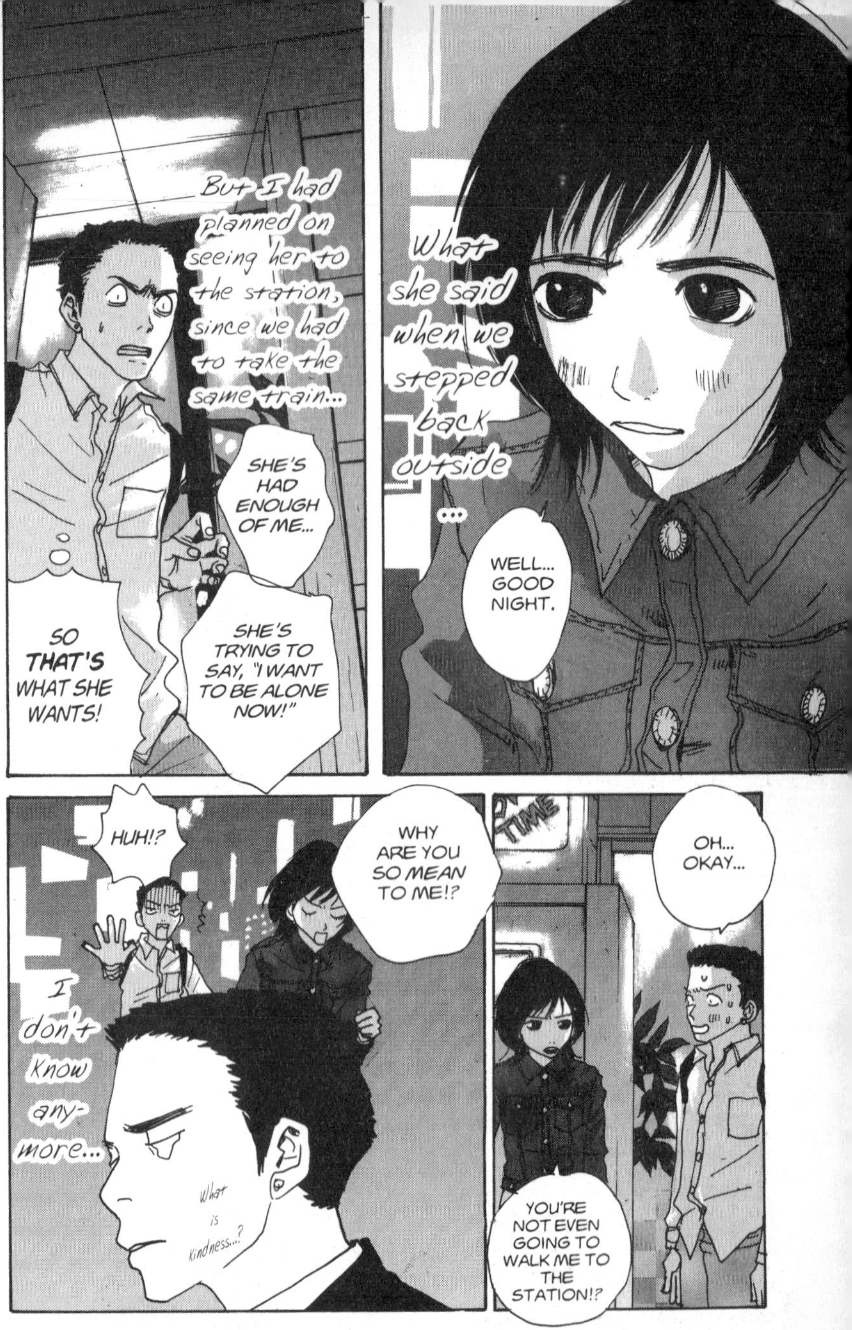
What she said when we stepped back outside...
WELL... GOOD NIGHT.
But I had planned on seeing her to the station, since we had to take the same train...
SHE'S HAD ENOUGH OF ME...
SHE'S TRYING TO SAY, "I WANT TO BE ALONE NOW!"
SO THAT'S WHAT SHE WANTS!
TIME
OH... OKAY...
YOU'RE NOT EVEN GOING TO WALK ME TO THE STATION!?
WHY ARE YOU SO MEAN TO ME!?
HUH!?
I don't know any-more...
What is kindness...?

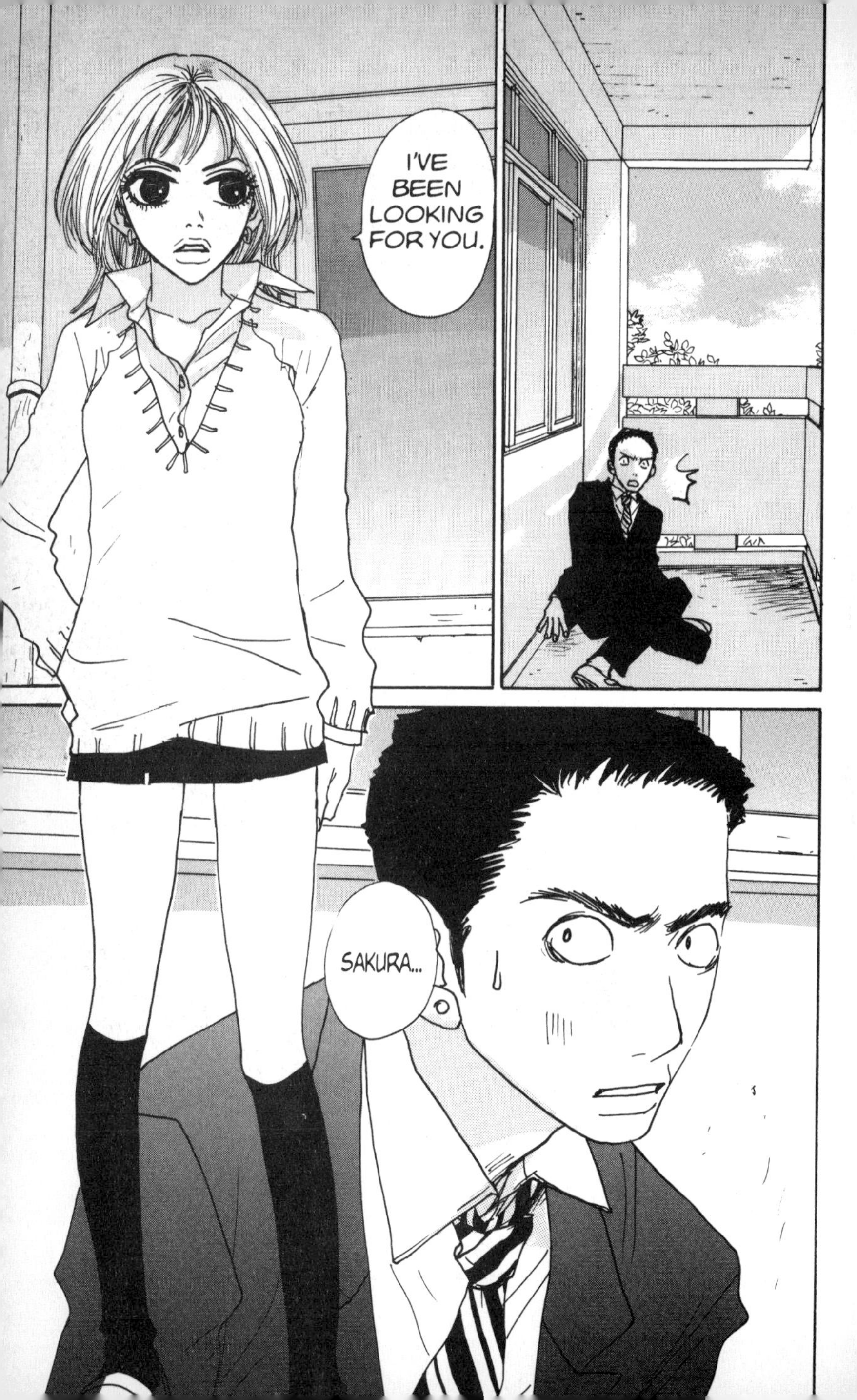
I'VE BEEN LOOKING FOR YOU.
SAKURA...

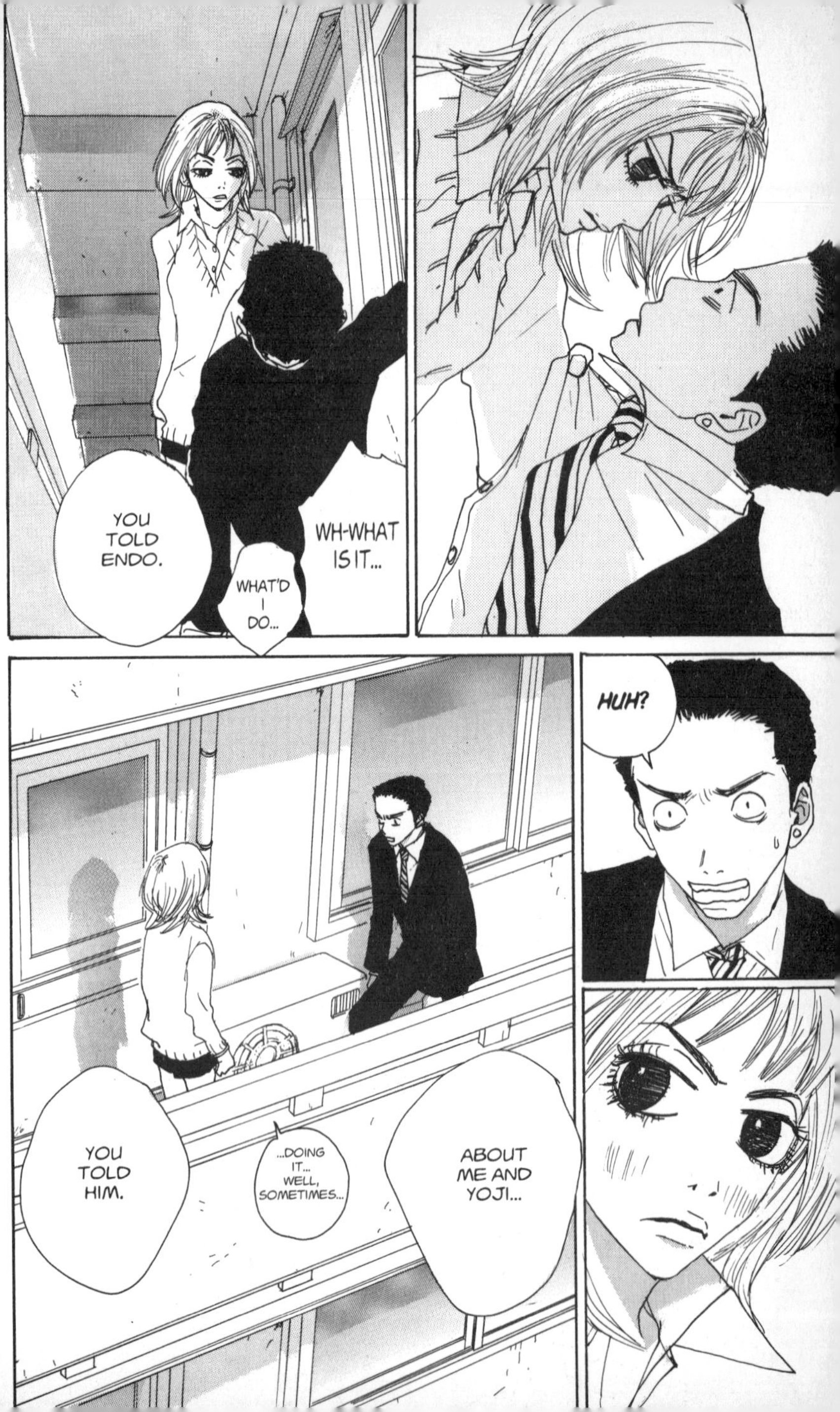
WH-WHAT IS IT...
YOU TOLD ENDO.
WHAT'D I DO...
HUH?
ABOUT ME AND YOJI...
...DOING IT... WELL, SOMETIMES...
YOU TOLD HIM.

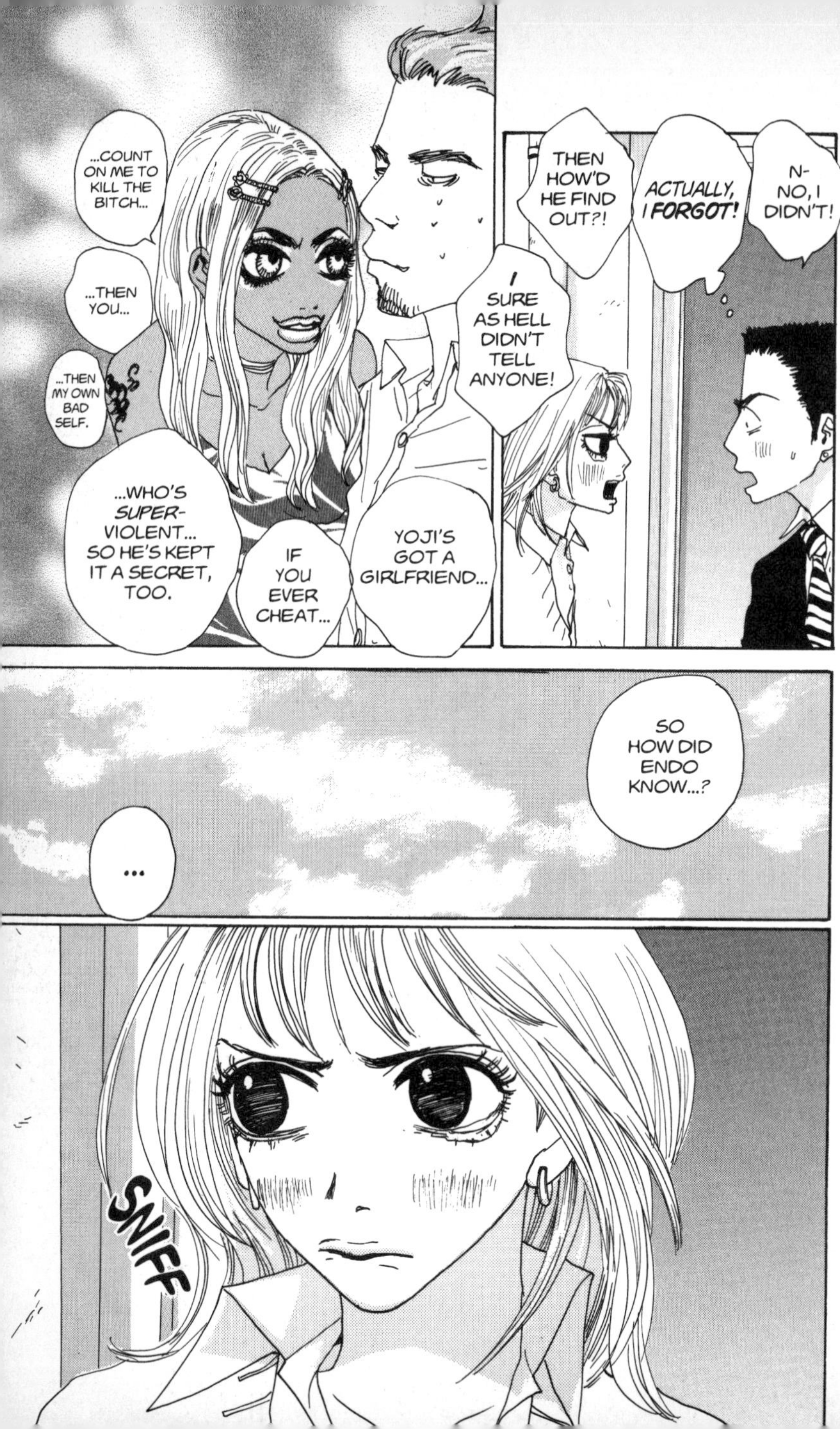
N-NO, I DIDN'T!
ACTUALLY, I **FORGOT**!
THEN HOW'D HE FIND OUT?!
I SURE AS HELL DIDN'T TELL ANYONE!
YOJI'S GOT A GIRLFRIEND...
...WHO'S *SUPER*-VIOLENT... SO HE'S KEPT IT A SECRET, TOO.
IF YOU EVER CHEAT...
...COUNT ON ME TO KILL THE BITCH...
...THEN YOU...
...THEN MY OWN BAD SELF.
SO HOW DID ENDO KNOW...?
...
SNIFF

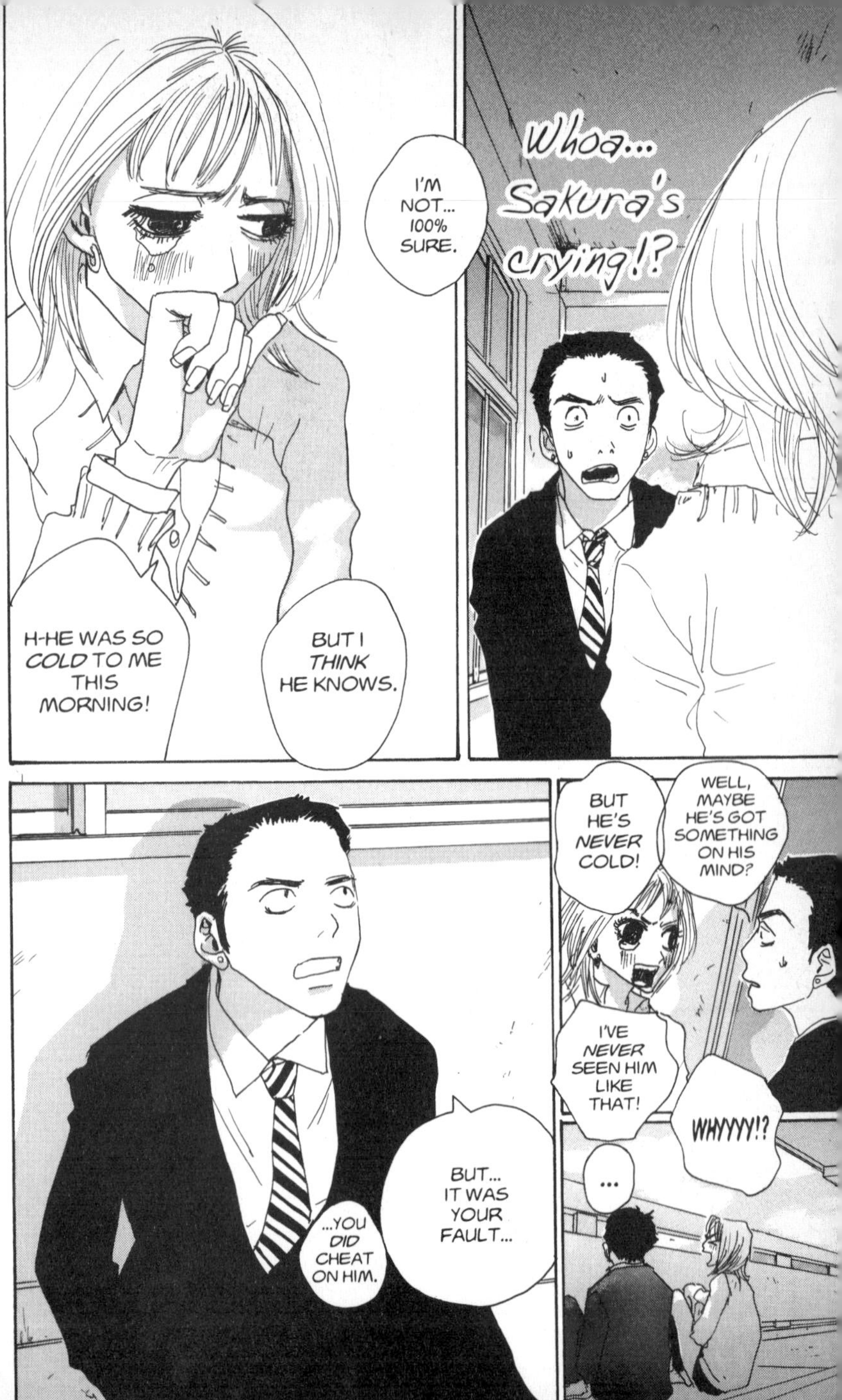
Whoa... Sakura's crying!?
I'M NOT... 100% SURE.
BUT I THINK HE KNOWS.
H-HE WAS SO COLD TO ME THIS MORNING!
WELL, MAYBE HE'S GOT SOMETHING ON HIS MIND?
BUT HE'S NEVER COLD!
I'VE NEVER SEEN HIM LIKE THAT!
WHYYYY!?
...
BUT... IT WAS YOUR FAULT...
...YOU DID CHEAT ON HIM.

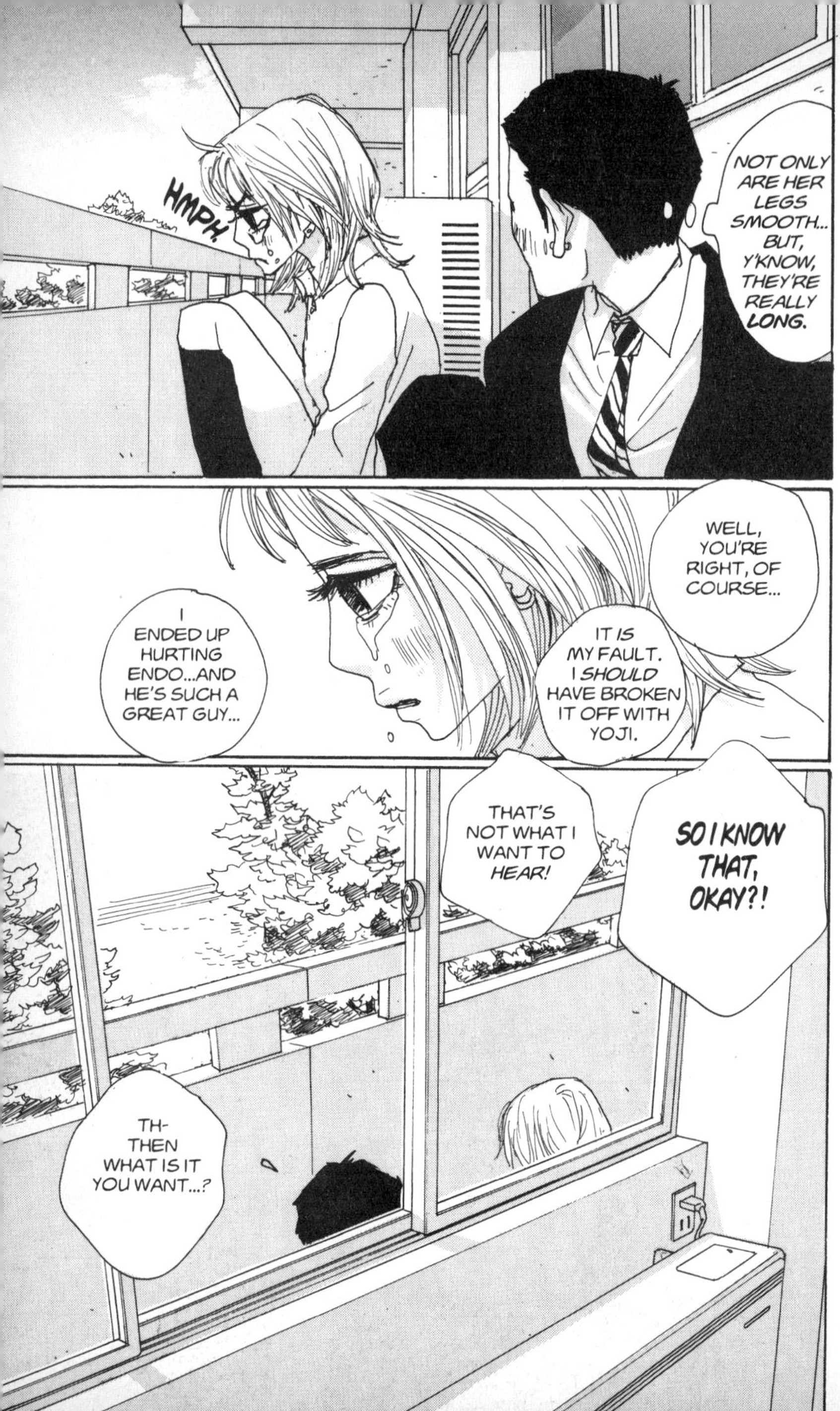

NOT ONLY ARE HER LEGS SMOOTH... BUT, Y'KNOW, THEY'RE REALLY **LONG**.
HMPH.
WELL, YOU'RE RIGHT, OF COURSE...
IT *IS* MY FAULT. I *SHOULD* HAVE BROKEN IT OFF WITH YOJI.
I ENDED UP HURTING ENDO...AND HE'S SUCH A GREAT GUY...
SO I KNOW THAT, OKAY?!
THAT'S NOT WHAT I WANT TO *HEAR!*
TH- THEN WHAT IS IT YOU WANT...?

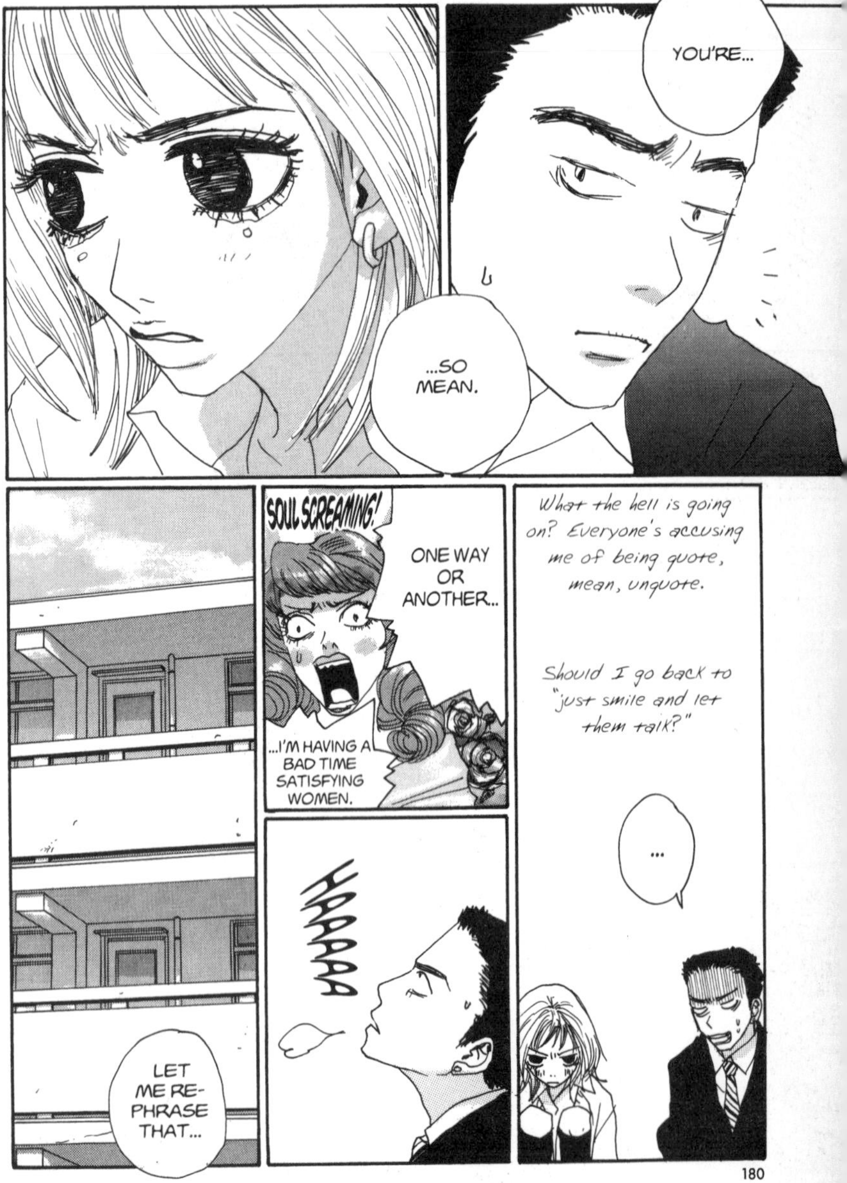
YOU'RE...
...SO MEAN.
What the hell is going on? Everyone's accusing me of being quote, mean, unquote.
Should I go back to "just smile and let them talk?"
...
SOUL SCREAMING!
ONE WAY OR ANOTHER...
...I'M HAVING A BAD TIME SATISFYING WOMEN.
HAAAAA
LET ME RE-PHRASE THAT...

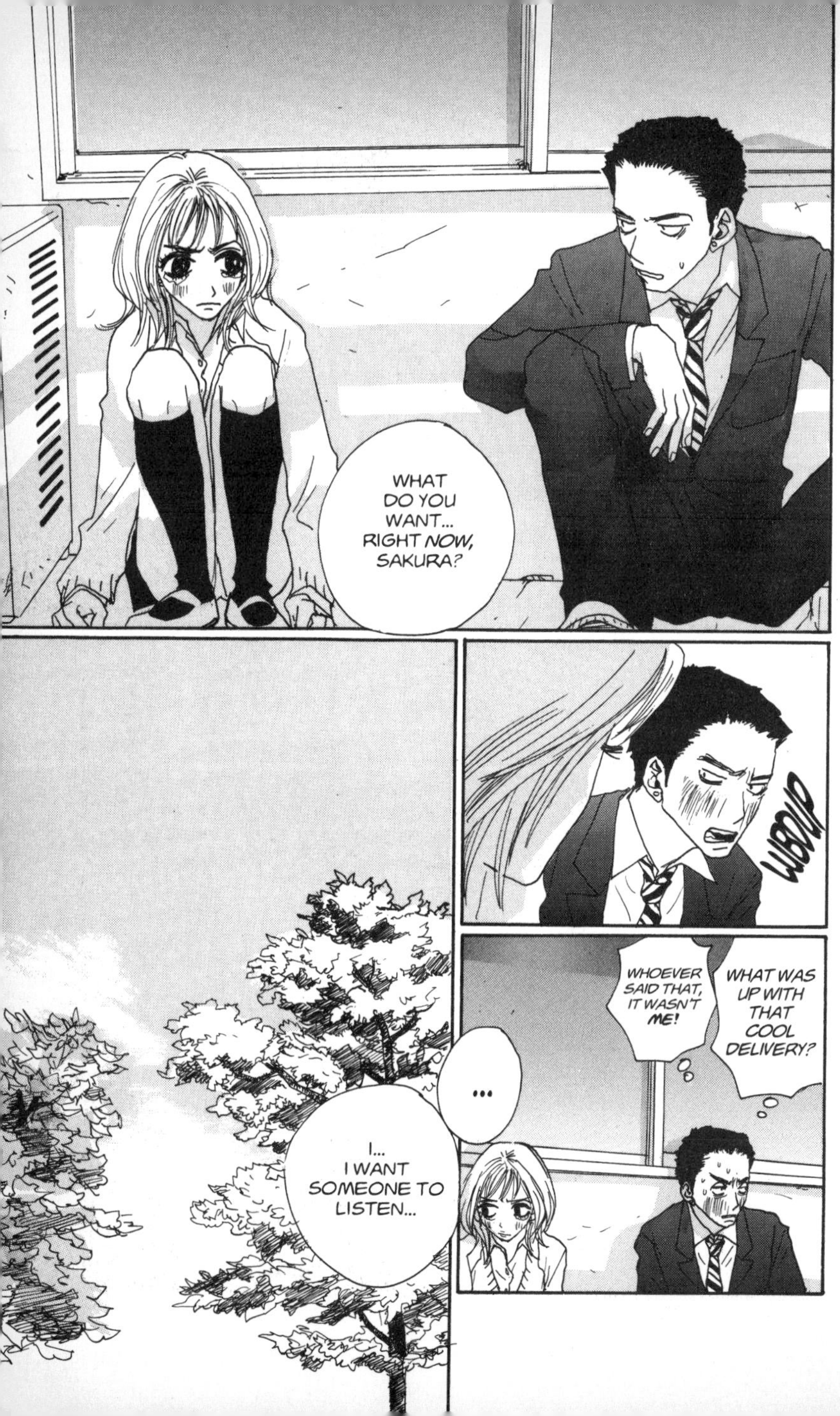
WHAT DO YOU WANT... RIGHT NOW, SAKURA?
WHAT WAS UP WITH THAT COOL DELIVERY?
WHOEVER SAID THAT, IT WASN'T ME!
...
I... I WANT SOMEONE TO LISTEN...

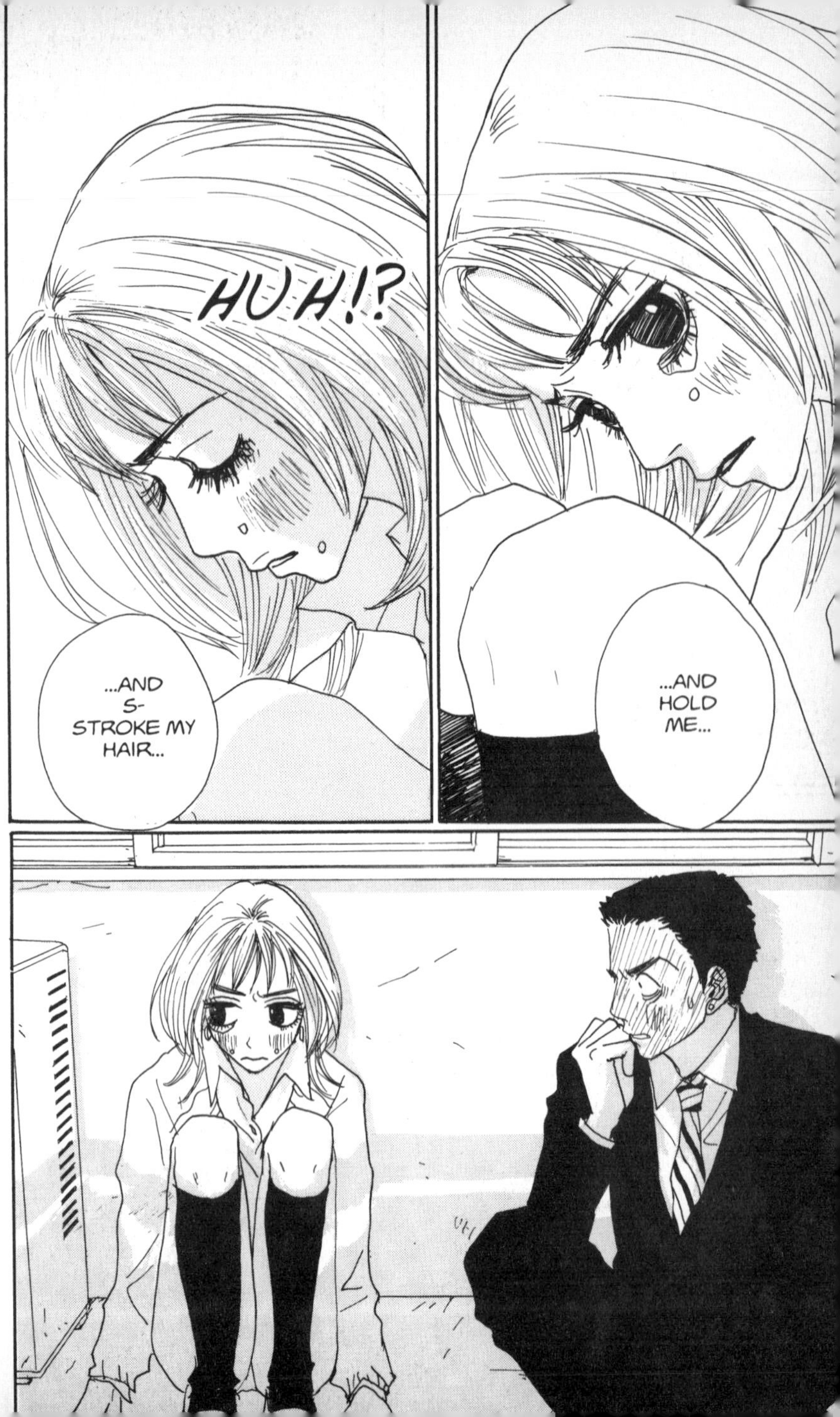
...AND HOLD ME...
HUH!?
...AND S- STROKE MY HAIR...

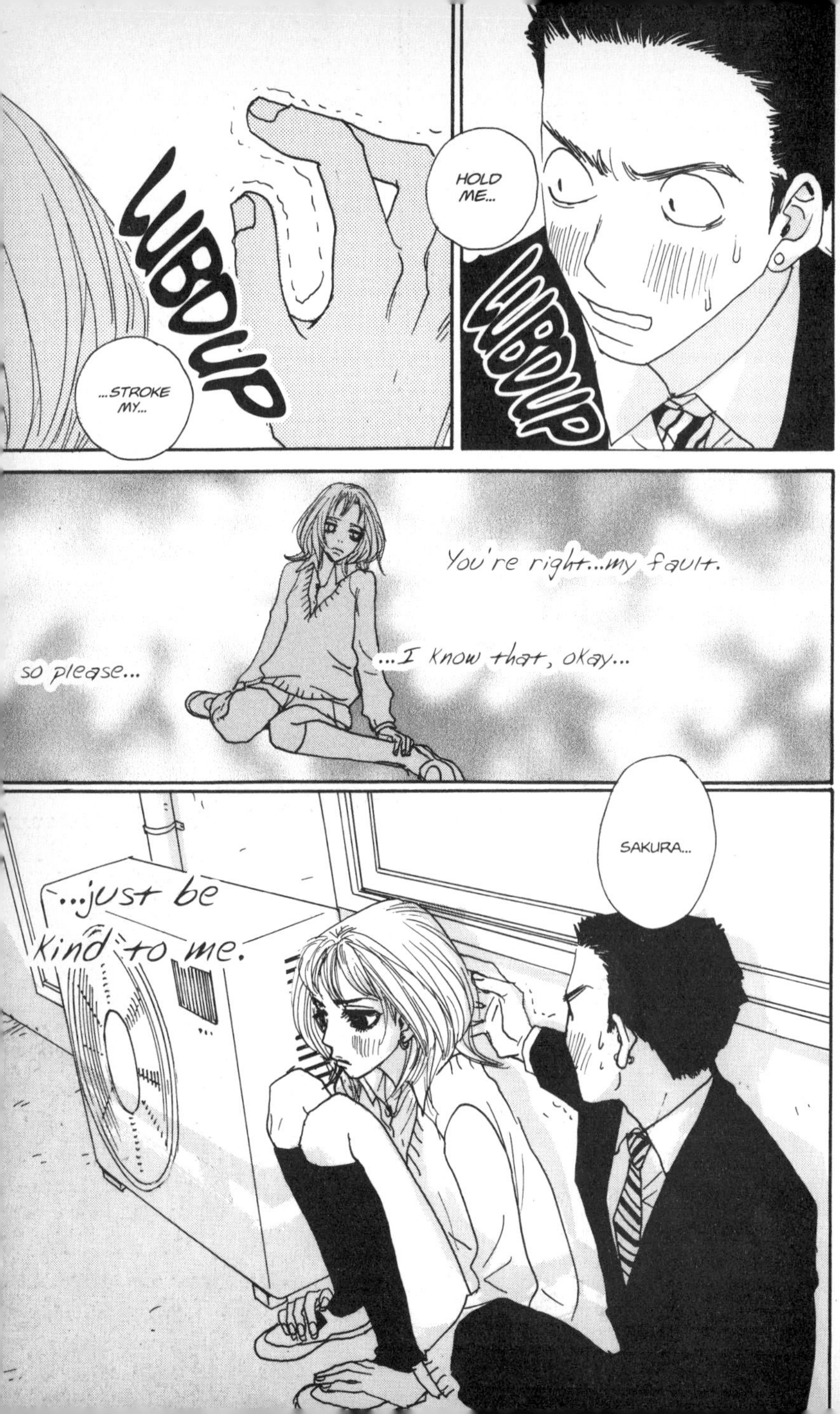
HOLD ME...
WUBDUP
...STROKE MY...
WUBDUP
You're right...my fault.
...I know that, okay...
so please...
SAKURA...
...just be kind to me.

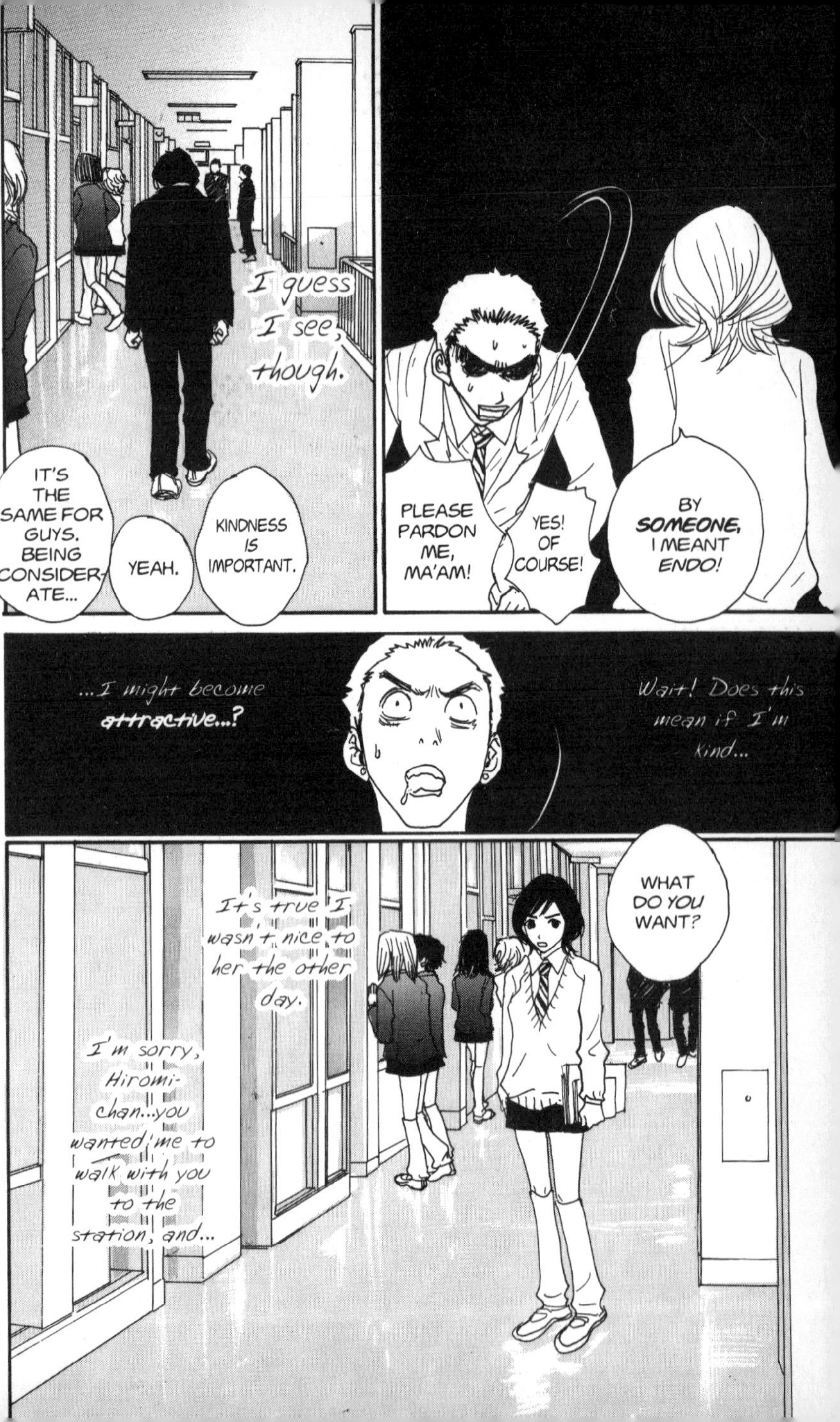
BY SOMEONE, I MEANT ENDO!
YES! OF COURSE!
PLEASE PARDON ME, MA'AM!
I guess I see, though.
KINDNESS IS IMPORTANT.
YEAH.
IT'S THE SAME FOR GUYS. BEING CONSIDER-ATE...
Wait! Does this mean if I'm kind...
...I might become attractive...?
WHAT DO YOU WANT?
It's true I wasn't nice to her the other day.
I'm sorry, Hiromi-chan...you wanted me to walk with you to the station, and...

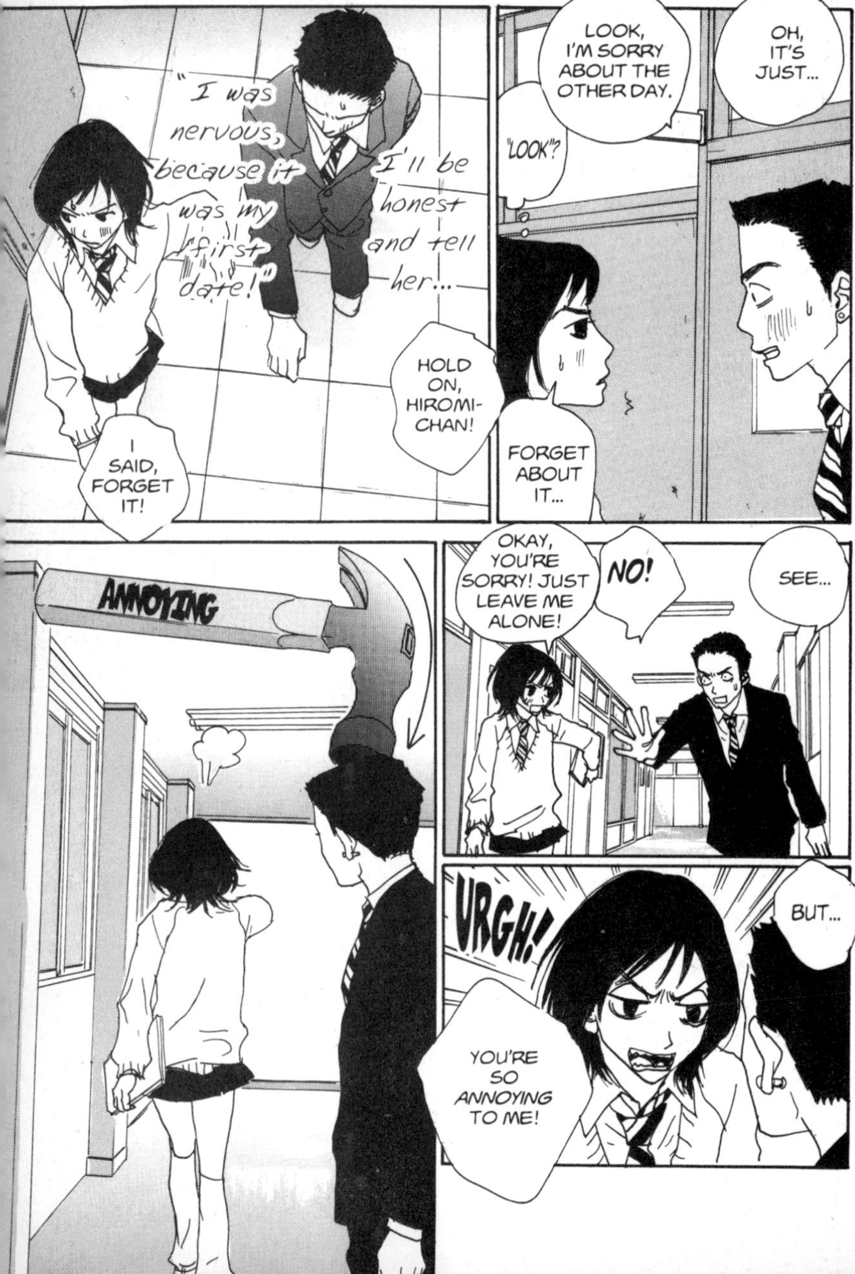
OH, IT'S JUST...
LOOK, I'M SORRY ABOUT THE OTHER DAY.
"LOOK"?
FORGET ABOUT IT...
I'll be honest and tell her...
"I was nervous, because it was my first date!"
HOLD ON, HIROMI-CHAN!
I SAID, FORGET IT!
SEE...
NO!
OKAY, YOU'RE SORRY! JUST LEAVE ME ALONE!
BUT...
URGH!
YOU'RE SO ANNOYING TO ME!
ANNOYING

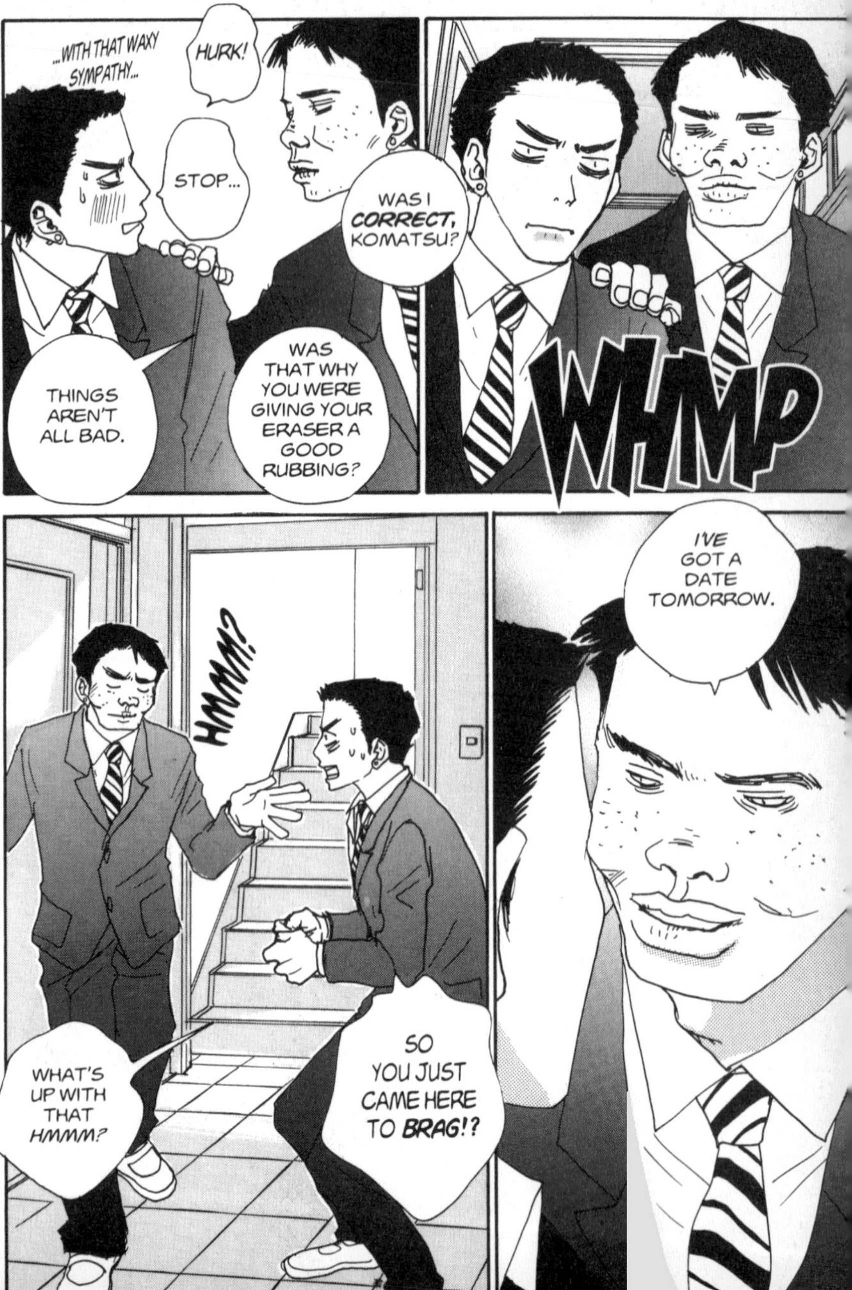
WHMP
HURK!
...WITH THAT WAXY SYMPATHY...
WAS I CORRECT, KOMATSU?
STOP...
WAS THAT WHY YOU WERE GIVING YOUR ERASER A GOOD RUBBING?
THINGS AREN'T ALL BAD.
I'VE GOT A DATE TOMORROW.
HMMM?!
SO YOU JUST CAME HERE TO BRAG!?
WHAT'S UP WITH THAT HMMM?

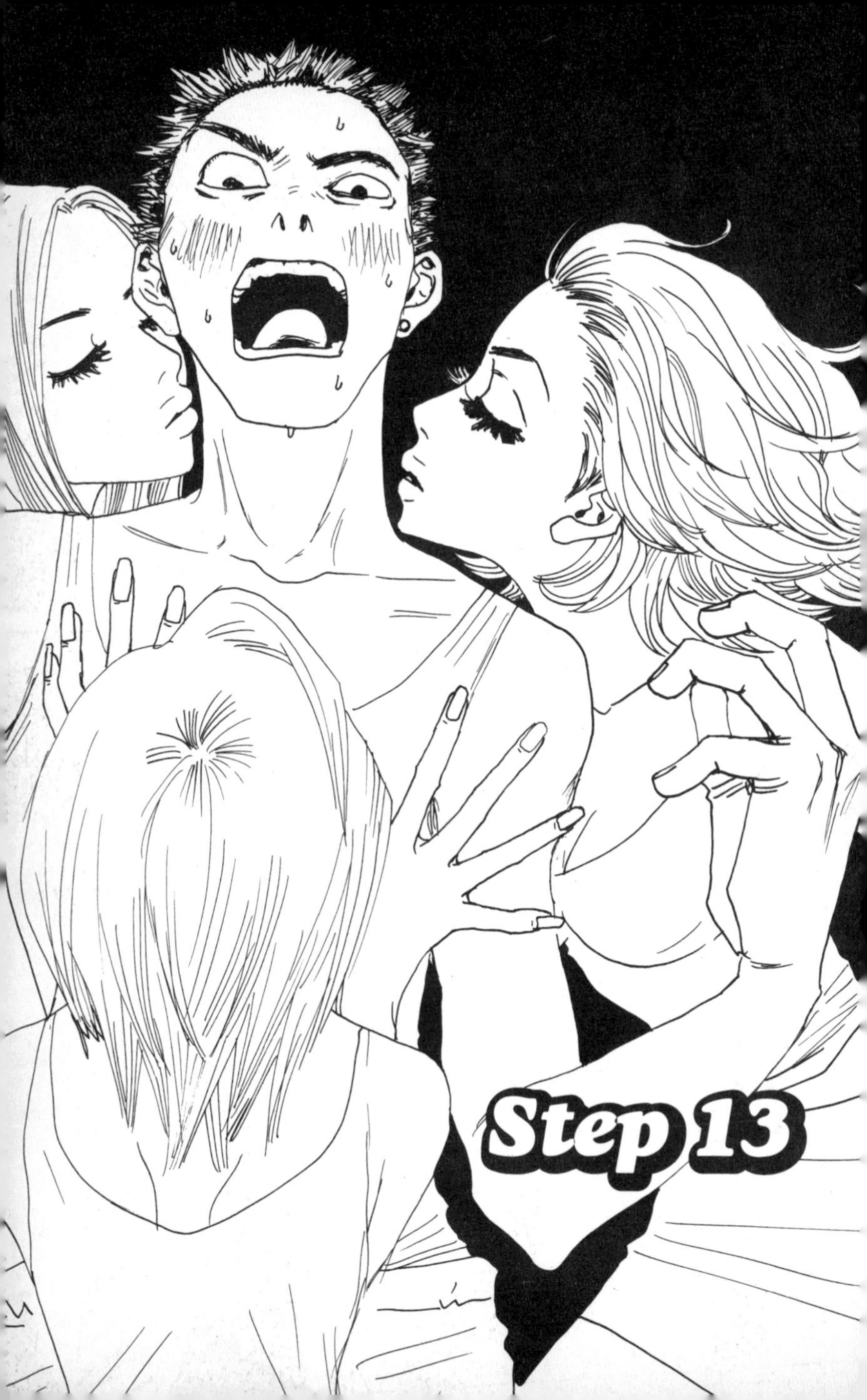
Step 13

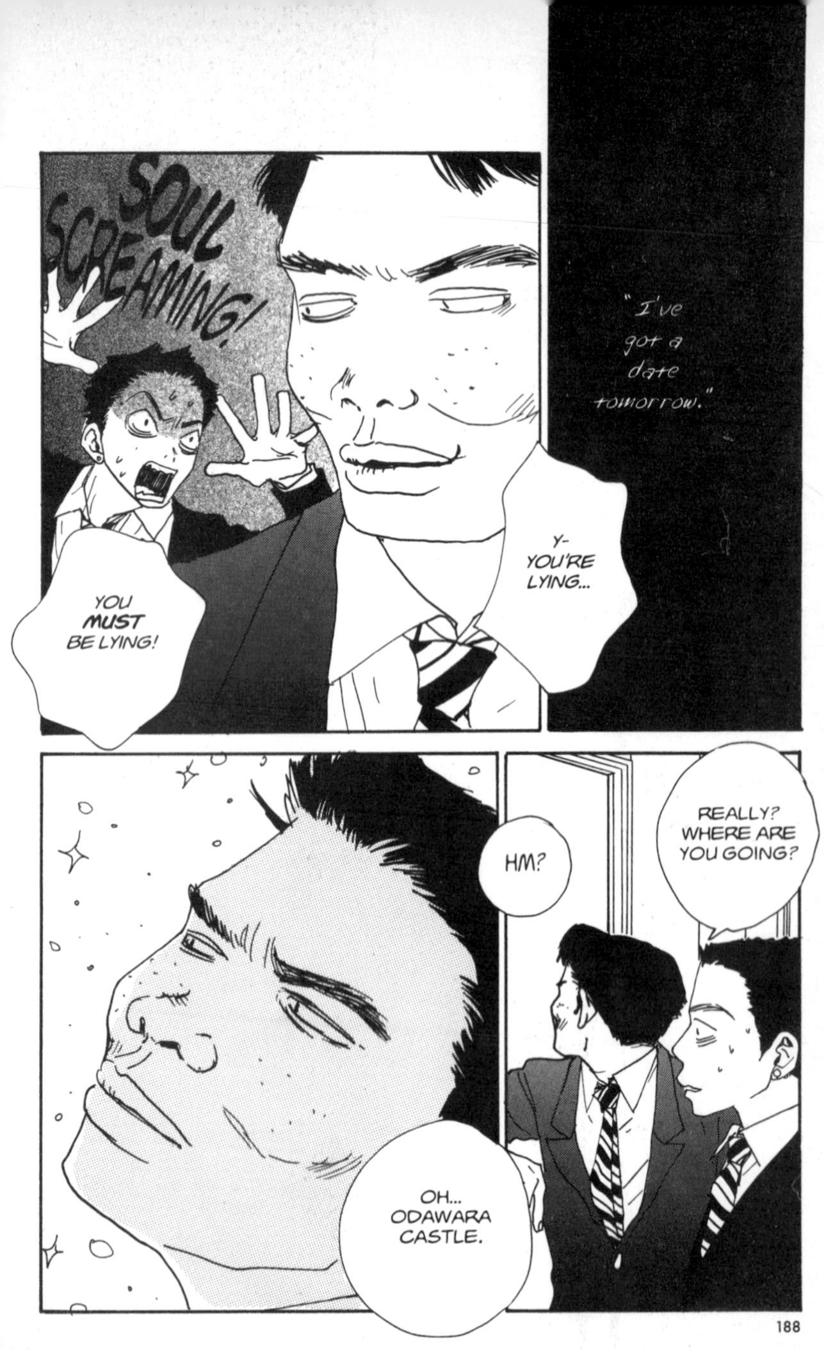
"I've got a date tomorrow."
Y- YOU'RE LYING...
SOUL SCREAMING!
YOU **MUST** BE LYING!
REALLY? WHERE ARE YOU GOING?
HM?
OH... ODAWARA CASTLE.

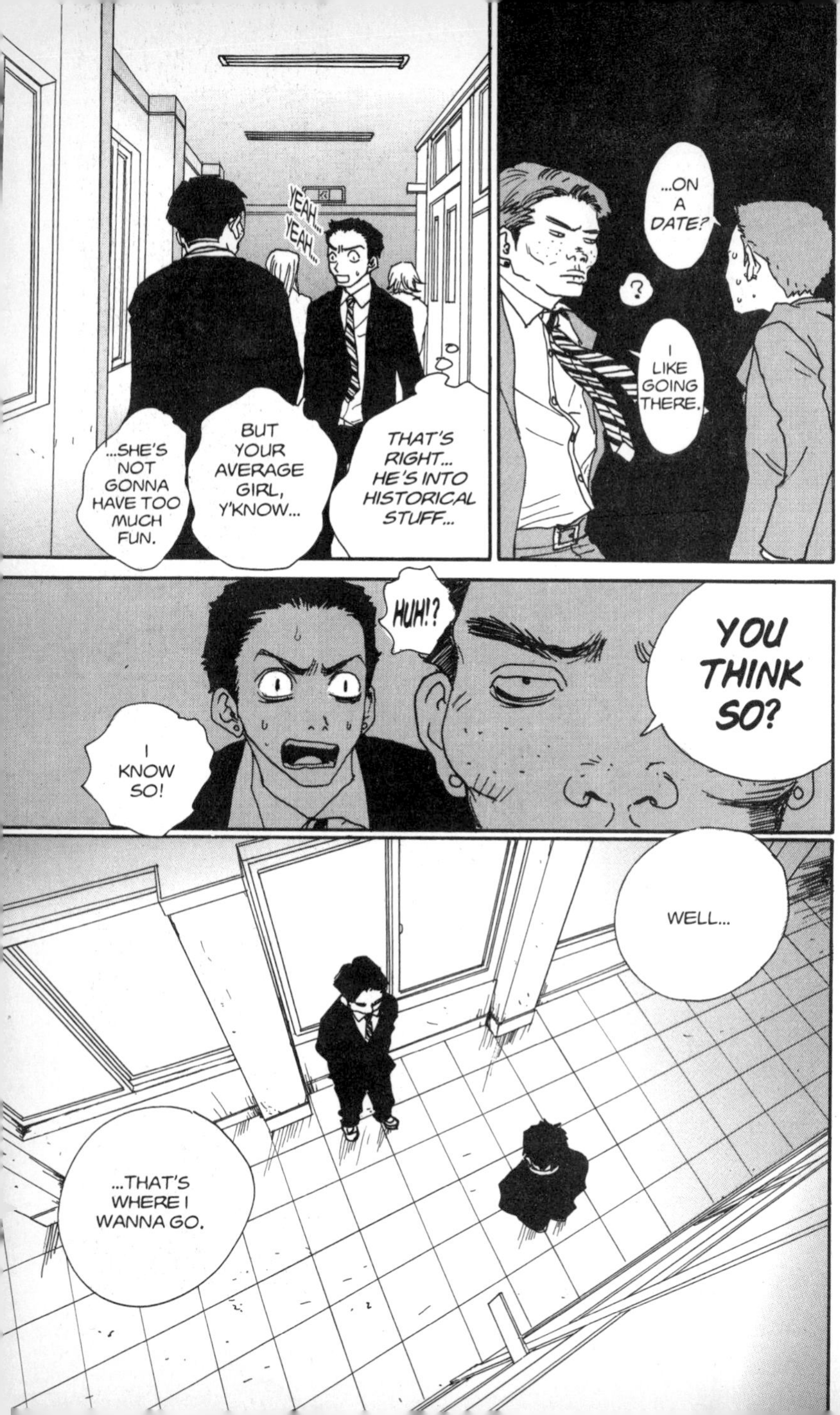
...ON A DATE?
?
I LIKE GOING THERE.
YEAH... YEAH...
THAT'S RIGHT... HE'S INTO HISTORICAL STUFF...
BUT YOUR AVERAGE GIRL, Y'KNOW...
...SHE'S NOT GONNA HAVE TOO MUCH FUN.
YOU THINK SO?
HUH!?
I KNOW SO!
WELL...
...THAT'S WHERE I WANNA GO.

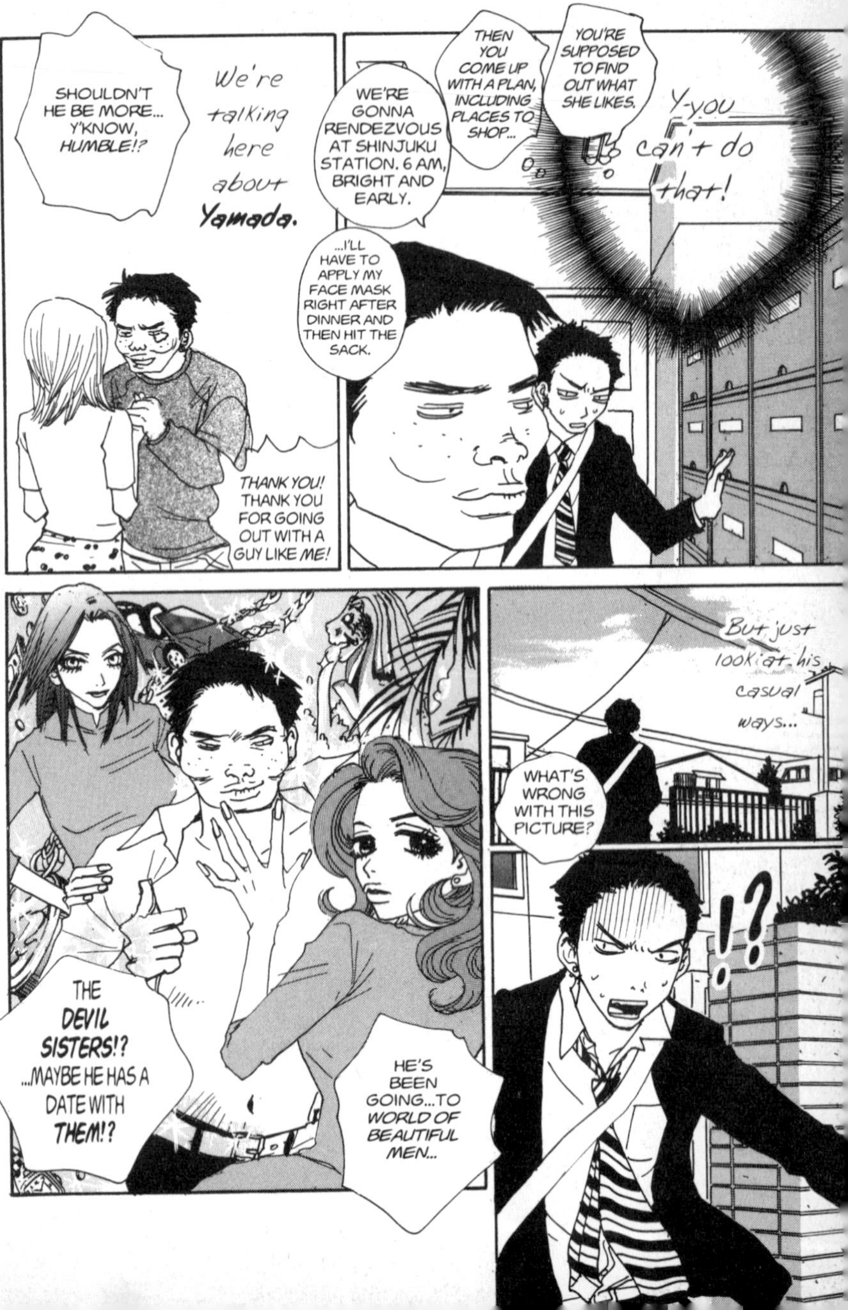
YOU'RE SUPPOSED TO FIND OUT WHAT SHE LIKES.
THEN YOU COME UP WITH A PLAN, INCLUDING PLACES TO SHOP...
Y-you can't do that!
WE'RE GONNA RENDEZVOUS AT SHINJUKU STATION. 6 AM, BRIGHT AND EARLY.
...I'LL HAVE TO APPLY MY FACE MASK RIGHT AFTER DINNER AND THEN HIT THE SACK.
We're talking here about Yamada.
SHOULDN'T HE BE MORE... Y'KNOW, HUMBLE!?
THANK YOU! THANK YOU FOR GOING OUT WITH A GUY LIKE ME!
But just look at his casual ways...
WHAT'S WRONG WITH THIS PICTURE?
!?
HE'S BEEN GOING...TO WORLD OF BEAUTIFUL MEN...
THE DEVIL SISTERS!? ...MAYBE HE HAS A DATE WITH THEM!?

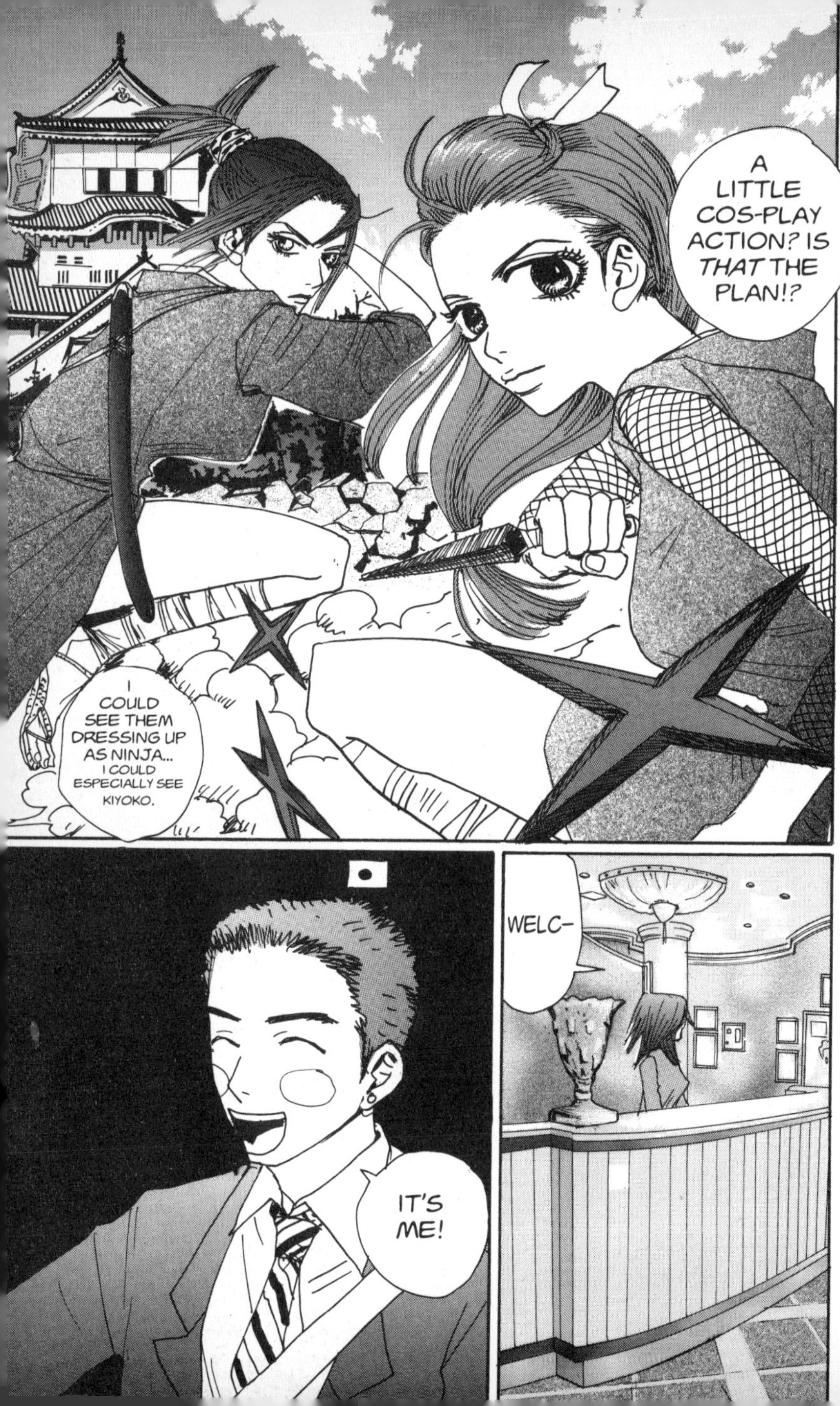
A LITTLE COS-PLAY ACTION? IS *THAT* THE PLAN!?
I COULD SEE THEM DRESSING UP AS NINJA... I COULD ESPECIALLY SEE KIYOKO.
WELC-
IT'S ME!

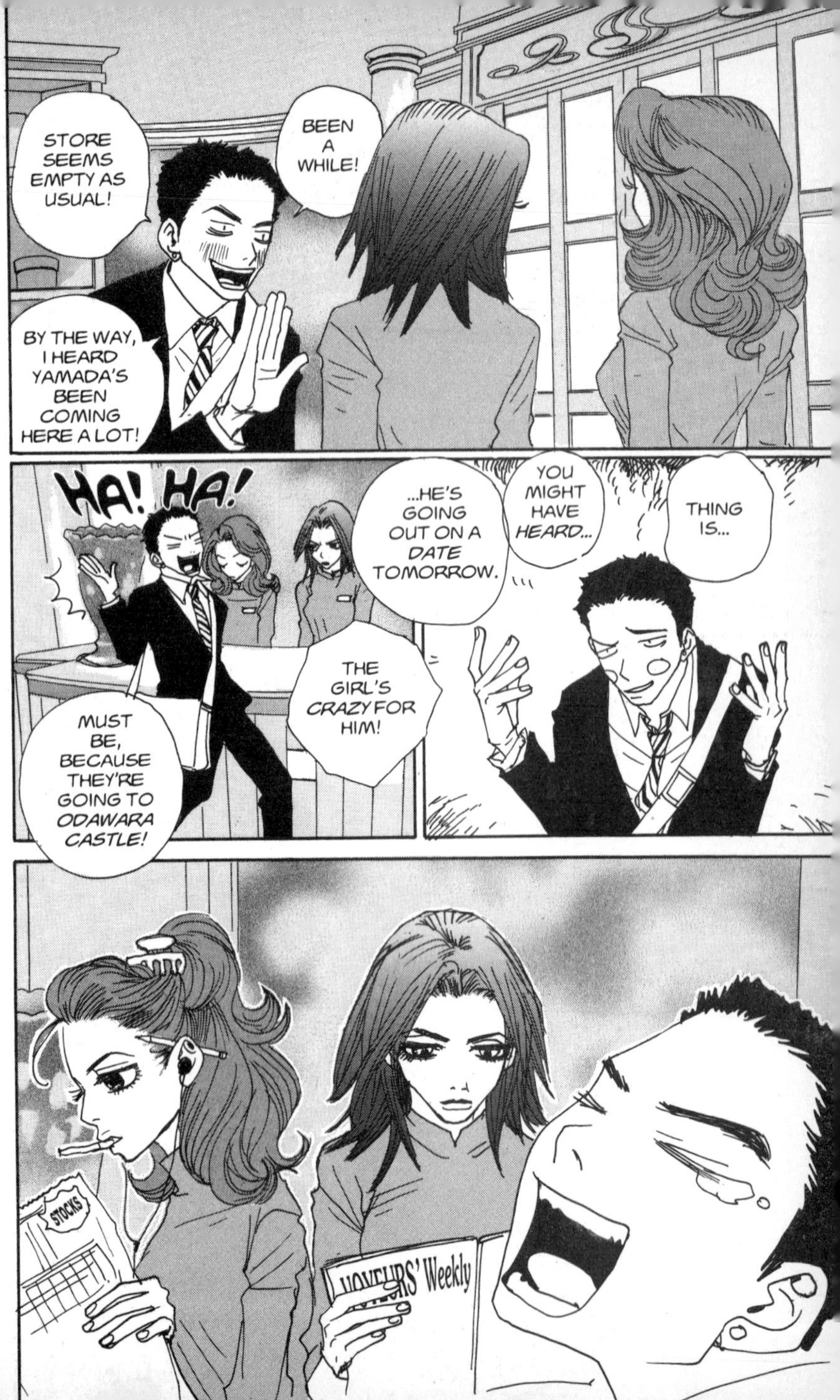
BEEN A WHILE!
STORE SEEMS EMPTY AS USUAL!
BY THE WAY, I HEARD YAMADA'S BEEN COMING HERE A LOT!
THING IS...
YOU MIGHT HAVE *HEARD*...
...HE'S GOING OUT ON A *DATE* TOMORROW.
THE GIRL'S *CRAZY* FOR HIM!
HA! HA!
MUST BE, BECAUSE THEY'RE GOING TO *ODAWARA CASTLE!*
STOCKS
VOYEURS' Weekly

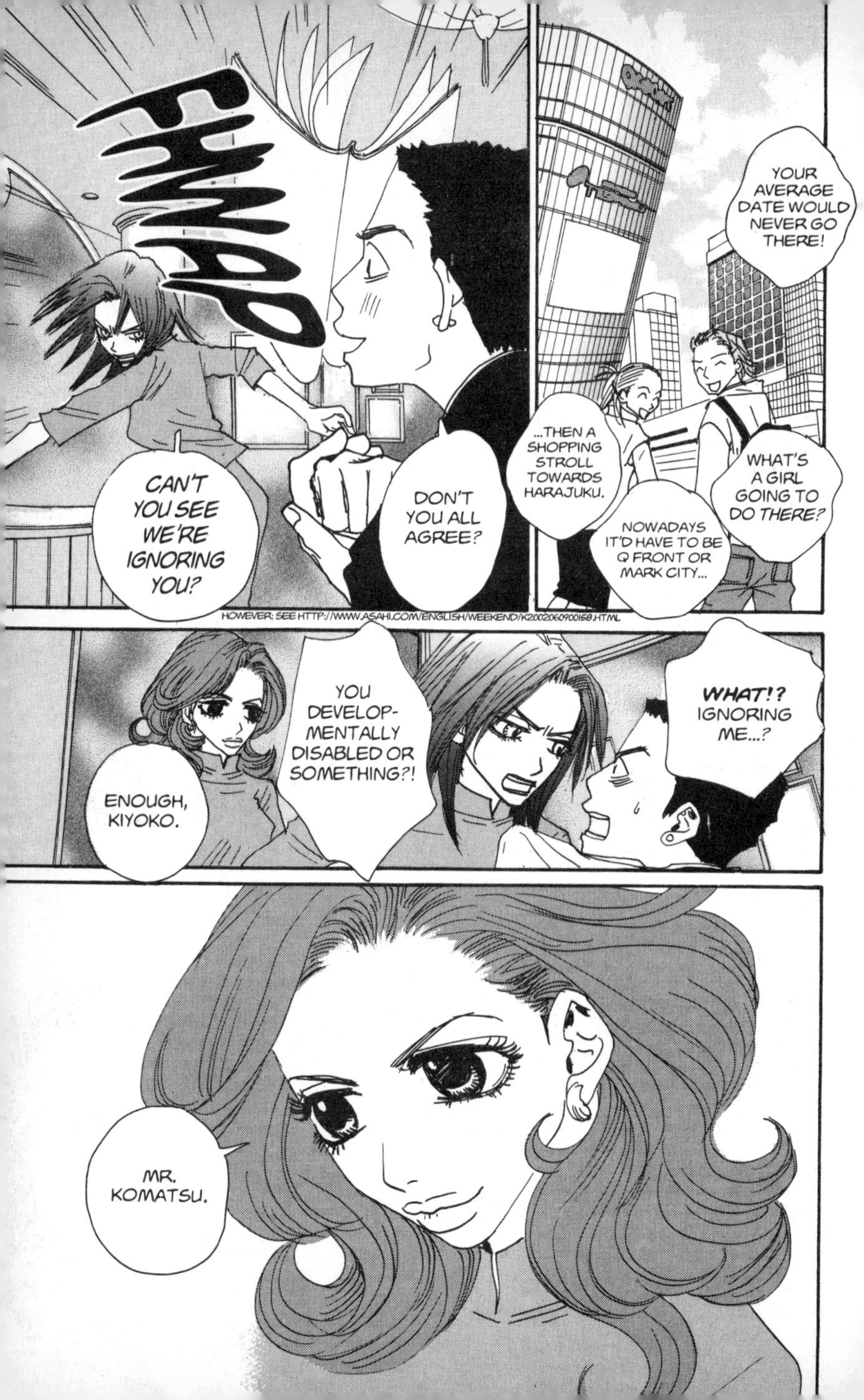
YOUR AVERAGE DATE WOULD NEVER GO THERE!
WHAT'S A GIRL GOING TO DO THERE?
...THEN A SHOPPING STROLL TOWARDS HARAJUKU.
NOWADAYS IT'D HAVE TO BE Q FRONT OR MARK CITY...
FWAP
DON'T YOU ALL AGREE?
CAN'T YOU SEE WE'RE IGNORING YOU?
HOWEVER: SEE HTTP://WWW.ASAHI.COM/ENGLISH/WEEKEND/K2002060900158.HTML
WHAT!? IGNORING ME...?
YOU DEVELOP-MENTALLY DISABLED OR SOMETHING?!
ENOUGH, KIYOKO.
MR. KOMATSU.

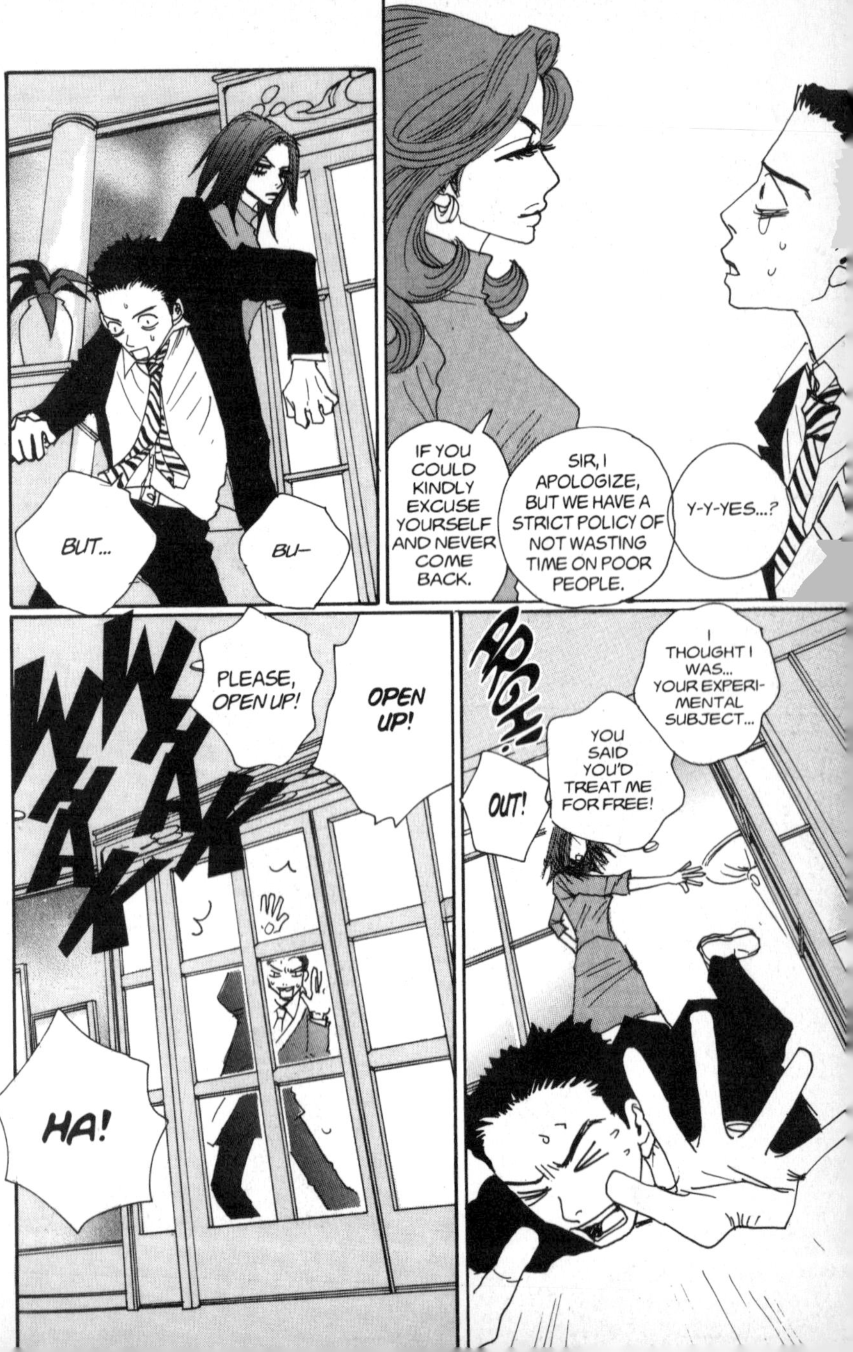
Y-Y-YES...?
SIR, I APOLOGIZE, BUT WE HAVE A STRICT POLICY OF NOT WASTING TIME ON POOR PEOPLE.
IF YOU COULD KINDLY EXCUSE YOURSELF AND NEVER COME BACK.
BU–
BUT...
ARGH!
I THOUGHT I WAS... YOUR EXPERI-MENTAL SUBJECT...
YOU SAID YOU'D TREAT ME FOR FREE!
OUT!
OPEN UP!
PLEASE, OPEN UP!
WHAK WHAK
HA!

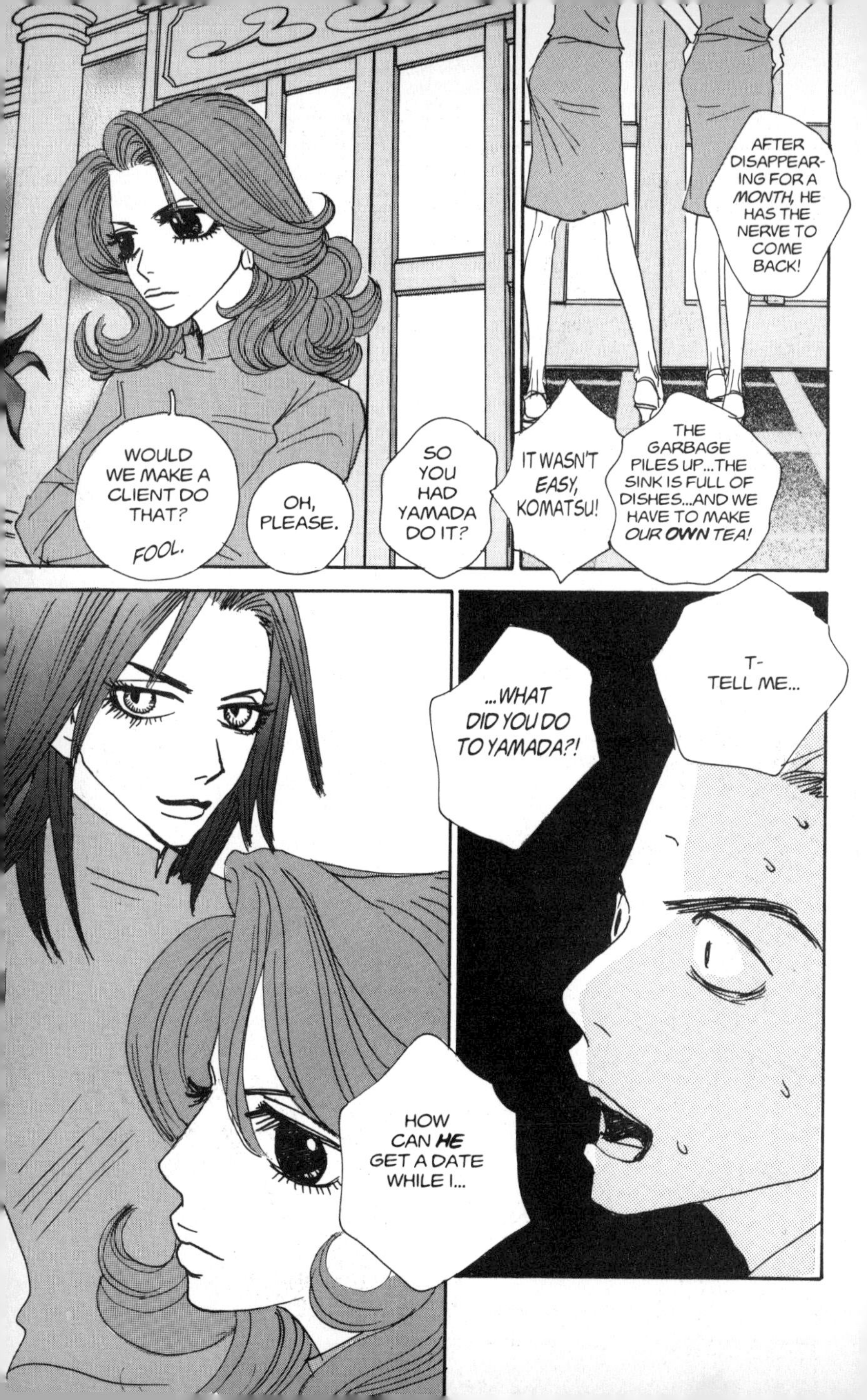
AFTER DISAPPEARING FOR A MONTH, HE HAS THE NERVE TO COME BACK!
THE GARBAGE PILES UP...THE SINK IS FULL OF DISHES...AND WE HAVE TO MAKE OUR OWN TEA!
IT WASN'T EASY, KOMATSU!
SO YOU HAD YAMADA DO IT?
OH, PLEASE.
WOULD WE MAKE A CLIENT DO THAT?
FOOL.
T-TELL ME...
...WHAT DID YOU DO TO YAMADA?!
HOW CAN HE GET A DATE WHILE I...

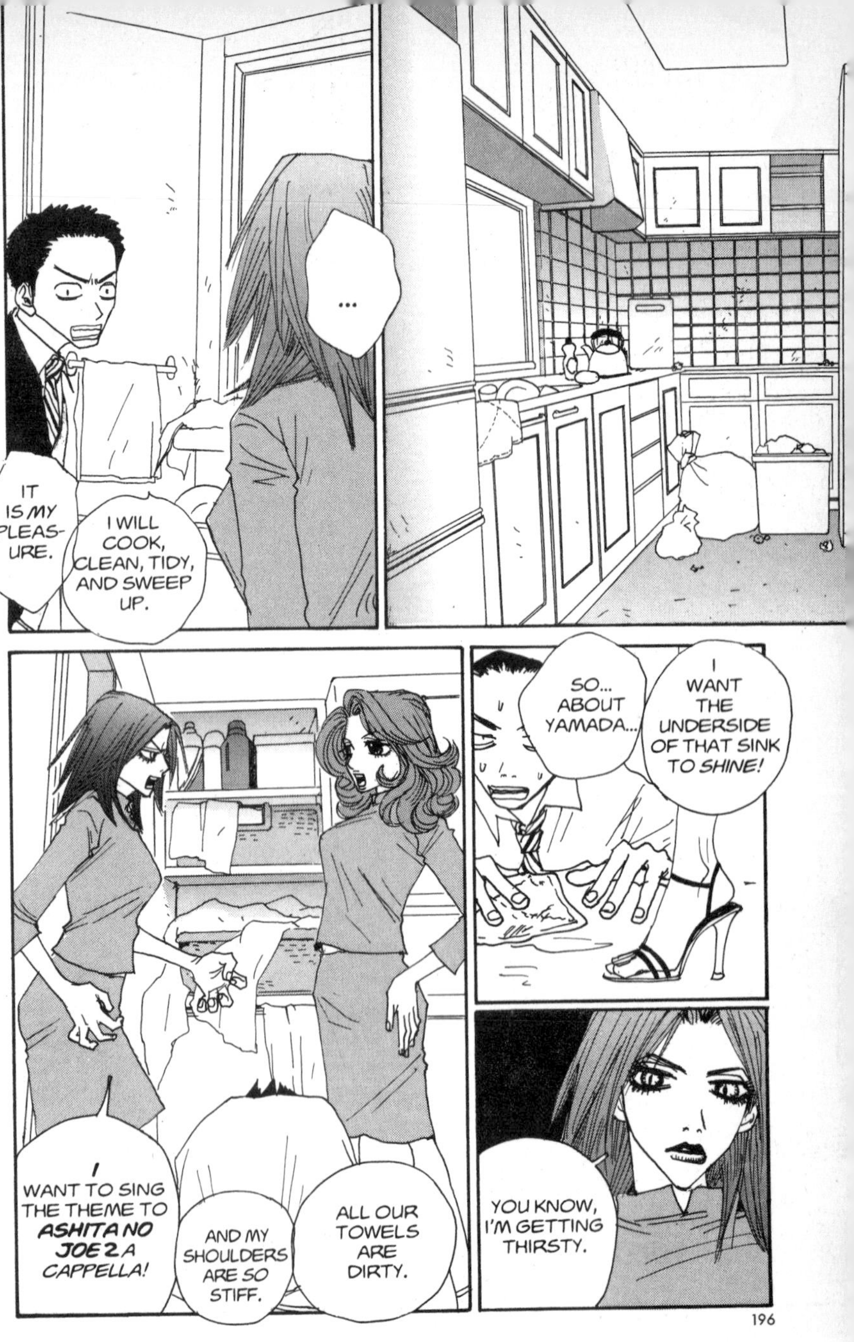
...
I WILL COOK, CLEAN, TIDY, AND SWEEP UP.
IT IS MY PLEASURE.
I WANT THE UNDERSIDE OF THAT SINK TO *SHINE!*
SO... ABOUT YAMADA...
YOU KNOW, I'M GETTING THIRSTY.
ALL OUR TOWELS ARE DIRTY.
AND MY SHOULDERS ARE SO STIFF.
I WANT TO SING THE THEME TO ***ASHITA NO JOE 2*** *A CAPPELLA!*

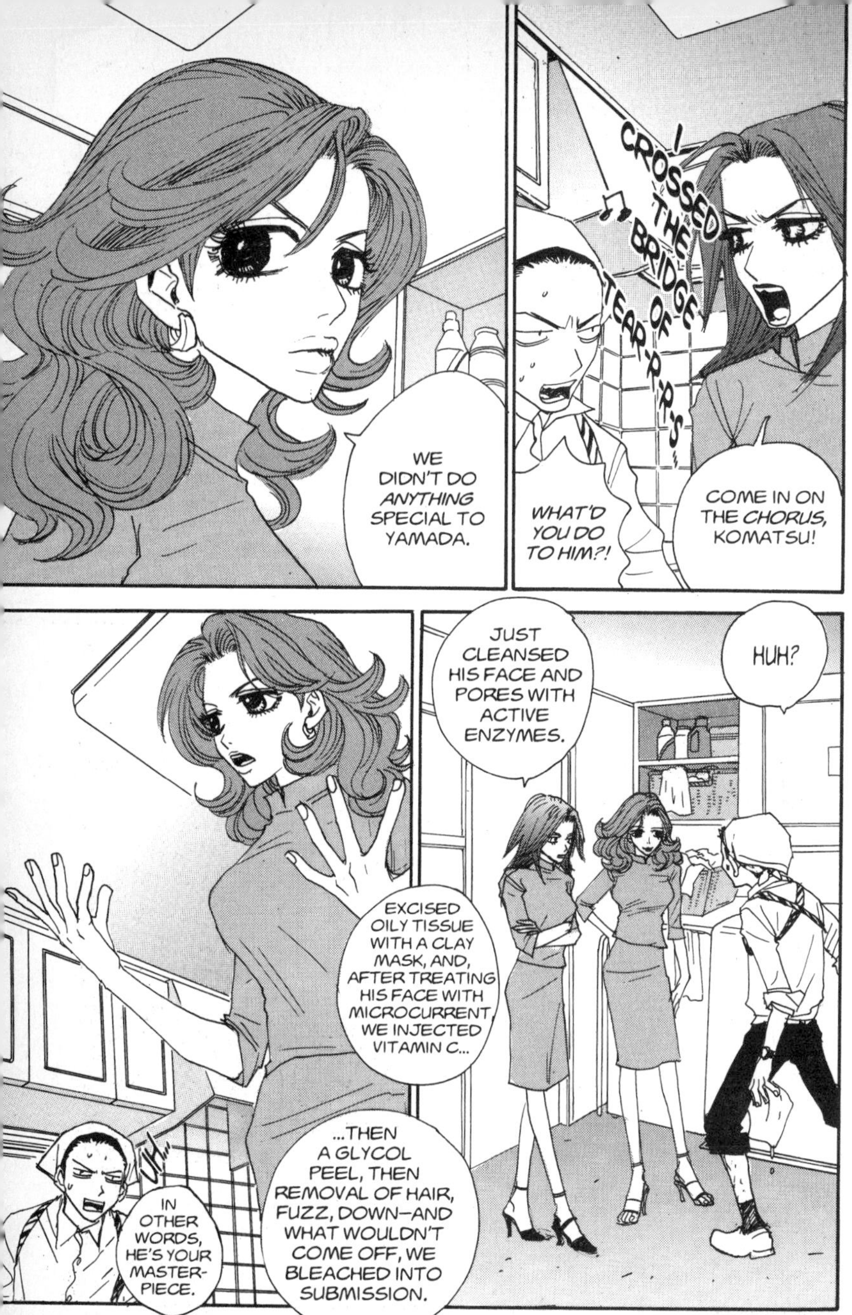
I CROSSED THE BRIDGE OF TEAR-R-R-S...
COME IN ON THE *CHORUS*, KOMATSU!
WHAT'D YOU DO TO HIM?!
WE DIDN'T DO *ANYTHING* SPECIAL TO YAMADA.
HUH?
JUST CLEANSED HIS FACE AND PORES WITH ACTIVE ENZYMES.
EXCISED OILY TISSUE WITH A CLAY MASK, AND, AFTER TREATING HIS FACE WITH MICROCURRENT, WE INJECTED VITAMIN C...
...THEN A GLYCOL PEEL, THEN REMOVAL OF HAIR, FUZZ, DOWN—AND WHAT WOULDN'T COME OFF, WE BLEACHED INTO SUBMISSION.
UH...
IN OTHER WORDS, HE'S YOUR MASTER-PIECE.

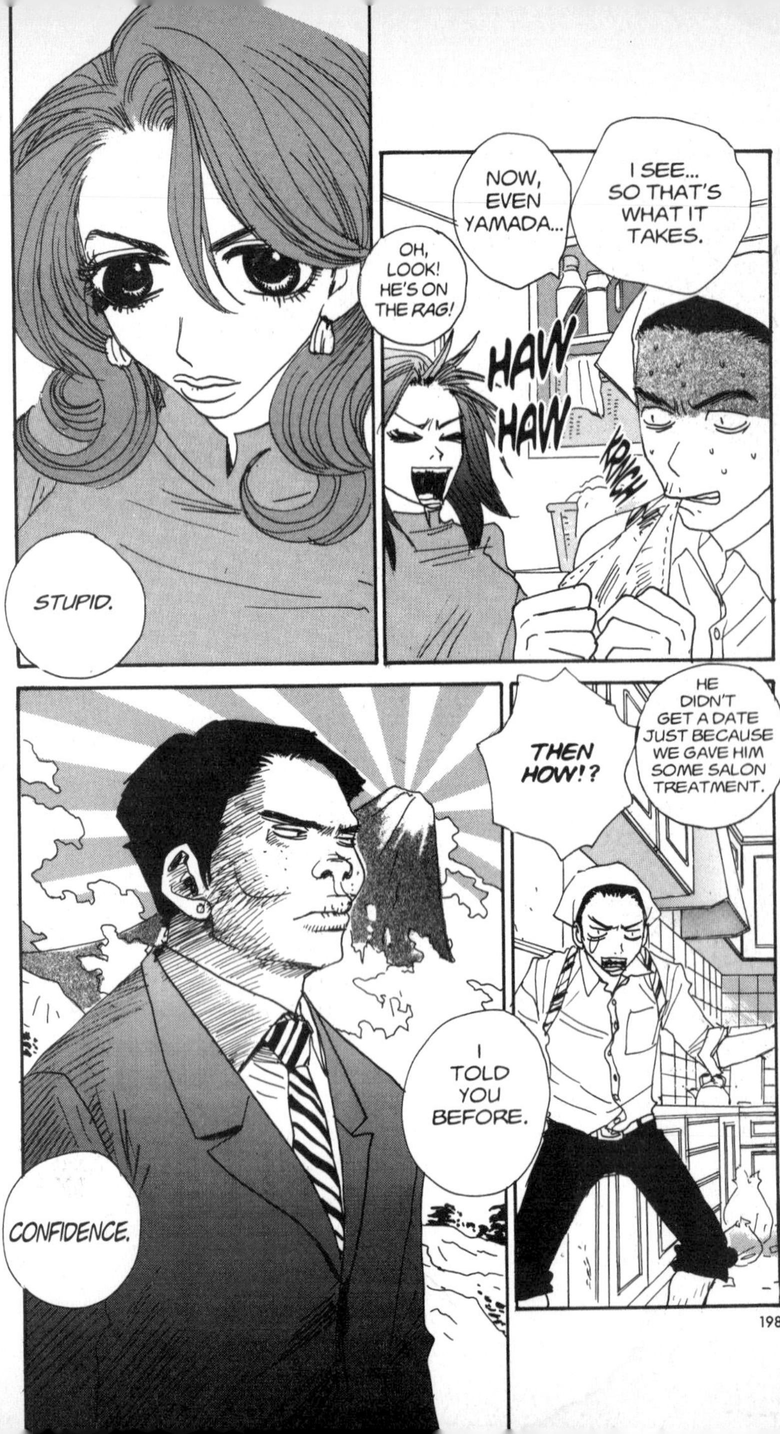
I SEE... SO THAT'S WHAT IT TAKES.
NOW, EVEN YAMADA...
OH, LOOK! HE'S ON THE *RAG*!
HAW HAW
KRNCH
STUPID.
HE DIDN'T GET A DATE JUST BECAUSE WE GAVE HIM SOME SALON TREATMENT.
THEN HOW!?
I TOLD YOU BEFORE.
CONFIDENCE.

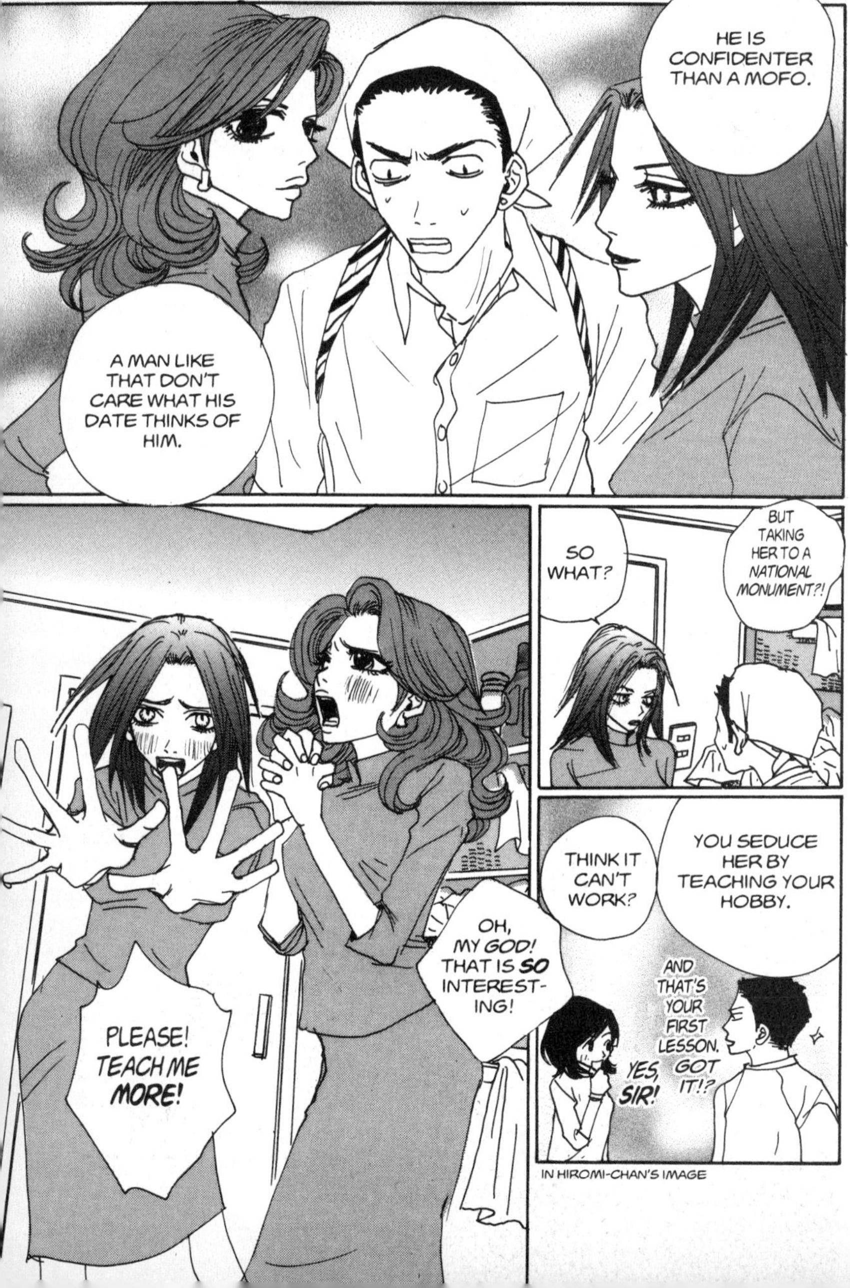
HE IS CONFIDENTER THAN A MOFO.
A MAN LIKE THAT DON'T CARE WHAT HIS DATE THINKS OF HIM.
BUT TAKING HER TO A *NATIONAL MONUMENT*?!
SO WHAT?
YOU SEDUCE HER BY TEACHING YOUR HOBBY.
THINK IT CAN'T WORK?
AND THAT'S YOUR FIRST LESSON. GOT IT!?
YES, SIR!
IN HIROMI-CHAN'S IMAGE
OH, MY *GOD*! THAT IS ***SO*** INTEREST-ING!
PLEASE! TEACH ME ***MORE***!

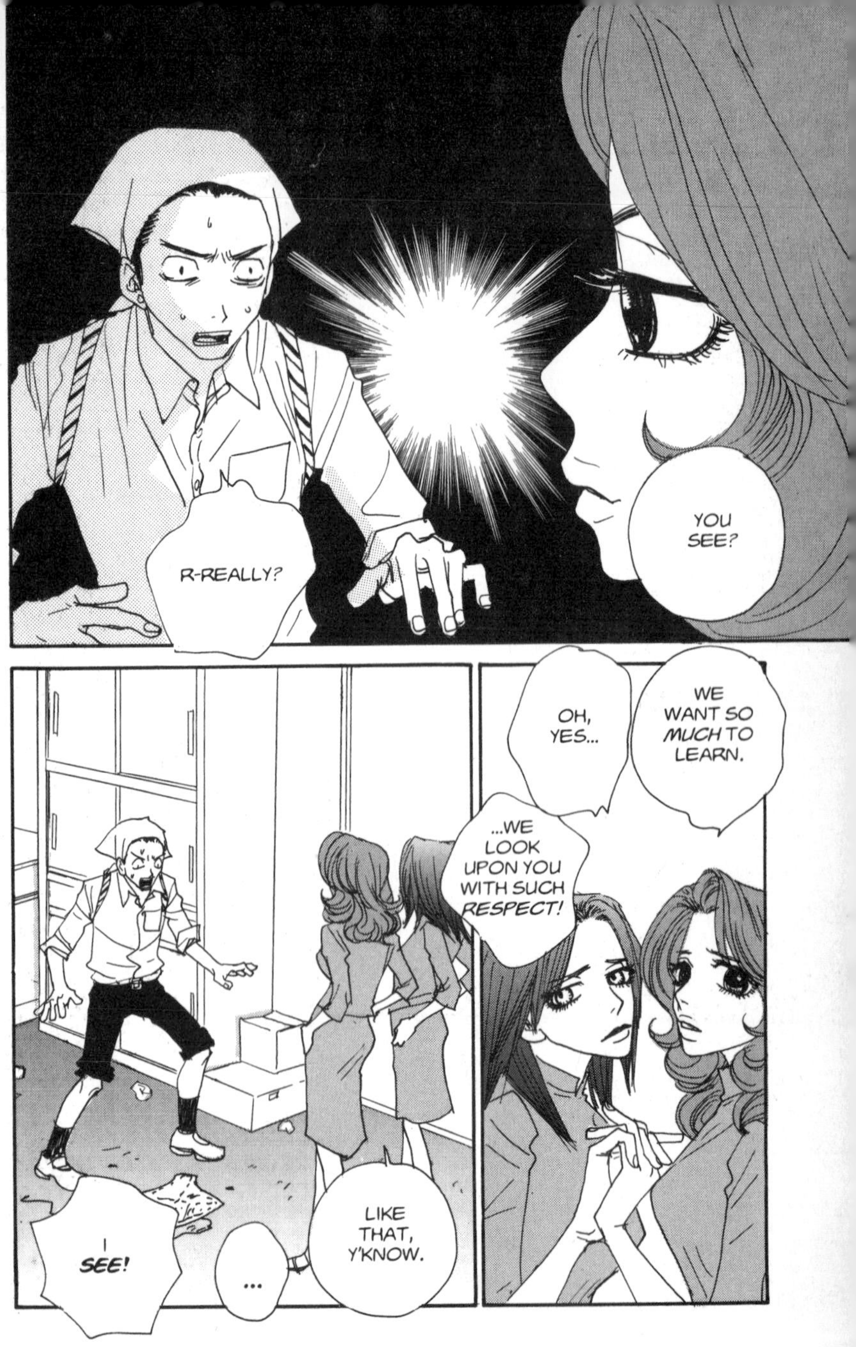
YOU SEE?
R-REALLY?
WE WANT SO MUCH TO LEARN.
OH, YES...
...WE LOOK UPON YOU WITH SUCH RESPECT!
LIKE THAT, Y'KNOW.
...
I SEE!

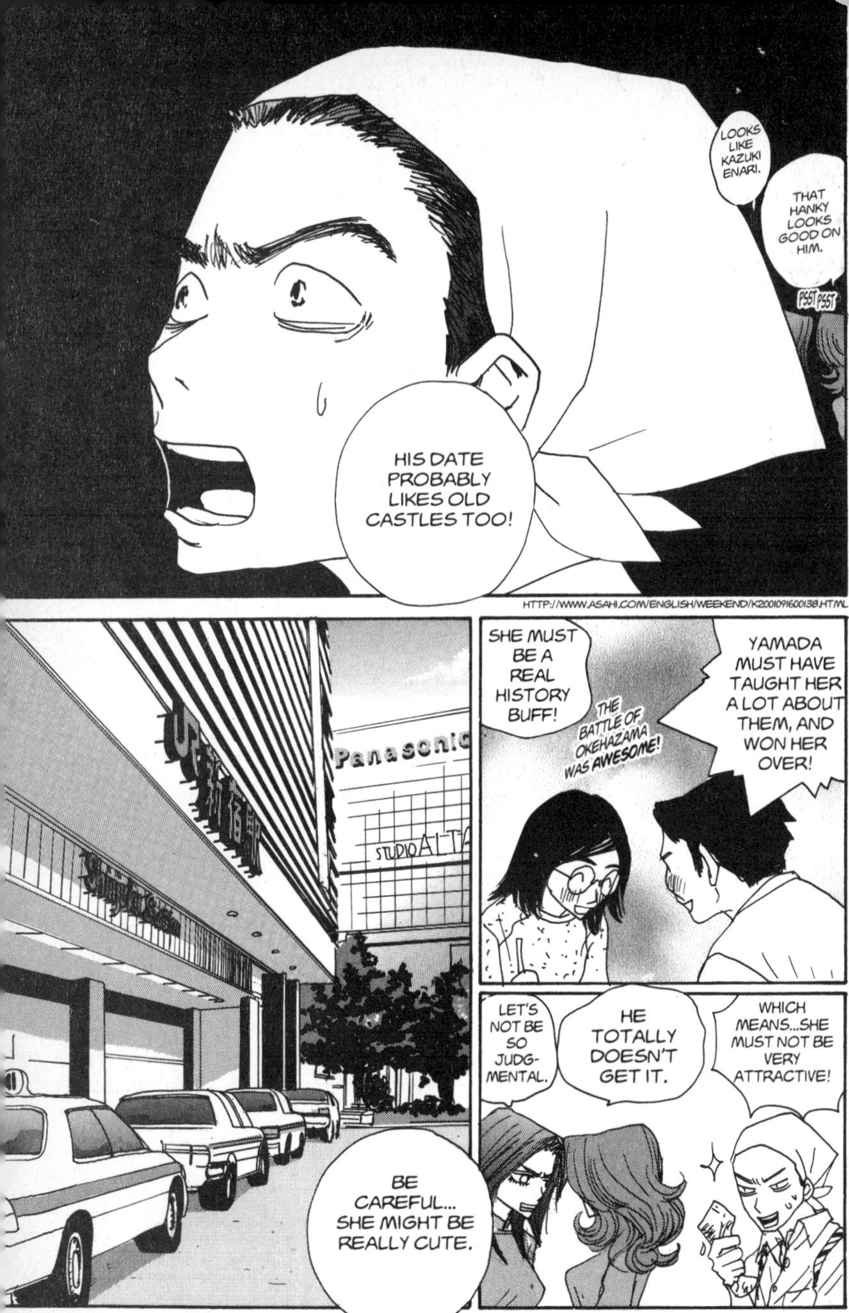
LOOKS LIKE KAZUKI ENARI.
THAT HANKY LOOKS GOOD ON HIM.
PSST PSST
HIS DATE PROBABLY LIKES OLD CASTLES TOO!
YAMADA MUST HAVE TAUGHT HER A LOT ABOUT THEM, AND WON HER OVER!
SHE MUST BE A REAL HISTORY BUFF!
THE BATTLE OF OKEHAZAMA WAS AWESOME!
WHICH MEANS...SHE MUST NOT BE VERY ATTRACTIVE!
HE TOTALLY DOESN'T GET IT.
LET'S NOT BE SO JUDG-MENTAL.
Panasonic
STUDIO ALTA
BE CAREFUL... SHE MIGHT BE REALLY CUTE.

HTTP://WWW.ASAHI.COM/ENGLISH/WEEKEND/K2001091600138.HTML

HTTP://WWW.CITY.TOYOAKE.AICHI.JP/ENGLISH/OKEHAZA.HTML

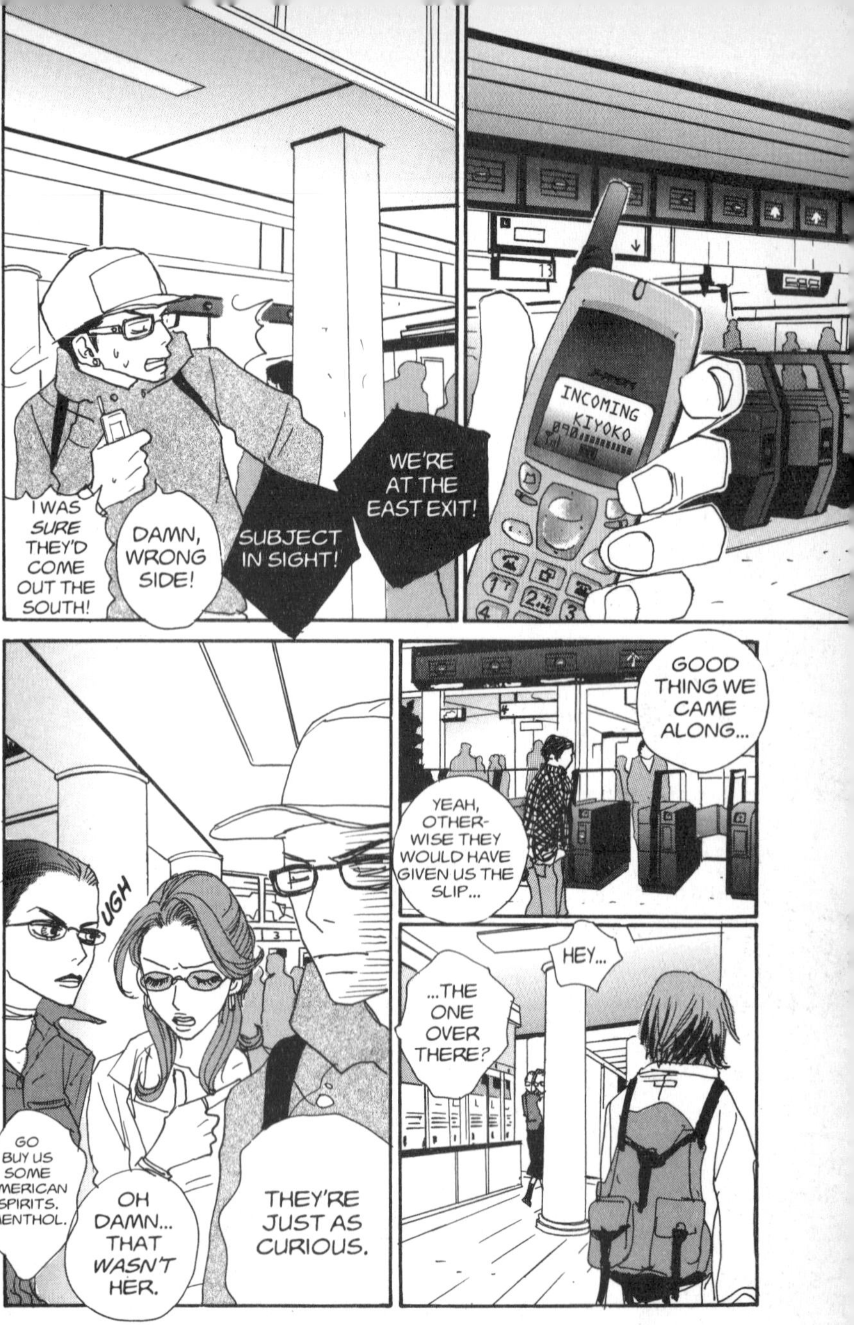
INCOMING
KIYOKO
SUBJECT IN SIGHT!
WE'RE AT THE EAST EXIT!
DAMN, WRONG SIDE!
I WAS *SURE* THEY'D COME OUT THE SOUTH!
GOOD THING WE CAME ALONG...
YEAH, OTHER-WISE THEY WOULD HAVE GIVEN US THE SLIP...
HEY...
...THE ONE OVER THERE?
UGH
THEY'RE JUST AS CURIOUS.
OH DAMN... THAT *WASN'T* HER.
GO BUY US SOME AMERICAN SPIRITS. MENTHOL.

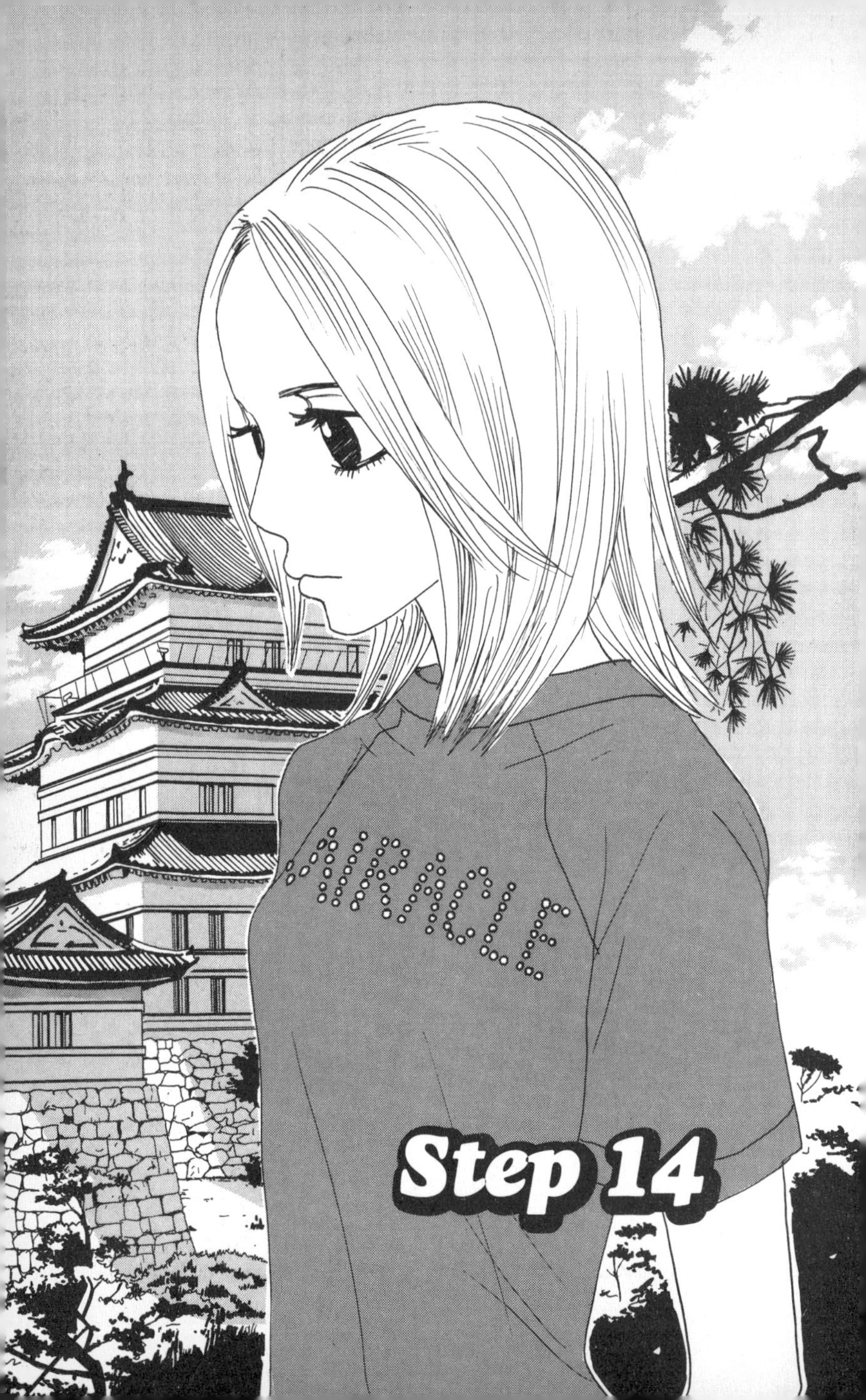
MIRACLE
Step 14

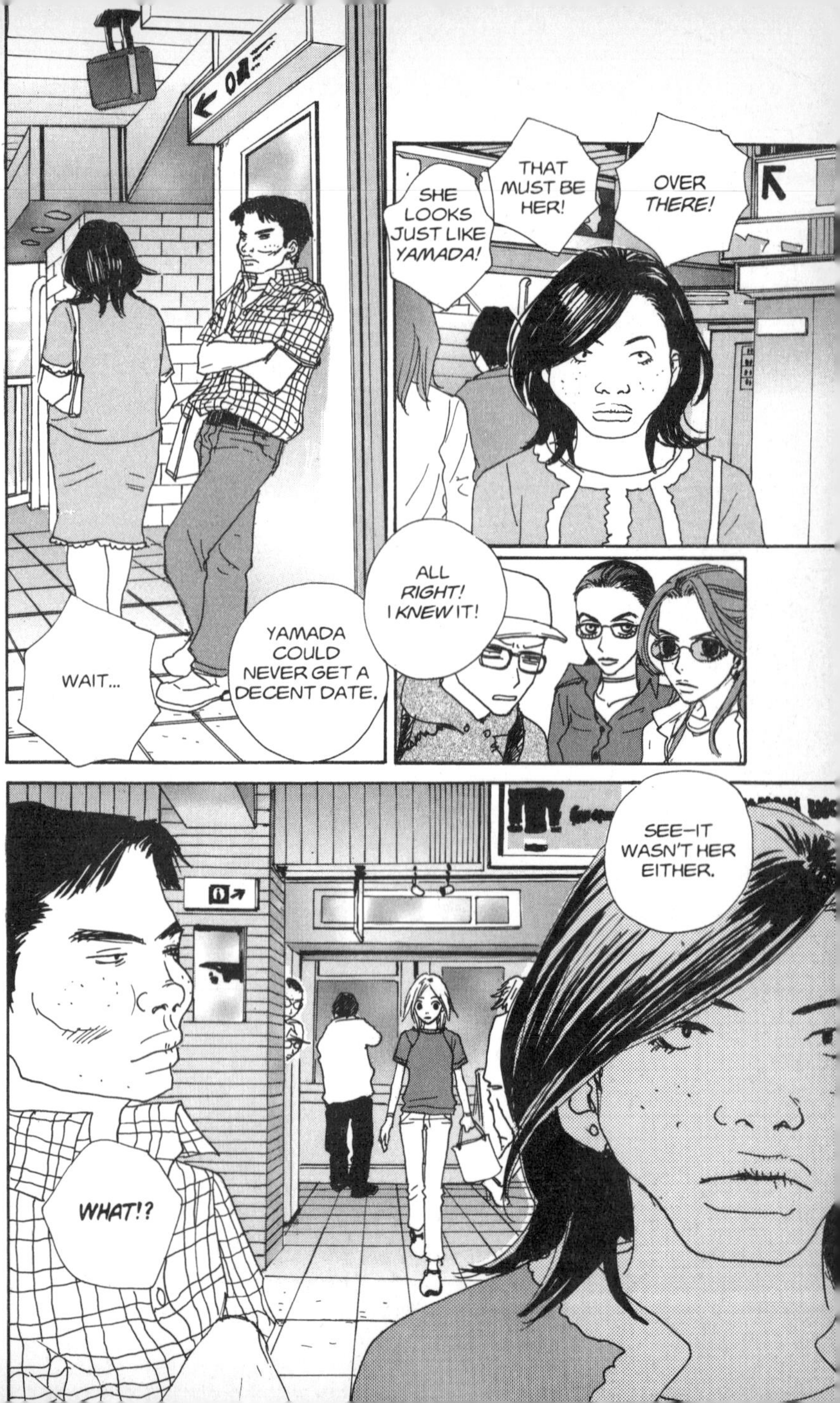
OVER THERE!
THAT MUST BE HER!
SHE LOOKS JUST LIKE YAMADA!
ALL RIGHT! I KNEW IT!
YAMADA COULD NEVER GET A DECENT DATE.
WAIT...
SEE—IT WASN'T HER EITHER.
WHAT!?

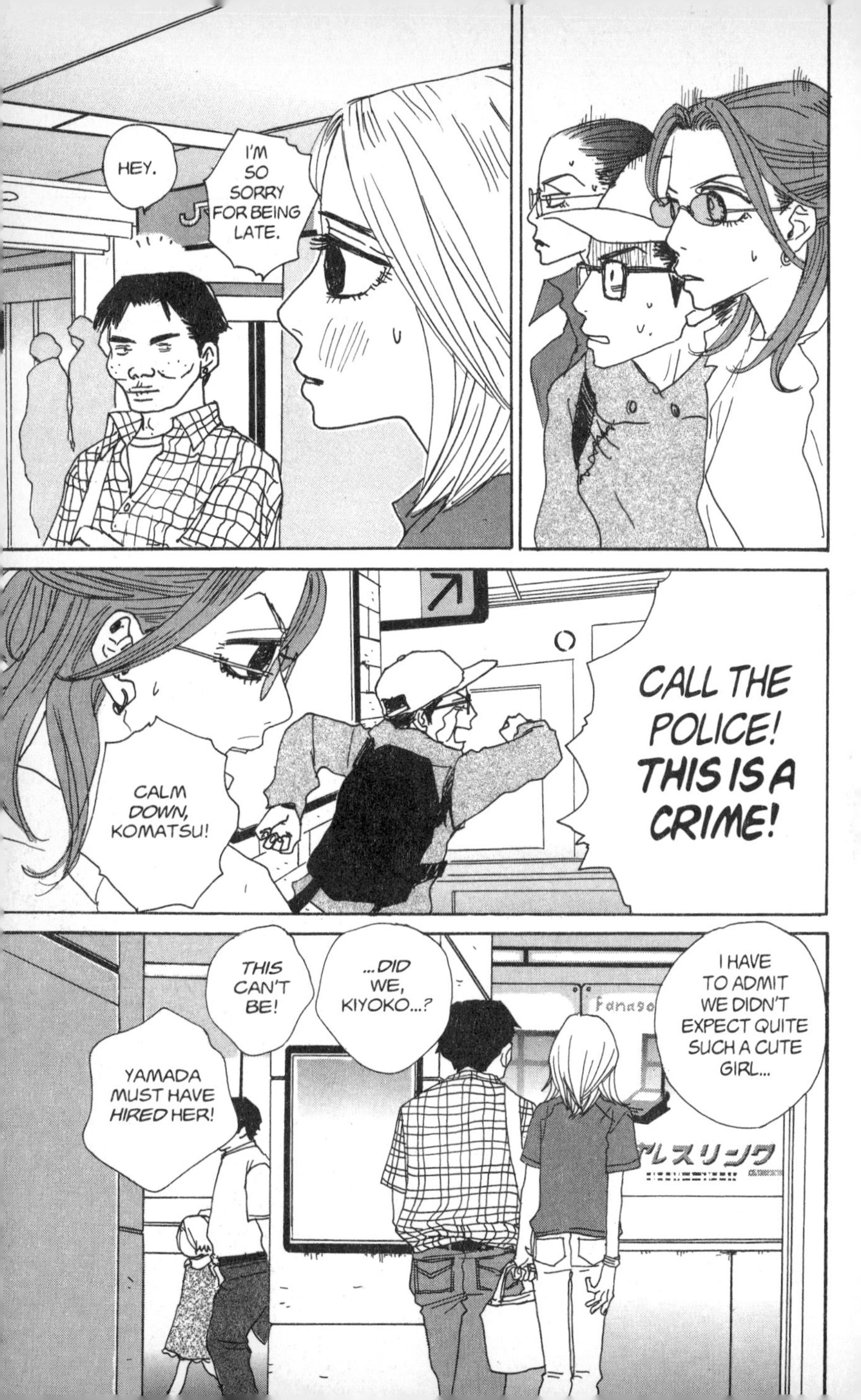
I'M SO SORRY FOR BEING LATE.
HEY.
CALL THE POLICE! THIS IS A CRIME!
CALM DOWN, KOMATSU!
I HAVE TO ADMIT WE DIDN'T EXPECT QUITE SUCH A CUTE GIRL...
...DID WE, KIYOKO...?
THIS CAN'T BE!
YAMADA MUST HAVE HIRED HER!

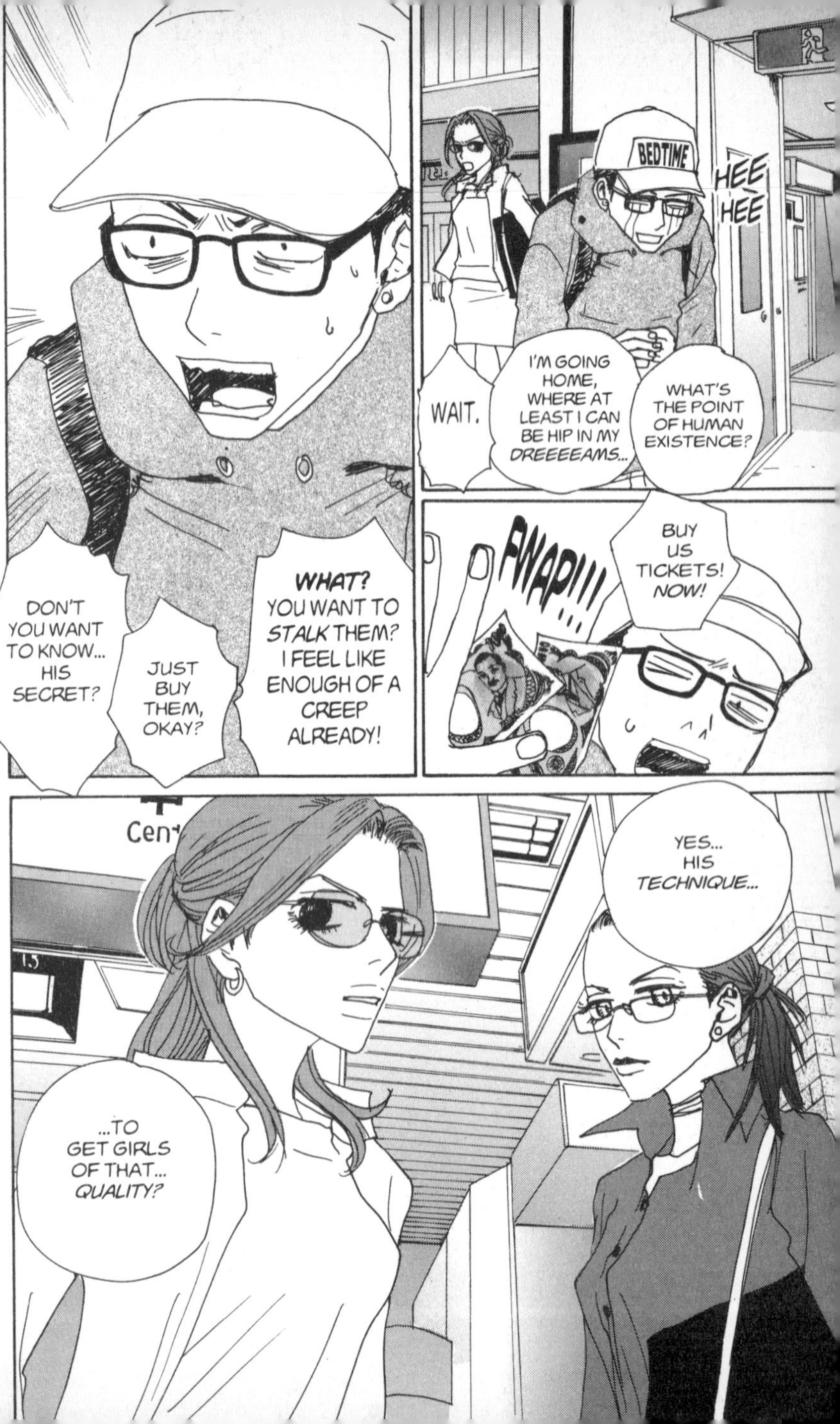
BEDTIME
HEE HEE
WHAT'S THE POINT OF HUMAN EXISTENCE?
I'M GOING HOME, WHERE AT LEAST I CAN BE HIP IN MY *DREEEEAMS...*
WAIT.
FWAP!!!
BUY US TICKETS! *NOW!*
WHAT? YOU WANT TO *STALK* THEM? I FEEL LIKE ENOUGH OF A CREEP ALREADY!
JUST BUY THEM, OKAY?
DON'T YOU WANT TO KNOW... HIS SECRET?
YES... HIS *TECHNIQUE...*
...TO GET GIRLS OF THAT... *QUALITY?*

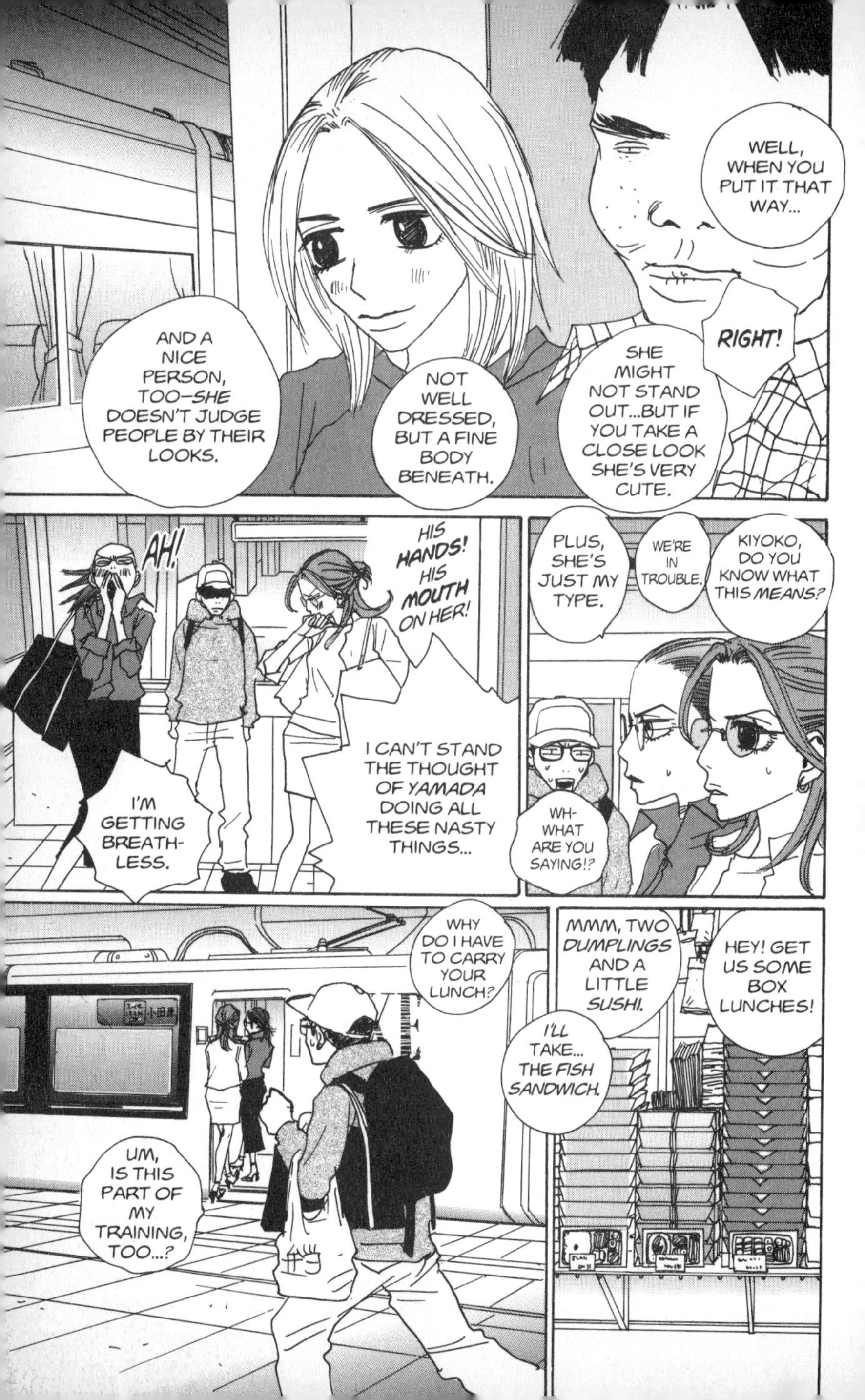
WELL, WHEN YOU PUT IT THAT WAY...
RIGHT!
SHE MIGHT NOT STAND OUT...BUT IF YOU TAKE A CLOSE LOOK SHE'S VERY CUTE.
NOT WELL DRESSED, BUT A FINE BODY BENEATH.
AND A NICE PERSON, TOO–*SHE* DOESN'T JUDGE PEOPLE BY THEIR LOOKS.
KIYOKO, DO YOU KNOW WHAT THIS *MEANS?*
WE'RE IN TROUBLE.
PLUS, SHE'S JUST MY TYPE.
WH-WHAT ARE YOU SAYING!?
HIS *HANDS!* HIS *MOUTH* ON HER!
AH!
I CAN'T STAND THE THOUGHT OF *YAMADA* DOING ALL THESE NASTY THINGS...
I'M GETTING BREATH-LESS.
HEY! GET US SOME BOX LUNCHES!
MMM, TWO *DUMPLINGS* AND A LITTLE *SUSHI.*
I'LL TAKE... THE *FISH SANDWICH.*
WHY DO I HAVE TO CARRY YOUR LUNCH?
UM, IS THIS PART OF MY TRAINING, TOO...?

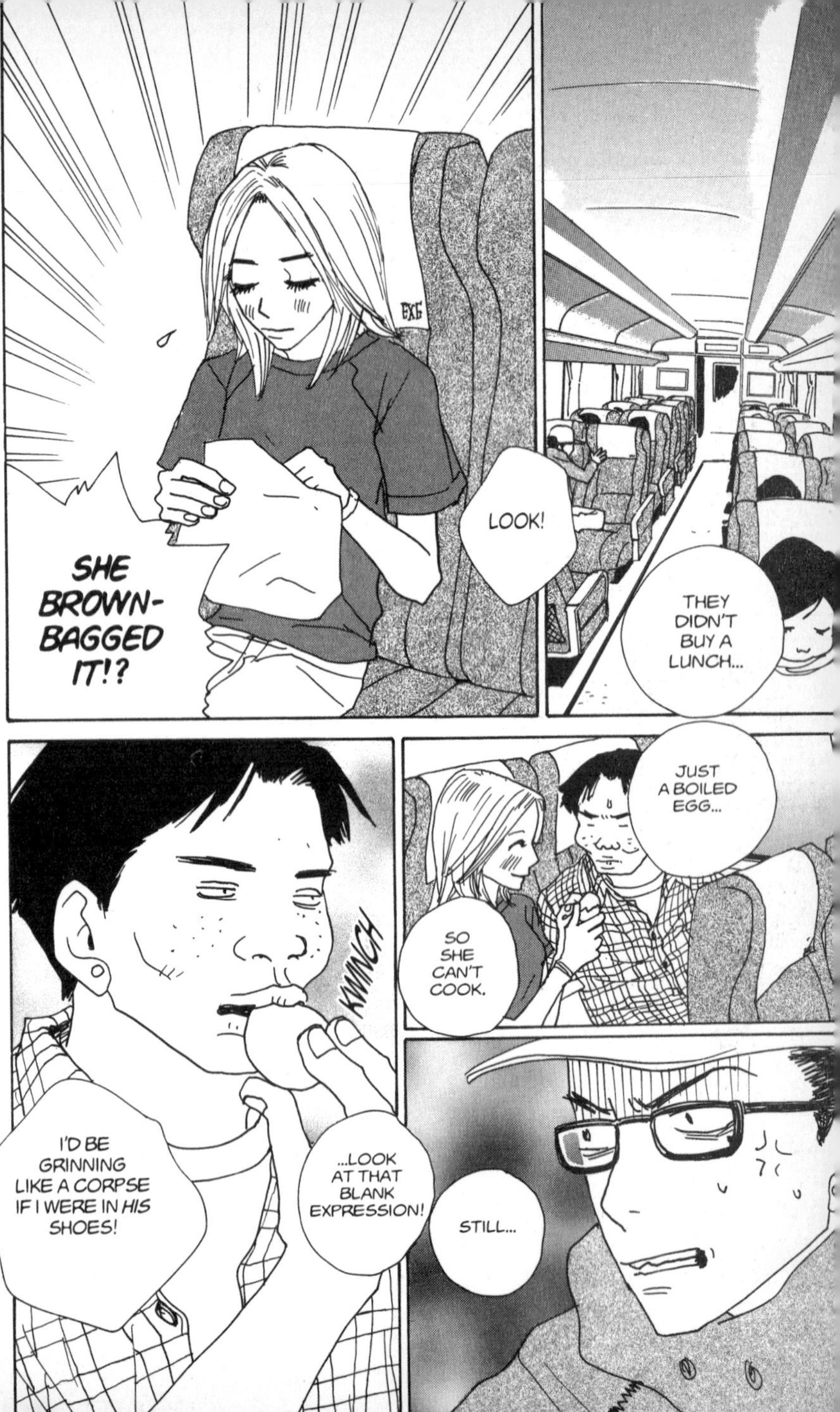
LOOK!
THEY DIDN'T BUY A LUNCH...
SHE BROWN-BAGGED IT!?
JUST A BOILED EGG...
SO SHE CAN'T COOK.
STILL...
...LOOK AT THAT BLANK EXPRESSION!
KWINCH
I'D BE GRINNING LIKE A CORPSE IF I WERE IN *HIS* SHOES!

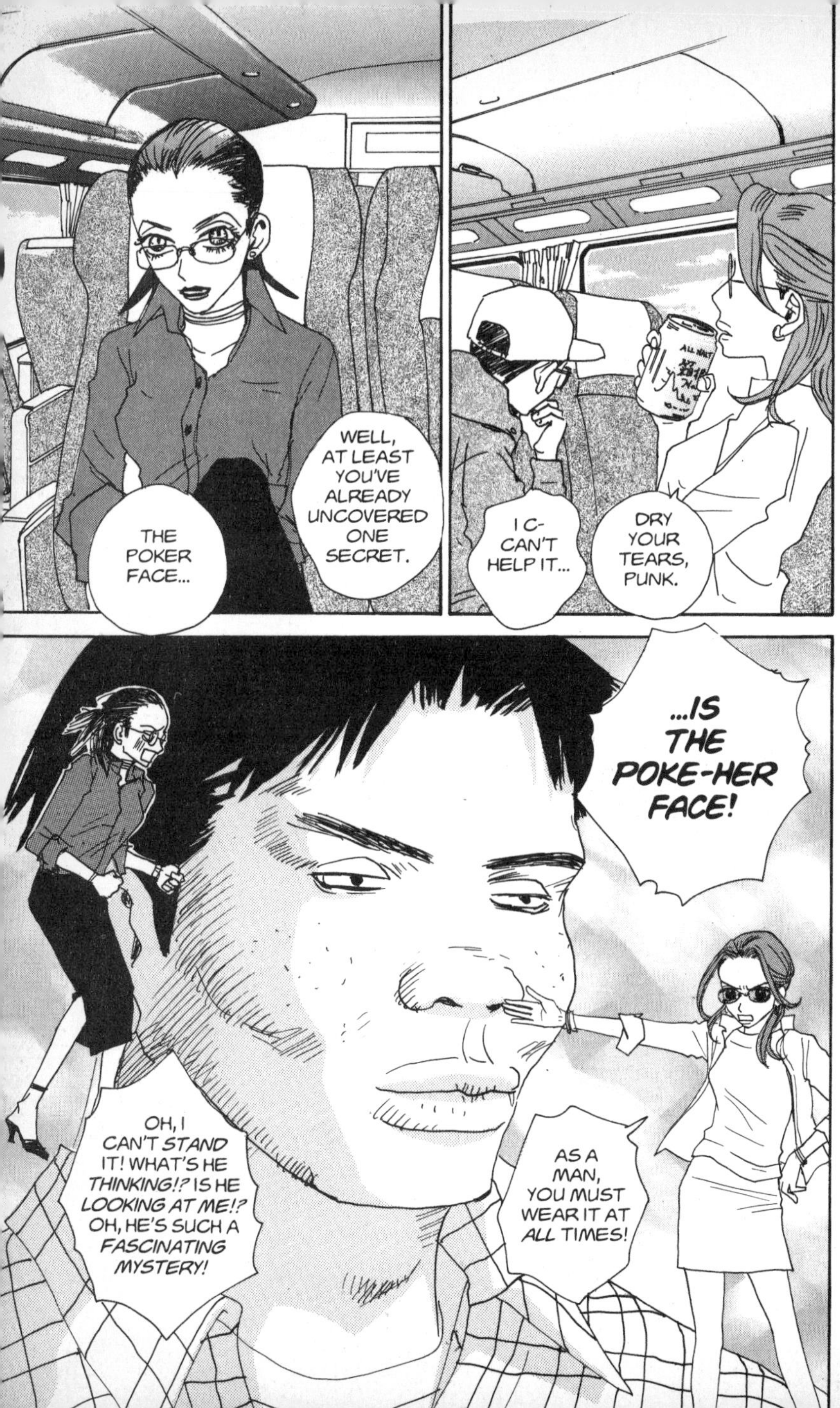
DRY YOUR TEARS, PUNK.
I C- CAN'T HELP IT...
WELL, AT LEAST YOU'VE ALREADY UNCOVERED ONE SECRET.
THE POKER FACE...
...IS THE POKE-HER FACE!
AS A MAN, YOU MUST WEAR IT AT *ALL* TIMES!
OH, I CAN'T *STAND* IT! WHAT'S HE *THINKING!?* IS HE *LOOKING AT ME!?* OH, HE'S SUCH A *FASCINATING MYSTERY!*

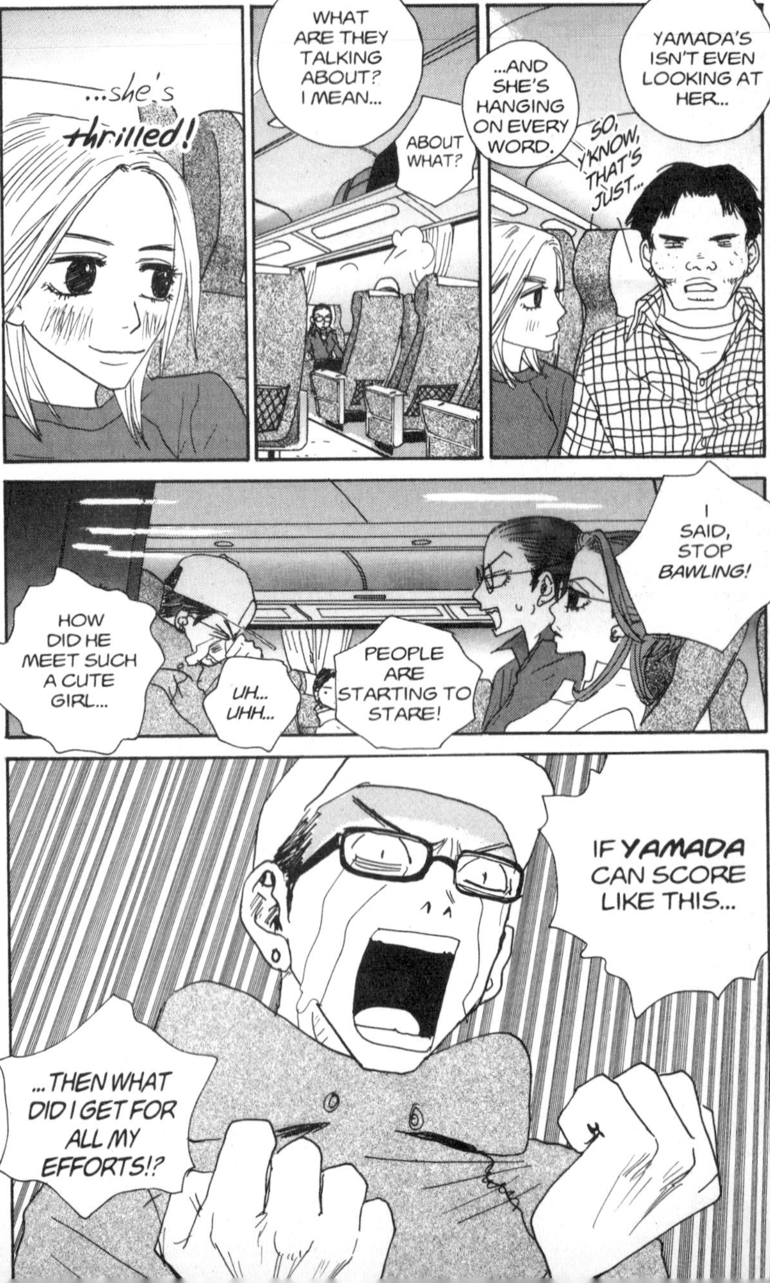
YAMADA'S ISN'T EVEN LOOKING AT HER...
...AND SHE'S HANGING ON EVERY WORD.
SO, Y'KNOW, THAT'S JUST...
WHAT ARE THEY TALKING ABOUT? I MEAN...
ABOUT WHAT?
...she's thrilled!
I SAID, STOP BAWLING!
PEOPLE ARE STARTING TO STARE!
UH... UHH...
HOW DID HE MEET SUCH A CUTE GIRL...
IF YAMADA CAN SCORE LIKE THIS...
...THEN WHAT DID I GET FOR ALL MY EFFORTS!?

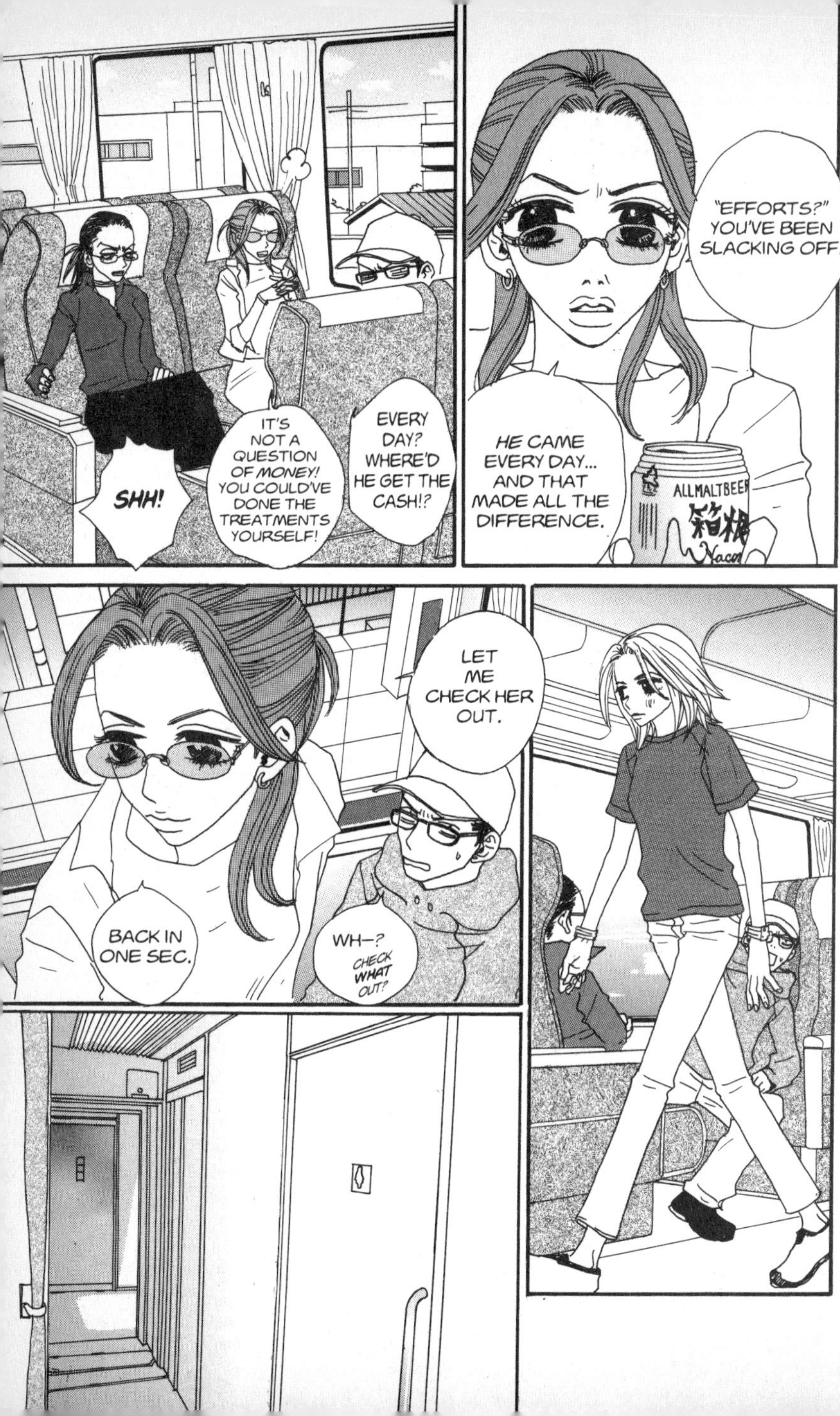
"EFFORTS?" YOU'VE BEEN SLACKING OFF.
HE CAME EVERY DAY... AND THAT MADE ALL THE DIFFERENCE.
ALLMALTBEER
箱根
EVERY DAY? WHERE'D HE GET THE CASH!?
IT'S NOT A QUESTION OF *MONEY!* YOU COULD'VE DONE THE TREATMENTS YOURSELF!
SHH!
LET ME CHECK HER OUT.
WH-? CHECK **WHAT** OUT?
BACK IN ONE SEC.

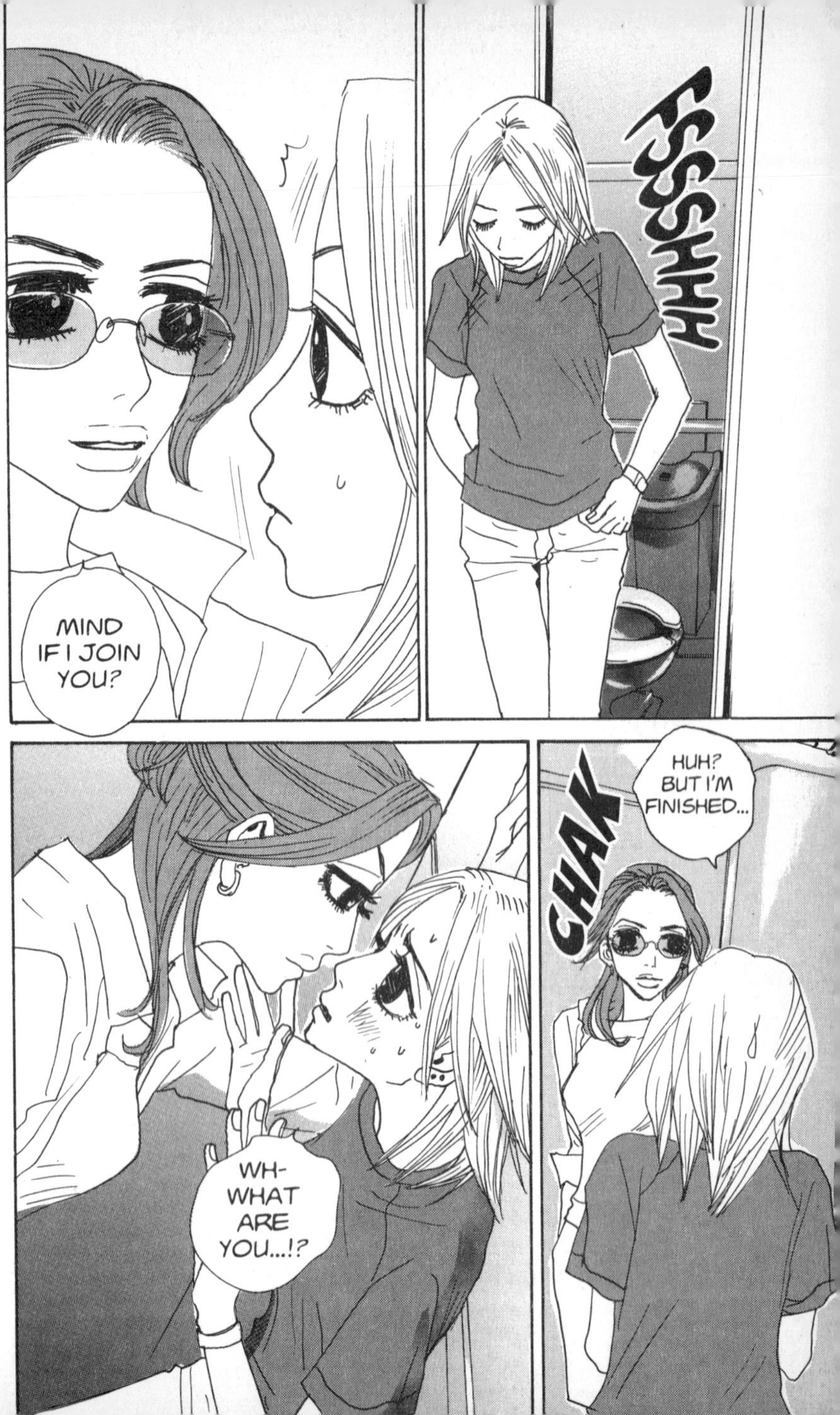
FSSSHHH
MIND IF I JOIN YOU?
CHAK
HUH? BUT I'M FINISHED...
WH- WHAT ARE YOU...!?

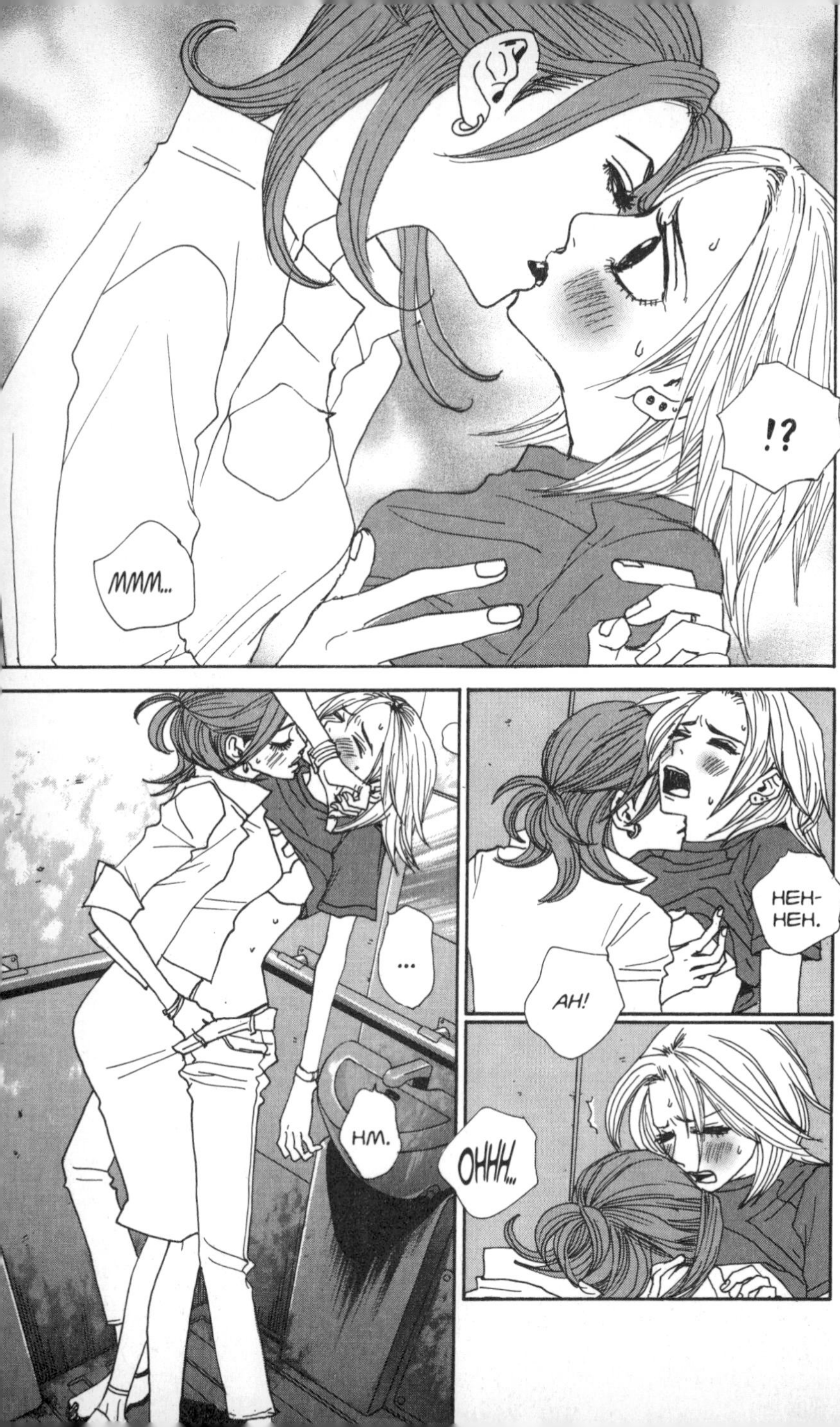
!?
...
MMM...
HEH-HEH.
AH!
OHHH...
...
HM.

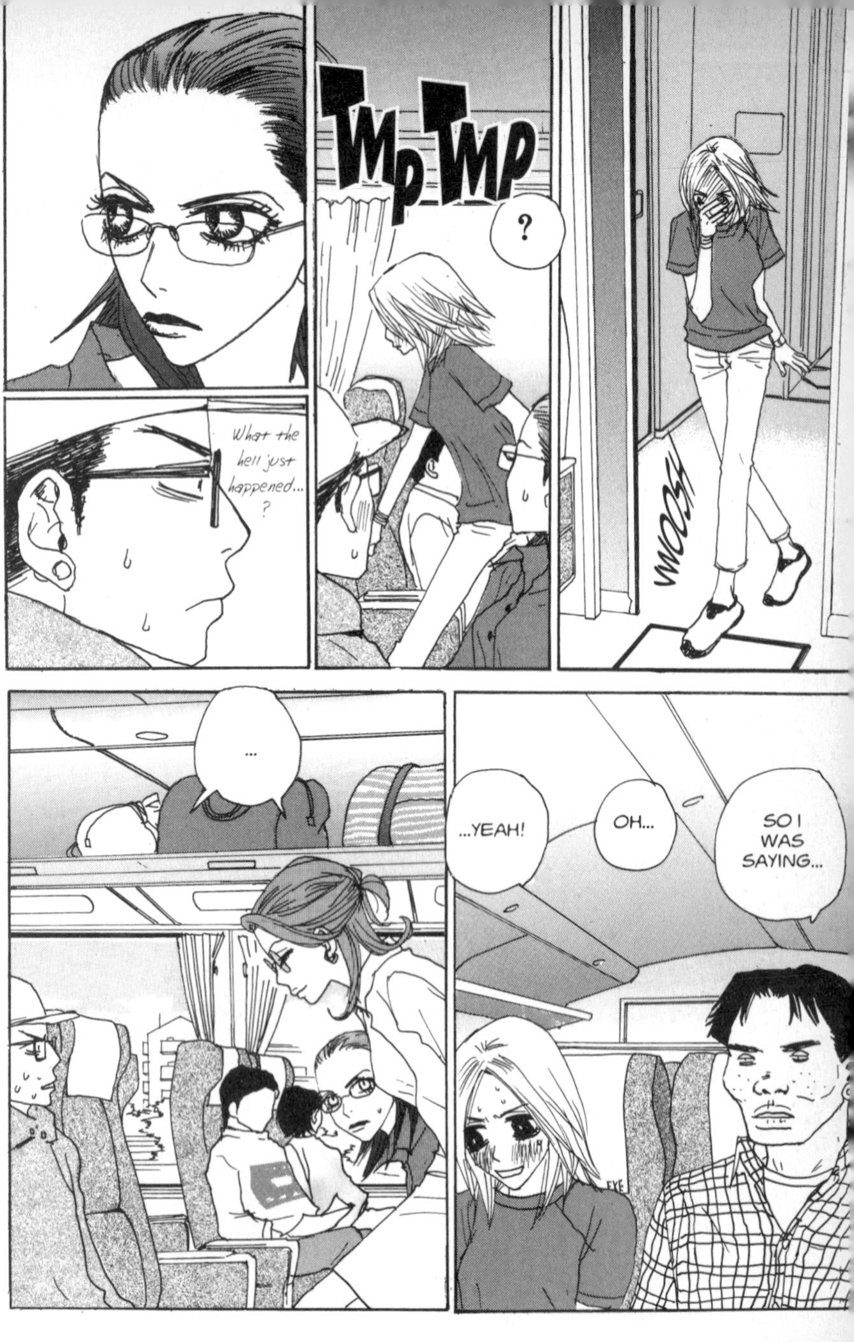
WOOSH
TMP TMP
?
What the hell just happened...?
SO I WAS SAYING...
OH...
...YEAH!
...

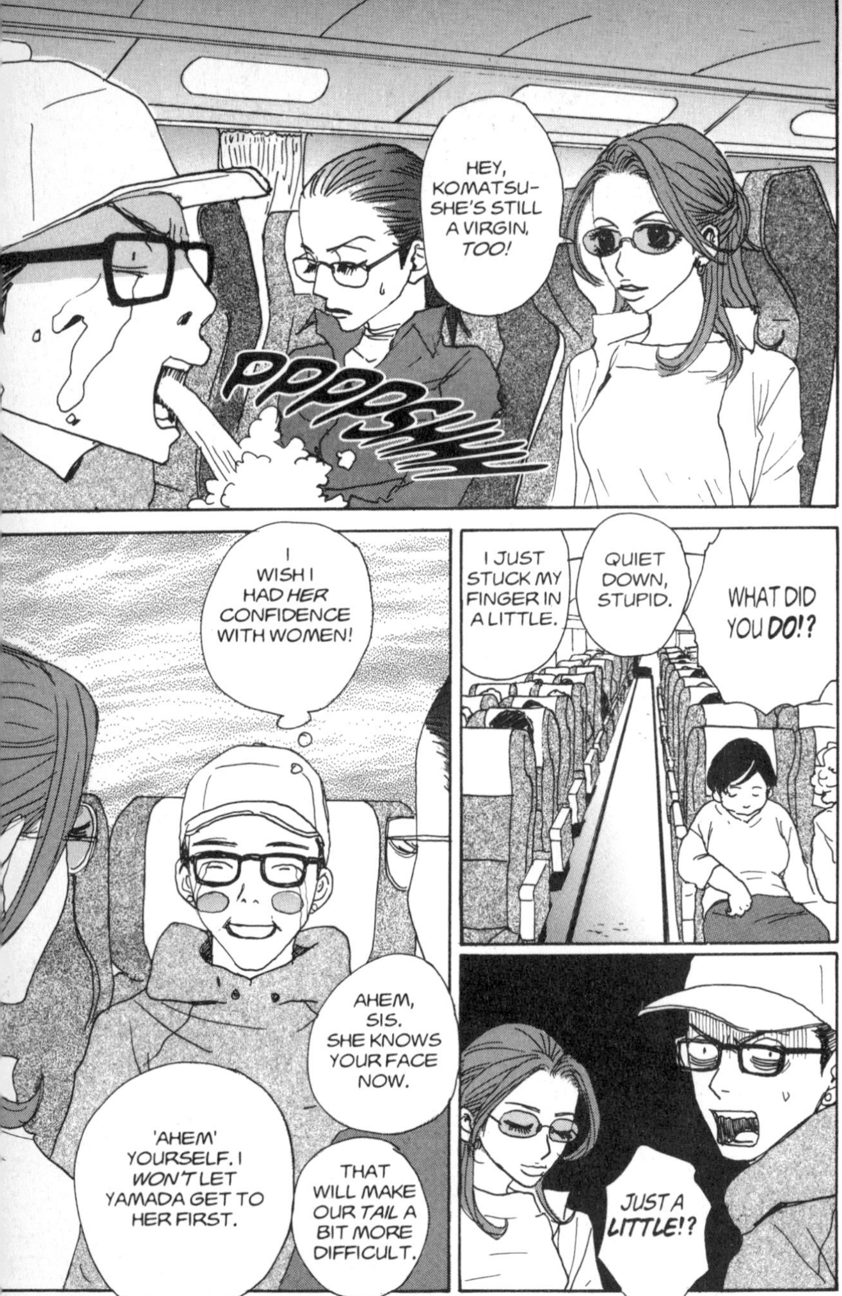
HEY, KOMATSU- SHE'S STILL A VIRGIN, *TOO!*
PPPPSHHHH
WHAT DID YOU **DO**!?
QUIET DOWN, STUPID.
I JUST STUCK MY FINGER IN A LITTLE.
JUST A **LITTLE**!?
I WISH I HAD *HER* CONFIDENCE WITH WOMEN!
AHEM, SIS. SHE KNOWS YOUR FACE NOW.
THAT WILL MAKE OUR *TAIL* A BIT MORE DIFFICULT.
'AHEM' YOURSELF. I *WON'T* LET YAMADA GET TO HER FIRST.

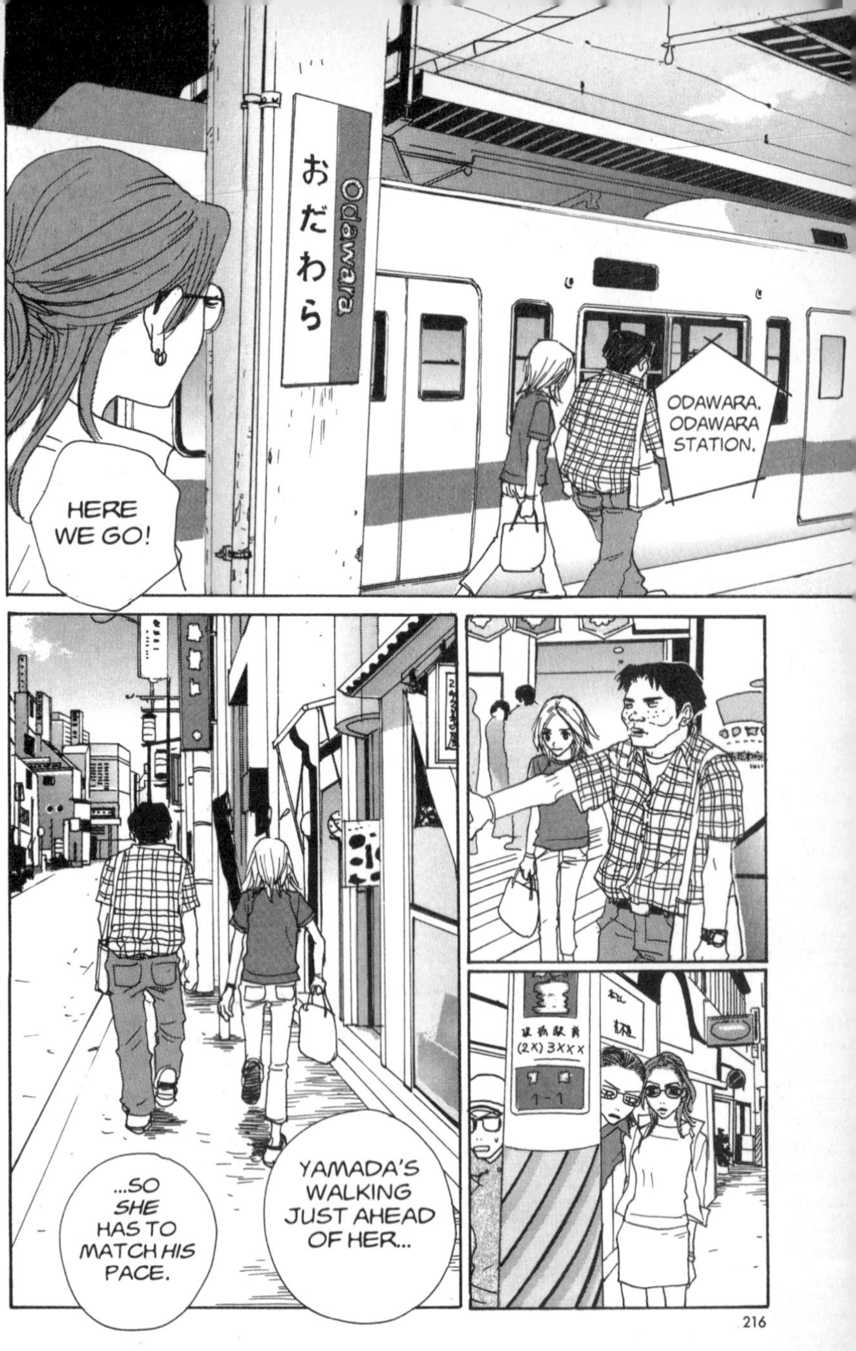
おだわら
Odawara
ODAWARA. ODAWARA STATION.
HERE WE GO!
YAMADA'S WALKING JUST AHEAD OF HER...
...SO SHE HAS TO MATCH HIS PACE.

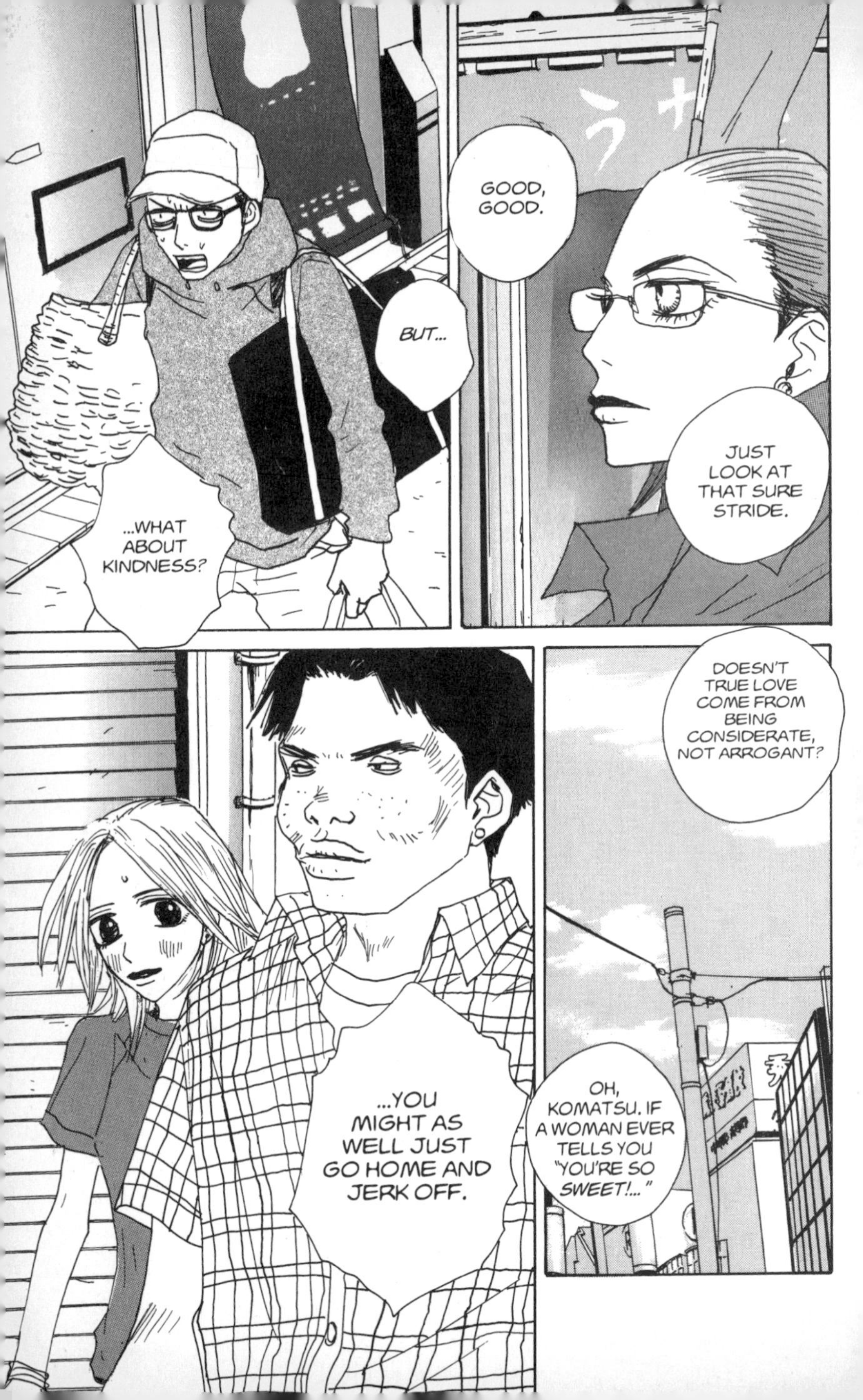
GOOD, GOOD.
JUST LOOK AT THAT SURE STRIDE.
BUT...
...WHAT ABOUT KINDNESS?
DOESN'T TRUE LOVE COME FROM BEING CONSIDERATE, NOT ARROGANT?
OH, KOMATSU. IF A WOMAN EVER TELLS YOU "YOU'RE SO *SWEET!*..."
...YOU MIGHT AS WELL JUST GO HOME AND JERK OFF.

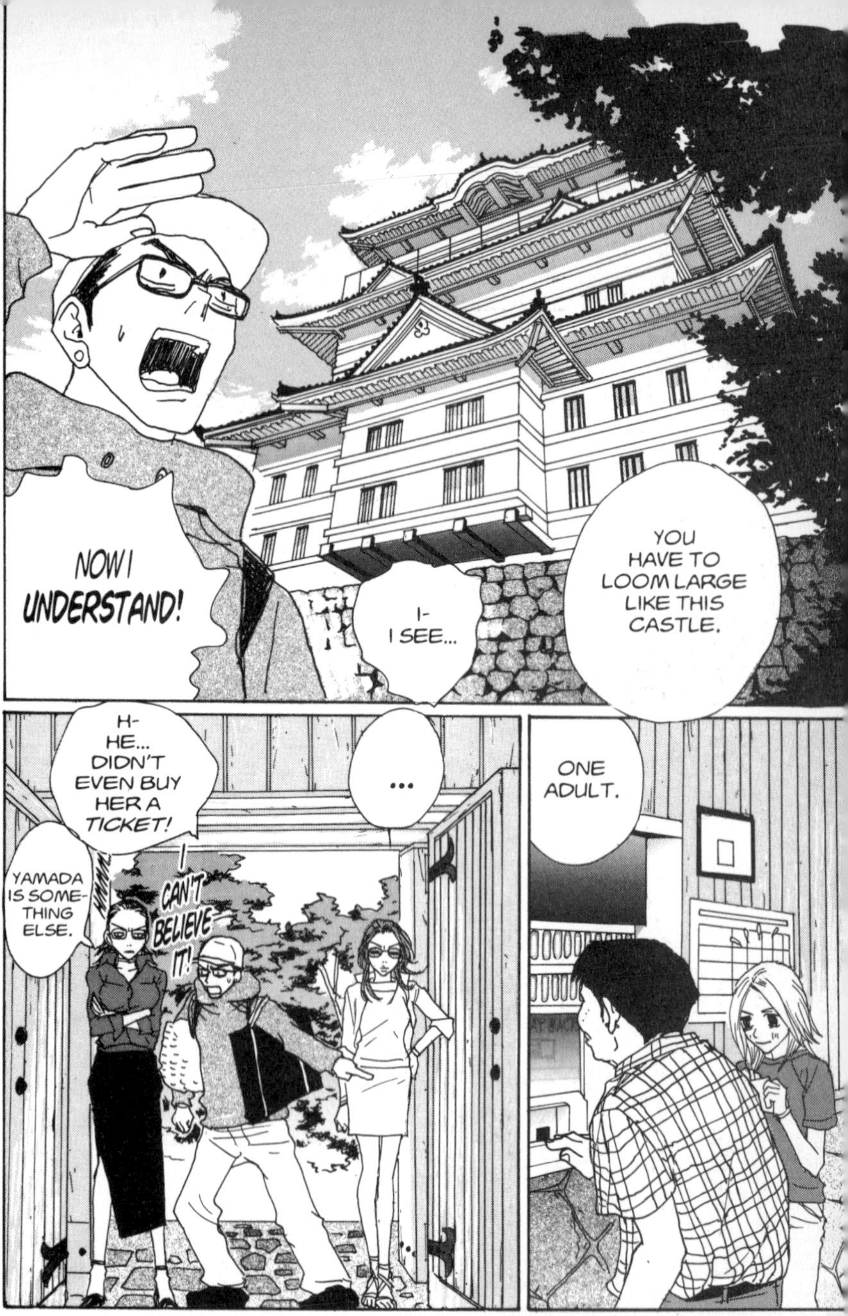
YOU HAVE TO LOOM LARGE LIKE THIS CASTLE.
I- I SEE...
NOW I UNDERSTAND!
ONE ADULT.
...
H- HE... DIDN'T EVEN BUY HER A TICKET!
I CAN'T BELIEVE IT!
YAMADA IS SOME-THING ELSE.

TO BE CONTINUED IN ***FLOWERS & BEES VOL. 3!***

THE ADVENTURES OF...

AFTERWORD BOY!

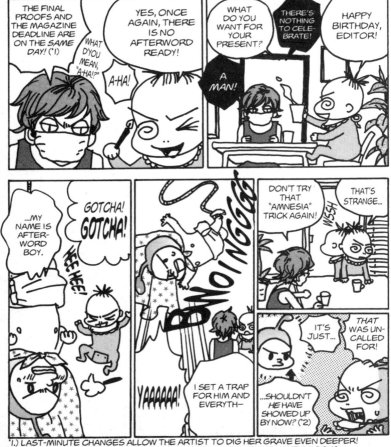

HAPPY BIRTHDAY, EDITOR!
THERE'S NOTHING TO CELEBRATE!
WHAT DO YOU WANT FOR YOUR PRESENT?
A MAN!
YES, ONCE AGAIN, THERE IS NO AFTERWORD READY!
THE FINAL PROOFS AND THE MAGAZINE DEADLINE ARE ON THE *SAME* DAY! (*1)
WHAT D'YOU MEAN, "A-HA!?"
A-HA!
THAT'S STRANGE...
DON'T TRY THAT "AMNESIA" TRICK AGAIN!
WISSH
THAT WAS UN-CALLED FOR!
IT'S JUST...
...SHOULDN'T *HE* HAVE SHOWED UP BY NOW? (*2)
BWOINGGG
YAAAAAA!
I SET A TRAP FOR HIM AND EVERYTH—
GOTCHA! GOTCHA!
...MY NAME IS AFTER-WORD BOY.
HEE HEE!

*1.) LAST-MINUTE CHANGES ALLOW THE ARTIST TO DIG HER GRAVE EVEN DEEPER!
*2.) APPEARS IN VOLUME 1 AS WELL. WHY DON'T YOU BUY IT AND HAVE A LOOK?

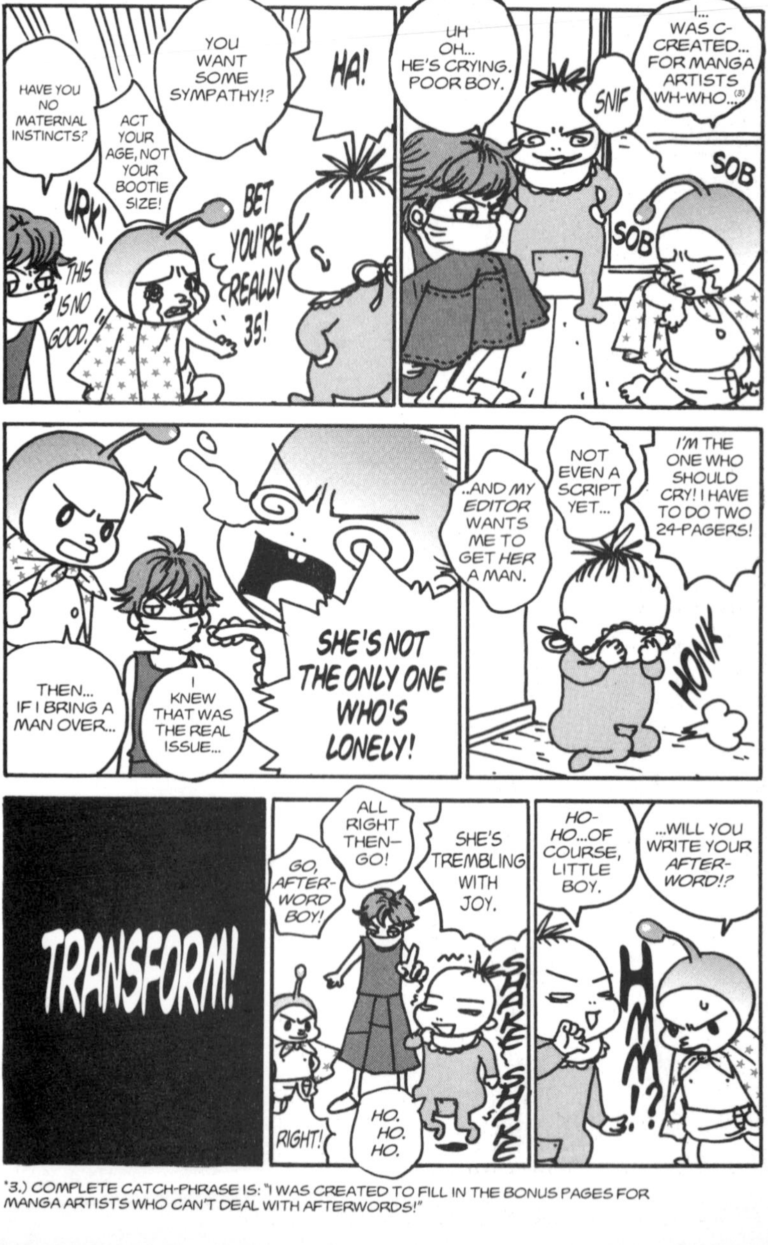
I... WAS C-CREATED... FOR MANGA ARTISTS WH-WHO...[3]
SNIF
UH OH... HE'S CRYING. POOR BOY.
SOB
SOB
HA!
YOU WANT SOME SYMPATHY!?
BET YOU'RE REALLY 35!
ACT YOUR AGE, NOT YOUR BOOTIE SIZE!
HAVE YOU NO MATERNAL INSTINCTS?
URK!
THIS IS NO GOOD.
I'M THE ONE WHO SHOULD CRY! I HAVE TO DO TWO 24-PAGERS!
NOT EVEN A SCRIPT YET...
..AND MY EDITOR WANTS ME TO GET HER A MAN.
HONK
SHE'S NOT THE ONLY ONE WHO'S LONELY!
I KNEW THAT WAS THE REAL ISSUE...
THEN... IF I BRING A MAN OVER...
...WILL YOU WRITE YOUR AFTER-WORD!?
HO-HO...OF COURSE, LITTLE BOY.
HMM!?
SHE'S TREMBLING WITH JOY.
ALL RIGHT THEN-GO!
GO, AFTER-WORD BOY!
SHAKE SHAKE
HO. HO. HO.
RIGHT!
TRANSFORM!

*3.) COMPLETE CATCH-PHRASE IS: "I WAS CREATED TO FILL IN THE BONUS PAGES FOR MANGA ARTISTS WHO CAN'T DEAL WITH AFTERWORDS!"

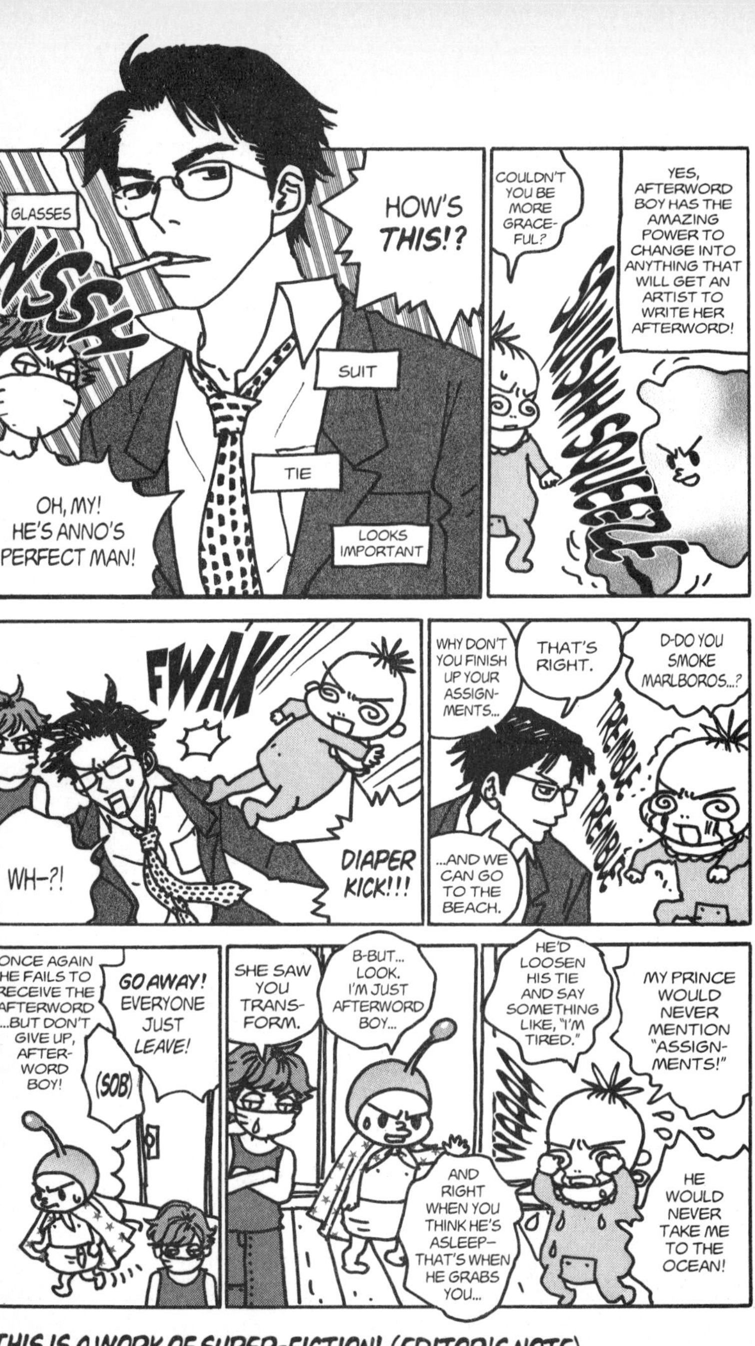
YES, AFTERWORD BOY HAS THE AMAZING POWER TO CHANGE INTO ANYTHING THAT WILL GET AN ARTIST TO WRITE HER AFTERWORD!
COULDN'T YOU BE MORE GRACE-FUL?
SQUISH SQUEEZE
HOW'S THIS!?
GLASSES
WSSH
SUIT
TIE
LOOKS IMPORTANT
OH, MY! HE'S ANNO'S PERFECT MAN!
D-DO YOU SMOKE MARLBOROS...?
THAT'S RIGHT.
WHY DON'T YOU FINISH UP YOUR ASSIGN-MENTS...
TREMBLE TREMBLE
...AND WE CAN GO TO THE BEACH.
FWAK
DIAPER KICK!!!
WH-?!
MY PRINCE WOULD NEVER MENTION "ASSIGN-MENTS!"
HE'D LOOSEN HIS TIE AND SAY SOMETHING LIKE, "I'M TIRED."
HE WOULD NEVER TAKE ME TO THE OCEAN!
B-BUT... LOOK. I'M JUST AFTERWORD BOY...
AND RIGHT WHEN YOU THINK HE'S ASLEEP—THAT'S WHEN HE GRABS YOU...
SHE SAW YOU TRANS-FORM.
GO AWAY! EVERYONE JUST LEAVE!
ONCE AGAIN HE FAILS TO RECEIVE THE AFTERWORD ...BUT DON'T GIVE UP, AFTER-WORD BOY!
(SOB)

TO BE CONTINUED (UNTIL THE AUTHOR GETS MARRIED)

THIS IS A WORK OF SUPER-FICTION! (EDITOR'S NOTE)